BUYING ART ON A BUDGET

BUYING ART ON A BUDGET

What to Buy and Where to Buy It in the U.S.A.

by Joanna Eagle

Hawthorn Books, Inc.   Publishers   New York

For my mother and father, and for George

First Edition: 1968
Second Printing: 1969

0330

Contents

Good Art Is for Everyone

In the early 1920s, a girl still in her teens and on her first job used to browse in the New York City art galleries during her lunch hour. This in itself was somewhat unusual as generally only the very rich frequented the art galleries at that time. Only a few galleries in the city were devoted to showing modern art, and she tells how she used to haunt two of them. She recalls one painting she wanted very much, and she went back day after day to look at it in the gallery window. Finally she worked up her courage to ask the owner if she could pay a little each month until the full cost of the picture was realized. The dealer, amazed and taken aback, laughed both at her and at the idea of paying for art on time. The answer was "no."

The young girl, humiliated and angry, decided that someday she would make it possible for persons like her to buy art. The neophyte art buyer was Edith Gregor Halpert, who as gallery director, artist's wife, lecturer, and exhibition organizer has done more than any other individual in the United States to make that ambition a reality.

With the opening of her Downtown Gallery of Contemporary Art in New York in 1926, Mrs. Halpert was able to give encouragement to the many struggling artists who so sorely needed it. She had the patience to wait as long as seven years for an artist to sell, as was the case with painter Jack Levine. Ben Shahn, Stuart Davis, Arthur Dove, Charles Sheeler, William Zorach—to name just a few—all started with her. She was also interested in American folk art, regarding the earlier anonymous American artists and craftsmen as "ancestors" of her artists, and in 1929 she inaugurated the American Folk Art Gallery. Both art establishments were pioneering ventures which proved highly successful in stimulating the public's taste and appreciation for American art.

Perhaps Mrs. Halpert's greatest contribution was to bring original art to the average American, to make it possible for him to buy art for his home. In 1926, the same year she opened her Downtown Gallery, she inaugurated her now famous "Christmas Shows,"

1

in which smaller works by her gallery artists were specially priced. These shows were designated for the more modest buyers only, but sometimes Mrs. Halpert's wealthier patrons would try to buy anyway. "We could always tell them by their handmade shoes," she recalls, "but it was harder when they sent their secretaries." She tells how she recently went through her files and found that her most faithful customers through the years were the ones she started off with these shows.

It's difficult to realize that Christmas shows once didn't exist, because now almost every gallery across the U.S. has them. It's also hard to remember when installment buying of art—going back to Mrs. Halpert's early rebuff—didn't exist. There are several obvious advantages to buying on time, which Mrs. Halpert realized very early. Aside from taking home art he might otherwise be unable to buy, the installment purchaser doesn't have to compromise on quality and can buy better, more expensive art. Also, like all the other merchandise the consumer purchases on time—homes, TV sets, cars, furniture, et cetera—art bought this way can be enjoyed sooner than if the buyer had to save up for it. Mrs. Halpert remembers that some years ago, when prices were somewhat lower, a good art collection could be built up by paying fifty cents a month. She also knows of at least one collection that was built up through the owner's denying himself a status car. And now, of course, one can rent paintings, prints, or sculpture so that the rental fee can be applied to the purchase price, as well as take art home for a two-week approval period to live with it—both natural outgrowths of Mrs. Halpert's innovations.

In a way, Mrs. Halpert has succeeded almost too well. She has always based her sales on the idea that a person must have a personal rapport with the art he's buying, and that her art should go only into "loving homes," but now some people are using her installment-buying plan to speculate in art for quick profits and to exploit the latest art gimmick instead of acquiring a real feeling for and knowledge of good art.

So often news accounts are devoted to these gimmicks, and the news is most often where the big money is. Yet in the present day millionaires are prohibited by taxes from buying on the scale they once did. More and more it is the persons buying out of low salaries or an allowance who comprise the art market. Few people know that Sotheby & Co. in London, the world's largest art auction house, rings up over fifty per cent of its business in art objects priced at under thirty pounds—eighty-four dollars—or that the largest percentage of sales is in the lower-priced categories. Many dealers with whom I have talked feel the best art collections are built up by persons who have to watch every penny closely and think through their purchases carefully, rather than by those who can be freer with their money.

When Mrs. Halpert opened her gallery in 1926, there were only six galleries devoted to showing modern art in New York City. Now there are close to five hundred in that city alone. A recent Tamarind Lithography Workshop, Inc., survey shows that the American public and its museums are buying at least five hundred million dollars worth of art annually; and it's also estimated that about ninety new museums open each year.

All of this is very healthy, as well as being the reason why this book was written. But buying art must be tempered with knowledge. The millionaire oilman-art buyer J. Paul Getty has written in his book *The Joys of Collecting* (New York, Hawthorn Books, 1965), "In order to be a successful collector of any type or school of fine art, an individual must learn as much as he can about it before he starts collecting. He must be able to recognize what he is looking for, and be able to recognize at least the more patent counterfeits." We can all take counsel from Mr. Getty, who is so astute in art he could have built a good collection on five cents or five million dollars. If you follow Mr. Getty's advice, you will find there are many places you can go to learn about art. In large and small communities across the United States, a combination of civic pride, new leisure hours, better education, and more money is causing a proliferation of art galleries, museums, theaters, concert halls, and cultural centers such as the country has never seen before. Not only the larger cities like New York, with its Lincoln Center, and Los Angeles, with its Music Center and spanking new County Museum, but smaller cities such as Atlanta and Kansas City are building centers for their arts. Much of the money is coming from the government and from private foundations, but a lot is also coming from local businessmen for purely commercial reasons. And there is nothing wrong with this business participation in the arts. There is a whole new breed of patrons who have replaced the princes and the Church of the past, and among them are not only wealthy corporations and individuals like the Rockefellers but people like you and me.

We can all become patrons—modest ones, to be sure, for yearly memberships of ten or fifteen dollars—by joining our local museums. Museums are perhaps most responsible for the current art interest, and are still the best places to learn about art. Through museums—better called culture centers—we can come in contact with beauty, and beauty concomitantly becomes a force in our daily lives. Many of us have found we cannot live .without beauty, and this realization has resulted in the current flourishing of art galleries and the increased buying of art. Going from looking at art to wanting it, then to buying it, is a very natural progression. In many ways, the museums have created the new audiences which not only look but buy for enjoyment rather than for investment and which now comprise the largest art-buying public in the history of the United States. The museums have improved taste to the point where it is now passé to put up a reproduction rather than an original work of art.

At the pace most museums operate these days, the rest of us seem merely to be riding along on their coattails. The usual program during a month at your local museum is enough to make your head spin. Formerly these institutions were rather musty, remote places where you went on a rainy day or when you had nothing better to do. They were thought of purely as repositories for beautiful objects. This, of course, is still their main function, but now you see young mothers and their children milling in during the week for art classes and joining the guided tours through the galleries. The whole family often goes on weekends to see the latest traveling exhibition and perhaps to hear some special lecture on the exhibit. Evenings during the week there may be a choice of movies, concerts, a formal opening for a visiting exhibition which may feature champagne and a seven-piece band, or a meeting of the museum's "Collectors' Club," where museum personnel advise members on buying art, usually on the installment plan. And then there is always the rental gallery, where you may look at the new work that has come in and decide to buy the painting you have been renting for the past few months—the rental fee applied to the final cost, of course. These are only a few of the services most American museums currently provide, and others will be discussed further along in the book.

A few months before he died, President John F. Kennedy flew to Amherst College in Massachusetts to take part in a ceremony honoring poet Robert Frost. Kennedy had decided to speak on the theme of poetry and power used by Frost at the Presidential Inauguration.

"I look forward to a great future for America," Kennedy said, "a future in which our country will match its military strength with our moral restraint . . .

"I look forward to an America which will not be afraid of grace and beauty . . .

"I look forward to an America which will reward achievement in the arts as we reward achievement in business or statecraft . . .

"I look forward to an America which commands respect throughout the world not only for its strength but for its civilization as well . . ."

America has, in many ways, achieved the leadership in the arts about which Kennedy was talking. New York has replaced Paris as the world's capital of art. America's artists are looked to the world over for their uniqueness and their innovations. With growing leisure and wealth, there are both more artists and more art buyers in the United States. And for the first time in its history, the United States affords opportunities for its average citizens to enjoy the great pleasures of owning original art.

This book is limited to art priced under a thousand dollars, but most of the art discussed is in the ten- to five-hundred-dollar price bracket. With rental, installment-plan, and approval merchandising methods, art is now available to everyone who isn't downright penniless. The painter Maurice de Vlaminck once said, "Good art is like good cooking; it can be tasted, but not explained." This book is designed to increase your great pleasure in "tasting" art and, by directing you to what might be comparable to certain ingredients and spices, hopes to help you appreciate the flavor of the art you see and buy. As an occasional art buyer myself, I have never regretted anything I have bought. I have only regretted the things I did *not* buy. So whether you're buying only one or two paintings for your home, or beginning a lifelong love affair with art, I hope this book will be a handy guide, your Baedecker through the world of art.

The Joy of Looking

Remember that there are parts of what it most concerns you to know which I cannot describe to you; you must come with me and see it for yourselves. The vision is for him who will see it.

Plotinus

Plotinus' advice is another version of the timeless saying, "Beauty is in the eye of the beholder." In our discussion of buying art, the questions of beauty and of taste are going to come up again and again. Our conception of beauty depends on many factors: our Western heritage, which determines, to a large extent, our art standards; our personal ideas on art; the way we live; our moods; our tastes; how much art we've seen beyond the Western spectrum. Yet, we must decide for ourselves what is beautiful or, basically, what appeals to us. It is only then that we can begin to buy.

Taste is another matter. Some are born with it and the rest of us can aquire it by training our eyes and broadening our art experiences. But while good taste is one of the easiest things in life to acquire, the old saw, "I know nothing about art, but I know what I like," is still the claim of too many. The cocktail party art experts who launch into heated attacks on "those crazy paint throwers" are usually the same people who take time to learn about other subjects—their own businesses, for example—before offering opinions on them. For some reason, art all too often brings out the beast in us.

It's surprising how many people think that any kind of art they don't immediately like or understand is bad or worthless. Most beginning cooks wouldn't try to prepare a meal without first consulting a cookbook. Yet a lot of people launch into art buying knowing next to nothing about it. Like business, or playing the piano, or traveling, art takes a certain amount of effort and knowledge in order to reap its rewards.

Someone once asked the late pianist "Fats" Waller, "Hey, Fats, what is swing, Fats?" to which he replied, "Boy, if you gotta ask,

you ain't got it." Obviously Fats was born with "swing," just as
many are born with taste. Yet, for those of us born without taste,
a lot can be learned from those who "got it." Try to meet and
know people with taste—your local museum curator, for example
—and see what they like and what they buy and for what reasons.
You can also learn from the art you look at while buying or while
going to exhibitions or museums.

"The power to 'see beautifully,' " the Washington, D.C., art collector and pioneer Duncan Phillips once said, "is almost all there is
worth bothering about in art." Most of us can see, in the sense
that we can pick out light and objects. Yet to "see beautifully" is
another story. I have a friend who now buys quite a lot of art, but
who tells me he never really "saw" art until he met his wife, an
artist.

MUSEUMS

Probably the best way to learn to "see" is to join your local
museum and to become an active member. There you will find
other art lovers from whom you can learn. There you will also find
the best in art—what is called "museum quality"—selected by persons with taste. And there you can, over the years, develop your
taste, remembering, as the great English art critic John Ruskin once
wrote, "The temper by which right taste is formed is character-
istically patient. It dwells upon what is submitted to it . . . it is
good ground, retentive . . . And the pleasure which it has in
things that it finds true and good, is so great, that it cannot possibly
be led aside."

American museums began their mushrooming growth as late as
the 1770s, and it's often hard to believe that a museum as enormous
and as excellent as the National Gallery of Art in Washington,
D.C., was only twenty-five years old in 1966. America's public collections are made up of the extraordinary excellence of her private
ones, many of which have been donated to her museums. Unlike
Europe, with its mighty patrons of Church and State, its Hapsburgs,
its Napoleons, its Richelieus and Mazarins, who filled its museums
with art treasures, United States museums continue today to develop and expand with the gifts of art lovers, old and young,
wealthy and not-so-wealthy.

The first function of a museum is to delight, to give pleasure. Go
to museums and look for the sheer joy of looking. There is much
to learn from both the old and new masters. The more you study

Secretary of State Dean Rusk at the black-tie opening of the exhibition "Contemporary Art from Yugoslavia," 1965, Corcoran Gallery of Art, Washington, D.C. (*Courtesy Corcoran Gallery of Art*)

Festival of Arts, 1966, Milwaukee Art Center, Milwaukee, Wisconsin. (*Courtesy Milwaukee Art Center*)

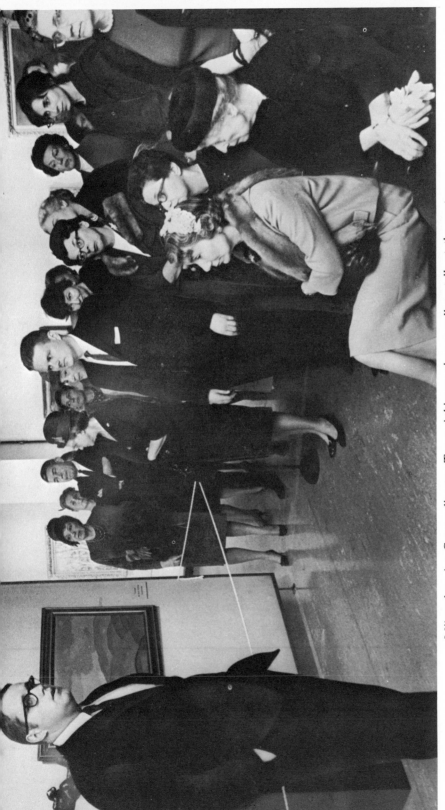

Milwaukee Art Center director Tracy Atkinson gives a gallery talk at the center. (*Courtesy Milwaukee Art Center, Milwaukee, Wisconsin*)

a certain painting, and the more times you go back and look at it, the more you will enjoy it. Art yields its full pleasures slowly, somewhat like a friendship that mellows and grows richer with the years. There is no adequate substitute for educating the eye, or for looking at original art.

But when you go to a museum, don't turn your excursion into a survival test: take a few galleries at a time—especially if children are along—and, if possible, study up on the exhibits before you go. Dr. Raymond S. Stites, curator of education at the National Gallery of Art, points out that children like to recognize art they have seen before. If a child has studied a reproduction of a famous painting, such as a Rembrandt *Self-Portrait,* he will be interested and excited when he sees the original.

Try and plan your tour ahead of time by reading the museum's guide book first and obtaining a floor plan of the museum. These are usually available at the museum sales desk. Know where the restaurants and rest rooms are, and your visit will be much pleasanter. And don't forget that your feet usually give out long before your eyes. Also find out when lecture tours are scheduled and, if you have a group, arrange your visit with the museum's educational office beforehand. Many museums now have Audio-Guides, personal earphones which give a running commentary on the exhibits, and which usually can be rented for about twenty-five cents.

Most museums charge around ten dollars for an annual individual membership, fifteen dollars for a husband and wife. For this, there are usually an almost dizzying number of benefits and activities from which to choose, making museum membership one of the best bargains around. First, of course, is the permanent collection, which you can enjoy for years on end. Then there are often traveling exhibitions with their attendant gala openings (all free if you are a member), plus lectures, catalogues, tours, films, and so on. Year-round there are lectures and classes both in creative art and in the history of art. There are also free subscriptions to the museum bulletin and the monthly calendar of events, as well as discounts on art magazines such as *Art News* and *Arts.* Museum personnel will often advise on your art purchases; in fact, many museums have special days of the week set aside for people to bring in art they are considering buying and have out on approval, or art of their own they want authenticated. (See the chapter on authentication for a further discussion.) There are often members' rooms where you can relax, meet your friends, read, and talk. And often there are chartered art tours to Europe, where special arrangements are made to visit collectors and artists.

In addition, many museums have "Collectors' Clubs," organizations made up to help members buy art. The Virginia Museum of Fine Arts in Richmond, for example, has its Collectors' Circle, with a very active membership. The program includes a series of talks by such art experts as Dorothy Seiberling, art writer for *Life* magazine; advice by the museum curators on what to buy; and an annual showing of the members' purchases called "Collectors' Choice." The Walker Art Center in Minneapolis has a similar program, and so do many other museums around the country. If your museum doesn't already have some of the programs outlined above, perhaps you could start one. Most museums are in crying need of volunteers.

Several museums send out mobile units of both art reproductions and originals to shopping centers in their communities. The Virginia Museum was a pioneer here; and the Arkansas Art Center in Little Rock, the Museum of New Mexico at Santa Fé, and the Detroit Museum, among others, also provide this service.

Museums are also utilizing show-business techniques. Many, like the Brooklyn Museum, are planning displays with sound—using the language and music of other civilizations, the voices of artists speaking on their work, and the simulated sounds of ancient ceremony and ritual. The Museum of Modern Art in New York City now has weekly jazz concerts during the summer in its Sculpture Garden. And the Smithsonian Institution in Washington, D.C., has set up a carousel on the mall and a military band organ in the outdoor restaurant pavilion of one of its new buildings.

A little-known service of museums is the selling of art. They often do their best to hide this fact, but it's true. For some strange reason, museums still have the old-fashioned idea that it's undignified to put a price tag on a painting. Usually a traveling exhibition of contemporary art or a show of original prints will be for sale. If a work of art is labeled "lent by the artist" or "lent by such-and-such gallery," the work is usually for sale. Inquire at the sales or information desk for the list of works available and for prices. The sales desk of a museum is perhaps the most obvious place to buy art, and objects there do have price tags. These shops are fairly recent innovations, and their quality varies. Some are devoted solely to selling guide books, catalogues, and reproductions. Others, like that of the Museum of the American Indian in New York City, are

highly sophisticated stores with high-quality original art. Both the
Indian Museum's director, Dr. Frederick Dockstader, and the
shop's manager, Mrs. Mary Williams, make buying trips to Indian
reservations to select the excellent art you will find there. Unfortunately, many sales desks are run by volunteers who know little
about the merchandise; however, this should improve over the
years as museums get more public support. Too many still sell
souvenir-type items, but the good ones are truly educational ex-
tensions of the museums. Museum rental galleries, discussed earlier,
rent art with advantageous options to buy.

It's more fun to go to museums than to read about them; but
the several excellent guides to museums in the United States are
useful both for telling you more about the museums in your community and for listing museums in cities you may be visiting. *The
Handbook of American Museums* ($8.00, The American Associa-
tion of Museums, Smithsonian Institution, Washington 25, D.C.) is
the most complete listing available and includes historical houses as
well as both art and science museums. The Association also publishes *Museum News,* a monthly publication devoted to news about
museums. While the *Handbook* is *the* book for useful and needed
facts, Eloise Spaeth's *American Art Museums and Galleries: An
Introduction to Looking* (New York, Harper & Row, 1960) is an
entertainingly written, lively account of the major art museums in
the country. She also includes some commercial art galleries in certain selected cities. *Museums, U.S.A.: A History and a Guide* (New
York, Doubleday, 1965), by Herbert and Marjorie Katz, takes a
light vein in describing museums, but does go into the historical
aspects of museums more than do the other two books. W. Aubrey
Cartwright's *A Guide to Art Museums in the U.S. (Southeast Coast
Section)* is now somewhat outdated (New York, Duell, Sloan &
Pearce, 1957) but still has excellent descriptions of the major
museums in that section of the country. S. Lane Faison, Jr.'s *Art
Tours and Detours in New York State* (New York, Random
House, 1964), as well as his *A Guide to the Art Museums of New
England* (New York, Harcourt, Brace, 1958) are the best guides
to these respective areas. See also *Traveler's Guide to America's
Art* by Jane and Theodore Norman (New York: Meredith, 1968).
You will find these books well worth the time and money invested
in terms of the pleasures you will reap from them.

ART GALLERIES

Paris, December 10, 1869

My Dear Sir:

... It is really pitiful to see how most of the people who want to buy pictures set about it. More often than not they are advised by persons who are either fools or rogues, so they buy horrors at very high prices. Yet I, who want to trade fairly and prevent my clients from falling into traps, have the utmost difficulty in succeeding. I have to fight all the time against the people who stand to gain by closing their eyes to the truth. ...

... I have had no word from either Mr. G. or Mr. F. I am sorry I have been unable to do anything for these gentlemen. Please assure them that if they care to trust me, I will never send them anything but good pictures. I am, and always shall be ready to take back anything I have sold, provided I am not specially asked for works that happen to be fashionable, greatly sought after and very dear one day, but not worth a penny the next.

So wrote the French art dealer Paul Durand-Ruel in a letter to an American collector when the dealer's fortunes were at their lowest ebb. In effect, he was stating his creed of art dealing and the faith that made him the champion of the French Impressionists when all of Paris laughed at him. He later added, "A genuine picture-dealer ought to be . . . an intelligent connoisseur, ready if need be to sacrifice what seems to be his immediate interests to his artistic convictions; he should prefer to fight speculators rather than joining in their activities." The story of this particular pioneer is well worth reading in Pierre Cabanne's *The Great Collectors* (New York, Farrar, Straus, 1963).

You will find that most art dealers, like Durand-Ruel, are in the business because they love it. Of course there are as many kinds of art dealers as there are kinds of people—after all, they're human beings, too—and you may find a few cheaters as well as foresighted, devoted, generous men like Durand-Ruel. The dealer will make all the difference when you visit a gallery, and pretty soon you'll learn to recognize a scalper when you see one. I recently visited an exhibition where the dealer's assistant dogged my every step, remarking on the paintings, obviously hoping to make a sale. This kind of thing is fairly unusual, however, and hasn't happened to

Giorgione (c. 1478–1510): *The Adoration of the Shepherds.* (Venetian.) Panel.
Height: 35¾ inches. Width: 43½ inches. Samuel H. Kress Collection, National
Gallery of Art, Washington, D.C. (*Courtesy National Gallery of Art*)

Museum of Contemporary Crafts, New York. (*Courtesy American Craftsmen's Council, New York*)

me in years. Only occasionally will you have an unpleasant experience.

While we're talking about looking at art—and next to visiting museums, going to galleries is the prime method of training your eye and your taste—let's talk about buying too, because this is eventually what you're going to do. You'll find that most dealers welcome the casual browser and that few press sales on you. Contrary to what most people think, galleries are open free to the public and are not expensive clubs reserved for the wealthy few. You'll find only one or two commercial galleries with an entry fee. Galleries vary from small rooms in framing shops to larger, more comfortable establishments.

When you first start visiting galleries, you can be very frank and tell the dealer your price limit; he will, in the long run, appreciate this and you will benefit from sound advice geared to your budget. There is no harm in asking prices as you browse, and it is a good idea to do this on your first gallery rounds. It commits you to nothing, and any good comparison shopper does it. Don't be afraid to show you don't know much about art; and after you've found several galleries you like better than others, try to become friendly with the dealers. The investment in this friendship will be well worth the time and effort.

Be sure that you go to a reputable dealer. I, and the contributors to this book, have tried to select only reputable galleries for listing. You can always consult with your local museum curator as to a gallery's reputation. A good dealer offers many advantages. He offers comfortable surroundings which are quiet and well lighted for browsing and where, usually, nobody bothers you. He often permits a few days to several weeks approval period, in which you can take your purchase home and live with it in your home surroundings. He will advise you on good, low-priced art with which to begin your buying until you are sure of your taste. He can arrange for paying on time without interest (the normal procedure is twenty per cent down with six to twelve months to pay, but this is a highly personal matter and some dealers allow only three months.)

Don't forget that galleries are basically stores with merchandise to sell. The late avant-garde architect Frederick J. Kiesler once expounded his theories on galleries in an article for *Art News* magazine, in which his designs for New York's World House Galleries, based on his concept of "flowing space," were illustrated.

A Gallery is a place where pictures and sculptures are sold. It's a market-place under a solid roof. In Hellenic times, any artist of public repute, who sold a piece of art privately, was liable to be condemned as a prostitutioneer; eventually he was imprisoned; or, as in the case of Phidias, left to die. We put even Death to work for better prices and profit all around. Yet today the artist's best friend, for acquiring food and fame, is the dealer. A good gallery is therefore a market-place where various artifacts (let's call them by the proper name) are sold, and sold for good money. . . .

There are many types of these "stores." Some have what is called a "stable" of artists, artists who are members of that gallery and who participate in one-man and group shows there. Others have a greater variety of art and artists. If you know who is on a gallery's roster, you can ask to see the artist's work even if it isn't on display. The dealer will then show you his stock in the back rooms (dealers are usually glad to show all their artists, not only those on exhibit), or will direct you to the artist's studio. The gallery's financial arrangement with the artist varies—and so, therefore, will the prices—but it's usually better to go through a dealer. Remember that, in the long run, the dealer will be your best friend.

More about art buying will be discussed under the "How and Where to Buy" section of this book, but it's well for both buying and looking to keep in mind the gallery "season." The art market, especially in New York City, slackens during the summer months, when galleries either close down completely or shorten their hours. The best shows are usually scheduled for the winter, and the more reasonable prices are posted during the "Christmas Shows" in December. Hours are most often ten a.m. to six p.m. daily, but many galleries, like the museums, now stay open during the evening hours. Closing days are normally Sundays and Mondays, but this varies with the individual gallery. (Such information is listed in the book's gallery guide.) Don't be afraid to go into galleries where you have to ring the doorbell (that's just so they'll know you're coming), or to phone for an appointment first if the dealer opens his gallery "by appointment only." Many of the better dealers are doing this these days, so that they can spend their free time better serving you. And be sure to get on the gallery's mailing list. In this way, you will get announcements of the current exhibitions and invitations to the exhibit openings. These can be very lively affairs where you will meet artists and other art aficionados, and get first option on the new art work.

OTHER PLACES TO LOOK

There are so many places to look at art, other than museums and art galleries, that they are almost too numerous to list. Historical houses, usually administered by local historical societies, are fun to visit and good places to train your eye. Almost everyone is selling art these days, and, therefore, there are plenty of opportunities for looking. The department stores are perhaps the biggest and most recent entries in the art sweepstakes; almost everyone is familiar with Vincent Price's art program for the Sears Roebuck chain. But Sears is by no means the only department store with quality art for sale. The May Company, based in St. Louis, has initiated several excellent, even important, art exhibits, such as the Primitive Arts show and sale in 1963 and the Greek and Roman Art exhibition circulated in 1965. Both were done with great care, selected by art experts, and only the highest quality art was offered. Rich's in Atlanta, the J. L. Hudson Store in Detroit, and Macy's in New York are a few more of the many which come to mind. Shopping centers, restaurants, even churches and synagogues are putting on art displays, and, while the quality usually varies, the art requires no effort to look at—it's right there. And don't forget your local university and art school, which give most of the cultural impetus in small towns.

Many United States businesses have found it a good policy both for employees and customers to hang art in their offices. Although few have the taste and the money of the Chase Manhattan Bank in New York, which reputedly has spent over a half million dollars on its art and which has some of the best art experts in the city on its art advisory board, more and more businesses have come to the view that the artist and his works are useful not only as good business and public relations, but are part of their obligation to reinvest some of their wealth in the nation's cultural future. Hallmark Cards, Inc., has long conducted artists' competitions which are connected neither with Christmas nor cards. I.B.M. has been building up its collection since 1939 by buying outstanding paintings by living artists all over the world. Clairol, Inc., annually holds a competition from which it buys paintings for its offices. General Electric commissions several paintings yearly and circulates its rapidly growing collection. These are only a few of the growing number of businesses supporting America's artists; for a complete listing, consult the "American Business Supports Art" section in the *Arts* magazine booklet *Art in the U.S.A. and Where to Find It, 1965, Summer/Fall.*

Two more opportunities for looking at art which don't occur to most people are visits to artists' studios and visits to the homes of private collectors. These are often quite easy to arrange. Artists are usually receptive to visitors, as long as an appointment is made ahead of time and the visit does not drag out into a matter of hours. Many museums and local art groups arrange tours to artists' studios, and these shouldn't be missed. It is interesting to see how an artist works and a visit can often give you important insights into his thoughts and feelings. Many of my artist friends in New York have color postcards of paintings of Old Masters tacked up on their walls, and interesting fabrics, fruits, and flowers around their studios. I remember well, also, the home of a Japanese abstract calligrapher I visited in Tokyo whose studio was filled with gleaming black rocks from the northern Japanese island of Hokkaido. He told me their shapes often inspired his bold calligraphic distortions. And when I visited sculptor David Smith's studio in Bolton Landing, N.Y., with some friends, the place looked like a welding factory where indeed, Smith had received his training for the starkly abstract welded-steel sculpture he produced.

It is often more fun to see a private collection in a home than to wander through an enormous museum. You will find that many collectors are very proud of their art and happy to show it off. Some may collect in the art area in which you're especially interested. Here, again, your local museum can be helpful in directing you, and will advise on which collectors will be receptive. You can then write or telephone for an appointment. Many museums, such as the Corcoran Gallery of Art in Washington, D.C., give showings of art from local collections every few years. The Corcoran has been specializing in modern collections in the Washington area, and these exhibits are always fascinating to visit.

ART REPRODUCTIONS AND ILLUSTRATED ART BOOKS

Back in 1920, when America's most popular automobile was the Model T, several leading New York art dealers joined forces in an all-out campaign to get auto entrepreneur Henry Ford interested in buying Old Master paintings. Headed by the usually shrewd Joseph Duveen, the dealers made up a costly three-volume set of elegantly bound books. These were a collection of handsome color reproductions of what they selected as the hundred greatest paintings in the world. It was to be a gift for Ford. The dealers then embarked for Michigan, confident they would have a customer.

Ford was delighted with the pictures, pointing to the ones he thought especially beautiful. Finally, Duveen tactfully suggested that Ford might like to buy some of the originals. "But, gentlemen," Ford said, "what would I want with the original paintings when the ones I have right here in these books are so beautiful?"

It was probably the only time in his life that the irrepressible Joseph Duveen was at a loss for words (Duveen subsequently went on to sell millions of dollars worth of original art to Joseph E. Widener, Benjamin Altman, Samuel H. Kress, John D. Rockefeller, Jr., William Randolph Hearst, and Andrew Mellon). Today, a sales gimmick such as volumes of reproductions would never be used by a dealer. The appreciation of the unique qualities of original art has changed greatly since Ford's day, and Henry Ford II, reportedly an expert collector of modern paintings, has paid hefty sums for his art.

General taste has been greatly improved in the Unitetd States since the 1920s. While it was perfectly acceptable even five or ten years ago to hang a reproduction of a Rembrandt or a Rubens in your living room, it is now generally felt to be much more pleasurable to have an original print or a watercolor (which may have the same price tag as an expensive reproduction).

And this is as it should be. As people's tastes improve, they can see the distortions and the failings of the usual reproduction made by photo-mechanical methods. A machine-made article always lacks the touch of the artist's hand. There are usually color discrepancies and the inevitable change in scale and size that distort the artist's original conception. Try buying some of the reproductions usually sold at a museum's sales desk, and take them upstairs to the originals. You're bound to see the difference.

Sculpture reproductions are, to my mind, even worse than facsimiles of paintings. Again, there are the usual differences in scale and size. And, I feel, there is usually a strangely frozen quality about them.

I'd like to add that reproductions are fine, and indeed necessary, as educational aids and as teaching tools. I constantly use color slides in my art history lectures. Reproductions are valuable as illustrations for art texts and for becoming familiar with works of art. But they should be used solely as introductions to seeing, and for persons who cannot go to art museums often. Otherwise, they should be used to enhance the pleasure of a visit to a museum or art

"*And Terence Conran has designed these legs which screw in and turn it into a rather in-touch coffee table.*"

Courtesy *Punch*.

gallery where original art can be viewed. And as mentioned before, reproductions are valuable in preparing children for museum visits.

You may be wondering why so many museums sell reproductions. Many sell them as educational aids or as souvenirs, while others are simply behind the times in the upsurge of taste in the United States. This also may change in a few years, and you may then find more and more originals being sold at the sales counter.

Reproductions may also be helpful in your initial experimenting with art in your home. You may want to experiment with some to test what you like in the way of color, texture, line, and form. Several great collections have grown out of such experimentation. Joseph Hirshhorn, who recently gave his entire collection to the Smithsonian Institution and who is one of America's greatest art buyers, comes from a poor immigrant family of thirteen children. Even when he was very small, he would cut out romantic landscapes and appealing animals from calendars and pin them up on the wall near his bed. When he began making his fortune, the first original art he purchased very closely resembled that on the calendars. Now a multimillionaire with changed, but still definite, tastes, Hirshhorn still picks out all his own art, has no art advisers.

The Samuel Marxes of Chicago are a similar case. They started off "collecting" with a Rouault reproduction. It was so handsomely framed and so well displayed in their living room that many of their friends thought it an original. This gave the Marxes an impetus to buy originals; and now they have built up a noteworthy collection of twentieth-century European paintings.

Reproductions are valuable for introducing you to original art. Many of us are hindered by demands of job, profession, or home and cannot often get to museums and to the lectures given at museums. In such cases it is sensible to study reproductions in the many excellent art books on the market. But, here again, it's wise to exercise caution. Many art books are lavishly illustrated and extremely expensive, more expensive than an original print, a drawing, or a watercolor. Expensive art books may look good on your coffee table, but why not have good, original art on your walls for the same price or less? Some art books can run as high as three hundred dollars, and there's a lot of good art around for this price. And remember that a mechanically made reproduction can never gain in value, while original art almost always does. This is not to discourage you from owning such books and reading about art, but is a recommendation that you choose books for the excellence of their texts, rather than for their excellence in photo-mechanical color work. The bigger art books with many color plates and little information are rarely worth their weight in gold or silver or green-backs. And there's always the local library where you can borrow them free.

I'd like to point out, however, that several publishers offer excellent illustrations as well as excellent texts. Skira, in Switzerland, and the New York Graphic Society come first to mind, while Harry N. Abrams, Phaidon, and Praeger are also good. One of the best series on art history put out to date is the Metropolitan Museum's *Art Seminars in the Home.* The series of color portfolios, with accompanying explanatory text by *New York Times* art critic John Canaday (formerly Education Director of the Philadelphia Museum of Art) are excellent. Each portfolio goes into some style or school of art such as Expressionism, Impressionism, or Realism; and the reproductions, while sometimes fuzzy, are perfectly adequate for giving you a general idea of the work of art.

READING, RADIO, TV, ART COURSES

Reading never replaces looking, but it is an important adjunct to it. Useful knowledge and information, on everything from art critiques to current news to art history, can be gained from the popular journals and newspapers as well as from certain art books. For local art purchases, it's a good idea to consult your city newspapers. While most newspapers, and magazines for that matter, underestimate the current American art hunger, many feature Sunday art reviews, calendars of art events, announcements of visiting art exhibitions, and advertisements for art festivals and antique fairs.

Unfortunately, the quality of the criticism tends to vary greatly, especially on the smaller city newspapers. Even in the larger communities, there is usually only a part-time art critic writing for the Sunday paper, and art news doesn't even exist on some of the smaller papers. In order to find out the particular qualities of an exhibition, check the reviews against your own reactions. See what the critic writes about it and how you feel about it. You can train your eye and sensibilities by reading the better art magazines such as *Art News, Art in America, Antiques, Arts, Art Voices, Craft Horizons, Art International,* and *Horizon*—available free in your public or museum library as well as by subscription. In this way, by reading and looking, you can get some idea of how good your local critic is. *Art News* and *Arts* are especially valuable for their monthly New York and cross-country art calendars listing the major art shows across the United States; and from their "Competitions and Scholarships" and "Where and When to Exhibit" sections you can often find the dates of shows opening near you. *Art News* also publishes a "Summer Art School Guide" every May, and an "Art Travel Guide" citing the major art festivals, galleries, museums, and exhibitions in Europe, Latin America, and Canada in their summer issue. Many of the art magazines review newly published art books, especially at Christmas time, and every December *Art News* and *Craft Horizons* publish illustrated art-buying features. And for you who live in or go to New York City, the *New Yorker* magazine publishes a weekly listing of the city's art shows (arranged in order of the artists' last names) in its "Goings On About Town" section, giving short descriptions of each exhibit. *The Art Gallery,* available for fifty cents at most galleries and museums, and by subscription, lists news of exhibitions across the nation. The *New York Arts Calendar,* also fifty cents, concentrates on art news in that city. Even the supermarket magazines like *Family Circle* and *Woman's Day* run excellent articles on art from time to time.

Your local librarian can help you with your special fields of art collecting, and there are certain reference books that you should find helpful. Among the many excellent art dictionaries on the market, Mervyn Levy's ninety-five-cent paperback, *The Pocket Dictionary of Art Terms* (Greenwich, Conn., The New York Graphic Society, 1961), is succinct and informative. It is sold at many museum sales counters. If you're confused by such terms as chiaroscuro, baroque, offskip, or pointillism, just look them up in this handy booklet—be sure to take it with you when you go to museums and galleries. *The American Art Directory* is the most valuable general art guide being put out today. Published by the American Federation of Arts in New York City, it lists national and regional art organizations in the United States; museums, art associations, and organizations by states; art schools; art museums, societies, and schools in Canada; major museums and art schools abroad; children's and junior museums; the major art magazines and newspapers that carry art reviews, with the names of their critics; scholarships and fellowships; sources of various types of exhibitions; and traveling exhibitions and art booking agencies. *Art Prices Current,* published every June by the Art Trade Press, Ltd., London, and listing yearly art auction prices, will inform you of current values. *The International Directory of the Arts,* published in four languages, is a good directory of museums, galleries, universities, art schools, art and antique dealers, and private galleries, and is especially useful if you're planning a trip to Europe or the Far East. *Who's Who in American Art* is a good directory of American artists, critics, and museum personnel.

Libraries are invaluable for the art buyer. There are literally thousands of public, private, and museum libraries all through the country. They are usually generously stocked with books on art; in fact, many have special divisions devoted solely to this subject. The staffs of these art divisions are usually extremely helpful and knowledgeable. You will soon learn that art reference books are usually numbered in the seven hundreds, according to the Dewey Decimal System, and that many art divisions also circulate mounted color reproductions.

It is at the library that you will find the many windows which will open your vision to the drama of art. The critic Aline Saarinen, writing in *The Proud Possessors* (New York, Random House, 1958) has beautifully set down what an art book should do in her description of Bernard Berenson's work: "His writings, from the earliest handbooks to the latest essays are not only scholarly art history, but also *a rare summons to see and feel and understand the work of art as an event itself*" (italics mine). Good art books do *do* this; and you'll be able to recognize the excellent ones after a while. Later in this book I will be recommending certain books to you, and I hope you will find them useful as a guide to your knowing and your seeing.

Exhibition catalogues are also an excellent way to become knowledgeable. A collector friend of mine keeps up with news of art by reading the art magazines; then he writes for catalogues of exhibitions in which he is interested. He feels this is a good way of training his eye; and, in reading a good, serious introductory essay to the exhibit catalogue, he learns about the particular field of art the exhibition covers.

The radio is another source for widening your art horizons. Interviews with artists, listings of cultural events in your city, and programs by art critics are only a few of the usual radio offerings. The National Gallery of Art has a "Radio Picture of the Week" program, in which a museum staff member discusses one of the Gallery's paintings. You can order reproductions of the series to be discussed ahead of time and study the painting along with the curator's discussion. This is good practice for the whole family.

Television, also, is devoting more of its programing time to art. Through TV, you can visit the Louvre, the White House, or the Kremlin, with the experience enhanced by a perceptive narrator. Aline Saarinen's appearances on the "Today" show have given art on TV a great shot in the arm. At this point, however, the BBC, in

England, has done much more than we have, and how much art will appear on TV in the United States will probably ultimately depend on the development of color TV. Still, the educational stations are doing more and more along these lines, and it is hoped that they will do more in the near future. Although art on TV is always somewhat distorted by both the curvature and smallness of the screen, it is probably the most immediate means of bringing art into the home.

Finally, do try to take some kind of course on art and aesthetics at your local college or university. Adult education courses are blossoming forth much the way art appreciation is, and many courses are given in the evenings for working people and for homemakers. There, through the instructors and lectures and the slides shown, you can trace the many varied and fascinating paths art has taken through the ages.

You can also do this through art films. Your local museum and art association are bound to have many showings during the year. Further, a group can get together and rent them from the many organizations, such as New York's Museum of Modern Art and Metropolitan Museum, that offer them for nominal sums, especially if you're renting a series.

CONSULTING ART GROUPS

Certain organizations, many of which are listed throughout this book, can be very helpful to art buyers. If you are interested in purchasing the work of a certain painter, write the Museum of Modern Art or the Metropolitan Museum, both in New York City, for names of reputable galleries handling that artist. If you want to find out quickly where your favorite contemporary painter is showing, write The Art Information Center, 11 W. 56th Street, New York City (247-2350); they provide service free of charge. Local art groups and organizations will be listed in *The Art Directory*. The Art Dealers Association of America (575 Madison Ave., New York City) is an extremely reputable outfit which carefully screens its membership. You can write them for a free listing of their members, who are selected from only the most scrupulous and knowledgeable dealers in the United States. Each is an outstanding and representative authority in the field or fields of art in which he is active. The Association strives to elevate ethical standards in the art trade and also runs an important appraisal service both for individuals and for the federal government. (See the section on appraisals.)

TYPES OF ART

The beginning art lover will quickly realize that he is faced with a bewildering array of goods. Which museum should he visit on his one free Sunday a month, a museum of modern art or one with paintings of historical interest? Which gallery should he start to frequent—with an eye to future buying—an antique shop or one that specializes in original prints?

I will try to answer some of these questions in the section on what types of art are available for under a thousand dollars, but there are still other questions. What medium is the one for you? For that matter, what is a medium? Quite simply, it is the material from which a work of art is created. You can easily look up the following definitions in any good art dictionary; but here, briefly, are some characteristics to look for.

Oil paintings are made of ground pigments mixed with some kind of oil, usually linseed. Their particular quality is the reflection of light within the pigment. Oils are also extremely pliant. They are usually shiny, and vary from very thin, smooth surfaces to thick, rough texturing. Traditionally the invention of oil painting is credited to two fifteenth-century Flemish brothers, Hubert and Jan van Eyck. So popular did oil painting become that it almost immediately replaced the previously favored fresco and tempera techniques. Oil painting is an essentially Western practice, and was not used in the Far East until recently. Oils may be near the top of your art budget, and you probably won't be buying the great names in this medium. However, it is here that you can test your more adventurous taste and buy from the "undiscovered" artists.

Watercolors are ground pigments mixed with water, in which gum is the usual binder. This medium is usually prized for its transparent, luminous, abbreviated qualities; some artists, however, like the American watercolorist John Marin, have thickened their colors for the opaque effects of *gouache*. The Oriental ink-and-brush techniques are essentially watercolor ones, and in Chinese and Japanese scrolls you can see the multitude of ways in which water-with-color can be handled. Western watercolors are usually framed under glass; and you will notice that in a great many the artist has allowed the white of the paper to sparkle through in the untouched areas. As I will discuss in the graphics section, water-

Peter Paul Rubens (1577–1640): *Sketch for the ceiling of a banqueting hall, Whitehall, London.* (Flemish.) Oil. Height: 31¼ inches. Width: 27⅞ inches. Collection of the Minneapolis Institute of Arts, Minneapolis, Minnesota. (*Courtesy Minneapolis Institute of Arts*)

John Marin (1870–1953): *Maine Islands.* (American.) Watercolor. Height: 16¾ inches. Width: 20 inches. 1922. The Phillips Collection, Washington, D.C. *(Courtesy Phillips Collection)*

(Left) Replica of *A Muse*. (Roman.) First century A.D. Collection of the Minneapolis Institute of Arts, Minneapolis, Minnesota. (*Courtesy Minneapolis
Institute of Arts*)

(Right) Constantin Brancusi (1876–1957): *The Yellow Bird*. Height: 37¾ inches.
Circa 1912. Collection of the Minneapolis Institute of Arts, Minneapolis, Minnesota.
(*Courtesy Minneapolis Institute of Arts*)

Tucson, Arizona, potter Maurice K. Grossman working on the potter's wheel.

colors are usually moderate in price and are an excellent area in which to buy. *Casein,* made with a milk-curd base, is similar to gouache in its thickened qualities but is somewhat easier to manipulate. Three older techniques are: *tempera,* in which egg yolk is the main ingredient; *encaustic,* a melted wax medium; and *fresco,* so popular with the Renaissance painters, a painting method in which ground pigments are painted directly into wet plaster for large wall decorations or murals. *Pastels,* or colored chalks; *charcoal,* which is made by charring animal or vegetable substances; and *pen and ink* and *pencil* are used in the drawings too often neglected by collectors.

Sculpture requires a high degree of technical skill and, because of the materials used—wood, stone, clay, and bronze and other metals—can often be more expensive than the other mediums. Sculpture is traditionally *modeled* or *carved* from wood or stone but it may be *welded* or *cast* in any of a variety of metals. Plastics and wax are currently popular with contemporary sculptors, along with the welded metal forms. A little-known form of low-cost sculpture to buy is the *maquette* that a sculptor makes in preparation for his larger works. Essentially these *maquettes* are smaller studies, and are comparable to the drawings painters execute for their paintings. My Washington, D.C., collector acquaintance, Henry Hecht, puts it this way; "There are the same aesthetics, the same patina, the same balance." Some sculptors will do a series of *maquettes*; and you may be able to buy such a whole series quite reasonably. Don't neglect this area in your buying. *Constructions* are essentially built-up forms which border between painting and sculpture, and which are made from a variety of materials such as clay, wood, metal, and paper. This approach to art has been the stimulus for many of the more exciting art trends in the art of the twentieth century. When paper is the medium, constructions are most often called *collages.*

Ceramics are usually made on a potter's wheel, a flat, circular stone that is turned quickly by means of a foot pedal, and on which the clay takes shape. Other methods are *coil building,* in which coils of clay are laid one on top of the other and the sides smoothed (this is the most ancient technique for making pots), and *slab building,* a form of construction with slabs of clay. Many of today's potters combine slab and wheel-thrown techniques for what is popularly called *ceramic sculpture.*

There are a great many *original print* techniques (for a fuller description, see the section on graphics). Prints are multi-originals which are made by pressing one material against another. An artist first creates an image on or in one of many kinds of materials—stone, metal, wood, silk, linoleum, et cetera—and then presses the paper against this material to make the print. Original prints are *not* to be confused with "prints" made by machine processes. Different kinds of prints, depending on the materials used, are called *engravings, etchings, aquatints, lithographs, silk screens,* and *woodcuts.*

How and Where to Buy

No one person can give you infallible advice as to the "what," "where", and "when" of art buying. I can only give you the benefit of my experience as a writer and lecturer on art and as an occasional buyer, as well as what I have learned from friends who buy frequently. As I emphasized before, taste is an essential ingredient of successful buying, but this should not be a problem if you've read the previous section. There are as many sources for buying as there are for looking, and an attempt will be made to describe some of them here. And just as you prime your eye by looking at as many works of art as possible, so also you must constantly compare what you like in art and its prices, in order to get your best value both in pleasure and dollars.

ART RENTAL

"Giving a Christmas party? Art Lending will cater the paintings," was the call that went out to members of the Washington, D.C., Gallery of Modern Art several Decembers ago. Renting art for a party in your home is only one of the many reasons for renting before you buy. The main reason, of course, is that renting the art you *think* you like assures you of *really* liking the object long after you've purchased it. When you are going to buy art, I can't recommend any method more highly than renting first.

Many art dealers, of course, will let you take art home on approval, for a period of anywhere from two days to two weeks. Renting gives you a somewhat longer period in which to test your taste. The minimum rental period is usually two months, and the very nominal fee can be applied later should you decide to buy.

Inga Heck, director of Rental Services of the Corcoran Gallery of Art, Washington, D.C., runs one of the most unusual rental galleries in the United States. Started in 1962, when Mrs. Heck first joined the Corcoran, the gallery is the only one in the country to work with local interior decorators in setting up sample rooms in which the decorating is planned around a work of art—which is for rent, of course. The rooms, which are designed for both homes and offices, are changed about three times a year, with cocktail openings scheduled at each change.

Not all museums set up their rental galleries with as much care and imagination as Mrs. Heck, but many across the country make quality art available to their members on a rental basis. I recently visited the Philadelphia Museum of Art and was very much impressed by both the quantity and the quality of the art offered in the enormous white room that serves as their rental quarters. The Museum of Modern Art in New York City is rightly famous for the exhibitions in its rental gallery, culled from over ninety New York City art galleries. The purchase prices range up to $850, and sizes are limited to thirty-six by forty-eight inches for framed works and to seventeen inches for sculptures. All works are insured by the museum, and they can even be rented through the mail.

The Corcoran selects its rental objects from dealers in New York and Washington, D.C.; and prints, sculpture, ceramics, and paintings are offered in its spacious, attractive galleries. For an object with a sale price of $125, the rental is five dollars for two months; for a $126-to-$200 sale price the rental is ten dollars, and so on. If you've ever rented a TV, tape recorder, or typewriter, you will realize how very reasonable these prices are. Everything is insured, and the renter must pick up and return his own art.

Mrs. Heck tells me that quite often persons come into the gallery wanting to buy, never having heard about renting art. Often these are persons to whom reproductions are no longer satisfying. They want to fill an empty space on their wall without really knowing what they want or what they like. Mrs. Heck usually tries to persuade them to rent first and buy later, and most are pleased with this arrangement. Business people, too, come into the Corcoran to rent art for their offices. At first they move gingerly around the contemporary paintings like husbands at a lingerie counter, but these businessmen often grow to like the art so much that what was rented for an office goes home as a purchase, or stays permanently on the office wall, rather than being returned to the gallery. This was the case with the Federal Deposit Insurance Company, which was built near the Corcoran in the 1960s. "Acres and acres of beautiful, bare walls," as Mrs. Heck described them, had to be filled. The company first rented paintings, then decided to buy the whole lot outright. As in the case of other renters-turned-buyers, the company was then referred to individual galleries where various buying arrangements, including purchase on the installment plan, could be made.

"Art and Offices" exhibition, Rental Gallery, Corcoran Gallery of Art, Washington, D.C. Furniture by Herman Miller, Inc., with American Indian crafts.
(*Courtesy Corcoran Gallery of Art*)

Mrs. Heck tells me that the most common reasons for renting are the following: for a party; to replace one's own art while it is being reframed; for a temporary stay away from one's home (for example, there are many transients in Washington who leave their art at home but who want something while they're living in the Capital); or, in the case of a wedding present, to see if the newlyweds really like it. Many bachelors rent art and like to experiment, Mrs. Heck says, but it is usually the women who eventually want something more permanent. The prime reason for renting, of course, is to deepen your appreciation for art with contact, to confirm your taste before you invest your money.

GALLERIES

The telephone company, in advertising its very useful Yellow Pages, advises that "your fingers do the walking." While this is normally good procedure, it is better that you, not your fingers, do some walking around, at least at the beginning of your art-buying safaris. Comparative shopping in art is absolutely necessary, and where better to do this than in your local art galleries?

It used to be that one would have to journey to New York to get any reasonable selection of art and galleries from which to choose. But this is no longer true. Today every sizable U.S. city is practically jumping with opportunities to buy art. And the galleries constitute the major percentage of these opportunities.

There are rules in every game or trade, and among the musts of the art game is to put yourself in the hands of a reputable art dealer. As I mentioned before, many are in the business because they love it, and many are only too eager to help the beginning art buyer. Remember that art buying is nothing new—indeed, the Romans were enthusiastic collectors and auctioneers— but it was only in the nineteenth century that the skilled, professional art dealer came into his own. Dealers want others to share their love of art and that is why I urge you to go to a well-established dealer during the fledgling stage of your buying. Later you can be more adventurous when you're sure of what you want and of prices; but, at least at the beginning, the bargain basement is not for beginners. You'll find also, as you shop around for art and make the price comparisons you would on any purchase, that art at the bigger galleries, auction houses, and antique shops is sometimes less expensive than at the smaller ones.

Some of the advantages of a good dealer have already been mentioned in the section on looking at art. First, dealers encourage you to browse. As you're browsing, many questions will cross your mind: what is the status of the painter? how do his prices compare with those of other artists and other galleries? what is the place of this particular style in the artist's *oeuvre* as a whole? are the paintings of good or bad quality? which of the two paintings hanging side by side is better?

A good dealer will attempt to answer these questions honestly, and not try to force a work of art on you. In fact, most of the dealers I know prefer to start a beginning buyer with something not too costly and let him try out his purchase in his home for a while until he is more sure of his taste. Dealers will try to encourage your natural bents, answer your specific questions, and try to bring you along somewhat as a teacher does a student. In fact, many galleries have special advisory services for businessmen to help them with art-buying programs for their offices.

It is generally unwise to try to circumvent the dealer in your buying. Some people try to cut out the dealer's percentage by buying directly from the artist. If you bypass the dealer, you will miss out on the many advantages he offers, especially in the long run of your buying. (You can, of course, select your purchase in the artist's studio while making the business transaction through the dealer.) Henry Hecht, a Washington, D.C., collector, has many artist friends and could easily buy from them. But he likes the approval period in the home that so many dealers give. He also likes to have an option on exchanging the particular work he's buying for another by the same artist at a later date. It is quite easy to have this arrangement written into the bill of sale; many dealers, Hecht tells me, will guarantee taking back any work of art for its full value or for at least eighty per cent of its value, if the object is returned in good condition, and if another purchase is made. The advantages of this kind of agreement are obvious. In addition, a dealer, if he likes you, will telephone you if something comes into the gallery which he thinks will interest you. And, finally, if you like something at a gallery, the dealer will usually put it away for a few days while you're thinking it over. Another friend of mine recently saw what he described as a Renaissance-style portrait set in a beautiful frame in a gallery window. The price was eighty-five dollars, the value of the intricately carved, gilded frame itself. When he went back the following weekend, it was gone. "The one that got away" wouldn't have if he had walked right into the gallery and taken an option on it.

In buying art, be sure to have the dealer write the particulars of what you're purchasing—name of artist, school (if there is one), medium, year executed, and so on—on the bill of sale. Then, if the article is not what it purports to be, the dealer is obliged to take the article back for a full refund. This is particularly useful in buying older art or antiques. No reputable dealer will refuse to write these particulars out for you, *but they must be in writing if you expect a refund.*

At the beginning, you will want to sample the many varieties of art, and you may become friendly with several dealers. After a while, however, your own tastes will probably begin limiting themselves quite naturally and your interests will intensify in one direction. You may become interested in a certain artist; or in one medium, such as sculpture; or you may decide to concentrate on something like carved Spanish chests, as a friend of mine in New York recently did. It is especially then that you will begin to rely heavily on one dealer, and that the dealer will become the best friend you can have in your art buying.

AUTHENTICATION

Just as valued a friend as your art dealer will be the art expert who checks on your purchases. This could be your local museum curator or a staff member of your local college, university, or art school. An art expert is one who, through education and training, has a particular knowledge of an artist, period, or school. The collector J. Paul Getty has written, "Before you invest, investigate; the cost of having an independent authority expertize a work of art *before* . . . [you] buy is the cheapest insurance any collection can obtain," and goes on to point out that the local university or college art historian is one of the great unplumbed sources of authentication. "These people," Getty continues, "are not there only for writing or teaching, and many people are afraid of them because of their titles like 'Professor' and 'Doctor.' " I think you'll agree Getty has a point.

Museum curators are the most sought-after authenticators, but many people are unaware that museums set aside certain days during the week for this service. (These will be listed in the museum listings in this book.) You have to make an appointment beforehand, because museum curators are often overworked, underpaid, rather harried individuals who would like to help but who are limited in time. The curator will counsel, but he is usually prohibited by law or his museum director from giving a money appraisal. Museums have had too many litigations concerning authentications for the curator to put himself out on a limb.

One of the many stories about authentication is the "Jade of Ho" anecdote about an art find in China in the eighth century B.C. The story goes that a minor but very honest official named Ho was digging in his garden in the state of Ch'u one day when he came across an ancient piece of sacrificial jade. Ho did not even consider keeping it for himself because traditionally in China all antiques are the property of the government. He immediately went to the court and presented the piece of jade to the Duke of Ch'u. The piece was handed to the duke's experts, who pronounced it an imitation.

Ho protested vehemently, and the experts were so incensed they persuaded the duke to remove Ho's right foot as punishment for attempting to deceive the head of the state.

Ho was now lame, but he kept the jade and polished it lovingly from time to time. When the old duke died and a new one came to power, Ho again went to court and presented his jade.

This time he lost the other foot and was reduced to the status of a helpless beggar. But when again the dukedom passed into other hands Ho again went to court and, poor, weeping, and emaciated, told his story to the new duke. He wept not for himself, he said, but for the beautiful jade which had been so maligned. Again, the jade was examined and this time the experts agreed that it was a genuine antique.

This is the classic story of how experts disagree; but there was also the time when the art dealer Joseph Duveen wanted the famed Renaissance art scholar Bernard Berenson to authenticate a certain painting as a Giorgione. Berenson insisted it was a Titian (Titian was Giorgione's pupil, and early Titians are often very Giorgionesque; however, since there are many more Titians around, they are less valuable than works by Giorgione, who died early and left few paintings). Duveen, who wanted to make a better sale, was incensed at what he called Berenson's "stubbornness," and it was even rumored at the time that the two painters, who had been good friends on earth, started having violent quarrels up in heaven. The disputed painting, which now hangs in the National Gallery of Art and which is titled "The Adoration of the Shepherds"—and credited to Giorgione—is such an obvious masterpiece the controversy no longer seems important.

Authentication is often a very tricky matter, but your local museum curator or college art professor can usually tell you something about the quality of your purchase and usually come close to telling if it is what it is purported to be (needless to say, most of us are not in the market for Giorgiones or Titians). It is always wise to check your purchase in this manner while you have your art out on approval, as everyone likes to receive the full value for what he's paying. You can also improve your own authenticating talents by first carefully training your eye and researching the kind of art you're buying, learning the many little clues to authentication which the experts use. Learn something about the collectors' marks which are often stamped on drawings, prints, and works in other mediums; look for signatures, and for the marks of honorary societies and estate signatures. As these usually appear on graphics, they will be further discussed under that section. If you're buying an early Willem de Kooning you will know he used housepainter's paints, and will recognize a clever copy in oils. Or if you're buying a Rembrandt etching you will look up one of the *Catalogue Raisonnés* of his work and see where the number and subject fit into his work. These are only examples, and you will soon discover your own guide posts.

If there is no local authority for you to consult, you can write the Appraisers Association of America, Inc., 510 Madison Avenue, New York City 10022 (PL 3-5039), for their membership directory. This is an extremely reputable organization with members in more than two hundred categories and classifications (besides art, appraisers of industrial plants and machinery are also listed). As membership is open to individuals only, the listing is alphabetical, and it takes a little while to locate appraisers in your locale or city. It is well worth the trouble, however, and the little directory is free for the asking.

Another organization which performs outstanding authentication services is the Art Dealers Association of America, 55 Madison Avenue, New York City. Committed to the maintenance and improvement of standards in the art world, the Association also issues appraisals of art contributed to museums or to other non-profit institutions where the donor desires to take the market value of the gift as a deduction for income-tax purposes. The appraisal is executed by a committee of three who are supplied with certain documents on the work to be appraised. They work independently, and come to their own conclusions. In most cases involving modern works, appraisals can be issued on the basis of these documents and photographs. However, when an examination of the original is required, the owner must ship the painting to the Santini Brothers Warehouse in New York City for the committee to look at.

After the valuation has been made, a letter of appraisal is sent to the owner and a copy is sent to the Audit Division of the Internal Revenue Service in Washington, D.C. The modest schedule of fees charged for the Association's appraisal service can be obtained by writing to them. The art dealers who serve on the appraisal panels do so entirely without compensation and as a public service, while the appraisal fees are used to administer the Association's activities.

The Association, also without compensation, renders opinions as to authenticity and value, at the request of government bureaus, in both income- and estate-tax cases. If necessary, they will supply expert testimony at trials. The Association acts as a kind of watchdog in protecting the public from fakes and frauds. As an association, and having at its disposal the collective expertise of its members, the Association is in a position to act where no individual dealers would care or dare to. The Association did not hesitate to declare publicly in the summer of 1962 that approximately one-half of the works in the collection of Walter P. Chrysler, first at his own museum in Provincetown, Massachusetts and later at the National Gallery of Art in Ottawa, Canada, were not what they purported to be. Recently, when fake Franz Klines, Piet Mondrians, and Jackson Pollocks began to appear on the New York art market, the Association, at its own expense, retained an investigator to develop the facts. He obtained evidence which was turned over to the United States Attorney for the Southern District of New York, and an indictment on seventeen counts was obtained against the perpetrator of the frauds.

PRICES

As I have emphasized, you should ask prices on your first rounds of looking at art. Galleries are only too glad to give prices, and museums usually have price lists at their sales desks. It is the law of supply and demand that basically determines art prices. You have to consider first the artist's reputation and whether the work you want is characteristic of any one of his styles. Certain periods in an artist's *oeuvre,* for example, will be less expensive than others, such as Vincent van Gogh's "dark" period in Holland, when he painted "The Potato Eaters." While this period is now rising in value, his "Impressionist" style is generally more in demand. The condition of the work is also extremely important, especially from the point of view of resale. If you're spending quite a bit of money, buy only works in top-notch condition. Look for repainting and touching up and for overcleaning, especially in older paintings. I once bought a torn José Clemente Orozco etching in Mexico for four dollars and I've enjoyed that print as much as any whole one. The tear is almost unnoticeable and, as I'd never want to sell it, the resale value doesn't matter to me. In most cases, however, be sure the condition is impeccable, because restoration and repairing can often run into more than you've paid for your art.

Where and when an art object is offered for sale also affect the price. Prices are perhaps most advantageous at December "Christmas Shows." And it is sometimes a good idea to buy in the summer when galleries are not as crowded and prices are often made more attractive. (However, the demand for art continues to increase, so galleries may not have to continue doing this). Changing vogues and styles may raise prices one year, lower them them the next; this is especially typical of today's art prices, which reflect the all too quickly changing fashions in art. Needless to say, a work by an unknown artist is going to be cheaper than that by a "name." The age of the work and the identity of the previous owner also affect the price; if the art was in a well-known private collection or happened to belong to Napoleon you can be sure the price is going to be high.

It is usually unwise to sink all your money into one work of art, unless it's completely irresistible and will satisfy your art desires for a long time to come. Consider rather how much money you have to spend, then look around for several pieces that will fit your pocketbook.

It is also unwise to buy solely for a name, as an artist's production is usually uneven. Even Picasso has his bad days. And if you buy something you don't really like, even though it's by a "name," you will never receive your full measure of value or pleasure.

The medium of your purchase will also affect the price. An etching or drawing by Rembrandt is going to be much lower than any of his paintings. The same could be said of a modern artist like Franz Kline or Jackson Pollock. In original prints, the edition size (see the chapter on graphics), the condition, the date of execution, and the size of the print itself are all cost factors. Whether or not a work is signed is also important, especially for modern art. The general characteristics of the work, especially the subject matter, will add to the price. For example, a boxing scene by George Bellows will bring a higher price in any medium than the other subjects he treated. And with antiques, the time consumed in manufacture and the cost of the materials will both add to the price.

Also consider the costs of framing and restoration. The framing charges must always be added, because it is the frame that completes the work of art. If your purchase is already framed attractively, this is all to the good. The cost of framing can easily be forgotten when you're buying. I once paid more for a frame than for the art itself in the case of some temple rubbings I brought back from Bangkok. The rubbings were two dollars each, while the gilt frames and raw silk mats with which I surrounded them were thirty-five dollars each. Yet I felt it was well worth the expense, because it is the whole effect you take in, and the elegant designs of the rubbings demanded something comparable in the way of frames. I do not recommend this for everyone, however. If you're planning to pack and ship your purchases, you should also think of the costs involved, as well as the costs of insuring your art. And with that great antique "find" you discover at a local junk shop, remember that the cleaning and restoration and repairing can add up to quite a bit.

Perhaps most important of all, especially when you're investing in an unknown artist, is the fact that prices rise immediately when an artist dies. Too often it's only after death that an artist is rewarded, so let's do something about rewarding him in the here and now.

Remember that the price of *quality* art will never go down, and that this is the best kind of art to buy and to resell later if you wish. Buy what you like and what you love. Although we all like to see the price value of our art go up, buying solely for investment is the final degradation of art buying. Purchasing art for investment is very dependent on fashion and is at best a calculated gamble.

It is also wise to buy in art categories about which you know something. Learn the values and what is typical of the art and artists involved. But also be adventurous and don't be afraid to mix styles. Try to dig out neglected categories of art before they become fashionable and prices concomitantly high. (Remember that Victoriana was really "out" only five or ten years ago.) Young couples who are just married should consider the lack of space in most modern apartments and include graphics, which store easily, in their art buying. One of the best books I've read on adventurous purchasing and sound decorating is by the owner of San Francisco's famed Gump's store, Richard Gump. Titled *Good Taste Costs No More* (New York, Doubleday, 1951), the book gives valuable tips for fitting all kinds of art into your home with flair and taste.

AUCTIONS

When you've been buying art awhile and know your tastes and the market prices, start going to auctions: they are veritable gold mines for the young art buyer. Auctions have had a varied and colorful press; they range from the country auction, where the auctioneer mounts the block in his shirtsleeves, to the elegant, velvet-walled quarters of the Parke-Bernet Galleries in New York City. Whichever kind of auction you attend, the timeless advice of the auctioneer, "let the buyer beware," is given at the start of every auction. In other words, you pay your money and take your chances. Unlike the gallery dealer, the auctioneer guarantees nothing he sells as genuine, and therefore you have no cause for complaint if you find you've bought a fake. However, once you know what you're doing, you can often obtain excellent art for very little money. The bigger auction houses like Sotheby & Co. in London do a large part of their business in the lower price ranges; sixty-eight per cent of the items auctioned in the 1965-66 season sold for $280 or less, and twenty-eight per cent for fifty-six dollars or less.

Art and literary auctions are a long-time tradition in Holland, and were introduced to England in 1676. It was not until 1744, however, that Samuel Baker of Russell Street, Covent Garden, held the first of a continuous series of sales which made him the first professional art and book auctioneer in England. Baker's firm, since then known as Sotheby's (pronounced "suth-er-bees"), claims to be the oldest auctioneering firm in the world, and they're still going strong in London. In fact, so booming has business been since the 1920s that Sotheby's recently merged with its United States rival, Parke-Bernet (pronounced Bernett, *not* Bernay). This auctioneering cartel now has the most formidable array of art experts and auctioneering resources of any firm of its kind in the world.

The new president of the Parke-Bernet Galleries is a six-foot Briton named Peregrine Michael Hungerford Pollen. Although Pollen comes from the kind of English nobility who inherit, rather than buy, their paintings, he is no snob. He worked his way around the world in 1955 when he was twenty-four, acting as gas-station attendant, market researcher, driver, aluminum worker, moving man, and pantry boy on a ship. He also, while at Oxford, performed the exploit of running a mile, riding a mile, and rowing a mile, all consecutively, and within the space of fourteen minutes (the challenge had been for fifteen).

Peter Wilson, chairman of Sotheby & Co., London, and the Parke-Bernet Galleries, Inc., New York. (*Courtesy Parke-Bernet Galleries, Inc.*)

Louis B. Marion auctioning Rembrandt's *Aristotle Contemplating the Bust of Homer,* Parke-Bernet Galleries, New York, 1961. (*Courtesy Parke-Bernet Galleries, Inc.*)

Returning from his trip in 1955, Pollen joined the Old Masters Department of Sotheby & Co., and became personal assistant to the astute, debonair, six-foot-four chairman of Sotheby's, Peter Wilson. Wilson , also from a moneyed family, joined Sotheby's in 1936. Becoming a partner two years later, he pushed the specialized type of auction sale, in which furniture was grouped together, or a special sale of jades was held. He is also a master of the Soft Sell. When is was rumored that novelist Somerset Maugham wanted to disperse his Impressionist painting collection a few years ago, Wilson, along with other would-be auctioneers, visited Maugham. Unlike his colleagues, Wilson never once mentioned the paintings. So, of course, it was Wilson who auctioned Maugham's collection.

Of a slightly different breed, but with the same passion for expertly auctioning beautiful objects, are the officers of the Parke-Bernet Galleries in New York. Louis J. Marion, Parke-Bernet's former president and now a member of the board, worked his way up in the firm from mailboy. In 1961, he expertly auctioned off the Erickson Rembrandt "Aristotle" for $2,300,000 in just under four minutes.

The late Hiram H. Parke and Leslie A. Hyam instituted Parke-Bernet's huge mail-order business during the war. Parke could see that a medium-price business would have to be instituted to supplement the more spectacular sales— a bread-and-butter business, so to speak—that would make the modest art buyer aware he could buy at a place like Parke-Bernet. James Brough, in his entertaining book *Auction!* (Indianapolis, Bobbs-Merill, 1963), describes the initial difficulties by quoting Hyam. "Let's face it," Hyam reportedly said, "there's a certain amount of resistance to coming in here. We have the reputation of being rather elegant and expensive. Many smaller people are afraid that things will cost too much, just as they might hesitate about going into Cartier's to buy a piece of smaller jewelry."

The plushness of the galleries themselves, with their velvet walls and thick piled carpeting, were obstacles to attracting wider audiences. However Hyam, who has a Cambridge University degree in physics, had one passion: the catalogs which are prepared for each auction. He took to heart that maxim of the last Sotheby, Samuel Leigh, who died in 1861, in his "Hints for a Young Auctioneer of Books": "Consider your Catalogue as the foundation of your eminence and make its perfection of character an important study." These catalogs are now the pride and joy of the firm, and it is their perfection, with the careful descriptions of the art, photographs, extensive bibliographies, and background information, that has succeeded in attracting a new type of buyer. Before he died, Hyam used to read each galley proof of every catalog, and the resulting accuracy has enabled the catalogs to pull in between fifteen and twenty per cent of each year's income through the mail orders that pour daily into the firm. Every serious art buyer in the United States should be on the master list. It is, as Brough puts it, probably the "world's most exclusive compilation of mail-order enthusiasts." With this tool, the buyer can write, telephone, or wire his bid in advance. Hyam quite accurately called the catalog a "kind of do-it-yourself kit for would-be collectors."

Expertly researched catalogs are only one of the many advantages the larger auction house offers. The house processes the works, identifying and describing them in the catalogs; and it presents only objects in good condition (if necessary, they are repaired by the firm before being presented for sale). In other words, you start out with selected, quality merchandise.

Auctions are usually announced in the local papers. For bigger events, information is carried in the major art and news magazines. Parke-Bernet also sends out monthly bulletins announcing their sales. These bulletins are free, but a nominal sum is charged for the catalogs. The bigger sales now have a great deal of glamor and prestige connected with them, so much so in fact that people have been known to arrive at Parke-Bernet on skis during heavy snowstorms. Many of the evening sales are now televised, with as much glitter and jewels attendant as at any charity ball.

Auction houses sell only on consignment: nothing belongs to them. An auction is usually held when a private collector, dealer, or estate wishes to liquidate a work of art or an art collection. The auction house works strictly on commission and functions chiefly as a middleman. The larger houses, as mentioned before, try to authenticate the objects they present, and they have on their staff many specialized experts. This is the main difference between buying at places like Sotheby's, Parke-Bernet, Christie's in London, or the Palais Galliéra in Paris, and a smaller auction house. Your catalog will be your Baedecker; and the viewing period before the auction will be your main opportunity for deciding on what you will bid. The works to be auctioned are always displayed at the auction house for a specified time before the sale (newspaper announcements tell when and for how long). During this period, you should examine the catalog carefully, and the objects even more carefully. If you wish, you can bring along an adviser. You can also obtain the auction house's estimates of anticipated prices on each object, and record them next to the listed item. Knowing your market prices for the art in which you're interested, you will find that auction prices are slightly lower. They do not include the assurances that any reputable dealer gives, however.

You will then be well prepared when you go to bid. Take the catalog along and set yourself a ceiling price, in terms of the market price and what you can afford. The auctioneer will begin with an opening bid, which someone in the audience usually meets. Try not to be the opening bidder. Wait awhile before you bid to see how the prices are going. You can enter the competition at any time; and the really important objects usually begin about halfway through the sale and continue until the last ten or twelve pieces are offered. You place your bid by raising your hand toward the auctioneer, although the more expert bidders may use such curious techniques as slumping further into their chairs, or giving a wink, a nod, or a twitch. You can even wait as late to bid as the auctioneer's final "fair warning" which means he is about to close the bidding, bang his gavel down, and declare the object "Sold!" Bidding this late is a little risky, as the auctioneer can choose to ignore your bid— but few ever do.

Bidding at an auction is much like gambling, and there are all the dangers of gambling here. You must have a firm idea of the limit you can afford, and what an object is worth. The auction atmosphere is very seductive and it is easy to get caught up in the excitement of the moment. Remember that very wealthy people go to auctions and that it is often impossible to outbid them. Yet, there is no question that some of the most wonderful buying coups by younger art buyers have been made at auctions, especially when less famous collections are being auctioned off or when some lesser lights are included in the furniture and *objets d'art* sales. Remember that at auctions where there are no real drawing cards there is likely to be less competition. This is also true when the weather's bad and during the summer months, especially during the noon sales. The major dealers are usually in Europe buying for the winter season while those who are left may not want to leave their businesses. In addition, many of the male buyers are at work, and their wives at home.

Auction prices are usually unpredictable, depending on who attends the sale, who wants what, and, quite often, the weather. While the Erickson Rembrandt sale went over the two-million-dollar mark, there are still many Old Master paintings which could top even that should they come up for auction. Then there is also what is called "bidding up" at an auction, where a dealer or collector tries to push prices up abnormally. One of the few examples of a pure, philanthropic impulse behind "bidding up" occurred in the late 1920s when the German art critic and writer Dr. Wilhelm von Bode was forced to have his art library auctioned off. Von Bode had advised the American dealer Joseph Duveen on the purchase of some of Duveen's first collections. But now von Bode was ill, poor, and going blind, and he needed money. When Duveen heard the sad news, he sent two emissaries to Germany to make high cross-bids so that von Bode realized a handsome sum through the auction. This, however, is unusual, and most bidding up is not so charitable.

One last word on auctions, charity auctions to be specific. The charity people are going to protest, but generally, if you're watching your pennies, it's better to steer away from them. The object here is to get money for the charity, and the prices are usually more than the dealer's price. If you're feeling charitable, go, but don't go for a bargain.

OTHER SOURCES OF ART

The current availability of art in department stores, supermarkets, and university and college art galleries, as well as in local banks, libraries, theaters, restaurants, churches, and synagogues is a recent phenomenon, and demonstrates how broad-based the appeal of art has become. Many more people also are buying on vacations than ever did before, and summer sales at resorts are booming right along. Some friends of mine who go to Martha's Vineyard every summer had a local artist do a beautiful portrait of two of their sons standing in the meadows of the island. As a result, my friends have a handsome painting of their children as well as a pleasurable year-long reminder of the delights of summer and vacation.

Department Stores

Perhaps the most exciting development in all this is the art programs that so many of the better department stores across the country have instituted. That of Sears, Roebuck and Company, begun in 1962, has been the most attention-getting and widespread. Headed by actor and sometime art expert Vincent Price, the shows are chosen by Price and a staff of three assistant buyers, and set up as a series of traveling shows that visit local Sears stores. The tall actor combines the selling tactics of a circus barker with graduate training in art history at Yale. From the exhibitions I've seen, the quality varies, but apparently it's better and bigger in scale than any of its competitors. Price shines at selecting original prints. When I saw one of the "Vincent Price Collections" in Honolulu, he had just bought up an important print estate, and I considered these the best art bargains there. I wasn't as enthusiastic about the paintings. Price buys in volume (I believe he bought close to two hundred art works in a single afternoon from a marathon sale of Hawaii artists), and since the Sears program started he has made art available in smaller towns and areas of the country which normally see little art.

Many other department stores and chains have followed Sears' example, and now almost every leading department store in the larger cities offers original art. E. J. Korvette has instituted a program which sends traveling shows to thirty-nine discount houses in nine states. Safeway had a rather short-lived art program for selling low-priced European paintings in their supermarkets, and may start it up again. Even the Woolworth store on New York's Fifth Avenue now hangs its paintings cheek by jowl to ladies' blouses and the lunch counter, and, as with all its other merchandise, rings the sale up at its checkout counters. Art can, of course, be purchased on credit in most of these stores, and usually all you have to do is flash your handy charge card.

By way of contrast, selling art in department stores is nothing new for the Japanese, and we still have a great deal to learn from them in terms of the quality of art offered and the presentation. Any fine department store in Tokyo, Kyoto, or Osaka will have its "art gallery," usually on the top floor. Many of the shows consist of historical art objects, what the Japanese call "National Treasures," borrowed from museums and private collectors. Other exhibitions may feature Japan's famed potter Shoji Hamada, or a showing of exquisite flower arrangements. Everything is done in the best of taste, a trait that does not always characterize the American department store efforts.

Traveling Exhibits

Another great disseminator of culture throughout the U.S. is the traveling art exhibition. Perhaps the first of these was in Honolulu,

Hawaii. Even before the Academy of Arts opened its doors there in 1927, it was decided that the children of island schools should have the opportunity to see and learn about famous paintings and artists.

Mrs. Charles Montague Cooke, later the founder of the Academy, used to take art educator Mrs. Norman Schenck on art pilgrimages about the island of Oahu. Not only was Mrs. Cooke's chauffeured car filled with original art objects from the Academy, but it was also weighted down with lunches, a baseball, and a bat. After Mrs. Schenck's art presentation, there would be lunch and a baseball game. Many of the children were the sons and daughters of imported Oriental plantation workers, and this was their first exposure to art. Well educated and wealthy now, they currently comprise some of the more important collectors on the island. Eventually the students began to come to the Academy, and Mrs. Schenck's talks were given within the building. The collection of pictures and objects that used to travel with lunch and baseball have now become part of the Academy's extensive lending collection, available to all the island teachers.

The larger traveling exhibitions services, such as those of the Smithsonian Institution, the Museum of Modern Art, and the American Federation of Arts, operate on a somewhat larger scale. Many of these exhibitions travel to small towns and college museums, and are perhaps the only opportunity for persons in small towns to buy good, original art. Many of the works included in the shows are for sale; and the circulating exhibitors usually receive no commission. The illustrated brochures of these traveling exhibitions are issued yearly and can be ordered free; the shows range over such diverse subjects as "Maine—Fifty Artists of the Twentieth Century," "The Philadelphia Tradition," "Modern Japanese Calligraphy," and "American Hardware." There is usually a price list which you can get from the museum or exhibiting group, and they will usually refer you to the artist or to the organization from which you can buy. The prices range from about thirty-five dollars to the thousands. The Museum of Modern Art shows are notable for the excellence of their prints, which start at about fifty or sixty dollars, and the Smithsonian's are interesting for their children's, architecture, crafts, history, photography, and science shows, which they send out in addition to art. The Smithsonian circulates about one hundred shows yearly to as many as five hundred towns and cities, and to groups including colleges and libraries. Some of their exhibits are surprisingly inexpensive to rent, some as low as fifty dollars. Smaller organizations which circulate shows mainly to arts and educational groups are listed in the *American Art Directory*.

Local Exhibitions and Festivals

Local art exhibitions and festivals are flourishing all over the country. You can hardly walk into a neighborhood library, bank, theater, church, restaurant, or synagogue without seeing some kind of an art display. The quality of these shows varies, of course, but they are an important part of the movement sweeping the U.S. that brings art to the people. The Jewish Community Centers are noted for the excellence of their art programs. Don't forget the student shows at your local art school and the art departments of the university or college. Student work can often be excellent, and it's usually quite inexpensive. Make it a practice to go to these shows, and you can be sure that at schools where the instruction is good, the student art will be of comparable quality.

Commissioning Art

Perhaps one of the best ways to buy art is to commission it. Commissioning art means that for a certain sum an artist will execute a work in the medium and on a theme which will please you. You probably think this will be very expensive, but it's not necessarily so. It's particularly practical in today's modern homes with their acres of glass walls. A professor in New York State recently built himself a handsome home with a splendid view of the Hudson River Valley. Wanting to make the most of the natural assets of the site, he used lots of glass. He found, however, that "while their daytime virtues were obvious, the walls let in the cold at night when the glass became a black pit, pulling the room out of shape visually."

The happy solution was to commission an artist friend to paint her version of the daytime view on old-fashioned window shades using acrylic paints. The room is now cozy and warm, and the professor and his family are surrounded by art. Obviously, all kinds of variations can be done on this idea. Commissioning is more often done in the crafts (see the section on crafts), but more and more people are now commissioning paintings, prints, and sculpture, usually for a specific use or for a special area of their home. Commissioning art is a time-honored custom, and one which should be exploited more fully today.

BUY WHAT YOU LIKE

Writing in *The Washington Post* at the time of the showing of his collection at the National Gallery of Art, Paul Mellon told this anecdote about his family. "One of our daughters brought home some Foxcroft School friends for lunch—and at the time we had a large and very beautiful but very impressionistic Van Gogh, of blue sky and waving wheat, in our front hallway. As they came in the front door one of the girls looked up at it and said in passing— 'Oh, who paints?' Not at all shattered or confused, the daughter said—'No one here. Da buys them in the store.' "

In the same article, "Da," who is the son of Andrew Mellon, gave some thoughts on art buying. The younger Mellon compares art collecting to the "childish pleasure of searching for odd or rare or beautiful shells on a beach . . . it is collecting trains, teddy bears, and dolls. *It is an attempt to preserve timelessly the bright vision of an instant, and to transform the object into part of one-self*" (italics mine). He tells how his wife, having a passionate love of flowers (she has personally designed two of the White House gardens), as well as being immersed in domestic life, was naturally drawn to the Impressionist painters. He tells how the pictures in their various homes "are lived with, constantly looked at, and loved."

But, even more important, "transforming objects into part of oneself" entails a great love of the objects themselves. The lesson for Mellon, and for you and me, is to buy only what we love, never, as Mellon puts it, "to buy a painting or drawing we would not want to live with or see constantly."

The maxim here is if you don't like it, don't buy it. There are many art "bargains" (nothing is a bargain if you don't really like it) that may tempt you. There are also many fads and fashions surrounding art today, many artists who, as the old song goes, are "here today and gone tomorrow." And so it will be with your money. There is good painting going on all over the country today, so don't be swept along on the tides of fashion that New York constantly generates, or think that New York is the only place to buy. The good, solid painting going on in Cincinnati, or Dallas, or Seattle rarely receives any publicity outside of its own area. Yet, if you live in Cincinnati, or Dallas, or Seattle, or cities like them, look around at your local artists and buy from them.

Remember that you and your family are the ones who are going to have to live with your art. No matter what your neighbors, or friends, or even your trusted art adviser may say, remember Mellon's devotion to and love for the object itself. The collector J. Paul Getty once wrote, "Someone once criticized my collection to Sir Alex Martin at Christie's, arguing that I collected in unrelated categories, that my collection lacked the singleness of purpose and the concentration that he, the critic, felt should characterize a collection. The critic concluded his tirade by disdainfully sneering, 'Paul Getty buys only what *he* likes!' " Let's hope we all have the courage to do the same.

Your Art in Your Home

FRAMING, MOUNTING

There is an interesting re-creation of a conversation between the painter Georges Seurat and some of his artist friends in Irving Stone's *Lust for Life*:

> "We get through with a canvas. Then what do we do? We turn it over to some fool who puts it in a hideous gold frame and kills our every last effect. No, I propose that we should never let a picture out of our hands until we've put it into a frame so that it becomes an integral part of the picture."
> "But Seurat, you're stopping too soon. Every picture must be hung in a room. And if the room is the wrong color, it will kill the picture and the frame both."
> "That's right. Why not paint the room to match the frame?"
> "A good idea," said Seurat.
> "What about the city that the house is in?"
> "Oh, Georges, Georges, you do get the damnedest ideas."

I first saw this little interplay of artistic exaggeration in a book titled *The Right Frame, A Consideration of the Right and Wrong Methods of Framing Pictures* (New York, James H. Heineman, Inc., 1964), and I firmly believe that everyone who buys art for his home should own this little bible of framing. *The Right Frame* is by framing expert Henry Heydenryk, who runs what is probably the largest framing establishment in the country at 141 West 54th St., New York City. Heydenryk comes from a long tradition of framing going back to 1845, when his grandfather established a framing shop in Amsterdam. As a small boy, Heydenryk used to play in the shop, watching the skilled craftsmen carve frames for original Rembrandt paintings and sometimes helping in smoothing down the wood or gilding one of the frames. Heydenryk came to this country to study business in 1927 but found that the lure of paintings and frames was too much for him. He started his framing enterprise in New York in the 1930s, and at first it was an uphill struggle. Recently, however, it has not been uncommon for celebrities like Marlene Dietrich, Shirley Booth, and Greta Garbo to convene in his shop at the same time. But even more impressive than his celebrity trade are the many museum customers, such as the Whitney Museum of Art and the Virginia Museum of Fine Arts, for whom he does so much work. His reputation for craftsmanship and dependability, and his belief in fine framing as a fine art, have done a great deal to bring a respect for quality framing in this country.

Much of this, of course, has been a natural outgrowth of the gradual rise in taste in the United States. Most people have now come to realize that a frame is an essential part of a picture, that a suitable frame can indispensably heighten the good points of a painting or a print. Heydenryk's two books, *The Art and History of Frames* (New York, James H. Heineman, Inc., 1963), which deals mainly with the history of framing, and *The Right Frame,* which is more concerned with the importance and techniques of good framing, have no doubt had considerable influence.

Also important was Heydenryk's exhibition, "Framing, Right and Wrong." A number of years ago the Virginia Museum of Fine Arts in Richmond found that the poorly framed entries of participants in the competitions for the Virginia Biennale made it difficult to judge the artistic content. The museum's curator asked Heydenryk to prepare an exhibit demonstrating the need for proper framing. So popular was the exhibit that it has traveled to hundreds of museums in almost every state of the Union and is regularly booked ahead for a period of two years. The exhibition received accolades from the press, and it was partially from that exhibit that the idea for Heydenryk's *The Right Frame* was born.

In both the exhibit and the book, Heydenryk has succinctly and interestingly explained the "rights" and "wrongs" of picture framing and the fact that a fine frame should be as well designed and as durable as any piece of fine furniture. He also explores some of the complexities implied in Seurat's "conversation" concerning the relation of the frame both to the art it encloses and to the room interior of which it is a part.

The fine art of framing is too often neglected by even tasteful art buyers and lovers. I recently visited some friends whose home had been beautifully decorated with wall-to-wall carpeting and even wall-to-wall draperies. The owner of the house had some very fine watercolors by a prominent artist, and almost immediately led us to the sofa above which they were arranged. Then our host very proudly told us what a bargain he had gotten with his fifty-cent frames purchased at the dime store.

The noted painter Edgar Degas once said, "The frame is the reward of the artist," and, to quote Heydenryk, "it is also the enduring reward of the owner of the picture." Any work of art which is worth buying is deserving of a proper frame, and even an old map can look like a masterpiece once it is treated to a suitable mat and frame. Always keep in mind that the frame you put around a work of art can be as important as the art itself.

While there are literally hundreds of books published yearly on painting, sculpture, architecture, et cetera, there is little available on the history and importance of framing. In his *Art and History of Frames,* Heydenryk relates how "there have been frames almost as long as there have been paintings," and that there is evidence that frames existed in Egypt and Rome. He goes on to explain how today's framing developed from the architectural moldings made to fit panel paintings into the walls of thirteenth-century European churches. Out of this, framing became an independent, respected craft in the Italian Renaissance when panel painting came into its own. So also today the skilled framer must be regarded as a valued craftsman in his own right.

It is for this reason that framing is often expensive, but, *if you regard framing as the fine art it is,* you will agree that the money is well spent. Fine frames can even be economical in the long run, as they will probably never have to be replaced. There is an old story about the fourteenth-century painter Giotto, who was commissioned by the Doge of Venice to do a painting for a certain sum of money. When the Doge received the painting, he sent it back to the artist for framing. Giotto complied, but when he rendered his bill for both the painting and the frame, his fee had more than doubled. You can see from this little story how important the great artists of history have considered the often neglected and maligned frame.

Of course, there are fashions in frames just as there are those in interior architecture and home furnishings. The development of new materials, textures, and simplified designs, also, has accounted for many of today's innovations in frame making. And the many artists like Georges Seurat, John Marin, and John La Farge, who have designed and made their own frames, have also greatly influenced tastes in framing (La Farge reputedly carved the frame for his large "Scene in Tahiti" with motifs adapted from native Tahitian art).

Just exactly what, then, is a "frame"? Heydenryk describes how the "original picture frame" was simply "an opening in the forest foliage through which some caveman looked forth on a scene appealing enough to capture and hold his attention for perhaps several minutes before he was distracted by something else." It is not uncommon today to find such lookout points revered by primitive tribesmen, leaf-framed bowers where traditionally only chiefs or witch doctors were permitted to sit or crouch in isolated contemplation of the scene at hand.

"At some unknown date in ancient history," Heydenryk goes on to explain, "it became the practice to frame a special setting by constructing a crude doorway of timbers, and later rocks . . . The natural evolution was from rough slabs of stone, to the carved and massive doorways of the Egyptians, and ultimately to the arch."

"The important point here," Heydenryk stresses, "is that the picture frame, as a distinct element, originated with this whole concept of directing a viewer's eye through an attractively designed opening toward a scene entirely contained within the focal point of that opening."

You may also be asking yourself, "What should a frame do?" Basically, as Heydenryk has put it so well, a frame protects the picture, enhances it without entering into competition with it, and makes a transition between the limits of the picture and the wall it occupies or the composition with which it is involved. *Aesthetically the frame should complement the subject it surrounds.* Ideally, the frame should also remain harmonious and unobtrusive in order not to interfere with the effect of the art work it holds; yet it should still be handsome when noticed.

And as the painter Van Day Truex has written, "The framing of a painting or drawing is a *presentation* of that painting or drawing to the best advantage. It is a means of defining and emphasizing the picture's area in relation to the larger area of the room. It should enhance, embellish, complement and emphasize the picture. It should never overpower the subject. The frame acts as a sort of impresario, the picture remains the star performer, whether it's an original Botticelli or a Gauguin reprint." The frame, then, protects the work of art, it gives you something to grip without handling and perhaps hurting the art itself, and it will limit the surface so that your eye won't wander aimlessly.

There are many parts of a frame, some of which we do not see and are, therefore, often not conscious of. These components are all, every one of them, important for the proper framing of your art. You will become aware first of the frame's molding, its most salient element and the one of which you will be most conscious. The molding will often have some kind of decoration, in such forms as carving, scratching, combing, metal or stone ornaments,

Oak frame. (French.) Early Louis XIV style.
Gilded and hand-carved. (*Courtesy House of
Heydenryk, New York*)

I. Rice Pereira: *Abstraction*. (American.) Oil. From the House of Heydenryk
exhibition "Framing: Right and Wrong." This frame is an example of "correct"
framing, according to Henry Heydenryk, as it gives "weight" to the painting.
(Photograph by Alfredo Valente—*courtesy House of Heydenryk, New York*)

I. Rice Pereira: *Abstraction.* (American.) Oil. From the House of Heydenryk exhibition "Framing: Right and Wrong." This frame is an example of "incorrect" framing, according to Henry Heydenryk, as it is "too light" for the painting. (Photograph by Alfredo Valente—*courtesy House of Heydenryk, New York*)

Frederick Franck: *Seashell.* 1963. This framing demonstrates the possibilities of modern materials, here linen and brushed aluminum. According to Henry Heydenryk, the linen mounting "opens up" the space between the painting and the aluminum strip. (*Courtesy House of Heydenryk, New York*)

Artist unknown: *Emma Van Name.* (American.) Oil. Circa 1795. The gold leaf, concave molded frame is of the same period. (*Courtesy House of Heydenryk, New York*)

Henry Heydenryk: "Even an old map deserves better framing than it usually gets." (*Courtesy House of Heydenryk, New York*)

Salvador Dali (1904–   ): *The Gold Cube Cross.* 1960. Collection of the Owen Cheatham Foundation, New York. Frame by the House of Heydenryk, New York. (*Courtesy the Owen Cheatham Foundation*)

and the like. This is part of what makes this element attractive and pleasing to the eye. There will also be some kind of finish, which will be one of two types: the almost invisible ones, such as varnish, shellac, or wax, applied for purposes of protecting the frame, or the finishes which are meant to be seen, such as white or colored casein paste paint, bronze powders, gold, silver or bronze metal leaf, or other color matter for decorative purposes. Another very important element, also very much before your eye, is the mat, which is usually a flat piece of cardboard, pressed wood, or other material used within the frame to set off the picture and somewhat isolate it. It often forms the bridge from the picture to the frame and is an essential part, in terms of design, texture, and proportion, of your frame. It can be very small or very large, depending on the nature of the picture. Some modern artists have dispensed with mats altogether, framing right to the edge of the painting or print. This usually calls for a very "all-over" and diffused manner of painting, however.

The backing and the backing paper are necessary both as supports for the picture and as a way of sealing the picture from the rear to protect it from dust and changes in humidity. Glass, which is used to face a picture, is also very much in evidence and is used most often with watercolors, pastels, engravings, and other art works which do not have natural surface protections against dust and grime. The problem of glass as a reflecting surface that sometimes mars the picture's effect has not been properly solved, in my opinion. The glass usually used in framing does sometimes spoil the effect of the picture by the many reflections it gives off, while the new types of nonreflecting glass have a slight opacity which I find often distorts a picture and gives it the quality of a mechanically made reproduction. I feel it puts up a kind of wall between the picture and me, a distorted wall I do not like. So I personally prefer the old-fashioned kind around which I often have to crane my neck but through which I can, with effort, see what the artist is trying to do. Inserts, also called "liners," put beneath and within the outer moldings; hangers, which are the hanging unit on the back of the picture frame; and fitting strips, which may be attached to the outer edge of a canvas or panel for protection, are some of the hidden goodies in the complex and skilled craft of framing.

Enhancing your art with a frame, then, should be very simple. But here you get onto dangerous ground. Just how should the frame enhance the picture? Should it bring out the red tones of the work? Should it increase the depth? Should it emphasize the horizontals, or the verticals? The problem is simplified if you realize that there are, basically, two main questions: to relate the picture by way of its frame to its surroundings in the room, and to relate the picture to its frame. Often, the frame will be the bridge between the generally two-dimensional quality of the picture and the richer textures of the interior in which it is placed.

You must also think of it as a bridge to the other pictures in the room, and to their frames. First, you consider the color of your walls. A soft white or gray has been found to be the best "frame" for your framed art, but a neutral, textured cloth background like burlap or Japanese grass cloth has also been found to be very nice with certain kinds of art. The great art scholar and collector Bernard Berenson preferred either white or a shade of green for his walls, as the best backgrounds for his Italian Renaissance paintings with their gold grounds. Warm woods, such as the walls of the Rembrandt Room at the National Gallery of Art, or the warm damasks with patterns used in the Metropolitan Museum in New York can also enhance certain art works. The important thing to remember is that the wall and general decor of the room should be suitable to your picture and to its frame. You'll find, also, that, if you redecorate, you'll have to move your art around to fit in with your new color and wall schemes. Then, you should also think of the period of your picture and the period of the frame. Ideally these two should coincide, but it isn't at all necessary to match the style of the frame to the rest of your decor. Sometimes, a very elaborate Baroque type of frame can look magnificent in a starkly modern home where it gives the room some richness. Some friends of mine in Brooklyn, New York, inherited an old portrait with an intricately carved gilt frame around it. They live in an old house built in the early 1820s with wide pine flooring, high ceilings, and magnificently large rooms. The painting, as it hangs above the dining-room fireplace overlooking their contemporary furnishings is the showpiece of that room.

Your next consideration will be the relationship of the picture to its frame. This is admirably answered by Heydenryk's "Ten Commandments" for framing (The Right Frame):

1. The width and pattern of the molding must bear relationship to the design and "weight" of the picture. A painting with simple, uncomplicated design calls for a plain molding; a much-detailed compostion is best balanced by a rich design in the frame, with ornamentation called for.

2. A receding molding (one slanting toward the wall) or a rather flat profile will suit two-dimensional paintings best.

3. A concave molding (one slanting toward the painting) will enhance the feeling of perspective suggested by a composition in depth.

4. Strong, bold patterns (such as Rouault's paintings) demand powerful lines in the frame, to contain the composition.

5. A delicate, feathery, airy composition (such as a Vertès) calls for the same "frivolous" feeling in the frame.

6. A linear composition (such as a Feininger) calls for a repeat of this fine, lineal quality in the frame.

7. Inserts, or contrasting colors, will help to separate the ornamentation or pronounced color in a frame from those in the picture and will enhance the feeling of perspective.

8. Mats for watercolors and prints should be chosen to accentuate the significant colors. White is seldom ever right, because it tends to flatten the picture and darken it by contrast.

9. Only in the matter of glass protection do pastels and watercolors call for special treatment. A gouache can be as strong in color and pattern as any oil, and should be framed accordingly.

10. Key the colorings in frames to hues in the picture. A general guide is that warmly toned pictures (in which reds, browns, and yellows predominate) are most appropriate in warm-toned frames; whereas cool colors (blues, greens, blue-blacks, whites) are likely to go best in frames that have silvery or similar cool tones.

You should also consider the special problems involved in framing contemporary art and original graphics, and in the mounting of sculpture (mounting is also a kind of "frame"). Heydenryk points out that the owner of modern pictures has more freedom to exercise his framing tastes with the many new materials—cork, linen, burlap, sand—now more available to him than to his art-loving predecessors. Many contemporary painters now compose their works so that the compositions quite literally spill out beyond the picture boundaries, the wall becoming an extension of the painting. This "all-over" kind of painting, so popular with painters like Jackson Pollock and Franz Kline, demands a whole new attitude toward framing and light. James Johnson Sweeney, then director of the Guggenheim Museum in New York City, was constantly faced with this problem when mounting new shows at that museum. He finally concluded that a white tape bound tight around the stretcher sides of a canvas suggested a reflection of the background, and supported his "wall-as-frame" solution for the framing of modern paintings. This "wall-as-frame" concept, in which placement, background, and lighting create the "frame," has been found suitable by many museums and galleries for certain of today's problems in framing. However, doing this in one's own home requires that the wall be, first, a suitable color, and second, that a complex lighting system be installed so that the light becomes, in effect, an integral part of the "frame."

Original graphics also present special framing problems; and it is best to consult the Print Council of Amercia in New York City and the Tamarind Lithography Workshop, Inc. in Los Angeles. (See the section on graphics.) Tamarind has put out several of their *Fact Sheets* on the framing of prints, cautioning you to direct your framer to use only one hundred per cent all-rag paper, two or four ply, for mat board, or inert fabrics such as linen, cotton, or silk (pulp paper contains chemical properties that turn the paper brown and can, in time, cause the print to become brittle and to crack). Tamarind also cautions against the dangers of taping down a print with any of the normally used adhesives, such as brown gummed paper, scotch tape, cellophane tape, or masking tape, and recommends the use of rich flour paste or a Japanese paper hinge. They warn, too, that suspension of a print between two sheets of glass can expose it to dampness caused by condensation.

Just in case the high cost of good framing may be frightening— and prohibitively expensive—for you, there are "frame-it-yourself" ensembles that are useful both for short-term framing and for protecting your art. Sold in most art-supply and framing establishments under the trade names of Braquette and Pic Frame, these small brackets of clear plastic or stainless steel fit around the top and bottom of the picture. It is wise to get the picture backed and glassed first, however, so that the brackets have something to clamp to. The brackets are sturdy and unobtrusive, and are almost no strain on the budget. They are also a good way of deciding whether you like a picture enough to invest in more expensive framing, and provide much better protection for your art than rolling it up (rolling often breaks the picture, no matter how carefully it's done.)

Mounting sculpture can be even trickier than framing pictures, and a great deal more difficult. Many framers are not equipped to mount sculpture, and one recently told me he gets only about three calls a year for this. In buying sculpture, try to get the sculptor himself to provide the base or go to a competent cabinetmaker who has an eye for art. If the sculpture is small and doesn't need mounting, you can just attach felt to the bottom and leave it at that. Heydenryk emphasizes that the "visual weight" of the whole composition—the sculpture and its stand—is important here. The sculpture mount is every bit as important as your picture frame; both are most definitely "the reward of the artist."

Perhaps the classic example of misframing can be seen by even the most casual visitor to the Louvre Museum in Paris. The Empire frame with its "precise, severe 'scoop molding' with plaster-cast ornamentation" came into fashion under Napoleon, who dictated that all the Louvre paintings should be embellished à l'Empire. So overwhelming is the impact of these frames that Gertrude Stein was once moved to write, "The Louvre at first was only gold frames to me gold frames which were rather glorious, and looking out of the window of the Louvre with the gold frames being all gold behind within was very glorious. I always like, as well as liked looking out of windows of museums. It is more complete, looking out of windows in museums than looking out of windows anywhere else. . . ." And many another visitor to the Louvre has enjoyed the view through the windows rather than looking at all those gilt frames.

Overframing, such as at the Louvre, is the situation when the frame overwhelms the art and calls attention to itself. It is, however, not the only pitfall in framing. Underframing, in which the frame doesn't enrich the picture in any way, is another serious mistake (an example of this is the severe, thin black frame which used to be put around all prints). You have to be careful in matting, also, and make sure the color, texture, and proportions of the mat are suitable to the art. An insert or mat can give additional perspective, open up the work, and let the picture "breathe." Perhaps the cardinal sin, one often committed, is attempting to "pick up the colors in the room" in the mat or frame; often this only results in killing the colors in the painting itself.

My advice, here, as in the case of buying your art, is to put yourself in the hands of a reputable framer, someone you can trust, who will take the time to advise you, and who has a large stock of frames and mats. You will find that the choices of framing are never simple, and can be as big a challenge as the choice of your art. You will discover that a reliable framer will be every bit as valuable to you as a trusted gallery dealer.

PLACEMENT, LIGHTING

This brings us to the hanging, displaying, and lighting of your art. It has been said that a work of art creates its own environment, and this has recently been further confirmed by the development of "Environmental Art" in the United States. The canvases of the Abstract Expressionists were "environmental" in that they were often so large they would completely dominate any space into which they were put. The Orientals long ago realized that art extends itself, an idea taken up by Charles Lang Freer when he planned the Freer Gallery of Art in Washington, D.C. In writing about the planning of the museum, Agnes Myer has said, "Mr. Freer often stated that the objects in each room should be few, with ample distances between them . . . he had learned from the Orientals *the need that beauty has for broad spaces in which to expand and radiate*" (italics mine). The gallery, therefore, has only a small percentage of its collection on view at any given time, and art is frequently rotated from the storage quarters below to the galleries above. A modification of this system could be an excellent plan for your own art.

The placement of a painting will depend on many things. The nature, size, and proportion of the painting are major considerations, of course, while the decor of the room in which it is to be hung, and the personal tastes of the owner, are also important. There is almost as much creativeness in hanging a picture as there is in painting it. There is, however, nothing worse than buying a painting because, as one friend informed me, "the pinks pick up those of my living room." A painting should, of course, complement your color scheme, but should be displayed to its best advantage and should not merely be an accent for some decorating plan.

Not only are the *in*doors of where a painting is hung to be considered, but what is *outside* as well. The collector Paul Mellon describes it this way; "There is also a relationship to be considered between the subject matter and the *over-all* feeling of a painting, and the out-of-doors as actually seen beyond the windows and the doors. We are not apologetic about having a large proportion of seascapes at the seashore or country landscapes in the country, leaving the more city-like paintings and portraits for the city—not necessarily because they *are* seascapes, etc. and more 'appropriate,' but because in general their colors and atmosphere blend with the colors and atmosphere of the actual environment."

You may also be wondering about mixing mediums and different styles of art in one room. This can be done, and it *should* be done, but always with taste. You may be interested to know that the Mellons juxtapose works by different schools, periods, and nationalities in the same room. And they never hesitate to hang drawings, prints and watercolors with oils. "At Cape Cod," Mellon has said, "a Winslow Homer painting and a Homer drawing live tranquilly in the same living room (which looks out to sea) with a Monet, a Boudin, a Boudin watercolor, a Redon landscape, a Berthe Morisot and a modern American Primitive." Or perhaps it could also be put this way: who would go to Europe on holiday and just visit one city, Rome, for example? Perhaps on the third or fourth trip, but certainly not on the first, and probably not on the second. It would be absurd to limit your traveling, and it is just as absurd to surround yourself with only one kind of art.

Lighting, unless you are an art buyer on a large scale, is best left to the experts and the museums. I have been in the homes of many prominent collectors and I have yet to see a satisfactory lighting arrangement. A little brass lamp is usually hung above a painting with an unsightly electric cord drooping down the wall behind it. Or glaring spotlights installed in the ceiling take away the coziness that usually goes with a home and manage to massacre the paintings as well. Remember that the best light for paintings is natural light—indeed most artists while painting or sculpting favor a cold, north light through a skylight—and it is this natural light that should be simulated. In view of this, it is somewhat ironic that paintings are usually seen and enjoyed at night when artificial light is used. It is wise to call in a lighting expert if you want to rig up a lighting arrangement. Some of the solutions which framing and lighting expert Henry Heydenryk lists in his book *The Right Frame* are overhead fluorescent or other lighting fixtures set into the ceiling to simulate a skylight; ceiling spotlights with pinhole openings; wall spotlights; long "pencil" or "finer" lights set in brackets over the picture, and usually attached to the frame (these can be placed at the bottom of the frame); or the "Heyden-Ray" frames, which contain a series of thin, incandescent bulbs concealed in the molding itself (a Heydenryk invention for especially dark paintings in dark surroundings). If you want to read further on lighting problems, I highly recommend this book (see also the section on framing).

ROTATION

Sit back, relax, enjoy your art—but don't let it become an unseen habit. After having had your art around for several years, there always come the moment when it begins to recede into the background and you don't really "see" it any more. This is the time to take your cue from the Orientals and rotate your art buys. The Eastern custom of rolling up paintings and calligraphies into boxes, and taking them out for only short periods of time to savor and enjoy, has the advantage of preserving the eye's freshness of vision, its capacity for delight. Somehow, our custom of hanging art on walls and leaving it there makes it go stale all too quickly and prevents us from getting our full measure of pleasure. Put away that painting which you no longer look at with fresh eyes, and bring out something new. Or exchange hallway and living-room pictures. A collector friend tells me that the many requests he receives for loaning out paintings force him to rotate his art—and that he feels this forced rotation is a very good thing.

Although today's smaller homes and apartments make it difficult to store your art, try to rig up some sort of safe storage area—such as wooden racks—in one of your closets. Closets should never become a helter-skelter jumbling of your art buys, and it's relatively inexpensive to buy wooden storage racks or have them made to specifications by a carpenter. A closet with racks, where you can put away your art from time to time, will greatly help in the enjoyment and preservation of your art objects. Graphics are usually the easiest kind of art to store and, therefore, to rotate. (See the Tamarind Lithography Workshop, Inc. designs for storage coffee tables and chests in the section on graphics.) Remember that it's usually better not to show all your things at once. I know many persons who now favor the "grouping" arrangement of paintings and prints, in which several art works are arranged together on a wall. Personally, I don't recommend this, although I will admit these arrangements break up the often monotonous and sterile room design that characterizes most modern apartments.

CARE

Good art rarely requires much care, and the little it needs is ably explained in Carolyn Keck's inexpensive paperback, *How to Take Care of Your Pictures* (New York, The Museum of Modern Art

Frank Sullivan, National Gallery of Art restorer, at work in the studio. (*Courtesy National Gallery of Art, Washington, D.C.*)

and the Brooklyn Museum, 1964). Mrs. Keck and her husband, Sheldon Keck, have for many years been official restorers of paintings for both museums. In this very readable handbook, Mrs. Keck gives valuable tips not only on how to care for art, but also how to hang, light, frame, and ship it, as well as how to give first aid in event of water or fire damage. This book is an indispensable aid for any art buyer and art lover.

If your art needs a good cleaning or restoration job, take her advice, and mine, and go to a professional. Your local museum can probably direct you; but you can also write The International Institute for Conservation of Historic and Artistic Works, c/o The National Gallery, Trafalgar Square, London, W.C.2. IIC members can be found in over forty countries, and you will be put in touch with the one nearest you by writing this address.

Among the general rules for caring for art in the home is the placement of prints and drawings away from strong sunlight, as the sun will quickly fade them and discolor the paper. It is always wise to frame your graphics under glass; and you should direct your framer to use either a fabric or an all-rag paper for the backing and surrounding mat. Pulp mat board contains chemicals that cause browning and cracking of the paper. This can be a great problem for museum curators, who often inherit print collections in sorely damaged condition. In dusting your oils, a soft camel's hair or sable brush, a soft feather duster, or cheesecloth with a wad of cotton in it is suitable. *Never* use a damp cloth or sponge. And in cleaning your sculpture or ceramics use the dusting attachment of your vacuum cleaner for the recesses; for this, the shorthandled vacuum cleaners like those used for cars are the best, according to a restorer friend of mine. And finally, expose your art to as few violent temperature and humidity changes as possible; they can wreak havoc with your objects.

INSURING YOUR ART

A suitable insurance policy written on your art is perhaps the best care you can give it. You can either insure your art along with the goods listed on your regular policy, or you can have a separate fine arts insurance policy written on it. The first important step is to take stock of what you've got (reporting all new buys to the insurance company immediately after purchase), making up an itemized list with careful descriptions of each article, and an estimate on the market value of each object. As your art may increase in value, it is always a good idea to keep abreast of current market prices and inform your agent of the increases. Most of us are careless insurers, until something happens. Then, as the old saw goes, it's "closing the barn door after the horse has been stolen." Don't have the heartbreaking experience of losing your art through fire, breakage, or robbery without compensating insurance. See your insurance agent and discuss the problem with him; he is the one who will give you the best advice. And don't forget that if you're shipping art via Railway Express, you can get a Fine Arts All Risk insurance policy in addition to the nominal amount allowed in Railway Express's customary contract.

SELLING, GIVING AWAY YOUR ART

Don't be disheartened if you find your tastes change as your interests grow. This is almost inevitable and quite natural. It happens to the great art collectors, and it will happen also to the more modest buyer. The prominent primitive-arts collector Raymond Wielgus has said about his art, "The collection is in a process of continual modification. I do not feel irrevocably committed to any particular piece. Each work is open to reevaluation and *must constantly prove itself and be proved.*" And Judge Irwin Untermeyer's collection has been described as ". . . refined by prudent and careful weeding—as essential in good collecting as in good gardening."

Most great collections are the result of much "weeding." A friend of mine describes art buying as "going through phases, and having to separate these phases." In the end "you have to be ruthless," she says. Even if you're buying just a few things, you will find that taste almost always changes with the training of the eye. Art is so much a part of you that, as you change, your feelings on art will too. You may find that you have outgrown some of your earlier purchases and want to replace them. There are several ways of doing this. If you have originally made an agreement with the dealer that he would take the object back, and exchange it for another, you're all set. Or the dealer may agree to sell the object on consignment, charging you a commission of about twenty-five per cent. Still again, you can try to sell through an auction, although you might not realize as good a price here. Or perhaps a friend who likes the object very much and who has admired it in your home would welcome it as a present.

Probably the best way of "giving away" your art is to donate it to a museum, a school, or a library. The gift can be deducted from your income tax as a charitable contribution. Perhaps the most famous tax deduction in history was the millions of dollars-worth of art that Andrew Mellon gave to found the National Gallery of Art. We can't all be Andrew Mellons, of course, but with this type of art gift, you can derive great satisfaction from the enrichment you give the entire community. Incidentally, the gift also benefits the artist as it gives him greater exposure than he would get in your home.

Many persons have also made financial and personal sacrifices to give great works of art to museums, buying specifically for the museum rather than for themselves. Such was the case with the Robert Woods Blisses, who embellished Dumbarton Oaks, in Washington, D.C., with its beautiful gardens and famous collections, and subsequently moved down the street so that the public could enjoy the gardens and the art. This kind of joy in giving is typical of the true art lover, of his wish to communicate the unique values of art to his fellow humans.

Original Art Priced Under $1,000

On July 20, 1938, the American art collector J. Paul Getty was in London attending an auction at Sotheby & Co. Europe was on the brink of World War II and, while the sale was fairly well attended, there was as Getty describes it, "an almost desultory air about the bidding." Getty, however, was out to get some good buys. The paintings, many of which had hung in the Tuileries and which were originally part of the collection of the late Jaime III of Bourbon, were "enough to make any collector's mouth water." And, significantly, among the sale items listed in Lot Number 49, were three "after-Raphael paintings."

Like the astute collector he is, Getty not only examined the paintings the day before the sale but sought the advice of the well-known English portraitist Gerald Brockhurst on one of the "after-Raphaels" titled "Madonna di Loreto." Brockhurst had a hunch that the foreshortening of the Virgin's right arm was the touch of the master and not of a follower, and that this painting might actually be Raphael's famous long-lost picture of that subject.

The bidding was generally slow, and Getty first obtained two flower pieces attributed to Van Huysum for fifty-five pounds—in those days, approximately $275. The bidding for the "after-Raphael" opened at ten pounds, about fifty dollars. Getty increased his bid only slightly, and someone else topped the bid by just a few more pounds. And so it went until Getty purchased the painting for forty pounds or roughly two hundred dollars.

Twenty-five years later, Getty shipped the painting, which had become one of his favorites, to his home at Sutton Place, England. There the prominent London art dealer and expert Colin Agnew saw it and was astounded to find that Getty thought it a Raphael. Agnew did, however, suggest a thorough cleaning and "stripping." And when the painting emerged from all the overhauling, it was shiningly evident that it was indeed a Raphael. Today, after being authenticated by authorities on fifteenth- and sixteenth-century Italian painting, it hangs in the Raphael Room of the National Gallery in London and is insured for ten thousand times the price that Getty originally paid for it.

76

Unfortunately, things have changed since 1938. Great art "coups" such as Getty's depend on particular circumstances as much as on the individual. It is true that Getty had had the foresight to get an expert opinion on his "after-Raphael" purchase before he bid. But it is also obvious that, had it not been for the impending war, others with the same astuteness might have been present.

We can all learn from Getty's art-buying methods, but it is also well to remember that the price of art, like that of pineapples or peaches, depends on supply and demand, and that even "after-Raphaels" don't come on the market very much any more. Yet, there are certain art fields which are still available for buyers like you and me, and which will remain areas for good art buys for some time to come. Some, like the so-called primitive arts have only recently become fashionable. Others, such as Far and Middle Eastern art, have either been neglected or have only recently become available. Many types, such as Early American art and graphics, have been around for a long time and are only now being looked at with new eyes; we value our early Americana for its simplicity and craftsmanship, and we currently prize drawings and sketches for their spontaneity and "first-hand" appeal.

So let's take a good look at the art fields still lying within our one-thousand-dollar-and-under budget, and prime both our eyes and our knowledge before purchasing. Getty didn't get that Raphael by accident. He had spent years going to museums, art galleries, and auction houses, all the while studying up on the categories of art which he buys. It is so you can study your special interests that I have included information on publications and organizations that will help with your particular field of buying; which public collections are noted for the art in which you're interested; introductory books for your field of interest; current going prices and tips on how to buy in your area; categories within your field; and places to buy.

The art fields currently lying within our budget are American art from about 1750 to 1900; certain kinds of European and American antiques; the arts of the North American Indian; the contemporary crafts of pottery, silverwork, textile designing, and so on, which are now in the midst of a vigorous renaissance; the Far Eastern arts of Japan, China, and Korea; the arts of India and South Asia; graphics, a field which includes drawings, all kinds of *original* prints, and watercolors—a category that is still reasonably priced and one of the best fields for the beginning art buyer; the traditional arts of the Middle East, from such countries as

Iran, Turkey, Arabia, Egypt, Syria, Iraq, and Lebanon; modern art of the Western world from the turn of the century on; and what are known as the "Primitive Arts" of Africa, Oceania, the Americas, and prehistoric Asia and Europe.

Art categories beyond the scope of this book and beyond the ordinary pocketbook are the now very high-priced French Impressionists and Post-Impressionists, such as Pierre Auguste Renoir, Vincent van Gogh, and Camille Pisarro, who were ignored and ridiculed in their lifetimes but who are now so fashionable that only millionaires like Paul Mellon can amass a goodly number of them; the so-called French Moderns, Pablo Picasso, Henri Matisse, Maurice de Vlaminck, and Raoul Dufy, among others, also very high priced; the Old Master Italians, from the early fifteenth-century masters to the late eighteenth-century Venetians, most of them now in museums; the seventeenth-century Dutch and Flemish schools, including Rembrandt van Rijn and Peter Paul Rubens, who rarely, if ever, appear on the market; the eighteenth-century British painters, like Thomas Gainsborough and George Romney, great favorites of the American "Robber Barons," who practically bought them off the market; the "Old Master French" painters, such as Jean-François Millet and Jean Baptiste Camille Corot; the frothy, gay French Rococo of François Boucher and Jean-Honoré Fragonard; the new highly popular and very expensive German Expressionists—like Emile Nolde and Ernst Kirchner—forerunners of our own Abstract-Expressionist School in the United States; the very scarce Spanish painters, such as El Greco and Diego Velázquez; the Flemish Primitives, such as the Van Eyck brothers, who reputedly invented oil painting; the sixteenth-century Germans, like Albrecht Dürer and Hans Holbein; and the older, more established Americans, Gilbert Stuart, John Singer Sargent, Winslow Homer, et cetera.

These, and other categories, such as Medieval and most Greek and Roman art, are usually very expensive; many are just not available. So enjoy them in the museums and concentrate on buying the high-quality, reasonably priced art which still abounds. The following sections may help you with an art interest you've already developed, or may lead you into fields the availability and pleasures of which you may not know.

And in your buying, remember that J. Paul Getty has said, "Banal as it may sound in this glib and brittle age, the beauty that one finds in fine art is one of the pitifully few and lasting products of human endeavor. That beauty endures even though nations and civilizations crumble; the work of art can be passed on from generation to generation and century to century, providing a historical continuity of true value."

AMERICANA

You're likely to become interested in Americana while rummaging through your local thrift shop or by delving into your family's attic. Mary C. Black, the energetic director of the Museum of Early American Folk Arts in New York City, is a case in point. Growing up near Pittsfield, Massachusetts, she was exposed as a child to the best in early Americana. Then, when she inherited several works by the noted Early American painter Erastus Salisbury Field, her interest quickened. Like many other lovers of this kind of art, Mrs. Black proceeded to find out everything she could about what she had inherited, and now says, with great satisfaction, "I know more about him than his own relatives do!"

A good way to explore this field is to buy what appeals to you and restore what you're inherited, then delve into the historical aspects of your purchases. The historical, as well as the aesthetic, quests are, as Mrs. Black demonstrates, equally enjoyable and important here. It's fun to trace the genealogy of your art and the many historical societies that have mushroomed, especially those in New England, are usually happy to help you. The directory of the American Association for State and Local History (132 9th Ave., North, Nashville, Tenn., $2.00) will tell you how to reach the historical society nearest you.

The Americana field, which encompasses American art from about 1750 to around 1900, is a large one and is only gradually being sorted out by experts and buyers; for example, it's often hard to tell exactly where "old" and "new" Americana begin and end, and the term "Early American" covers a multitude of sins and virtues. And while the finer examples of American art are now often very near the top of our thousand-dollar budget, good things are occasionally found in out-of-the-way antique stores and at country auctions in New England, New York, Ohio, and Pennsylvania. It's always a good idea to collect Americana from the section of the country where you happen to be living; that way, you get the best pieces for the best prices (you're probably not going to get a good piece of Boston cabinetry in Virginia, for example).

It was Mrs. John F. Kennedy who, through her redecoration of the White House, was instrumental in reviving the popularity of

Isaac Sheffield (1798–1845): *New England Ship Captain.* (American.) 1835.
Collection of the Museum of Early American Folk Art, New York.
(Courtesy Museum of Early American Folk Art)

Artist unknown: *Gabriel* weathervane. Circa 1870. (American.) Collection of the Museum of Early American Folk Art, New York. (*Courtesy Museum of Early American Folk Art*)

Artist unknown: *Flag Gate*. (American.) Circa 1840. Collection of the Museum of Early American Folk Art, New York. (*Courtesy Museum of Early American Folk Art*)

Artist unknown: *Eagle*. (American.) Pine woodcarving, originally painted. Height: 56 inches, including base. Wingspread: 15 feet, 11 inches. Nineteenth century. From Tilton, New Hampshire, and believed to have come from the Naval Shipyard at Portsmouth, New Jersey. Collection of the Shelburne Museum, Inc., Shelburne, Vermont. (Photograph by Einars J. Mengis—*courtesy Shelburne Museum, Inc.*)

V. L. Vance: *Flask* (American, made in Ohio.) Pale, smoky green glass. Height: 8⅝ inches. Thickness: 2⅜ inches. Width: 4⅝ inches. Nineteenth century. Collection Harry Hall White, Detroit. (*Courtesy National Gallery of Art, Index of American Design, Washington, D.C.*)

American art. She made even the most average citizen aware of what she was doing by publicizing her efforts, getting contributors, and putting out a handsomely illustrated catalog (obtainable for $1.25 by writing The White House Historical Association, Washington, D.C.). John Walker, the director of the National Gallery of Art, wrote in the catalog's introduction, "The gifts from private individuals have been as varied as they have been touching. They have ranged from paintings and drawings costing many thousands of dollars to a piece of velvet of exactly the right period, color, and design to cover two chairs which Lincoln once used." By making the White House truly belong to the people, Mrs. Kennedy brought about a new appreciation of our history and our art, which, as I have pointed out before, always go hand in hand. Mrs. Lyndon B. Johnson is continuing this interest, and working closely with a White House Committee on Fine Arts which seeks outstanding examples of American art and which brings them to the White House for consideration.

Americana really begins with what is known as Early American Folk Art. Flourishing from around 1780 to 1850, folk art is naïve art, usually created out of a simple yearning for something of beauty. Untaught, itinerant artist-craftsmen traveled over the northeastern United States to paint the stiff, American "Primitive" portraits now so appealing to eyes attuned to modern art. Tradesmen turned their hands not only to inn- or shop-keeping, but also to making signs, weather vanes, and carved statues to draw the trade; one of these is the famed cigar-store Indian.

Edith Gregor Halpert, one of the first dealers in this category, has written, "The earliest signs were symbolic. This form of imagery was brought directly from England or other home-lands on the Continent and, in turn, relates to the distant past. The history of Trade Signs carries us back to ancient Egypt, Greece and Rome. Signs bearing the symbols of the baker's *Sheaf of Wheat*, the vintner's *Cluster of Grapes*, etc. were discovered in the ruins of Pompeii and Herculaneum. In time, other traditional types were added—the heraldic, emblematic, illustrative and humorous, each identifying the artisan's trade, specific wares, inns and hosteleries." Yet, it is interesting to note that one of the most popular and enduring of the American folk arts, that of the bird lure or decoy, was adopted from the Indians by the American colonists.

From the beginnings of the American Revolution to the Civil War, the self-taught artist flourished and produced his very appealing and unusual unstereotyped forms that drew on the variety of cultures forming America at the time. American folk art is essentially the art of the middle class, as Mrs. Black has written, "created by and for its members." It flourished in the northeast, where the middle-class artisans and craftsmen worked and lived. It was here that persons who were essentially trained in the crafts turned their skills to making beautiful objects. Sign, coach, and house painters produced portraits and landscapes; ship carpenters carved figureheads, ornaments, and shop figures; and hunters and sportsmen carved decoys. Even the genteel ladies of the "Female Academies" turned out illustrated copy books, mourning pictures, embroideries, and paintings on velvet. Sometimes clumsy, but always charming, these early efforts are appealing both as history and as art, and are an asset to any home and decor.

Back in the 1900s, however, the story of Early Americana collecting was not such a happy one. When the collector Electra Havemeyer bought her first cigar-store Indian for twenty-five dollars at the age of nineteen, her mother, who had taken Electra on innumerable sightseeing trips abroad and who herself collected Rembrandts and Manets, was quite understandably upset. And when she visited her daughter after Electra's marriage to J. Watson Webb and surveyed the American furniture, patchwork quilts, carved eagles, and weather vanes that filled the newlyweds' house, she asked in exasperation, "How can *you, Electra, you* who have been brought up with Rembrandts and Manets, live with such American trash?"

As Aline Saarinen writes (*The Proud Possessors*), Electra Webb's collecting urge had originally been instilled in her by her mother, though it expressed itself in a somewhat different direction. Undaunted, Mrs. Webb progressed to numerous other Early American art categories until ultimately she was to acquire some one hundred and twenty-five thousand objects and fill a museum village at Shelburne, Vermont. She started with quilts, rugs, furniture, pewter, glass, ceramics, toys, carriages, sleighs, tools, folk art, bonnets, hatboxes, and decoys, and progressed later to collecting somewhat larger objects such as a covered bridge, a lighthouse, a stone jail, a wooden meeting house, a completely equipped country store, a schoolhouse, and several dwellings specifically for her "museum." She also added a locomotive and, to top it off, the S.S. *Ticonderoga,* the last sidewheeler in the world to be in service. All this, which was at first stuffed away in bureau drawers (not the larger pieces, of course), is now presented in the unique outdoor museum she created in the rolling Vermont hills.

In recognition for her contributions to the appreciation of Americana, Mrs. Webb was awarded an honorary Master of Arts degree from Yale University in 1956, one of only five women ever to be so honored. Needless to say, this was especially gratifying in view of the title "American trash" that Electra Havemeyer's mother had given her collection in 1912.

It was much easier to find good Americana in the 1910s and 1920s than it is today, and unfortunately this field is rapidly rising beyond our price limit. Some excellent reproductions are made at Williamsburg, Virginia—things that you couldn't get as originals for fifty thousand dollars, Mrs. Black tells me—that are made in the original dimensions and materials. It might be well to look into this area if you're really interested in early Americana.

After 1850, trained artists like James McNeill Whistler, John Singer Sargent, Gilbert Stuart and Thomas Eakins began to appear. These painters are beyond our price range, but the drawings and prints of the artists for whom they opened the way are still available in several American cities: painters like Benjamin West; the artists of the social-protest "Ashcan School"; landscapists like Winslow Homer, George Inness, and Albert Bierstadt; American Impressionists such as Mary Cassatt (who was also Electra Havemeyer Webb's aunt); the American Frontier painters such as George Catlin, and the American Scene School of Thomas Hart Benton. I've seen framed drawings by Hudson River School landscapist David Johnson, unframed drawings by Benjamin West, and a large cache of drawings by "Ashcanners" Everett Shin, Arthur B. Davies, and Arthur B. Carles at New York's Graham Galleries, all well under five hundred dollars.

The reconstructed villages and outdoor museums which are scattered throughout the United States are perhaps the best places to look at American folk art. Among them are the Henry Ford Museum and Greenfield Village at Dearborn, Michigan (where the oldest windmill in the country vies with Thomas Edison's workshop and the courthouse where Lincoln practiced law); the village at Sturbridge, Massachusetts; the reconstructed Early American capital at Williamsburg, Virginia; the village at Cooperstown, New York, noted for its James Fenimore Cooper memorabilia; and the Shelburne, Vermont, museum complex.

All kinds of Americana are spread throughout United States museums, local historical societies, and city collections. The Museum of Early American Folk Arts, presently located in rather cramped second-floor quarters at 49 W. 53rd St., New York City, was founded in 1961 and is the first museum in that city devoted entirely to American folk art. Every show enters and leaves by a narrow flight of stairs or by the large window facing the street, the huge pane of glass of which is removed and replaced. Mrs. Black, the director, says the largest and most difficult object to install was a half-ton wood carving of George Washington that once graced the first arch at Washington Square in Greenwich Village, and which attracted quite a crowd at its arrival and departure hoistings and lowerings.

Other sources of Americana are the Abbey Aldrich Rockefeller Folk Art Collection at Williamsburg, Virginia; the American Wing of the Metropolitan Museum of Art, New York City; the Museum of the City of New York (its collection of early American doll-houses and dolls was one of my favorite childhood haunts); the Museum of International Folk Art of the Museum of New Mexico, at Santa Fé (the largest collection in this category in the U.S., which was formed by well-known designer Alexander Girard); the Maxim Karolik Wing of the Boston Museum of Fine Arts; the Corcoran Gallery of Art, Washington, D.C.; the Addison Gallery of American Art, Andover, Massachusetts; the Wadsworth Atheneum, Hartford, Connecticut; and the Currier Gallery of Art, Manchester, New Hampshire. These are only a few, and there are bound to be many more museums, historic houses, and collections near you.

When you are looking, it will be your local historical society or museum which will be the best source of information. Of the larger groups, the Archives of American Art of the Detroit Institute of Arts is a topnotch research collection of documentary material on American artists. You can write them at 5200 Woodward Avenue, Detroit 2, Michigan. Another research collection, chronicling U.S. crafts and folk arts from early colonial times to the close of the nineteenth century, is the Index of American Design at the National Gallery of Art. It is a collection of native design sources, painted in a special watercolor process, executed as a federal art project in the late 1930s. The Index will answer letters of inquiry, and circulates exhibits of these renderings to educational institutions.

Among the art publications, *Art in America, American Heritage,* and *Antiques* magazines are valuable, while *Woman's Day* now has a regular "Dictionary" feature on the subject.

There are so many good introductory books in this field that it is hard to choose among them. Some recommended to me are the *Gallery Book* of the Abby Aldrich Rockefeller Folk Art Collection, Williamsburg, Virginia; Alice Winchester's paperback book, *How to Know American Antiques* (New York, Signet Key Books, 1951); Harold Eberlein's and Abbot McClure's *The Practical*

Book of American Antiques (Philadelphia, J. B. Lippincott Co.); the Shelburne, Vermont, *Museum Pamphlet Series* on such diverse topics as bandboxes and quilts; Erwin O. Christensen's *The Index of American Design* (New York, Macmillan, 1950); Alice Ford's *Pictorial Folk Art, New York to California* (New York and London, Studio Publications, 1949); Jean Lipman's *American Folk Decoration* (New York, Oxford University Press, 1951); Eric Sloane's *ABC Book of Early Americana* (New York, Doubleday, 1963); and Alice Morse Earle's information-packed *Home Life in Colonial Days* (New York, Macmillan, 1898), now out of print but found in most libraries and secondhand book shops.

NORTH AMERICAN INDIAN ART

Like the rest of American art, that of the American Indian is close to our hearts and land. Collecting it is one of the few opportunities Americans have of coming in contact with a living culture that is part of their heritage. Many of us live near American Indian reservations or crafts outlets, and still more of us drive through the huge Indian preserves scattered through the United States on vacations. There we look at the Indian villages, observe their traditional customs, and often buy some of the silverwork, woven baskets, and pottery that are for sale. Like his white artist brother, the American Indian needs your interest and patronage, for often his art is one of the few ways of making a living currently open to him. Many of the objects are quite handsome and show fine craftsmanship, but, like the other arts here listed, they need careful screening and selection.

An almost unique institution for the fostering of young Indian art talent is the recently established Santa Fé Institute of American Indian Arts in New Mexico. There, the students are taught a special regard for Indian culture, and the values of that culture from which they can draw creative inspiration. The students range from sixteen to twenty-three years of age and often produce quite abstract work, remarkable for its strong design qualities. Supported by the U.S. Bureau of Indian Affairs, it is one of several important training grounds for future Indian artists.

One of the first exhibitions of these artists was at the reopening of the Art Gallery of the Department of the Interior, Washington, D.C., in 1964. The gallery, on the seventh floor of the South Interior Building, was once the pride of former Secretary of the Interior Harold L. Ickes, who had arranged for changing exhibitions

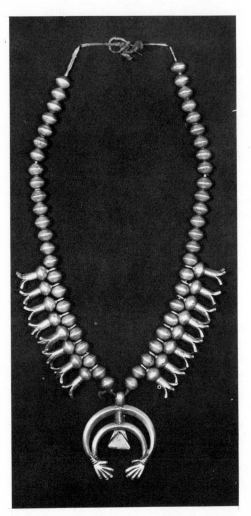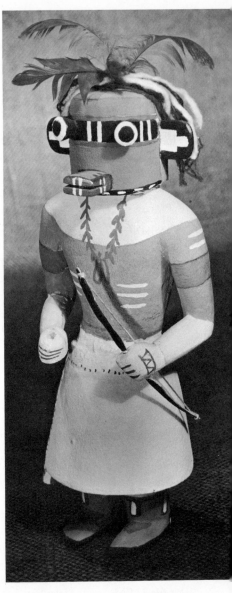

(Left) Navaho artist: *Necklace* (*Squash Blossom*). (American Indian, New Mexico.) Silver. Length: 15 inches. Collection of the Museum of the American Indian, New York. (*Courtesy Museum of the American Indian, Heye Foundation*) (Right) Artist unknown: Ho-ole kachina doll. (American Indian, Hopi.) Collection of the Museum of the American Indian, New York. (*Courtesy Museum of the American Indian, Heye Foundation*)

John Penatac, twenty-six-year-old Eskimo craftsman from King Island, Alaska, forms a piece of silver jewelry during the 1964–1965 Nome MDTA Designer-Craftsman Training Project. (*Courtesy U. S. Department of the Interior, Indian Arts and Crafts Board, Washington, D.C.*)

A display of typical work for sale at the Museum Shop, Museum of the American Indian, New York. (Left to right, top to bottom) a Navaho ·rug (New Mexico), a Papago tribe hand-woven basket, made from a yucca plant (Arizona), a Cherokee hand-carved ceremonial buffalo mask (North Carolina), a Hopi willow plaque (Arizona), a Hopi kachina doll (Arizona), a coil-built Zia Pueblo pottery vessel (New Mexico), a highly polished black-ware vessel (New Mexico), and shell and turquoise necklaces (New Mexico).
(*Courtesy Museum of the American Indian, Heye Foundation*)

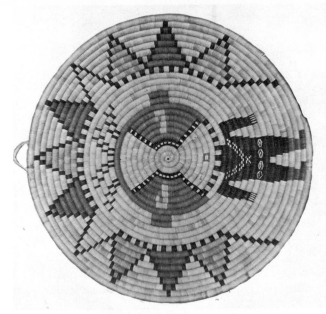

Artist unknown: *Basketry Plaque.* (American Indian, Hopi.) Coiled weaving. Depth: 15 inches. 1925. (*Courtesy Museum of the American Indian, Heye Foundation*)

Artist unknown: Mask. (Seneca, New York.) Corn husk. Length: 15 inches. Collection of the Museum of the American Indian, New York. (*Courtesy Museum of the American Indian, Heye Foundation*)

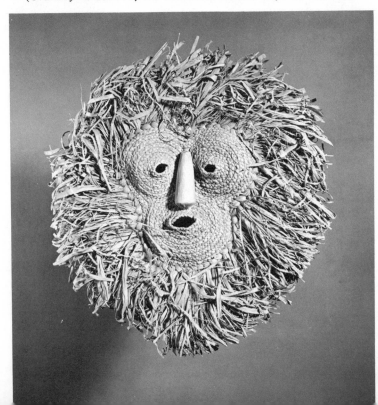

Interior of the Sales Building, the Institute of American Indian Arts, Santa Fé, New Mexico. (Photograph by K. Wiest—*courtesy Institute of American Indian Arts*)

Artist unknown: Dance mask. (Kuskokwim Eskimo, Anvik, Yukon River, Alaska.) Carved wood. Length: 17 inches. Collection of the Museum of the American Indian, New York. (*Courtesy Museum of the American Indian, Heye Foundation*)

Maria Martinez: Pottery jar. (Pueblo, San Ildefonso, New Mexico. Height: 7 inches. Circa 1958. Collection of the Museum of the American Indian, New York. (*Courtesy Museum of the American Indian, Heye Foundation*)

during the 1930s. However, the gallery had languished under dust since the outbreak of World War II until Mrs. Stewart L. Udall, wife of Secretary Udall, was poking around the buildings and discovered the galleries. Since then there have been a variety of fascinating shows, reflecting Indian arts from all over the country.

Perhaps you aren't lucky enough to live in Washington or in one of the cities where quality Indian art is available. But you may be planning a vacation that takes you through an Indian reservation. Here you are in luck because many American museums distribute information which you can obtain in advance. The best ones to write for advice are the American Museum of Natural History, New York City; the University of Pennsylvania Museum in Philadelphia; the Museum of the American Indian, Broadway at 155th St., New York City 10032; and the Indian Arts & Crafts Board, Room 4004, U.S. Department of the Interior, Washington, D.C. 20240. The Indian Arts & Crafts Board is equipped for almost any question you may have; it publishes an illustrated *Fact Sheet* of approved Indian-owned arts and crafts organizations and outlets, complete with names and addresses and what kind of art is sold at each outlet; a bibliography of recommended books on Indian arts; as well as maps of former Indian-owned lands and of the present reservations. It also issues informative sheets on the state of Indian art today and the marketing of Indian crafts. In addition, the monthly magazine *Smoke Signals,* available on request, prints current news about the field. All are free. And if you wish to investigate still further, the Bureau of Indian Affairs, U.S. Department of the Interior, publishes booklets of a more sociological nature. These, too, are available at no charge.

In addition, the Museum of the American Indian has an extensive selection of 35mm color slides of selected objects from their collection. You can obtain this list, and their recommended bibliography, "Books About Indians," by writing them directly.

Frederick J. Dockstader, head of the museum and an outstanding authority on Indian art, recommends the following guidelines for your buying: when you arrive at your destination—be it Yellowstone Park or the great inter-tribal Indian Festival at Gallup, New Mexico, that is held every August and that has plenty of war whoops and art for everyone—buy Indian art of the area you're in, i.e., don't buy Sioux art while in Navajo country, for instance. In this way, you can get good advice from the local man at the trading post; he is usually knowledgeable about his own tribe, but less so about others. As there is just as much faking—objects made especially to deceive—in archeological American Indian material as in other fields, choose carefully, and always let good design and craftsmanship be your guides. Regarding mail orders, which Indian arts and crafts outlets do fill, Dockstader suggests it is usually better not to order by mail if the purchaser can visit any of the several Indian crafts outlets. Robert Hart, general manager of the Indian Arts & Crafts Board, concurs, saying, "Although the outlets on our *Fact Sheet* will fill mail orders, essentially 'beauty is generally in the eye of the beholder.' Basically, you're buying one of a kind and when you order from a photo, you can only see the quality and type of design. Everything else is going to vary."

It's often possible to buy direct from the artist. In Santa Fé, New Mexico, for example, the Indians come in from the reservation to sell their wares in the colorful main plaza, sitting under the portico of the Governor's mansion. At fiesta time, which is usually around Labor Day, the best wares are brought in and dances are also performed. You should also try to visit the many Indian villages and reservations which welcome visitors and where you can often personally visit the artist at his home.

There are several first-rate public collections of Indian art, and many that show Indian arts of their locale. Among the better exhibits recommended by Dockstader are the Philbrook Art Center, Tulsa, Oklahoma, with the best collection in the United States of American Indian paintings by Indians (their big annual exhibition is usually mid-May through June); the Museum of New Mexico and the Institute of American Indian Arts in Santa Fé; the Museum of the American Indian in New York City; the Denver Art Museum; the American Museum of Natural History in New York City; Halls 9 and 11 in the Museum of Natural History of the Smithsonian Institution, 10th and Constitution, Washington, D.C. (also rather confusingly called the U.S. National Museum); the Colorado Springs Fine Arts Center; and the Art Gallery of the Department of the Interior, Washington, D.C.

For local interest, there are the Seminole Art Center, Dania, Florida; the Portland (Oregon) Art Museum; the Henry Art Gallery of the University of Washington, Seattle; the Emily Cowles Museum, Spokane, Washington; the Museum of the Plains Indian, Browning, Montana; the Southern Plains Indian Museum, Anadarko, Oklahoma; and the Sioux Indian Museum, Rapid City, South Dakota.

There are many good introductory books on all phases of Indian art. Remember the reading lists of the Indian Arts & Crafts Board and of the Museum of the American Indian. Some of the literature I've enjoyed includes Dockstader's *Indian Art in America* (Greenwich, Conn., The New York Graphic Society), the most comprehensive survey available of all Indian art in North America; Erwin O. Christensen's *Primitive Art* (New York, Viking Press, 1955); Miguel Covarrubias' *The Eagle, the Jaguar, and the Serpent* (New York, Alfred A. Knopf, 1954); E. S. Curtis' *The North American Indian* (Cambridge, Mass., Harvard University Press, 1903-30, 30 vols.); Frederick H. Douglas and René D'Harnoncourt's *Indian Art of the United States* (New York, Museum of Modern Art, 1941); Dorothy Dunn's article, "The Development of Modern American Indian Painting: Southwest and Plains Area" (Santa Fé, New Mexico, *El Palacio,* 1951); John Sloan's and Oliver La Farge's *Exposition of Indian Tribal Arts* (1931, 2 vols.); Oscar B. Jacobson's and Jeanne d'Ucel's *American Indian Painters* (Nice, C. Szwedzick, 1950, portfolio); and Pál Kelemen's *Mediaeval American Art* (New York, Macmillan, 1943, 1956).

ANTIQUES

Jim and Barbara Ketchum are a young couple with a baby and a Late Federal-style townhouse that they recently bought on Washington's Capitol Hill. Jim, who also happens to be the Curator of the White House, is working on restoring their home, which he facetiously describes as currently being "early fraternity and late drugstore." Like most couples just starting out, Jim and Barbara don't have much to spend on art, but they do know where to get the bargains.

Jim was recently doing some work with the New York Historical Association in Cooperstown, New York. There he heard about a flea market where the farmers' wives of the Cooperstown area load up wagons with things from their attics and bring them into town to sell. Before the day was over, he had purchased a very large "flow-blue" serving platter (which Jim describes as the "prize of our dining-room table") for $7.50, a Charles Dana Gibson pen-and-ink sketch for six or seven dollars, a mid-nineteenth-century brass coal scuttle for ten dollars, and a sterling-silver Victorian-style bird cage for ten dollars (Jim tells me it looks magnificent filled with Christmas tree balls at Christmas time).

Like many of us, the Ketchums like to buy on vacation. They recommend buying in the country and have a favorite place in Massachusetts where they always stop each summer. They feel that half the fun in collecting antiques is the going out and searching, and becoming friendly with a good dealer. They point out that

The Green Room, the White House, Washington, D.C.: this Federal-style parlor handsomely displays a chandelier with urn shaft and sparkling festoons, the famous portrait of Benjamin Franklin by David Martin, and a late eighteenth-century English Axminster carpet in the classic Adam style. (*Courtesy the White House*)

The Parke-Bernet Galleries, New York, during the pre-auction exhibit of the Helena Rubinstein Collection, April, 1966. (*Courtesy Parke-Bernet Galleries*)

The Empire Guest Room, the White House, Washington, D.C.: the American Empire style furniture includes a sleigh bed which probably once belonged to John Quincy Adams. (*Courtesy the White House*)

The Lincoln Bedroom, the White House, Washington, D.C.: the two velvet-covered slipper chairs on each side of the bed were sold after the Lincoln administration and were returned to the White House in 1961. (*Courtesy the White House*)

many dealers are in the business for the love of it, and will do much to help and encourage the young buyer. Jim, who started going to country auctions with his father when he was four years old, now has a three-hundred-fifty-dollar-a-year budget with which he's buying antiques for his home. So, you see, it *can* be done.

Antiques are defined by the U.S. Customs Office as objects made before 1830, but can be more adequately characterized as objects about one hundred years old or more. But then, you should also think of what Ketchum calls "potential antiques" or "antiques of the future"—such as those of the later nineteenth century. Antiques present a highly varied, international field for buying, ranging from England, to the Orient, to France, Spain, Germany, Holland, Belgium, and Italy, to the United States. Such diverse items as ceramics, glass, prints, pewter, furniture, metalwork, textiles, firearms, folk art, rare books, and toys are included. Despite the moans of auctioneers and dealers that the supply is fast diminishing, there are still many reasonably priced antiques around. Dealers usually welcome the beginning buyer on a limited budget, and will give valuable advice and counsel when starting you off. Good objects are not always expensive, and I'll presently point out several bargain categories in which you can begin purchasing.

One important caution: don't buy something merely because it's old. Perhaps, as Richard Gump writes in his book *Good Taste Costs No More,* it's because we're a relatively new country that we're unduly impressed by age and antiquity. We associate special characteristics with certain historical periods and, when these characteristics are handsome and beautiful, they are a good reason for buying. Quality and beauty, unfortunately, are not always the handmaidens of age.

Ketchum cautions the beginning buyer to have a wary eye when he is starting to collect and doesn't have much money, and recommends that you concentrate on one or two types of antiques until you know what you want. It is always wise to go to a reputable dealer who is knowledgeable in the category in which you're collecting; even the most conscientious dealer can't be expert in every category of antiques. This, by the way, is also a good way to get a bargain. Consult the advertisements and travel guides of *Antiques, Art News,* the *Spinning Wheel,* and *Hobbies* magazines for good shops in your area. Buy only in shops where the prices are plainly marked, and make the dealer write the particulars about the purchase—date, period, condition, material, country of origin—on the sales slip. Then, if the goods are not what they are purported to be, the dealer must take them back and return your money. And don't forget that dealers are quite often susceptible to compliments on their wares, and will sometimes lower their prices for an enthusiastic customer. In addition, there are many country auctions and the larger auctioneers and dealers like Parke-Bernet in New York City and Sotheby's in London. Surprisingly, prices are sometimes lower at these bigger galleries than at the smaller ones (see the section on auctions).

Babette Craven, the former antiques editor of *Art News* magazine, tells me there are many bargains in antiques, although bargains are difficult to find in the eighteenth- and nineteenth-century categories. She advises that in ceramics and china, which seem to be a natural collecting field for women, you may want to begin with eighteenth-century English porcelain cups and saucers; some may start as low as fifteen dollars. They are extremely practical in today's smaller homes and apartments, and make good ashtrays or cigarette containers. You can hold the ware up to transmitted light (not ordinary daylight) and, in time, you'll begin to know the date and place of manufacture by the color gradations. You can build a collection around one kind of ware—such as the output of one factory—or one particular shape, pattern, or use. Chinese blue-and-white porcelain is presently quite reasonable, as is old Dutch Delft.

Or you can begin with any of the thousands of English, French, German, or Chinese enamel boxes that abound on the market. Small and usually extremely handsome, they begin at around a hundred dollars. Silver spoons, to be selected by pattern or factory, often begin around ten or fifteen dollars. Snuffboxes and patchboxes are handy containers for today's tranquilizers and aspirins; this is a wide field, and the best items are the seventeenth-century French boxes. Small eighteenth-century china animals and figures are still reasonable, as are many kinds of metalwork such as Roman bronzes, medieval locks and keys, English pewter, Japanese *tsubas* or sword guards, and English brass, pewter, and copper containers. Mrs. Craven also points out the neglected fields of fan collecting and of the black paper silhouettes so popular in the last century. Both are very attractive when framed and mounted alone or as a wall arrangement. These are only a few areas in which you can start; you'll find many more, depending on the section of the country in which you live.

Another antique-collector friend, Lawrence Ross, of *Connoisseur* magazine, points out that good reproductions of upholstered furniture are often reasonable and, unlike most reproductions, will have a good resale value. This is particularly true of wing chairs and sofas made fifty to seventy years ago by quality craftsmen.

For information about antique buying, you can often turn to your regional art and antique dealers associations. These are groups organized to insure fair trading and marketing practices; the largest are the Art and Antique Dealers League of America, Inc. (807 Lexington Ave., New York City 10021) and the National Antique and Art Dealers Association of America, Inc. (50 E. 57th St., New York City 10022). There are, in addition, many excellent publications devoted to the antiques field. The monthly travel guide and and advertisements in *Antiques* magazine have already been recommended; the guide lists reputable antique shops by state, town, address, and telephone number, with a brief description of each store's wares. *The International Antiques Yearbook,* published at 555 Fifth Ave., New York City, has a good, selected list of United States dealers; and there is also a *Great Lakes Directory of Antique Dealers* published for those living in that area.

The three English publications *Connoisseur, Burlington Magazine,* and *Apollo* are all excellent, as is also the French magazine *Connaissance des Arts. Art News* runs a monthly column on auction sales, titled "Coming Auctions"; while the English *Country Life* and *Country Life Annual* (published at Christmas) make pleasant, informative reading. *Hobbies* and *Spinning Wheel* are written in folksier styles but present a wealth of valuable features such as monthly calendars of antique shows, ads for auction and antiques exhibits, a buying-and-selling page, book reviews, directories of antique dealers, and listings of seminars or classes in the various antiques fields. All of the above are available through subscription or at your public or museum library.

Your local librarian can also help you in your reading in specialized areas. Mrs. Craven warns that, as a rule, you should beware of the how-to-collect type of antiques book: she feels they are usually much too general and are of little value. Rather, read books written on special antiques categories. I especially recommend, for buying antiques, Edwin G. Warman's *Antiques and Their Current Prices, A Listing of The Values of Over 32,000 Antiques* (Uniontown, Pa., E. G. Warman, 1963). Also good is Mastai's *Classified Directory of American Art and Antiques,* published every four or five years and the best buying guide around (New York, B. Mastai). *The Antiques Collector's Yearbook,* published in Europe, is a good shopping guide. Another good dictionary, recommended by Mrs. Craven, is Louise Ade Boger's and H. Batterson Boger's *The Dictionary of Antiques and the Decorative Arts* (New York, Charles Scribner's Sons, 1957). For ceramics, read John Goldsmith Phillips' *China-Trade Porcelains* (Cambridge,

Mass., Harvard University Press, 1956), William B. Honey's *Old English Porcelains* (London, Faber & Faber, 1948), and Alice Morse Earle's excellent and very basic *China Collecting in America* (New York, Charles Scribner, 1892). For furniture, anything written by Robert W. Symonds is bound to be good, as are also Wallace Nutting's *Furniture Treasury* (New York, Macmillan, 1954), Marion Day Iverson's *The American Chair* (New York, Hastings House, 1957) and Russell Hawkes Kettell's *The Pine Furniture of New England* (New York, Dover, 1962). Ruth Webb Lee's *Early American Pressed Glass* (Wellesley Hills, Mass., Lee Publications, 105 Suffolk Road) is the standard work on the subject; while George and Helen McKearin's *American Glass* (New York, Crown, 1966) and E. Barrington Hayes' paperback *Glass Through the Ages* (Baltimore, Pelican, 1964) are also good. And C. Jordan Thorn's *Handbook of American Silver and Pewter Marks* (New York, Tudor) is just what it says it is. There are many excellent encyclopedias of antiques, all of which, along with the books here recommended, can be found in your library.

CRAFTS

The seventeenth-century Japanese poet Basho once wrote, "Since there is no rice, let us arrange these flowers for a lovely bowl." This saying by Basho is a perfect illustration of the Eastern lack of distinction between what we call the "crafts" and the "fine arts." Essentially, because his bowl had a definite, functional use, Basho was talking about a crafted object, but because it was also used for something purely beautiful—the arranging of flowers—it could also be called a product of the fine arts. The Japanese make no distinction between the two, as we do in the West. In fact, in Japan today, a painter usually tries to exhibit with a potter because he knows the pots will draw the crowds. Yet, the rather outdated distinction between fine arts and crafts is now fast disappearing even in the United States, or, at least, becoming much less sharp. Certainly the same artistic impulses go into both, especially when one thinks of Iranian lusterware, Islamic prayer rugs, and Venetian Murano glass as no less beautiful for their having been designed for use.

With the Industrial Revolution in the nineteenth century, it was felt here that handicrafts would never be needed again. But, somehow, machine-made goods never quite took the place of handmade objects. The latter, as David Cort wrote in *The Nation,* make us feel good, and they get better the more we use them. And in using them we feel something of the creative joy of the human being who created them.

Like many others, a Putnam County, New York, housewife and mother of four felt the need for these disappearing objects and decided to do something about it in the Hudson River community in which she lived. The housewife was Aileen Osborne Webb, who started Putnam County Products to help the unemployed during the Depression and later turned it into the American Craftsmen's Council, which now has over twenty-five thousand members. In a sense, the whole American crafts movement can be said to have sprouted from Putnam County string beans and wooden footstools. A tall, strong person who looks like the craftswoman she is, Mrs. Webb is almost singlehandedly responsible for the crafts renaissance sweeping not only this country but the entire world.

Crafts are handmade objects, usually created for daily use, and are made with a variety of techniques and materials. Ceramics, or pottery, are made of clay, and are hardened by being "fired" in a hot oven, or kiln. Ceramics can range from the very delicate, thin porcelain of your finest table settings to thicker, rougher high- and low-fired wares. Metals are popular crafts materials today, as they were in the past: silver is used for flatware and hollow ware; iron and bronze make other cast objects; and gold, silver, and copper are used for jewelry. Glass is another very old crafts category, and can be used in a variety of ways in the home. Stained glass can look magnificent when displayed in front of windows with the light shining through and glinting off the colors. At the Corning Glass Center in Corning, New York, you can not only look at the glass displays in the museum, but also watch the glass being blown in the factory. Textiles, still another category, may be printed, woven, imprinted with the hot wax process called batik, stitched, painted, or appliquéd; while thicker textiles are classified as rugs. A handsome, rough-textured Scandinavian rug can make a compelling focal point for any room on either floor or wall, and you might consider this rather than a painting as the design focus of your decorating. Plastics and enamels are also popular with today's craftsmen, and new possibilities with these mediums are constantly being explored. Wood is still a popular material; as is the leather used for bookbinding.

The crafts renaissance, begun with the Putnam group, was further nurtured by the Handicraft League of America in the 1930s. The League was chartered as a foundation under its present name in 1943. What was then needed was a school to train craftsmen

Nik Krevitsky working on stitchery. (Tucson,
Arizona.) 1966.

Nik Krevitsky: *Remembrance*. (Tucson, Arizona.) Stitchery. 1964. Collection of Mrs. Alma
Lesch, Shepherdsville, Kentucky.

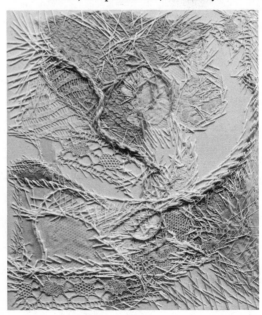

Erica Karawina: *The Fountain.* (Honolulu, Hawaii.) Fused and leaded glass. Height: 14 inches. Width: 10 inches. (*Photograph by Stan Rivera*)

Potter Teruo Hara with Kobo Group pottery displayed behind his home-workshop, Warrenton, Virginia.

Martin Amt with his collection of Early American salt-glazed pottery, Washington, D.C.

Frank Patania, Jr.: *Necklace.* (Tucson, Arizona.)
Sculptured and fitted silver with
semiprecious stone.

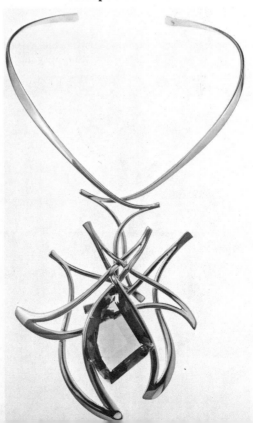

Ellen King: *Planters.* (New York.) (Photograph
by Burk Uzzle—*courtesy American Craftsmen's
Council, New York*)

Potter Joseph Vitek forming a pot on the wheel, Kobo Group workshop,
Warrenton, Virginia.

Ellen King: Covered jars. (New York.) (Photograph by Burk Uzzle—*courtesy American Craftsmen's Council, New York*)

and, after a rather circuitous journey from Dartmouth College in 1946 to Alfred College in 1948, the League finally settled down at the University of Rochester, which offers courses and facilities in all the crafts. Although no work is sold directly from the university, its graduates usually set up shop immediately and market their wares through another Webb project, America House, at 44 West 53rd St., New York City.

The American Craftsmen's Council, across the street from America House at 20 West 53rd St., provides a great number of services for both the craftsman and the public. In addition to having a rapidly expanding membership, it is the center for some 125 regional crafts organizations (you can write the A.C.C. for the organization and outlets nearest you); sponsors regional, national and international craftsmen's conferences; keeps a file on over twelve hundred recognized craftsmen, with colored slides of their work for use by architects, students, and designers; maintains the only crafts museum devoted solely to shows of contemporary craftsmen; runs a library; issues a newsletter; and provides a slide-rental service.

One of the Council's more valuable contributions is the publishing of *Craft Horizons,* a magazine devoted solely to the crafts. It undoubtedly contains the best answer to any question you may have. The magazine lists a calendar of crafts exhibitions by state and city; it has a where-to-show column; and it features articles on various craft exhibitions, the work of individual craftsmen, or even the crafts of a whole country (one issue, for example, was entirely devoted to design in Japan). In addition, it prints critical reviews of exhibitions around the country. *Outlook* is the Council's more specialized newsletter and is issued free to council members. The Council also puts out handsome catalogs for exhibitions at its Museum of Contemporary Crafts at the above address (almost next door to the Museum of Modern Art).

The energetic Mrs. Webb wasn't content to stop with the United States, however. In June of 1964, the A.C.C. sponsored the First World Congress of Craftsmen in New York City in order to establish some formal kind of worldwide craftsmens' organization with the purpose of educating craftsmen and public alike to the great values, economic and cultural, inherent in the crafts. With only about fifty expected, some two hundred fifty delegates from more than forty-nine countries poured into Morningside Heights for the conference at Columbia University. Among the glassblowers, silversmiths, potters, weavers, and batik designers who attended was a young mother from the Andes with her four-month-old baby. From this conference grew the World Crafts Council. Its leaders hope that meetings like the one at Columbia can be held every five or six years, and that some sort of central place can be established where inquiries can be made for information on crafts in any given country.

The whole crafts area is an excellent place for the beginning buyer with little money. Because of the general attitudes in the Unitd States toward crafts, they are usually priced well below the "fine arts." Yet buying can sometimes be a problem if there are no active crafts organizations, artists, or crafts outlets in your town or city. Many shops devoted solely to crafts find it a rough go and sometimes have to shut down. More often, craftsmen get a local reputation in their community and sell directly to their neighbors with no merchandising overhead; this is good for buyers, as it reduces the price and provides personal contacts with the potter, metalsmith, or textile designer. In this case, you can get a unique handcrafted rug for about the same price as a quality machine-made one, and handsome craft furniture at about the same cost as the comparable factory-made product. From time to time, the A.C.C. publishes a list of reputable crafts outlets, but as craft shops come and go so quickly it's hard to keep it up to date. Florence Eastmead, of America House, feels that purchasing directly from the craftsman is the best and cheapest way to buy, and she points out that crafts are spread all through the United States and are not centered in the cities or in New York. She recommends that you look into fairs and festivals, and also at the art department of your local university. Consult your local newspaper for crafts exhibitions and competitions, and read *Craft Horizons* for news of shows of craftsmen in your area. The magazine publishes a yearly illustrated "Christmas Shoppers' Guide" of carefully selected items which can be ordered by mail.

The crafts field is perhaps one of the easiest in which to commission a specific piece for your home. You can take a tip from the Baron Elie de Rothschild—and you don't have to be a Rothschild to do this—who believes in encouraging the making of contemporary decorative objects. In his home on the Rue Masseron in Paris, Rothschild has an elaborately convoluted coffee table made from an elm root, which he commissioned the French artist Stahly to make, as well as a stand for his television set which he commissioned from Cézar in 1962. Teruo Hara, a Japanese-born potter who teaches at the Corcoran School of Art in Washington, D.C., recently started a subscription "Ceramic of the Month" with this in mind. With his Kobo Group, a kind of craftsmen's cooperative,

Hara is producing for a mass market while still retaining the hand-craft element. He and his group, located in an old Warrenton, Virginia, house such as might have inspired Edgar Allan Poe, monthly turn out handsome sets of coffee cups, creamers, cereal bowls, and the like, for members of the "Ceramic of the Month" club.

Of course, there are other phases of crafts than the contemporary one. My friend Martin Amt collects early American salt-glazed pottery. Amt became interested in collecting when he began studying with Hara in 1962, and now sells some of his own work in order to buy the Early American. Mainly storage jugs made in the Central Atlantic area from about 1815 to 1890, these Early American crocks are usually wheel thrown and sport a cobalt oxide blue decoration which was sometimes stenciled. All are functional—there is even a spittoon—and are highly classic and restrained in their appeal. Amt, who now has over forty of these jugs, usually finds them in junk shops or hidden away in antique shops. He tells me that some are as low as five dollars, and that he's never paid more than fifteen.

Crafts are all around you, both old and new. While the Council's museum is probably the only one in the country devoted exclusively to showing contemporary crafts, the following are noted either for their permanent collections or for their changing exhibitions: the Corning Glass Museum, Corning, N.Y.; the Pasadena (Calif.) Art Museum; the San Diego (Calif.) Fine Arts Gallery; San Francisco's M. H. de Young Museum; the Denver Art Museum; the Bridgeport (Conn.) Museum of Art, Science and Industry; the Art Institute of Chicago; the Wichita (Kan.) Art Museum; the Flint (Mich.) Institute of Arts; the Newark (N.J.) Museum; the Albany (N.Y.) Institute of History and Art; the Everson Museum, Syracuse, (N.Y.); the Munson-Williams-Proctor Institute in Utica, (N.Y.); Philadelphia's University Museum; the Dallas Museum of Fine Arts; the Norfolk (Va.) Museum; the Atlanta (Ga.) Art Association; Raleigh's North Carolina Museum of Art; the Worcester (Mass.) Art Museum; the Milwaukee (Wis.) Art Center; the Columbus (Ohio) Gallery of Art; Santa Fé's Museum of New Mexico; the La Jolla (Calif.) Art Center; New York City's Cooper Union Museum; the Albright-Knox Gallery in Buffalo (N.Y.), and the Butler Institute of American Art at Youngstown (Ohio).

For books, you can again consult the A.C.C. for their recommended reading list, which is free to members, and read *Craft Horizons,* which regularly reviews new books in the crafts field in each issue. The Council also publishes a handy manual titled

Crafts for the Aging, which describes the fundamentals of the basic crafts and is valuable for young and old alike (*Crafts for Retirement, A Guidebook for Teachers and Students* is similar.) For ceramics, A.C.C.'s handsomely illustrated catalog, *Forms from the Earth: 1,000 Years of Pottery in America* (around $2) and Bernard Leach's *A Potter's Book* (London, Faber, 1940) are basic. For glass, look at Kay Kinney's *Glass Craft* (Philadelphia, Chilton, 1962); for textiles, study David B. van Dommelen's *Decorative Wall Hangings* (New York, Funk & Wagnalls, 1962); and for crafts in wood, consult E. and F. Andrews' *Shaker Furniture* (New York, Dover).

EXOTICS

Far Eastern Art

There is more of this art around than you think, and much of it is still reasonably priced—especially if the dealer doesn't know what he has and you do. Since there are so many shadings to the terms "Far Eastern" and "Oriental," let me define them here as the arts of Japan, Korea, China, and of the South Asian countries of India, Pakistan, Cambodia, Thailand, Vietnam, Nepal, Indonesia, Malaysia, Laos and the Philippines. As you might surmise, in such a diversified group of countries there is a great variety of artistic styles and expressions. Actually, people have no more business lumping them together than they do calling the East "mysterious." Part of this lumping, however, stems from the symbolic wall of lacquer and porcelain long ago erected by the Chinese and Japanese themselves, and the unavailability of many of their arts until just a short time ago (the Chinese at first despised Westerners as "barbarians" and would only let them buy what the Chinese considered their "minor arts," such as a lacquer and ceramics; it was only in the 1920s and '30s that the Chinese let Westerners see their treasured paintings and calligraphies).

Now another "wall" has been erected by the United States Treasury Department, which, since the Korean War, has put an embargo on all goods, including art, made in North Korea, Communist China and North Vietnam. The buyer must present proof in the form of bills of lading, insurance policies, museum catalogs, or the testimony of a Westerner (the Office of Foreign Assets Control feels a Chinese dealer's word is often not reliable) that the Asian goods were outside the Communist countries before December 17, 1950. So you can see it's rather complicated and has, of course, shot prices up, as the source of supply is now so limited. The law is a thorn in the side of Chinese art scholars, art curators, and art buyers. The well-known Oriental art collector Avery Brundage, who has given over six thousand Asian art objects to the M. H. de Young Museum in San Francisco and who started collecting over thirty years ago, now finds he has to collect mainly through dealers in Hong Kong. He recently pointed out, "Every Communist country has laws forbidding the export of art objects, and we have a law forbidding their import, which is a stupid law. We should encourage bringing in art." It is to be hoped the law may be revised in the future and that the market for these beautiful objects, therefore, will be changed considerably.

It is curious, but true, that few of the great collectors in this field have started out with much knowledge of Chinese history, language, or art. George Eumorfopoulos, an English businessman, was one of these. Collecting in London before others had begun to appreciate the Chinese aesthetic, he made almost no mistakes in judgment although he knew nothing about the artist and collector seals and marks that usually adorn every Chinese scroll. He was one of the first to appreciate and acquire Han and T'ang Dynasty pottery tomb figures and animals, when even the experts laughed at them. King Gustav Adolf VI of Sweden, whose collection of over two thousand early Chinese art objects toured this country in 1966-67, started buying in 1907 as a very young Crown Prince. His first purchase, for sixty crowns in a London antique shop, was an octagonal porcelain dish of the Ch'ien-lung period. The Prince later went on to more serious study and collecting under the many learned Swedish scholars in this field. But it is interesting that he started without special preparation but with that sixth sense the Chinese call *K'ai men chien shan,* meaning "Open the door and you see the mountain."

Yet the acquiring of Chinese art has by no means been confined to the rich. You may have some Chinese object—a household teapot, a lacquered chest, a painted screen—in your home, and not realize it is Chinese. That is because the appeal of certain types of Chinese art is so universal that one is not particularly aware of their subtle appeal until one stops and thinks about it. It is also interesting to note that the great scholar of Italian Renaissance art, Bernard Berenson (or "B.B.," as he was better known), collected many outstanding examples of Far Eastern art in his home, and once said that if he could begin once more, "I would devote myself to China as I have to Italy."

There are two main categories of Chinese art, that made for export and that made for the native taste. George Washington had a complete dinner service of Chinese export porcelain, which you can still see at his home at Mount Vernon, Virginia. These and other Chinese objects were brought to the United States by salty New England sea captains, and even today are still displayed in many Maine and Massachusetts homes. The Peabody Museum in Salem, Massachusetts, has perhaps the most interesting collection in the world of these wares from the China trade. Although some very beautiful collections of export porcelain have been brought together, such as the one of Mrs. John Allison of Honolulu, it is, as a rule, a good idea to buy objects made for the Chinese themselves.

In your buying, you may find that good, authenticated Japanese and Chinese paintings are usually higher than our thousand-dollar budget, that many *objets d'art* like ceramics, furniture, jades, and ivory carvings are much less expensive. And, of course, if you have a chance to travel in Asia, you can still get very good bargains. Mrs. Allison built up her collection while living in the Philippines and Japan (her husband is a former U.S. Ambassador in Tokyo). Someone else I know has a stunning collection of early Korean pottery from a two-year stay in Korea.

It is wise, as usual, to buy only from reputable dealers specializing in the field, who have the best selections at the most reasonable prices, and to get certificates of origin. Again, I urge you to get the particulars of your purchase written on the bill of sale. For beginning buyers, there are the intricately worked, often tiny Chinese snuff bottles, which begin around ten dollars, going up to two hundred and above; Chinese ivory carvings, many exquisitely shaped, are around a hundred dollars; carved Chinese jades, coral, or other semi-precious mineral carvings begin at thirty-five dollars; popular sword guards and *netsukes,* made in either bone or wood, can also be had for thirty-five dollars; Japanese ivory carvings range from sixty dollars to four hundred dollars; some very few small, early Chinese ritual bronzes begin at two hundred dollars— and the list could go on and on. You will probably have your best luck in finding and buying the Chinese "blues-and-whites" ceramics; they have been in this country longer than other Chinese objects and came in in bigger quantities than did the other arts.

Some other art categories that come to mind are the many authenticated Ch'ing and Ming paintings for seventy-five dollars and up at Simon Kriger's (712 12th St., N.W., Washington, D.C.), which Kriger got before the United States embargo went into effect;

Artist unknown: *Pi* (the traditional Chinese symbol of heaven). (China.) Green and brown jade. Attributed to the Han dynasty (circa 207 B.C.– A.D. 220) or earlier. Mounted on a separate, elaborately carved wooden stand. Outside diameter of *pi*: 17¾ inches. Inside diameter: 4½ inches. *(Courtesy S. Kriger, Inc., Washington, D.C.)*

Gallery of Japanese art, Oriental Wing, the Minneapolis Institute of Arts: a screen, "Swans and Willow Trees," circa 1556–1650 (far right); two of four doors painted by Sansetsu (1590–1651) depicting "The Eight Hermits" (nearer right); a sixth-century, black marble Kuan-Yin, Goddess of Mercy, in the gallery of Chinese sculpture (in the background). *(Courtesy Minneapolis Institute of Arts)*

The dancer Bali Ram before a copper gilt, fourteenth-century Avalokiteshvara (Goddess of Mercy), during a performance at New York's Asia House on the occasion of the exhibition "The Art of Nepal," 1964. (*Courtesy Asia Society*)

the handsome rubbings from the old Cambodian capital at Angkor Wat at the Weyhe Gallery (794 Lexington Ave., New York City), which are still available at that gallery for twenty-five dollars and up, but which may soon become scarcer because of the recent prohibition by the Cambodian government against making any further rubbings (the process is apparently wearing down the temple reliefs and destroying them little by little); the many excellent paintings done by contemporary Japanese and Chinese painters at New York's Mi Chou Gallery (801 Madison Ave.); and the wide selection of many Oriental goods at Gump's in San Francisco. You can find good Japanese paintings there for fifty dollars to seventy-five dollars in the racks at the back of the store. One of the nicest features of collecting Oriental decorative objects is the beautifully carved wooden stands that usually come with the pieces. And don't forget that Oriental things can be mixed with modern decor for stunning effects. John D. Rockefeller 3rd, who loves Asian things, and his wife, Blanchette, who is just as passionate about modern art, have handsomely mixed the two in their New York home. Now, as Aline Saarinen describes it in *The Proud Possessors,* a handsome, voluptuous Indian Gupta torso looks across the room at the ferocious black slashes of a Soulages abstraction, while a lovely Japanese Shinto wooden carving of a humble monk faces a Brancusi abstract sculpture entitled "Kiss."

Generally, South Asian art is very difficult to buy reasonably in this country; and prices have gone sky high since certain countries like Thailand and Burma have recently instituted harsh export embargos. When I was in Bangkok several years ago, I brought back a small gilded wooden Buddha for which I paid eighteen dollars (this price included shipping and crating). It is likely that this would be impossible today. But if you happen upon a piece in a shop in the United States and the dealer doesn't know the value of it, you might get a bargain.

The problem of fakes and copies is especially acute in Asian art. Among the Chinese, the copying of the old masters and models is not looked down on as it is in this country; rather, it is a revered, traditional manner of imbuing oneself with the spirit of the ancients, and is, in fact, one of the six main canons or rules of Chinese painting. For the Chinese, a later copy of an earlier work is not considered a rote imitation or forgery, but is a way of perpetuating what is admirable in the art that went before. As so many of the early Chinese scrolls are now lost, we are extremely fortunate to have these later copies. This custom or attitude is analogous to the singing of opera in the West, in which the singer performs the

same words and music but gives them his or her particular inter-
pretation. And so it is with the Chinese reinterpreting of the old
themes over and over again.

Aside from the honored tradition of copying, however, the
Chinese are among the cleverest members in the world of the not-
so-honored profession of forgery. There is not enough room here
to go into all their methods, but one instance I would like to cite is
the grinding up of the original clay from T'ang ceramic tomb figures
to make new ones. It may take years for you to spot a forgery, or
you may have a sixth sense about it immediately. A good guide
here is the usual one of buying from a good dealer. Even better is
to take the object on approval and have it authenticated by your
local museum curator or university professor.

This field may take a little more study than the others, but it's
well worth it. The best source of information about all kinds of
Orientalia is the John D. Rockefeller 3rd–endowed Asia House,
headquarters of the Asia Society, at 112 E. 64th St., New York
City (Pl 1-4200). Its gallery at the above address puts on outstanding exhibitions of Asian art, and the catalogs for these shows are
among the best references available for the layman. In the educational field, Asia House publishes a variety of teaching guides for
college and secondary-school teachers; runs an introductory course
on Asian affairs for primary and secondary New York City school-
teachers; sponsors a Program for the Promotion of Asian Literature which serves as a kind of writers' agent for placing Asian
subjects in magazines and books; runs a program of performing
arts that brings some of the best exponents of the Asian living arts
—theater, music, dance—to the United States; schedules an active
lecture program for members; runs an extensive library on Asian
subjects; schedules conferences; circulates traveling exhibitions;
and provides general information on Asia in answer to questions by
letter or telephone.

There are other organizations that have a variety of programs.
These are the Association for Asian Studies at Ann Arbor, Michi-
gan; the Japan Society, Room 1621, 250 Park Ave., New York
City; and the Asia Foundation, 200 E. 42nd St., New York City.
All have branches in several American cities.

The artist John La Farge once described the Freer Gallery of Art
in Washington, D.C., with its outstanding Asian art collection, as
"a place to go and wash your eyes." There are many United States
galleries displaying Asian arts, both large and small, for "washing
your eyes." No longer confined to the East Coast, they are, in
addition to the Freer, the Boston Museum of Fine Arts and the

Fogg Museum in nearby Cambridge, Mass.; the Peabody Museum, Salem, Mass. (repository of many objects brought in from the old Japan and China trade); the Metropolitan Museum of Art, New York City; the Nelson Gallery of Art, Kansas City, Mo.; the Museum of Fine Arts, St. Louis, Mo.; the Cleveland (Ohio) Museum of Art; the Seattle (Wash.) Museum of Art; in Chicago, the Art Institute and the Field Museum of Natural History (the latter is noted for its Hall of Jades); the Pillsbury Collection at the Minneapolis Museum; the Brundage Collection in San Francisco's M. H. de Young Museum; the University Museum in Philadelphia; and outstanding among the smaller collections are those in Cincinnati, New Haven, Denver, Detroit, Honolulu, and Indianapolis.

You will enjoy reading Lawrence Sickman's and Alexander Soper's *The Art and Architecture of China* (London and Baltimore, Md., Penguin Books, 1956); Robert T. Paine's and Alexander Soper's *The Art and Architecture of Japan* (London and Baltimore, Md., Penguin Books, 1955); Benjamin Rowland's *The Art and Architecture of India* (London and Baltimore, Md., Penguin Books, 1953); and Sherman E. Lee's *A History of Far Eastern Art* (New York, Prentice-Hall, Inc., and Harry N. Abrams, Inc., 1964) as surveys. Also recommended are Michael Sullivan's very readable *Introduction to Chinese Art* (Berkeley, Calif., University of California Press); James Cahill's *Chinese Painting* (Geneva, A. Skira, 1960); and Martin Fedderson's *Chinese Decorative Arts* (New York, Yoseloff, 1961), a good reference for the beginning collector. For bronzes, read William Watson's *Ancient Chinese Bronzes* (Rutland, Vt., Tuttle, 1962); for ceramics, William B. Honey's *The Ceramic Art of China and Other Countries of the Far East* (New York, Beechurst, 1954) and Hugo Munsterberg's *The Ceramic Art of Japan, A Handbook for Collectors* (Rutland, Vt., Tuttle, 1964); and for furniture, consult Gustav Ecke's *Chinese Domestic Furniture* (Rutland, Vt., Tuttle, 1962). In addition, the Foreign Areas Materials Center, 33 W. 42nd St., New York City (244-8480), publishes lists of available publications on Asia, offprints, book lists, and color-slide materials.

Middle Eastern Art

Just as enchanting as any Persian garden, Middle Eastern art is a marvelous and diversified field, one which is still reasonable because of the relatively few persons buying in this area. Islamic arts specialist Richard Ettinghausen tells me that the average person will find it difficult to purchase this art at its source because of

Artist unknown: Goat vessel. (Luristan.) Terracotta. Height: 5⅞ inches. Length: 7⅞ inches. Circa eighth to seventh century B.C. (*Courtesy Royal-Athena Galleries, New York*)

Artists unknown: (left to right) Boeotian statuette of a woman, terracotta, sixth century B.C. Height: 7 inches; Mycenaean idol, terracotta, circa 1300–1200 B.C. Height: 6⅛ inches; Boeotian statuette of a woman, terracotta, sixth century B.C. Height: 6⅞ inches. (*Courtesy Royal-Athena Galleries, New York*)

strict export embargoes, and that many of these art objects may actually be less expensive here than there. For any of the ancient or Islamic arts of Persia (now Iran), Iraq, Syria, Turkey, Egypt, Assyria, or Babylonia, the United States, therefore, is an excellent place to buy. And although the large "Seven Thousand Years of Iranian Art" and the "Art Treasures of Turkey" exhibitions which recently toured this country have increased public interest in the field and upped prices somewhat, costs are still extremely reasonable and cover a wide range.

Purchasing in this art field is mainly limited to a few New York City galleries, but two of them, the Safani Gallery at 960 Madison Ave. and the Royal-Athena Galleries, 1000 Madison Ave., carry on lively mail-order businesses through their illustrated catalogs. Jerome Eisenberg, the director of Royal-Athena, who is still in his thirties, has done much to heighten interest in the field by buying huge quantities of terra-cotta Syrian oil lamps, bronze and flint weapons, old Iranian arrowheads, ancient funerary figurines, Coptic fabrics, et cetera, and selling them at relatively low prices here (of course he has the four-figure-priced art, too). As part of his desire to provide ten-dollar- and twenty-five-dollar objects for the new collector, Eisenberg regularly stocks the sales desks of many United States museums. You can write him for the museum nearest you. These galleries, and the others listed under this category in the New York City chapter, are extremely reliable and will readily provide certificates of origin.

The less expensive items here are ceramics and the smaller bronzes. The Maboukian Gallery, at 1078 Madison Ave., for example, offers many small pots starting at around twenty-five dollars. The gallery's obliging Iranian owner, Mr. Maboukian himself, keeps a large store of inexpensive objects for the beginning collector, to whom he will often give a break.

You'll want to read and look as much as possible once you get "hooked" on this field. The major public collections are at the Metropolitan Museum of Art, New York City; the Walters Art Gallery, Baltimore, Md.; the Boston Museum of Fine Arts; the Freer Gallery of Art, Washington, D.C.; the Detroit Institute of Arts; the Cleveland Museum; and the Seattle Art Museum.

The best introductory book for the beginner is Roman Ghirshman's *Persia, From the Origins to Alexander the Great* (London, Thames and Hudson, 1964). Also good are M. S. Dimand's *A Handbook of Muhammadan Art* (New York, Metropolitan Museum of Art), Douglas Barrett's *Metalwork in the British Museum* (London, the British Museum), Donald N. Wilber's *Persian*

Gardens and Garden Pavilions (Rutland, Vt., Tuttle, 1962), C. K. Wilkinson's *Iranian Ceramics* (New York, Asia House, 1963), Richard Ettinghausen's *Arab Painting* (Geneva, A. Skira, 1962), aand W. G. Archer's *Indian Miniatures* (Greenwich, Conn., New York Graphic Society, 1960).

Primitive Arts

When the eighteen-year-old Jacques Lipchitz arrived in Paris in 1909, he was immediately attracted by the Primitive arts he saw in galleries and museums. Some fifty years later, in the catalog introduction to the showing of his collection at New York's Museum of Primitive Art, Lipchitz wrote, "I found (when I arrived in Paris) the so-called great art too pompous, too stiff. What at the time was called minor art was freer, more imaginative, more open to all kinds of unorthodox expression, all kinds of daring in the handling of materials."

Lipchitz also mentions that he has always collected as part of the learning process and that, as he had no one to guide him in his art tastes when he went to Paris, he went to museums and started collecting what especially attracted *him*. Now, more than a half century later, this famous sculptor has amassed thousands of primitive art objects and jokingly refers to his collection as "an illness with me."

Unfortunately, times have changed and the availability of good objects for very little money is a thing of the past. Julie Jones, a curator at the Museum of Primitive Art, tells me that most primitive-art collectors are not really wealthy and that the market is now becoming almost too high for them. The astronomical prices paid at the Parke-Bernet Galleries in 1966 for the primitive objects in the Helena Rubinstein collection makes this sad fact only too clear. But although prices have recently jumped considerably, it's still possible to purchase well. Or you can take the advice of Gerda Carlebach, who runs New York's Carlebach Gallery of Primitive Arts, when she says, "Buy expensive, quality pieces and pay on time." She adds that the gallery is always interested in starting the new collector off. However, you'd better start buying soon in this field, as increasing scarcity is rapidly becoming coupled with rising popularity. Some of the African nations such as the Congo and Liberia have instituted strict export regulations, although Latin America watches smuggling and illegal excavations go on right under the various governments' respective noses. Five hundred dollars can still purchase a very good piece, and any figure over that can buy objects of real importance. Under this figure, one can usually purchase handsome African ivory spoons for a hundred fifty dollars, surrealistic New Guinea fiber masks for around three hundred to four hundred dollars, African weapons for a hundred fifty to two hundred dollars, colorfully and intricately carved wooden totem poles from the Northwest United States or from Canada for five hundred dollars, and fierce African masks for around the same price. But remember, as primitive-art expert Allen Wardwell has put it so well, "Good money is for good objects," so know what you're buying.

The term "primitive art" is a catchall that covers just about every type of art not classified before 1900, usually the art of the peoples living outside the influence of both Western and Oriental civilizations. Wardwell, who is curator of Primitive Art at Chicago's Art Institute, points out that very sophisticated art from high cultures such as the Inca, Benin, Maya, and Aztec, and the humbler arts of the lower cultures of the Americas, Oceania, and Africa are included, as well as the prehistoric arts of Asia and Europe. One thing all of these peoples had in common, however, was a communal, highly religious type of society. Just as today's advertising is aimed at moving the goods, so also the art of primitive societies was aimed toward the gaining of certain objectives. In New Guinea, for example, art was deeply concerned with fertility. As you travel through Mexico, especially the Yucatan Peninsula, you can still see numerous images of their "Chac" (rain god), indicating these peoples' constant need for rain. And, again, like today's advertising, primitive art was usually created with rigid, carefully prescribed canons.

The appreciation of this field is still relatively new. Pablo Picasso and his Cubist colleagues in Paris were among the first to appreciate African art in the early 1930s and brought many of the stylizations of African sculpture into their own painting. You can see the powerful use of this African imagery in Picasso's huge masterpiece "Les Demoiselles d'Avignon," in which the figures are painted with African-like faces. This, in turn, started a new awareness of other neglected cultures, such as Pre-Columbian art (the art of the Americas before the coming of the Spanish), and the arts of the peoples of the South Pacific. The reason why that astute collector Nelson Rockefeller, whose fine personal collection is now housed in New York's Museum of Primitive Art, could make the spectacular, reasonable purchases he did is that he started buying in this field on a 1930 round-the-world trip. In Sumatra, he saw a knife whose handle was a carved head with human hair. A few years later, on a trip to Mexico, he became fascinated with Pre-Columbian art. Coupled with the daring (for that time) of his taste was the valuable advice he got from primitive-arts authority René D'Harnoncourt. Together they built up a stunning collection.

You have to be extremely careful when venturing into this field, Allan Wardwell cautions. He maintains that the most difficult part of collecting is knowing not where to buy, but what to buy. Wardwell does point out, however, that although they shouldn't have, many collectors started buying before doing exhaustive research and have learned from their initial mistakes. There is just as much bad primitive art as there is bad art in other fields, and you probably will make a few mistakes. Only experience will enable you to spot immediately that "just-right" quality, the quality that collector Raymond Wielgus calls "most easily recognized in its absence," that feeling of aesthetic strength that makes a work good or great no matter where or when it was made. Needless to say, an object should not be impaired by over-restoring, cleaning, and so on.

Wardwell also mentions that a nice aside to your buying choices can be the ethnographic or archeological importance of an object, where it fits into the development of a particular culture, and whether or not it is part of the mainstream of that culture's development, unhampered or weakened by alien influences. Much of primitive art is still classified as archeological and ethnological material, dating from before the days of its aesthetic appreciation; that's why you'll find so much of it still housed in natural history museums and ethnological public collections.

Wardwell also maintains that one sure test you have as to the authenticity of a primitive object is whether or not it has been used. Primitive art was not originally created to be displayed tastefully on the walls of mud huts. Rather it was created for a purpose: to kill off a rival chieftain, to induce fertility, or to bring sun or rain for the crops. Therefore, when you examine a mask, look for the marks that will indicate it was worn. Wardwell advises examining of its edges and back and surfaces to see if they are slightly damaged and rubbed. Examine it also for weathering. Remember that masks were used in ritual dances and ceremonies, whether rain or shine. If you want a free-standing figure, make sure it reveals the effects of standing outside some chieftain's hut. Look for indications of age, for encrustations from smoke, for small repairs done with native materials, and for the termite and insect damage typical of many primitive peoples' environments. In buying Pre-Columbian objects, look for the fine tracery of root marks that

(Left) Artist unknown: Animal mask. (Baoule-Senufo, Ivory Coast, Africa.) Carved wood. (*Courtesy Carlebach Gallery, Inc., New York*) (Right) Artist unknown: Mask (Bakete, Belgian Congo, Africa.) Carved wood painted with white and reddish paint. (Photograph by O. E. Nelson, New York—*courtesy Carlebach Gallery, Inc., New York*)

The sculptor Jacques Lipchitz with an iron
African mask from his collection of over
40,000 primitive works of art. Hastings-on-
Hudson, New York. 1966. (*Photograph by
JoAnne Murphy, New York*)

A table of primitive art objects in the sculptor Jacques Lipchitz's
studio, Hastings-on-Hudson, New York. 1966. (*Photograph by
JoAnne Murphy, New York*)

Artist unknown: Standing figure of a man. (Olmec style, Mexico.) Diopside-jadeite. Height: 23.9 centimeters. Collection of Dumbarton Oaks, Washington, D.C. (*Courtesy Dumbarton Oaks*)

Artist unknown: Double-spouted vase with a painted skull. (Coastal Tiahuanaco culture, Peru.) Height: 16.1 centimeters. Collection of Dumbarton Oaks, Washington, D.C. (*Courtesy Dumbarton Oaks*)

Artist unknown: Pot. (New Guinea.) Unglazed colors. Height: 10 inches. Width: 11 inches. (*Courtesy Carlebach Gallery, Inc., New York*)

often shows up if the piece was buried in the ground, as most of them were. Examine metal objects for corrosion, which results from ground burial. Stone objects will show weathering and eroding from long exposure to the elements, especially if made of limestone.

Certain fakes are obvious, but others are not. There are scientific instruments to detect forgeries, but Wardwell maintains that a sharp and well-trained eye can spot one almost as quickly. You yourself can examine how an object was made with a small hand lens or binocular microscope. Look for tool marks made by sophisticated tools—remember that primitive peoples originally had only rather crude tools with which to work. Ultraviolet light will sometimes show the amount of restoration or repair work done, especially on ceramics. For the experts, to whom you can go with your buys, radio-carbon tests are becoming very important. If you concentrate on gold objects, for example those made in Panama, you will soon be able to tell from experience those cruder objects made from rubber molds or those more delicate pieces cast by the original lost-wax (*cire perdue*) process. Look also for the stylistic conventions of the type of primitive art you're buying, what details characterize it, what materials were usually used, et cetera. A copy will lose much of the "just-right" quality by the use of distracting details and in weaknesses of carving.

Elizabeth Benson, curator for the Pre-Columbian Collection at Dumbarton Oaks, Washington, D.C., suggests you buy on approval and have your purchase authenticated before making your final decision to buy. Her recommendation about forgeries is to have a wary eye for things that look "old and beat up" and make sure the object is, as she puts it, "*logically* old and beat up." By this she means that a mask would be worn in certain places where it was attached to the head of a wearer and would not necessarily be worn elsewhere. She says there are "as many kinds of fakes in the world as there are people, and some are incredibly stupid, while others are just as incredibly clever." In her own special field of Pre-Columbian art, she knows that a Chimu motif would never appear on an original Mochica pot.

Another risk she mentions is that art students in the new African nations receive such superior training in the old traditions that it's often difficult to tell what's old and what's new.

For background information, you can write the Museum of Primitive Art, 15 W. 54th St., New York City; their catalogs of past shows, available for very reasonable prices and housed in their library, are excellent introductions for the beginning primitive-arts aficionado. For other good public collections, the following are among the best: the mammoth Melanesian and Polynesian collections in the Chicago Natural History Museum; the Museum of the American Indian, New York City; the Milwaukee Public Museum; the Buffalo (N.Y.) Museum of Sciences; the Peabody Museums in Cambridge and Salem, Mass.; and Philadelphia's University Museum. If you're traveling to Europe, you'll find that the natural history museums of almost every major city hold very good, carefully collected primitive art.

Wardwell recommends the following introductory books: Miguel Covarrubias' *Indian Art of Mexico and Central America* and *The Eagle, the Jaguar, and the Serpent* (both published by Knopf, New York); Wendell C. Bennett's *Ancient Arts of the Andes* (New York, Museum of Modern Art, 1954); J. Alden Mason's *The Ancient Civilizations of Peru* (Baltimore, Md., Penguin, 1957); H. Tischner's *Oceanic Art* (New York, Pantheon Books, 1954); Eliot Elisofon's *The Sculpture of Africa* (London, Thames and Hudson, 1958); Ruth Benedict's *Patterns of Culture* (Baltimore, Md., Penguin, 1946); Paul Wingert's *Sculpture of Negro Africa* (New York, 1951); L. Adam's *Primitive Art* (Baltimore, Md., Penguin, 1954); and Margaret Trowell's *Classical African Sculpture* (New York, Praeger, 1964).

GRAPHICS

Americans are fairly recent comers to the graphics field, for even though printmaking is a time-honored tradition in Europe, the purchasing, selling, and making of prints here remained a largely unknown or secondary category until only five or ten years ago. Even now, the making of prints and the potential market for them are greater than the outlets currently available for both printmaker and buyer. But more on that later.

Prints

Prints and drawings are perhaps the most available forms of art for the beginning art buyer. There are more of them around and their prices are within reach of almost anyone. The Print Council of America reports the phenomenal growth of interest both in the making and buying of prints in this country, and affirms the increasing recognition of the print as a major art form. Many more competitions and exhibitions of prints are held yearly and more prints are being sold to more people in the United States than ever before. No one school dominates, so that it's almost easier to find prints to suit your taste than it is paintings. There are reported to be over three thousand printmakers working in the United States alone, and the figure is going up all the time.

The print field is much wider and more complicated than the collecting of paintings. To know something about prints will help you to select better examples and to know why some prints are more expensive than others. A print is made by an artist who uses special crayons, inks, or other tools in drawing a picture or image directly on or into a material such as stone, wood, linoleum, or metal. After the image has been created, the artist transfers it by means of ink or other kinds of colors onto paper or cloth. Ideally, the artist performs this step himself, or in collaboration with a skilled artisan, and signs only those prints which are satisfactory to him. The artist inspects each "proof," discarding the ones that don't please him, and signing and numbering those that do. That is why you often see a number such as "20/24" at the right-hand bottom corner next to the artist's signature. This means the artist has printed twenty-four pictures from his original plate, stone, or woodblock, and this is the twentieth print of that series. When the edition is finished, or the plate begins to wear, the artist usually destroys the plate. The nice thing about prints is that they are all originals and that all the numbers made in a particular set (usually called an edition) are equally good. The idea of these print "multi-originals" can be somewhat confusing in our Western tradition, which usually ties originality to one of a kind, yet what could be better suited to our society than multiple originals?

As the noted print authority E. Maurice Bloch, curator of the Grunewald Collection at U.C.L.A., has pointed out, the uniqueness of the original print lies in the fact that it is pulled directly from the inked stone, copper plate, or woodblock drawn for that purpose. As Bloch says, *each impression that the artist pulls completes the art work anew,* because that print is different from the one that went before it, and because it also differs from those that will come after. This is in direct opposition to the popular impression that only the first proof of a print series is original, and that each succeeding impression is a reproduction of the first one. Just as a live performance of a violin concerto by a master like Heifetz differs subtly from his other performances of that particular concerto, so also will the proofs in an edition differ slightly from the others in that edition.

Prints, therefore, are works of art conceived and executed by artists who put every bit as much, if not more, work and imagination into a print as they do into a painting. As the well-known printmaker Leonard Baskin has written, "The print's eccentricity, one might say its special province, is its role as a popular art form." In fact, certain print types were developed just because they yielded larger and larger editions.

Prints, in addition, have the power of any original work of art to give the enduring aesthetic enjoyment so lacking in reproductions made by machine (also confusingly called "prints"). Before the invention of the modern machine processes of printing, handmade print illustrations were used in all kinds of popular media such as books, magazines, and newspapers; they were the only means by which images could be reproduced in multiple at that time. That is why prints by such acknowledged masters as Honoré Daumier, Francisco Goya, Winslow Homer, and even Rembrandt are still available at reasonable prices, many less expensive than those of some contemporary printmakers whose printing costs are much higher.

In addition, some of the finest early Japanese prints were "multiple originals," designed as advertisements for the great actors or plays, or as souvenirs of a play. And don't forget that many art experts think that Rembrandt's greatest work was done in the type of print known as etching, and that many quality Rembrandt etchings are still available for three hundred fifty dollars and under.

By contrast, photo-mechanical reproductions, usually run off high-speed presses by commercial printers in editions of many thousands and often in an enlarged or reduced version of the original—in itself a distortion—may be handsome examples of mechanical color-press work, but obviously do not have the artistic value or enduring quality of handmade prints.

I cannot emphasize enough that a print has just as much intrinsic value as a painting and should not be treated as a poor relation of painting. And although prints constitute one of the less expensive areas in which to buy, they are not merely cheap substitutes for other art mediums. Many of the greatest artists—Rembrandt, Dürer, Botticelli, Bruegel, Rubens, Goya, Picasso, Klee, and Braque—to name just a few in the West—and many distinguished Chinese and Japanese artists in the East, have been printmakers as well as painters. The contemporary painter and printmaker Robert Motherwell recently wrote, "Like all media, lithography has its own intrinsic beauties. *I like the possibility of making works [that are] less expensive to collect"* [italics mine]. But most of all, I like working with fine artisans in a country—this country—where they hardly exist, in comparison with France, Britain, Spain, South

America and the Orient." Another printmaker, Peter Paone, like Motherwell, likes printmaking because he can reach a bigger audience.

More and more United States exhibitions reveal the artist in more than one medium, as is common in Europe, and include prints and drawings in one-man exhibitions. Or an artist may have two simultaneous showings in different galleries, one of paintings and one of graphics. No one school predominates in the contemporary print field, and there are many styles that are very much alive and developing.

There is an almost infinite variety of print schools and types from which to choose and, while the field is broader than that of painting, it is easier to enter for buying than almost any other art category. The collecting of prints is also usually not limited by available wall space as is that of paintings, since prints are more easily stored and do not always require elaborate framing. The Tamarind Lithography Workshop, Inc., 112 N. Tamarind Ave., Los Angeles 90038, has developed several ingenious designs of end and coffee tables and chests for storing your prints. You can obtain plans and specifications for these repositories, to be put together by you or your cabinetmaker, by sending $1.50 to the above address.

There are several pleasures to be found in a print, aside from the functions of any work of art, which is to delight and illuminate. You can buy for the subject matter, purchasing such objects as the bulls of Goya or the fighters of George Bellows; or you can collect for the aesthetic love of the print. You can also buy for technical considerations, such as the rich velvety blacks given by the burr in etchings or for the vivid colors possible in serigraphy.

You have to decide for yourself how important it is to have wide margins (many print margins have been trimmed and, while this sometimes reduces the value in older prints, it usually doesn't show when they are matted and framed); for example, Whistler trimmed his own margins and Tamarind Workshop artists sometimes print without margins. And if an Edvard Munch print is trimmed, this is minor, as Munch's work is now very much in demand (and this is true of many other printmakers). You also have to decide how important the rarity of the print is to you; whether the technical quality of the print and its condition of preservation warrants a certain price; whether you want to buy a "name" artist like Rembrandt, or be content with one of his followers, such as Ferdinand Bol; or if the subject matters to you (some subjects by certain artists are rarer than others, and therefore more expensive).

The print collector Lessing J. Rosenwald started buying in the

1920s when he accidentally saw a print and bought it on the spur
of the moment. He went on to buy, through agents, at European
auctions. Perhaps his biggest coup was the purchase of the Martin
Aufhaüser collection in 1937. Rosenwald tells how Aufhaüser, a
Jewish banker from Munich, was quietly collecting the now almost
unobtainable fifteenth-century woodcuts and metalcuts in the 1920s
and '30s. These prints are the earliest and simplest form of printmaking in the West. They are almost all of religious subjects, in
one color, and were probably purchased by pilgrims for a few pennies as souvenirs of a far-off cathedral or pilgrimage site. Many
were subsequently pasted in books, and the ones that have survived
have mostly come down to us in this fashion. When Aufhaüser
bought, he always purchased anonymously, and not even his own
family knew about it. But when Hitler came to power in 1933, Aufhaüser sent his prints to Holland, and it was here that Rosenwald
first heard about them.

In 1937 the collector's son wrote Rosenwald from Montreal,
offering him the collection, but, although he sent a list of the collection which very much interested Rosenwald, the collector was not
sure he should buy it. Finally, one morning, Aufhaüser Jr. walked
into Rosenwald's office with a package under his arm that Rosenwald describes as looking like something from the the local deli-
catessen. But when the packet was opened, and Rosenwald saw
that every print was carefully mounted and protected, he bought
the whole lot outright. Rosenwald has kept the collection intact
within his own, creating a different collector's mark for it.

Rosenwald, who has done so much for prints in the United
States by helping to establish The Print Council of America (which
will be treated later in this section), currently houses his collection
of about twenty-five thousand engravings, etchings, lithographs,
mezzotints, drypoints, and woodcuts at his Alverthorpe Gallery set
in the rolling hills of Jenkintown, a suburb of Philadelphia. He has,
however, willed his entire print collection to the National Gallery
of Art and his illustrated books and reference materials to the
Library of Congress.

Rosenwald is, of course, a wealthy man to whom the chief considerations in collecting are, as he puts it "aesthetic quality, rarity,
and state of preservation." Others, such as a collector friend of
mine in Washington, D.C., buy for quite different reasons. This
collector, who works for the State Department, started buying
about ten years ago when he got what he describes as his "first
decent-sized apartment." Having limited resources with which to
buy art, he says he usually takes his time and thinks very carefully

before purchasing anything "to be sure I really like it." He tells me he almost always buys on the installment plan. A man of innate, superb taste, this collector's Georgetown house is now filled with woodcuts by Will Barnet, several "paper cuts" by Cassarella, a small "Op" work by Richard Anuszkiewicz which my friend feels shows his style as well as any of his larger works, a Stuart Davis casein, a small Jack Tworkov, a drawing by the sculptor Martinelli, and a José Bermudez drawing. As you enter the front hallway, there is an attractive arrangement of drawings, many by sculptors, which my friend recommends as a good "link" with their more expensive sculpture. This man is typical of the more modest collector who has built up a fine collection mainly of graphics and smaller works which he can afford.

Prices for prints usually run from about two to ten per cent of the cost of a comparable contemporary painting, so that several prints or drawings can usually be bought for the price of one painting. Although there is less chance of getting badly taken when buying prints, do some comparative shopping if you're spending over fifty dollars. Prints by famous Old Masters such as Hogarth and Daumier, whose paintings would be far beyond our thousand-dollar budget, are still available for ten and twenty dollars. Later Goyas can be obtained for twenty-five dollars and up. By "later Goyas" I mean prints that were pulled after Goya's death. His *Horrors of War* series, for example, could not have been printed in his lifetime because of its political implications. The reasonable prices for many Old Master prints is due to the fact that many of the plates— by Piranesi, Callot, Goya, and Hogarth, to name just a few—have remained in existence and have been reprinted from time to time. The original proofs are, of course, more desirable. Even the exquisite Japanese prints by such master printmakers as Ando Hiroshige and Utamaro can be had at fifty dollars, while the good ones go up to eight and nine hundred dollars, depending on the quality of the printing. And you can often get prints, especially the older ones, cheaper here than in Europe.

The lesson is self-evident: while the paintings of these masters are definitely out of reach, their prints are available, and usually very reasonably. And in many cases, the prints are equal, if not superior, to the paintings.

Among the pitfalls of print collecting is the overemphasis on numbering. While it is true that later impressions made in the drypoint and aquatint print mediums are weaker, usually all impressions of a given edition in the other print mediums are of equal quality. In fact, there is a certain stage in the etching process at which the plate is broken in but not yet worn that makes the middle numbers the best. It is an affectation to pay more for a lower number unless you're absolutely sure the lower numbers are superior to the higher ones artistically; the artist's signature on your print should guarantee its quality. The numbering of limited editions became a general practice in the 1920s, and editions today are limited in several ways. Sometimes the pulling of prints is stopped when a plate stops printing satisfactorily; or at other times the edition is arbitrarily limited to up the price. Leonard Baskin recently decried this practice when he wrote, "It is corrupt that plates and blocks which can give tens of hundreds are restrained to tens or a bit more. It is not only corrupt, it is stupid. The various print media were developed just because they yielded larger and larger editions. To exploit these very qualities for the perverse conceit of a minuscule edition is a function of an even more spurious species of conspicuous waste, i.e. ersatz rarity. Hence, welcome to any attempt to disperse prints more broadly." Unfortunately, however, many contemporary printmakers are forced to limit their editions to realize their quite sizable financial investment first in creating and printing the print, and then in distributing it.

Since some plates are strong enough to yield many proofs, impressions of excellent quality are still made from old plates today. The Louvre in Paris, for example, has a department, the Chalcographie du Louvre, devoted solely to this kind of printing, and sells such prints for only a few dollars. Of course this is not for the purists, although I am told the choice is extremely large and good. Another factor in the pricing of modern prints is whether the print is signed on the paper, or on the supporting material such as the stone or plate. The modern print is usually more valuable if signed on the paper or material on which the image is printed, although there have been cases in which certain artists have actually signed mechanically made reproductions on the paper and thus passed them off as originals. This is more commonly done in Europe than here.

Print prices vary, as those of most merchandise. Unknown artists' work is less expensive; and some dealers charge higher commissions and have higher markups than others. We have already pointed out that more is often charged for certain numbers in a print edition than others. Basically, print values are usually determined by: 1) the interest of the collector; 2) the rarity of the print edition; 3) the reputation of the artist; and 4) the condition of the print you're buying (this is sometimes tied in with the numbering, but only with certain print mediums).

Paul Gauguin (1848–1903): *Nave Nave Fenua.*
Ink drawing with watercolor. Circa 1894–1900.
Rosenwald Collection, the National Gallery of
Art, Washington, D.C. (*Courtesy National
Gallery of Art*)

Honoré Daumier (1808–1879): *Guizot.* (French.)
Lithograph. Collection of the Graphics Division,
Smithonian Institution, Washington, D.C.
(*Courtesy Smithsonian Institution*)

Artist unknown: *Allegory on the Meeting of Pope Paul II and Emperor Frederick III.* (German School, Ulm.) Colored woodcut. Circa 1470. Rosenwald Collection, the National Gallery of Art, Washington, D.C. (*Courtesy National Gallery of Art*)

·tist unknown: *Christ Appearing to Mary agdalene.* (French, Paris.) Colored woodcut. ·rca 1500. Rosenwald Collection, the National allery of Art, Washington, D.C. (*Courtesy National Gallery of Art*)

Leonard Baskin (1922–   ): *Children and Still Life.* (American). Woodcut. Rosenwald Collection, the National Gallery of Art, Washington, D.C. (*Courtesy National Gallery of Art*)

Will Barnet (1911–   ): *Wine, Women and Song.* (American.) Color woodcut. Height: 31½ inches. Width: 16½ inches. 1958.

Rembrandt van Rijn (1606–1669): *Eliezer and Rebecca at the Well.* (Dutch.) Pen and ink with wash drawing. Widener Collection, the National Gallery of Art, Washington, D.C. (*Courtesy National Gallery.*)

Käthe Kollwitz (1867–1945): *Self-Portrait with a Pencil.* (German.) Charcoal sketch. Rosenwald Collection, the National Gallery of Art, Washington, D.C. (*Courtesy National Gallery*)

Pablo Picasso (1881–   ): *Minotaur et Pêcheurs,* an etching from *Minotaur Aveugle.* (Spanish.) Rosenwald Collection, the National Gallery of Art, Washington, D.C. (*Courtesy National Gallery of Art*)

A three-drawer coffee table with brass or other base and formica top especially designed for the storage of original prints by the Tamarind Lithography Workshop, Inc. (*Courtesy Tamarind Lithography Workshop, Inc., Los Angeles, California*)

Augustin Hirschvogel (1503–1553?): *Landscape with Two Buildings Surrounded by Water.* (German School.) Etching. Rosenwald Collection, the National Gallery of Art, Washington, D.C. (*Courtesy National Gallery of Art*)

Francisco Goya (1746–1828): *Bullfight in a Divided Bullring.* (Spanish.) Lithograph. Rosenwald Collection, the National Gallery of Art, Washington, D.C. (*Courtesy National Gallery*)

The cost of contemporary prints, however, is determined by additional factors, such as the cost of production, which is higher today than formerly; the artist's own needs; and the cost of distribution (for example, a print will usually cost less if you buy from the artist rather than from the dealer).

Another problem in the buying and pricing of prints is that there are presently just not enough dealers handling them to keep up with the increasing interest. Or if the dealers handle prints they often do it improperly. Many times not only prints, but also watercolors and drawings, are stuck off in a corner of the gallery in what is known as a "print bin," where they often get covered with dirty fingerprints of browsers and easily get torn. Some dealers will not handle prints at all, or, when they do, too few of them know anything about the ones they handle. Ideally, a full-time graphics man should be hired, but it might also be difficult to find this kind of specialist. Artists and artisans are, therefore, too often isolated from collectors for lack of adequate channels of distribution. However, a New York City firm, A. D. Lublin & Co., has taken up the time-honored practice of commissioning print editions from artists and distributing them to dealers around the country. Lublin is a wholesaler, and more of them are sorely needed to help augment the distribution of prints from artist to customer. Another source is the agent or publisher who commissions and promotes individual works and suites, but these are still comparatively rare.

A few galleries are also commissioning artists and selling to a large mailing list through their illustrated catalogs. Roten, 123 Mulberry St., Baltimore, does this, as well as circulating print exhibitions. The Felix Landau Gallery, 702 N. La Cienega Blvd., Los Angeles, regularly sends out catalogs of contemporary original graphics available at the gallery, while the Associated American Artists, 605 Fifth Ave., New York 10017, does much the same thing. A look at A.A.A.'s background is interesting. Founded in 1934 by a group of artists including Grant Wood and Thomas Hart Benton, the gallery's purpose was to make original art available to the public at reasonable prices. Such has the quality been that the early A.A.A. print editions are now collectors' items. The R. E. Lewis Gallery, 555 Sutter St., San Francisco, also sends out mimeographed sheets of its excellent print and drawing stock. All these catalogs are profusely illustrated, so that it is possible to order by mail.

Of course, you can also buy from the printmaker: watch your daily newspaper for announcements of print shows and become familiar with the printmakers in your town or city. Often the problem can be solved by simply telephoning the artist and making an appointment to see his work at his gallery or studio. Remember that most printmakers teach to help augment their income, and you can usually reach them through your local university or art school. Also consult your newspaper or yellow pages to see if a print club is located in your city; these clubs usually hold shows and sell prints. It is still easier to buy in the larger cities than in the smaller ones; New York City accounts for slightly less than half the market for prints, while Los Angeles, Chicago, Philadelphia, Washington, Boston, Dallas, San Francisco, and Cincinnati account for roughly the second half. All of these have at least two fine arts museums; all have significant private print collections and active print curators, an art council, and a body of resident professional printmakers. Yet it is at the State University of Iowa that the Argentinian artist Mauricio Lasansky has organized and directed what has become one of the largest and most important centers of graphic arts in the United States, complete with circulating print exhibitions.

It is a good idea, both for buying and for print information, to join one of the several excellent print organizations that have recently sprung up. The International Graphic Arts Society, Inc., 111½ E. 62nd St., New York City, is a non-profit organization that commissions prints from leading international printmakers and offers them to IGAS members for extremely low prices. Membership is only fifteen dollars; for this, in addition to becoming a member, you receive a print from a selection of over fifty graphics. Once a member, you are obligated to choose at least three prints in the following two years—out of the eighty offered in IGAS's bi-monthly illustrated leaflets that are distributed to their members—for anywhere from eight to fifteen dollars. Of course, you can buy many more than these three prints and realize great savings, as IGAS's prices are usually a good deal lower than those of the galleries. The organization follows a balanced selection ranging from realistic to traditional to abstract and expressionistic, and attempts to make a fair presentation of all styles current both in the United States and abroad. Here you are assured of good screening as to technical competence and style, all at bargain rates. Since its founding in 1952, the Society has distributed more than sixty-two thousand original works of graphic art to its members. The Society is devoted to the idea of distributing graphic arts to as many persons as possible at the lowest possible cost and is succeeding admirably. IGAS also circulates exhibitions to colleges and universities all over the country free of rental fees; unfortunately, the prints in these are *not* for sale.

There are several other print clubs through which you can buy: the Cleveland Print Club, attached to the Cleveland Museum, and the Albany Print Club, part of the Albany Institute of History and Art, both put on exhibitions. The Philadelphia Print Club, 1614 Latimer St., is particularly active. And if you're interested in serigraphs, the National Serigraph Society, 38 W. 57th St., New York City, circulates shows in this print medium.

For print information of all kinds, write The Print Council of America, 527 Madison Ave., New York City. Founded by the collector Lessing J. Rosenwald, the Council helps the contemporary printmaker by circulating print exhibitions throughout the country and serves as an information and educational agency also. Among its services are a listing, issued three times yearly, of print exhibitions throughout the country; the publishing of a pamphlet titled "What Is An Original Print?" for the beginning print buyer (which I highly recommend); the publishing of books on prints such as Carl Zigrosser's *Prints, Thirteen Illustrated Essays on the Art of the Print;* a listing of print dealers throughout the United States; and distribution of The Print Exhibitions calendar, free to Council members, and twenty cents to non-members.

In addition, the magazines *Arts* and *Art News* carry reviews and announcements of print shows. A handsome magazine called *Artist's Proof*, published by the Pratt Graphics Art Center, 381 Broadway, New York City, is a magazine devoted solely to graphics and is issued semi-annually; this informative publication costs five dollars for two issues, and is well worth the price. The FAR Gallery, 746 Madison Ave., New York City, puts out a bulletin and publishes an excellent introduction to prints titled *An Introduction to Fine Prints—A Guide for the Layman.*

In your print buying and exploring you'll be faced with a bewildering array of print types. Your first decision will probably be whether to buy black-and-white or color prints. Black and white, usually favored by the past "greats" of the field such as Rembrandt, Goya, Daumier, is printmaking *par excellence*. The great French poet Paul Valéry analyzed the qualities of black and white as opposed to color in his *Petite Discours Aux Peintures Gravures* and found the qualities of the former closer to the spirit, and in the deepest sense poetic. The Chinese, too, both in their painting and calligraphy, long ago discovered that shadings of black through pearl gray to white implied much more than color ever could.

Yet, original color prints, such as color serigraphs and lithographs, are also most appealing, especially by modern French artists such as Picasso and Miró, and by the many contemporary American artists currently producing color prints.

Then, you will also have to make some kind of decision regarding print mediums. Briefly, there are four major ways of making original prints—relief processes, incised processes, lithography, and stencil techniques. The principle underlying the relief processes is that of cutting away any part of the surface of a flat block so that the desired image stands up to provide a printing surface. Woodcuts and wood engravings are the best known of the relief techniques, but other materials such as linoleum, lucite, cardboard, chipbard, composition board, plaster, and cut paper are also used.

The incised or intaglio processes are exactly the opposite of the relief techniques. Here, the printing areas are grooves, furrows, and indentations lower than the surface of the metal plate into which they are incised. These grooves and furrows are filled with ink in the printing process and become the image; the supporting material is most often some kind of metal plate, usually copper. Among the intaglio processes are engraving, etching, aquatint, mezzotint, and drypoint. When two or more of the intaglio methods are combined, as they often are, they are called "mixed method" prints.

Lithography is the process wherein the image is drawn on a stone, or a specially grained zinc plate, with a greasy crayon or ink. The texture of the stone is such that water adheres in an even film except where the grease has been applied. The stone is then covered with an oily ink, which adheres only to the greasy image, since there is a natural antipathy between oil and water. The greasy image remains in the stone after printing and the lithography process may be repeated again.

The basic principle of the stencil process is that of applying color or inks to the perforated or cutout sections of specially treated paper or silk screen so that the pattern or image comes through the cutouts to the surface to be printed. The printing industry calls this silk screen or screen printing, while in printmaking this technique is known as serigraphy. It reproduces color most effectively. As you look around, you'll notice that prints retain the sensual feel of the materials with which they're made; etchings retain the rich blacks of deeply incised lines; drypoints, in which furrows of metal and the burrs raised beside them by a sharp instrument hold pools of ink, are prized for their velvety blacks; lithographs often retain the cool, grainy texture of the stone; and woodblocks are usually rough grained like the wood of which they're made.

Contemporary printmakers, around whom much print collecting today centers, are carrying on experiments with all the print processes for extremely interesting new effects. By their experiments, they are demonstrating the enormous variety possible within the print mediums, and they present a great range of expression in printmaking. This new surge in the field has encouraged many artists to turn part, if not all, of their productivity to printmaking. In addition, two workshops, the Tamarind Lithography Workshop in Los Angeles and Tatyana Grosman's workshop on Long Island, have done much to further the production of contemporary lithographs. And the experiments being done on mechanical silk screens by such Pop artists as Andy Warhol and Roy Lichtenstein are adding new dimensions to the field.

There are several confusions about prints, which you should examine before you begin buying. Let me emphasize again that prints are originals, not mechanically made reproductions. For example, mechanically made prints in color are often called "color prints." Do not confuse these with original color prints such as color lithographs, color etchings, color woodcuts. Prints are not originals, even though signed by artists, if produced mechanically (unfortunately, some of the best known contemporary artists still do this; and the Print Council is attempting to set up a code of ethics for print dealers under which these mechanical reproductions would be distinguished from original prints and labeled as such.) Prints made after another artist's designs, such as those made by the French artist Jacques Villon between the years 1922 and 1930, usually bearing a double signature, can be called interpretive variations rather than exact copies, and can still be categorized as original prints.

In addition, several methods of reproduction so perfectly resemble the appearance of an original print that it is very hard to tell the difference, especially those reproductions that are made from heliogravure plates and that look almost identical to etchings or aquatints. For valuable tips on how to tell the difference, read Chapter 12 of Stanley Hayter's *About Prints* (New York, Oxford University Press). As with other kinds of art, go to a reputable print dealer or print organization when buying your prints.

Collectors' marks and artists' signatures are both important factors in your buying. Rosenwald tells me that the collectors' marks, what he calls the *provenance* of a print, are very important. These marks are somewhat similar to the collectors' seals you see so often on Chinese and Japanese scrolls. They are also called "collectors' stamps," and are usually found either in the margins or on the reverse side of the print or drawing. The marks are often quite interesting artistically, and take the forms of such things as crests, geometric patterns, numbers, Oriental marks, stamped initials. They can significantly add to the value of a print, since they indicate the print has been in an important collection. Rosenwald highly recommends Dr. Frits Lugt's *Marques de Collections,* which lists thousands of these marks, identifying them as to collectors and the collector's principal interests.

Other marks you can watch for are artist and estate signatures. Although an artist's signature does verify the work of art as genuine, many Old Master prints are unsigned. In fact, the signing of prints and drawings did not become common until the last century. However, today most artists make it a point to sign their works. After an artist's death, an estate signature is placed on the artist's unsigned works by the executors of his estate. Or an artist's wife or the executor himself will sign the work. These also add to the authenticity and value of the work.

A nice aside to your graphics buying could be the collecting of hand-printed art posters. The American Federation of Arts, 41 E. 65th St., New York City 10021, has recently inaugurated the List Art Posters program, in which top contemporary artists are commissioned to create original lithograph, woodcut, or serigraph posters in limited editions of one hundred. These posters are created for special cultural events—for example a symphony orchestra may apply to the A.F.A. to publicize a forthcoming series of concerts— and artists like Josef Albers, Richard Anuszkiewicz, Frank Stella, Leonard Baskin, Bruce Connor, or Theodoros Stamos are asked to come up with a poster design built around that event. The poster has, since the end of the 1800s with Toulouse-Lautrec, and later with Pablo Picasso, been an exciting art form, and the A.F.A., under a grant from the Albert A. List Foundation, has been seeking to revive it. Prices range from forty to a hundred fifty dollars.

And don't forget that old handmade book illustrations and old maps are easy and inexpensive to collect.

For looking at prints, the Print Council publishes a listing titled *Print Collections in the United States,* obtainable on request. The listing is alphabetically arranged by states and by names, and gives the number and a description of the prints in each collection. It is the best guide I can recommend. Among the better known collections are those of the Museum of Modern Art in New York City (modern and contemporary prints—they will answer letters of inquiry); the New York Public Library, New York City; the Brooklyn (N.Y.) Museum; the Boston Public Library; the Boston

Museum of Fine Arts; the Newark (N.J.) Museum; the Cleveland (Ohio) Museum; the Morgan Library, New York City; the Metropolitan Museum of Art, New York City; the Fogg Museum, Cambridge, Mass.; the Cincinnati (Ohio) Museum; the Library of Congress and the National Gallery of Art, both in Washington, D.C.; and Lessing J. Rosenwald's Alverthorpe Gallery in Jenkintown, Pa.

The best training for buying prints is looking, but for your reading William M. Ivins, Jr.'s *How Prints Look* (Boston, Beacon Press) is a good introduction. Felix Brunner's *A Handbook of Graphic Reproduction Processes* (New York, Hastings House, 1962) is an excellent guide to prints that explains, in careful detail and illustrations, more than forty print processes. *About Prints* by print pioneer Stanley Hayter has already been mentioned (Hayter has almost singlehandedly brought about the contemporary print renaissance through his teaching, writing, and exhibiting); and Gabor Peterdi's *Printmaking—Methods Old and New* (New York, Macmillan, 1959) is a standard in the field. I think you'll also enjoy Dorothy and Frank Getlein's *The Bite of the Print* (New York, Clarkson N. Potter, 1963), which is basically a history of printmaking, treating certain artists, especially the Satirists, in depth; and Carl Zigrosser's and Christa M. Gaehda's *A Guide to the Collecting and Care of Original Prints* (New York, Crown, 1965). Miss Gaehda's chapter on the care of prints is especially good. In addition, the Print Council will send you a recommended book list on request.

When I asked Mauricio Lasansky in Iowa for his advice to the beginning print collector, he wrote, simply, "My advice is to buy lots of prints." I hope, after reading this section, you will be off and running.

Drawings

"Drawing is the chamber music of art," says Carter Brown, the assistant director of the National Gallery of Art, by way of explaining the relative neglect of this medium. He does point out, however, that attitudes are changing; though the big money is still going for painting. What better, then, for the modest buyer than to collect drawings? As the good ones become rare, they will also become valuable. They are highly personal documents and often reveal the artist's artistic intentions better than do his paintings. As collector Henry Hecht puts it, "Drawings, to my mind, are the real quality of art." Drawings, in addition, are especially popular now because so much contemporary painting aspires to the qualities of drawing: reduction of means, spontaneity, the first-hand impression —a closeness to the artist's mind and being that is usually revealed only in drawing.

In addition, there is an almost infinite variety of drawing types. There may be just a fragile pencil line—Pablo Picasso is a master of this—when the artist has just picked up a pencil and made a simple sketch. Anybody who has been to art school knows the use of charcoal, a beautifully elastic medium that can be used for both rough and smooth lines, or for linear or tonal values. Pen and ink is another popular medium, and the flexibility of the steel nib pen is one of its most salient qualities. Other variations are brush drawing, sanguine pencil, conte crayon (a grease-based crayon) and pastels. And in today's smaller quarters, drawings, which are usually art works of modest size, don't get lost on your walls.

Prices are currently still very reasonable; and an increasing number of exhibitions devoted solely to drawings are being put on by American museums. In your buying, remember that drawings in the past were usually not signed and that attributions are therefore difficult, except for the collectors' marks (that is where your connoisseurship will come in). Remember also that you can usually obtain the quality of a famous artist's work for a mere fraction of what his paintings would get. Another suggestion I have for your buying is to purchase both a painting and a drawing of an artist and hang them together; you will quickly see how they enrich each other.

If you're seriously interested in collecting Old Master drawings, I recommend that you join the Master Drawings Association, 33 E. 36th St., New York City 10016, for an annual membership of fifteen dollars. For this you will receive four issues of their magazine, *Master Drawings*, which should answer all your questions about drawings. It is a handsomely illustrated publication with articles on the major masters and reviews of new exhibitions and books.

Watercolors

Watercolors are also included in the graphics category. Like drawings, they have long been looked down on, and that is one reason why prices are still low. Their qualities of spontaneity and reduction make them close to the Orientals. It is known that Cézanne diluted his oils toward the end of his life so that they would look like watercolor. In addition, he created many beautiful watercolor landscapes where much of the composition is filled with a shimmering light from unpainted areas of the paper. Other famous watercolorists have been Winslow Homer and John Marin, the latter giving to the medium a vitality and excitement which had been lacking before. Georgia O'Keefe and Charles Demuth also come forcibly to mind. Again, this is a highly flexible, varied medium.

MODERN AND CONTEMPORARY ART

On March 24, 1875, a civil servant in the French Customs Department bearded an insulting, clamorous mob at the Hôtel Drouot sales rooms in Paris to buy Monet's "Paysage d'Argenteuil" for one hundred francs. Few art movements have aroused the hatred and insults that the Impressionist movement did, and the crowd at the Hôtel Drouot was definitely in an ugly mood. Nevertheless, the customs official, Victor Chocquet, passionately loved Impressionist paintings, and stepped forward bravely at the sale to pick up his Monet purchase despite the jeers it then evoked. The painting has since been described as one of "dazzling brilliance, tremulous with light and joy, as though the artist had painted it in a state of ecstatic bliss." Yet, as Monet told Chocquet later on, he had actually been penniless and starving when he painted it.

Chocquet's otherwise colorless life as a customs official was lifted from its drabness by Chocquet's one "vice": his genuine and passionate love of paintings. He and his wife would deprive themselves of almost anything for a work of art, and it was not unusual for Chocquet to arrive home saying, "No chicken this Sunday, dear; I've found a little Daumier!" For years Chocquet bought works by Paul Cézanne, Pierre Auguste Renoir, Edouard Manet, and Claude Monet when he was their only patron. Often going without shoes he badly needed, and with no overcoat in the winter, Chocquet would pore over his new finds for hours and then, with his wife, would try to find space for them in their already overflowing little Paris apartment. Chocquet had no formal art training, only that instinct that the Chinese call *Yen ching yeh hsin* (with eye and heart). Instinctively he recognized beauty and quality in the avant-garde of his own time, and the objects that he collected sixty years ago on a very small salary have since sold for many times over what he paid.

In our own time, the late Duncan Phillips, who founded the Phillips Gallery in Washington, D.C., has done much the same thing. Not relying on the accepted in art, he collected American artists such as Childe Hassam, Arthur Dove, John Marin, and Charles

Demuth when they were as scoffed at as the Impressionists were in Chocquet's time. Phillips had what he called his "deliberate plan to try to understand the artists of my own day, instead of waiting cautiously for Time, the ultimate arbiter, to definitely measure their achievement." The shining example of Phillips' beautiful gallery, which is more like a comfortable and beautiful home than a museum, attests to the courage and taste of his choices.

The modern painter, whether he be abstract or naturalistic, is a pioneer just as much as are our modern spacemen, scientists, inventors, explorers, and moviemakers. This is what makes modern art more exciting, but also more difficult, than the art to which you may be accustomed. Columbus and the Wright Brothers suffered ridicule and neglect for years, while many of our greatest artists have received much the same treatment. Often they are viciously attacked, as was James McNeill Whistler for his painting "Portrait of the Artist's Mother" (actually titled "Arrangement in Grey and Black"). In 1877, the well-known art critic John Ruskin publicly sneered at several of Whistler's paintings which were on view in London at the time. Whistler promptly brought suit for libel against Ruskin for insisting that a painting be an exact, detailed, realistic picture of some object, scene, or event. Whistler felt, in his own words, that "The vast majority of folk cannot and will not consider a picture as a picture, apart from any story which it may be supposed to tell . . . As music is the poetry of sound, so is painting the poetry of sight, and the subject matter has nothing to do with harmony of sound or of color.

"Take the picture of my mother, exhibited at the Royal Academy as an 'Arrangement in Grey and Black.' Now that is what it is. To me it is interesting as a picture of my mother; but what can or ought the public to care about the identity of the portrait?"

Whistler was a pioneer in every sense of the word. He wanted people to look at his works as "harmonies" or "arrangements" without paying attention to the subject matter. Artists who came after him have gone one step further and left out the subject matter—or Whistler's mother—entirely, and depended solely on the language of form, color, paint, and line to convey their artistic message.

The modern or contemporary field presents the biggest art category on the market for testing your own judgment and taste. It is the category that is most available to you, and the art that speaks of your times. As Gerald Nordland, director of the San Francisco Museum of Art, has put it so well, "In collecting modern art, there is a unique joy in aiding a creative talent and watching that talent unfold. There is also a unique joy in watching the art of one's period unfold." Modern is the area of art that will give you the greatest sense of adventure and excitement, and this is what makes it so different from the arts already discussed. But one must, as Alfred Barr, the pioneering former director of collections at New York City's Museum of Modern Art, says, "Have open eyes and a free mind."

By definition, modern art is that art produced by artists born after 1800, while contemporary art is today's art and is created either by living artists or by those only recently dead. America's contemporary painters are perhaps more numerous and better patronized than any other living artists and, concomitantly, there is now for the first time in our history a distinctly American art—an American art that is copied the world over, while the world looks to New York City as its art capital. And while there is at present the largest group of artists producing in centuries, there is also the greatest number of choices and dilemmas for the art buyer. While the avant-garde leaders like Jackson Pollock and Willem de Kooning are now well established, it is still to be seen which of their followers will attain recognition and which will fall by the wayside. We do not have a history by which to judge and must rely—in the midst of a bewildering number of choices—on our own judgment as to quality.

In this age of high-powered publicity machinery and changing fashions in everything from food to automobiles, styles in art change rapidly and almost overnight. The Pop artist Andy Warhol has recently said that "now everyone has a chance to be famous for a day," and he wasn't joking either. You can never tell for certain which way the pendulum of taste is going to swing. Therefore, it is all the more important in this field to buy for those who *make*, rather than follow, styles; not to buy fashionable "names"; and to remember that good painting goes on all over the United States, not just at the art world's center, New York. So look around you at your local talent and buy from them. As art dealer Edith Halpert has put it so well, "There's a great difference between *con*temporary and purely temporary art."

Writing in an issue of *Arts* magazine, art critic Anita Ventura quotes a humorous little exchange between Pogo and "Little Awrful Annie":

"Now make your eyes go blunk," says Pogo to Annie. And, says Miss Ventura, "Her oval eyes turn pure white and empty."

Miss Ventura rightly points out that a great many people suffer a comparable "blunkness" when confronted with the art being produced today. Part of it is the variety and large range of choice. In fact, there are almost as many schools and types of modern art as there are ways of mixing a martini. However, the many "isms" and countries can be broken down into what is variously called Naturalism or Realism and what is known as Abstract or Non-Objective art. Basically, the first takes its inspiration from the world around us, and the artist's objects remain recognizable. For example, the adage that a barn is a barn and a tree a tree holds true here even though the artist may have shaped these objects to his own visual language. Andrew Wyeth is the American contemporary artist who has achieved the most recognition working in this modern mode; he, along with the greats of the United States tradition like Thomas Eakins and Winslow Homer, paints in what is essentially the American spirit. Contrary to popular belief, this kind of painting is not photographic; that is, it is not a pure duplication of the image that registers on the camera's eye, but is a transposition of reality into symbol.

The second, or Abstract and Non-Objective, type of modern art depends more on the artist's inner vision for its subject source; even when a painting begins with a real object, say our tree, that object is converted into a symbol of the artist's feeling about that tree. Much of this kind of art is dependent on twentieth-century psychological discoveries about man's inner and dream worlds. Surrealism, one kind of abstract art (usually not typed as Non-Objective, as it uses recognizable objects), juxtaposes places, objects, and time in paintings much in the way you may combine them in your dreams. Cubism is the breaking up of the picture plane into geometric patterns, in which natural objects are distorted to heighten the emotional effect. Picasso's talking of Cézanne's advice, "You must see in nature the cylinder, the sphere and the cone," is carried to a powerful extreme in many of his Cubist-style paintings.

Modern art has its roots in the 1860s with the Impressionist movement; the school derives its name from a painting by the French artist Claude Monet titled "Impression—Soleil Levant" ("Sunrise: An Impression"). The school was concerned with the fleeting effects of light falling on an object and on the juxtaposition of broken patches of primary colors. Rejected at the time, the Impressionists are now among the highest priced artists on the art market. The Post-Impressionists, painters like Paul Gauguin, Georges Seurat, Paul Cézanne, and Vincent van Gogh, modified the Impressionist cause in the 1880s with still more radical innovations: Gauguin with his flattened two-dimensional surfaces and dramatic cut-off compositions, Van Gogh with his short chopping

Painter Gene Davis in his Washington, D.C., studio. (*Courtesy Washington Gallery of Modern Art, Washington, D.C.*)

An early "happening" at the Reuben Gallery, New York, in the nineteen-fifties.

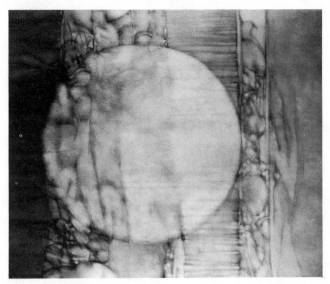

Robert Middaugh: *Moon: Persistant Image.* (American.) Oil on canvas. (*Courtesy Kovler Gallery, Chicago, Illinois*)

Grace Hartigan (1922–   ): *Vendor.* (American.) Oil on canvas. Height: 60 inches. Width: 68 inches. 1956. Collection of the Washington Gallery of Modern Art, Washington, D.C. (*Courtesy Washington Gallery of Modern Art*)

David Smith (1906–1965): *Untitled*. (American.) Brush drawing. Height: 27 inches. Width: 39¼ inches. 1960. Collection of the Washington Gallery of Modern Art, Washington, D.C. (*Courtesy Washington Gallery of Modern Art*)

Francis Bacon (1909–   ): *Study No. 6, After Velazquez's Pope Innocent X*. (English.) Height: 59½ inches. Width: 45½ inches. Collection of the Minneapolis Institute of Arts, Minneapolis, Minnesota. (*Courtesy Minneapolis Institute of Arts*)

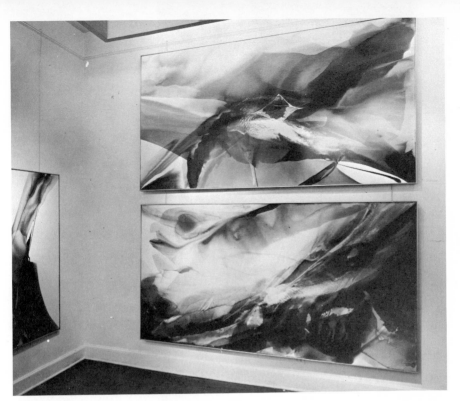

Paul Jenkins (1923–   ) : *Phenomena Day of Zagorsk* (top) and *Phenomena Sun Over the Hour Glass* (bottom), Martha Jackson Gallery, New York, 1966. (*Photograph by John D. Schiff*)

Peáro Friedeberg (1937–   ) : *Hands* and *Clocks.* (Mexican.) Wood. 1964. (*Courtesy Pan American Union, Washington, D.C.*)

Exhibition of sculpture by Reuben Nakian at the
Washington Gallery of Modern Art, Washington,
D.C., 1963. (*Courtesy Washington Gallery of
Modern Art*)

Raoul Hague: *Plattekill Walnut.* (American.)
Height: 35⅝ inches. Width: 28 inches. Girth:
18 inches. 1952. Collection of the Museum of
Modern Art, New York. (*Courtesy Washington
Gallery of Modern Art*)

Ellsworth Kelly (1923–   ): *Red-Blue.* (American.) Oil. 1963. Collection of the
Washington Gallery of Modern Art, Washington, D.C. (*Courtesy Washington
Gallery of Modern Art*)

strokes, and Cézanne with his preoccupation with geometric structure.

After that came the three greats of modern art, Pablo Picasso, Henri Matisse, and Paul Klee, and it is from their innovations that much of the rest of modern art has grown. Matisse's object to present form and color for its own sake has largely been realized; Picasso's Cubist experimentations are still being followed today; and Klee's exploitation of Surrealistic findings through an expressive line on often tiny formats did much to popularize the movement.

The Central European Expressionists, largely based in pre-World War II Germany, are another important group. Through deliberate distortions of forms, human features, colors, and placement of figures in space, the Expressionists evoke intense responses through their art. Our own Abstract-Expressionist or New York School, popular in the '50s and early '60s, is a partial outgrowth of both the German Expressionists and the French Impressionists.

More recently, the so-called Pop artists show the possibilities of interchanging realities, such as those of the billboard and comic strips, for real life. They take their cue from advertising art: beer cans become larger than life, comic strips take on a dimension beyond mere entertainment, and Marilyn Monroe becomes a symbol of all that's perplexing in modern American womanhood.

Artists have also turned to optical effects in painting (if you have astigmatism, as I do, this isn't for you) in which the colors change constantly depending on how the viewer moves and where he stands. Even more recently, the various modes of collage, construction, and "environment" have done away with the old-fashioned divisions between painting and sculpture; they account for some of the more exciting work being done today.

Because of the wide choice existing in this field, almost anyone can start buying contemporary art and like it. I have a young acquaintance, twelve-year-old Lisa, who buys out of her allowance and birthday money. Lisa, who has been collecting since she was seven, now has a very respectable collection, mainly of prints and drawings. She also corresponds with her artist friends, whom she has met through her parents, who collect on a somewhat larger scale, and has a scrapbook full of their sketches and autographs. Perhaps her most interesting pieces are a pair of small, carved wooden models that Mexican artist Pedro Friedeberg made for his "hands chair." I personally think that Lisa's are even more interesting than the finished versions, as Friedeberg attached feet to the hands in Lisa's model, but left the feet out of the finished pieces.

Some acquaintances of mine in Washington, the Philip Sterns, particularly like collecting sculpture, and it may have something to do with having five lively youngsters. Everyone is encouraged to touch the Raoul Hague chiseled wood form in the dining room, and the children regularly ride Reuben Nakian's "The Emperor's Bedchamber," which presides out in the garden. Mrs. Stern told me how Nakian, now in his seventies and recently honored with a retrospective at the Museum of Modern Art, came to visit and loved watching the children clamber over his work.

When a certain kind of art becomes popular, there is almost always a man and an institution behind it. In this case, Alfred H. Barr, Jr., now well into his sixties, is the man, and the Museum of Modern Art, for which he was until recently the director of collections, is the institution. Perhaps more than any other living person, Barr has made modern art and design an everyday part of American life. When the Museum was founded in the late 1920s by a group in New York City, Barr was teaching the first modern art course given in the United States at Wellesley College in Massachusetts. Not only did Barr lecture on the established art mode of painting and sculpture, but he included movies, theater, architecture, photography, and modern popular design as seen at the local dime store.

What Barr did essentially was to transfer his curriculum from Wellesley to New York, with the result that the Museum's highly active divisions now include not only those devoted to exhibiting painting and sculpture, but also sections devoted to films, photography, prints, architecture and industrial design (architect Philip Johnson was its first head), traveling art shows, an art-rental department, and an art school noted for its excellent children's program.

The Museum has been criticized by some of the public as being too "far out," and by artists and critics for "dragging its feet." It is both a treasure house of all kinds of art and an educational institution of the future. President Franklin D. Roosevelt, in a nationwide broadcast when he was in office, called it "a living museum, not a collection of curios and interesting objects," and its vitality is perhaps its most remarkable characteristic. Since its founding in 1927, it has tapped the very lifelines of modern art and translated them for public consumption. "For some reason," says the Museum's print curator, William Lieberman, "other museums lack the immediacy of our joint. People go individually to the Metropolitan or to the National Gallery. They go in pairs to the Modern. There's always something to be shared." And there is much to be gained by becoming a Museum of Modern Art member, even if you don't live right in New York City. Membership makes you eligible for free admission when you can visit, twenty-five per cent off the many catalogs, books, and paperbacks issued by the Museum's Publications Division yearly on all phases of modern art, and reduced annual subscription rates for *Arts, Art News,* and *Art in America.* The catalogs are excellent references for beginners in the modern art field, and the bibliographies, compiled by the meticulous Bernard Karpel of the library staff, are excellent guides to further research and exploration.

Another interesting feature is the talks given by A. L. Chanin on every phase of modern art in the Museum's galleries. I recently attended one of his talks—it happened to be on Expressionism—and even though it was dinnertime, he had an intent audience of about forty persons. Included in the lecture were discussions of such milestones of Expressionism, all at the Museum, as Oskar Kokoshka's double portrait of "Hans Tietze and Erica Tietze-Conrate," Max Beckman's highly symbolic triptych, "Departure," and Vincent van Gogh's "Starry Night," painted only a year before the artist's suicide. Chanin's clear, informative talk included what van Gogh wrote his brother Theo in Paris about the painting: "The night is so beautiful, and it's never been painted" and, even more significantly, "Death is the train one takes to the stars." Chanin lectures three times a week during most of the year. A sample schedule during one month included lectures on Italian Futurism; Tchelitchew and Dubuffet; Gauguin; van Gogh and Toulouse-Lautrec; Matisse; Léger; Jackson Pollock and American Abstraction.

These talks, publications, exhibits, and movies were all part of Barr's educating of the public, and are being continued by his successor, Bates Lowry. Barr has, indeed, accomplished the didactic function of a museum, and put into practice a favorite saying of his, "The most beautiful use of the word 'teach' that I know is in the caption of an engraving by William Blake—'Teach their souls to fly.' "

For your reading in this field, Barr has written one of the best introductions to modern art available, titled *What Is Modern Painting?* (New York, Doubleday, 1958). A paperback that sells for $1.25, it is succinct, clear, and entertainingly written. Barr's *Cubism and Abstract Art* (New York, The Museum of Modern Art), written in 1936, is still the standard reference on the subject. Other books recommended are two paperbacks by Sam Hunter, *Modern French Painting* and *Modern American Painting and Sculpture* (New York, Dell, 1962); Sir Herbert Read's *A*

Concise History of Modern Painting (New York, Praeger, 1959);
Edgar Richardson's *Painting in America* (New York, Crowell,
1965); Peter H. Selz's *German Expressionist Painting* (Berkeley,
Calif., University of California Press, 1957); Hilaire Hiler's *The
Painter's Pocketbook of Methods and Materials* '(Hackensack,
N.J., Wehman, 1956); Thomas B. Hess' *Abstract Painting: Background and American Phase* (New York, Viking Press, 1951);
and Paul Klee's *On Modern Art* (London, Faber, 1947). And if
you're planning a trip to Europe, don't miss buying *The Guide to
Modern Art in Europe* (New York, The Museum of Modern Art
and Pan American Airways).

Most United States museums, universities, and local art associations are currently building up excellent contemporary and modern
collections. Among the best are the above-named Museum of Modern Art; the Whitney Museum of American Art, New York City;
the Chester Dale Collection in the National Gallery of Art, Washington, D.C.; the Institute of Contemporary Art, Boston, Mass.;
the Barnes Foundation, a semi-private institution located near
Philadelphia (appointments must be made in advance, by letter, in
order to see the collection); the Art Institute of Chicago, famous
for its French Impressionist paintings; the Dallas Museum of Fine
Arts; the Houston Museum of Fine Arts (currently headed by
James Johnson Sweeney); the Carnegie Institute in Pittsburgh; the
San Francisco Museum of Fine Arts; and the museums of the Atlanta Art Association.

WHERE TO BUY

SOURCES OF LOW-COST ORIGINAL ART
IN THE UNITED STATES

The following listing is as accurate and informative as I, and the contributors, could make it. A great effort was made to find art professionals—writers, gallery directors, critics, artists—who thoroughly knew the art available both for purchase and looking in their respective cities. The listings, therefore, strongly reflect the taste and judgment of each contributor; they do not necessarily reflect my opinions or those of the publisher. The listings, too, are selective and are in no sense intended to be comprehensive. Don't forget the guides recommended earlier in the book—*The Handbook of American Museums* and *The American Art Directory* are two examples—which *are* comprehensive because they are listings per se.

In cities where contributors could not be found, the information was gathered by questionnaires sent to individual art galleries, museums, and historic houses.

Always keep in mind that the art market is a highly fluctuating one, a business that is constantly changing. And while many artists remain with one gallery for a lifetime, and certain galleries are passed from father to son at the same address for generations, there are many artists who do change their city and/or gallery, and just as many art outlets that move. It is always a good idea, therefore, to telephone before visiting a gallery or museum to check on the hours and days open. If you are a visitor in a strange city, remember that the tourist bureaus of each city often have helpful information on cultural outlets and events.

The galleries in each city fall under the *Where to Buy* sections. The *Where to Look* listings include mainly museums and historic houses, citing which items of original art are for sale in each. The *Information About Art* in each city will refer you to up-to-date calendars of art events and art critiques in local publications.

The art cited here is all priced under a thousand dollars, and is usually in the ten- to five-hundred-dollar range. The following abbreviations designate the categories covered: A—American art, old and new; An—Antiques; Au—Auctioneers; C—Crafts; E—Exotics (Far and Middle Eastern, Latin American, American Indian,

167

pre-Columbian, and primitive arts) (Eu—European art; F—Framers; G—Graphics; Mods—Modern and Contemporary art; A-R—Appraisals, Restoring; Install—Installment Buying; R—Rentals; M—Mail Orders.

The East

BOSTON, MASS.

By Jane H. Kay
Contributing critic, *The Christian Science Monitor,* and Art Critic, *The Patriot Ledger.*

Boston's "art flavor" is an academic one. Most of the better artists teach, too; or, in terms of making a living, teach mostly. Prices are below New York ones, both for local artists and for "names." There is no real "school," and no one style predominates. An artist like Gyorgy Kepes organizes his activities at M.I.T. and keeps turning out his major *Vision and Value* art series while painting handsome, glowing abstractions. The sculptor Mirko heads Harvard's important Carpenter Center of Design while basing his artistic reputation on handsome totem-like forms.

Teachers from the MUSEUM OF FINE ARTS SCHOOL (230 The Fenway, 267-9300) and BOSTON UNIVERSITY (855 Commonwealth, 262-4300) offer their wares at such galleries as the BORIS MIRSKI (166 Newbury, 267-9186) for substantial or average, but not exorbitant, prices (open 9:30-5:30 Mon-Sat). The RHODE ISLAND SCHOOL OF DESIGN in Providence sends evidences of its artist-teachers periodically.

Information about Art

A good guide for your looking and buying comes from a combined effort by the American Federation of Arts in New York and THE INSTITUTE OF CONTEMPORARY ART here. Titled *The Cultural Resources of Boston,* and published in 1965 as the first in a hoped-for series of cultural guides to major American cities, it covers not only the galleries but such cultural enclaves as the universities, the museums, drama and architecture. It is available through the Institute (100 Newbury, 262-0600). Other notices appear in the *Museum of Fine Arts Bulletin,* in university calendars

169

and in the local newspapers, which have a Sunday or once-a-week listing of art exhibitions.

Where to Buy

Geographically, Boston's art-going is easy to trace on foot along two main art-buying routes. For the first, start down Newbury Street from Berkeley to Fairfield (yes, it's alphabetic—Clarendon, Darmouth, Exeter, etc.). This narrow, car-crowded street is packed with shops and galleries, picture framers and interior decorator stores. Art ranges from the amateur to the avant-garde.

American artists of older vintage appear at CHILDS GALLERY (169 Newbury, 266-1108, open 9-5 Mon-Fri) and ADELSON GALLERY (134 Newbury, 266-6631, open 10-5:30 Tues-Sat), while artists from the Provincetown locale can be seen at the SHORE GALLERIES (179 Newbury, 536-3439, open 10-5:30 Tues-Sat) and those of conventional Wyethian inclinations at the COPLEY SOCIETY OF BOSTON (158 Newbury, 536-5049, open 10-5 Mon-Sat) and at DOLL AND RICHARDS (140 Newbury, 266-4477, open 9-5 Mon-Sat). Other galleries in this locale are the VOSE (238 Newbury, 536-6176, open 8:30-5:30 Mon-Sat), one of Boston's oldest art establishments, and CARL SIEMBAB (133 Newbury, 262-0146, open 10-5:30 Tues-Sat), specializing in photographs.

Lively, often more avant-garde and innovating stances are taken by artists like popster Richard Merkin and New Realist Symbolist Walter Feldman at the OBELISK (130 Newbury, 536-5432, open 10:30-5:30 Tues-Sat). A retinue of newcomers, including Al Rubin, are at the ELEANOR RIGELHAUPT GALLERY (125 Newbury, 266-5310). Handsome paintings by calligraphic expressionist Iqbal Geoffrey join other works at WARD-NASSE (118 Newbury, 267-3371, open 11-6 Tues-Sat), while good abstractions, vintage drawings, and sculpture can be found at the SWETZOFF (119 Newbury, 536-1990, open 9:30-5:30 Mon-Sat). Hannes Beckman and Gabor Peterdi show regularly at the KANEGIS (123 Newbury, 267-6735, open 10-6 Tues-Sat).

In addition, Stuart Denenberg and two women named Portia Harcus and Barbara Krakow last year opened very good new print galleries; the first, the TRAGOS (128 Newbury, 267-6860) furnishes both known artists like Lawrence Kupferman and lesser-known printmakers and artists at moderate prices; the second, aptly called HARCUS-KRAKOW (167 Newbury) supplies a quality

Main stairway, the Museum of Fine Arts, Boston, Massachusetts. (*Courtesy Museum of Fine Arts, Boston*)

Egyptian Gallery, the Museum of Fine Arts, Boston, Massachusetts.
(Photograph by Steven Trefonides—*courtesy Museum
of Fine Arts, Boston*)

Exhibition "London: The New Scene" at the Institute of Contemporary Art, Boston,
Massachusetts, summer, 1965. (*Photograph by George Alley*)

The Isaiah Thomas Printing Office, Old Sturbridge Village,
Sturbridge, Massachusetts.

An antique pillar and scroll clock by Connecticut clock-
maker Eli Terry at Old Sturbridge Village, Sturbridge,
Massachusetts.

roster of contemporary artists—Motherwell, Le Corbusier, Nevelson—at typical prices around two hundred dollars.

Two speciality shops along the route are ORIGINS (159 Newbury, CO 7-7249, open 11-5:30 daily, and summer by appointment) and R. M. LIGHT & CO., INC. (190 Marlborough, CO 7-6642, by appointment only). ORIGINS presents a section of Primitive and Ancient art for fifteen dollars and up, while R. M. LIGHT offers Old Master and modern prints and drawings for one hundred dollars and up. Both allow buying by installment, and will fill mail orders.

Cambridge provides a second though less packed art route. THE PAUL SCHUSTER GALLERY (134 Mt. Auburn, 876-1939) has many of the youngest, i.e. least expensive, artists of good quality (open 12-5:30 Mon, 9:30-5:30 Tues-Sat). THE GROPPER GALLERY (40 Brattle, 354-1130, open 11-6 Mon-Sat) has shows plus older masterprints; the new THOMSON GALLERY (1168 Mass, 868-1168) has prints in the middle price range by contemporary artists.

Boston's concentration of *antique shops* line Charles Street at the foot of nearby historic Beacon Hill, a colorful locale where eighteenth and nineteenth century paintings hang above furniture and china wares.

Boston, and its environs, house the usual diverse facilities for buying: art associations, universities, schools, libraries, theaters, restaurants, coffee houses, and department stores, not to mention framers and private homes. For contemporary craft shows, try Brookline's HARLEQUIN SHOP (700 Washington Street, 232-5505, open 9:30-5:30 Mon-Sat). Two other sturdy or offbeat enterprises are the CAMBRIDGE ART ASSOCIATION (18 Eliot, 876-0246, open 10:30-5 Tues-Sat and 2-6 Sun) and the BOTOLPH GROUP GALLERY (161 Newbury, 536-5862), a unique part-private, part-religious gallery with work by artists like Sister Corita and others suitable for church structures and individuals. BRANDEIS UNIVERSITY's pre-Christmas "Young Collectors' " show ferrets out samples priced under a hundred dollars by topflight talents chosen by the keen eye of its curator William Seitz (formerly of the Museum of Modern Art), with Thomas Garver, assistant. Periodically, too, some suburban synagogues and churches hold art shows and sales. SEARS, ROEBUCK & CO. sets up "Vincent Price Collection" exhibitions at various locales from time to time; while JORDON MARSH (450 Washington, 426-9000) has an annual amateur-oriented "Sea and Surf" competition. The tents of the BOSTON ARTS FESTIVAL failed to go up as usual in the summer of 1966; WINTERFEST, its supposed replacement, has mostly commercial wares. THE BOSTON PRINTMAKERS ANNUAL, an exhibition of prints by members and invited artists, is mounted every January-February at the Boston Museum of Fine Arts; and the BOSTON SOCIETY OF WATERCOLOR PAINTERS has its exhibition of paintings by members at the same institution every March-April. But the NEW ENGLAND ART TODAY, a juried, quality biennial, held at Northeastern University in April and May of odd years, is the only real substitute for the former Arts Festival.

Where to Look

Perhaps the richest cultural resource that Boston has to offer is its museums, many of them university ones.

The Museum of Fine Arts
465 Huntington, CO 7-9300

Towering above them all with its superior collections in almost any art field you can name, the museum is noted especially for the country's finest Asiatic art. Admission 50¢; free floor plan at sales desk; authenticating by appointment; staff restorer available to public; *Museum Bulletin* and *Calendar of Events* for members; noncredit courses with Tufts; admission 50¢ adults, 25¢ children; open 10-5 Tues-Sat, 1:30-5:30 Sun. 10-10 Tues, Oct-May; closed Mon, Christmas, New Year's, Thanksgiving, July 4.

Isabella Stewart Gardner Museum
280 The Fenway, 566-1401

Built by the energetic and legendary Mrs. Jack Gardner, the museum was originally designed as a magnificent Venetian palace. Its inner court is filled with flowers the year around, and much of the collection was chosen by the Renaissance art expert Bernard Berenson. The flowers, beautiful objects and Sunday concerts brighten many a gloomy Boston winter. Admission free; open 10-4 Tues, Thurs, Sat, with guided tours at 11; 2-5 Sun; closed Aug.

The Institute of Contemporary Art,
100 Newbury, 262-6000

As active as the Gardner but flashing closer to the contemporary scene, calling itself "an art center which doesn't collect," the Institute specializes in changing exhibitions of contemporary art. All works from these exhibits are for sale, and the Institute will put the potential buyer in touch with the artist or gallery. The Institute charges no commission. It also boasts the most thriving rental gallery in Boston, in a balcony overlooking its galleries. Works by many New England artists can be bought here in most media. Open 10-6 Tues-Sun, till 9 p.m. Wed; closed Mon, major hols.

De Cordova Museum
Sandy Point Rd., Lincoln, 259-8355
This renovated building on an old estate also espouses contemporary art and contemporary New England artists. It is an annex to the contemporary scene (only about 40 minutes from downtown Boston) with its shows sent by the Guggenheim, Smithsonian Institution, etc. Admission free; open 10-5 Tues-Sat, 2-5 Sun.

Some UNIVERSITY MUSEUMS you may be interested in visiting are those at HARVARD, which include one of the foremost university museums in the world, the FOGG; the PEABODY MUSEUM OF ARCHAEOLOGY AND ETHNOLOGY; the new glass-and-concrete, Le Corbusier-designed CARPENTER CENTER OF DESIGN, right next to the more traditionally styled Fogg; and the handsome, Medieval-style BUSCH-REISINGER MUSEUM, devoted to Germanic culture and notable for its magnificent Barlach sculptures. M.I.T. presents art exhibitions in its large HAYDEN GALLERY, and the BOSTON UNIVERSITY ART GALLERY also puts on periodic displays. NORTHEASTERN UNIVERSITY, WELLESLEY, TUFTS and PINE MANOR JUNIOR COLLEGE also feature occasional exhibits. BRANDEIS has changing shows in its Goldfarb Library; its ROSE MUSEUM is an important institution headed by former Museum of Modern Art curator William Seitz and presents some of the more important exhibits in the Boston area. Duchamp, Magritte, Bruce Conner are among recent artists shown.

Old Sturbridge Village
Sturbridge, Mass., 347-3362
A short drive from Boston, this is one of the outstanding historical museums in the United States with 36 exhibit buildings dating from 1790 to 1840. Reproductions of Old Sturbridge Village antiques, plus redware, woodenware, pewter spoons and buttons, etc. made on the premises by Village craftsmen, are available at the Museum Gift Shop. Open 9:30-5:30; closed Christmas, New Year's; admission for adults $2.50.

NEW YORK, N. Y.

By Joanna Eagle

New York has been named many times over as the world's art center. Emphasis in this huge, usually frantic, metropolis is on the selling of art, on the marketing of every conceivable style and fashion in art, and on the dissemination of art from countries the world over. It is true that over ten thousand artists live and work here, and exude a great creative vitality. Yet, it is New York as the world's major art marketplace, rather than as a center of creative art production, that is important. There is nowhere else, not even Paris, to parallel the variety and number of choices open to the art buyer as he strolls down Madison Avenue and its adjacent side streets, from the low Eighties to the Sixties, turning either west or east on 57th Street.

The salient truth here is that great taste and great dealers are synonymous, and that it is the foresighted and energetic dealers of this city who have set its art pace and tone. Despite the number of galleries in New York, it is rare to find two exactly alike or even similar. Galleries are extremely individualistic, reflecting the tastes of the men and women who run them. They range from the velvet-walled and plush-carpeted Old Master salons such as GEORGES WILDENSTEIN and M. KNOEDLER to nineteenth-century-flavored book and print shops like WEYHE and WALTER SCHATZKI. Above all, New York galleries are galleries with points of view. Sidney Janis, Pierre Matisse, Charles Egan, André Emmerich, and Leo Castelli are now almost legendary names; and it is they, and others like them, who have not only made their galleries highly successful and profitable but who have introduced major recent art styles (Janis and Castelli introduced the Pop and Found Art movements, respectively). Surprisingly, many of the most imaginative and enterprising dealers have been women. The contributions of Edith Halpert have been noted earlier in this book; Betty Parsons was among the first to push Jackson Pollock; Rose Fried was the pioneer United States dealer for the Neo-Plasticists (Mondrian, Albers, van Doesburg, Malevich, et cetera); Eleanor Ward introduced many important young painters in her once famous STABLE GALLERY Annuals; Eleanore Saidenberg represents several important artists, among them Picasso; Martha Jackson has also shown many notables; while Virginia Zabriskie and Eleanor Poindexter have done more than their share for younger, promising artists.

There are over five hundred galleries in New York today, and they reflect both the large production of American artists and the current American appetite for buying original art. Despite the great number of art outlets here, it is fairly easy to tour the galleries in a good day's walk (one gallery, THE MOBILE ART GALLERY, 118 E. 78th St., UN 1-6362, will even bring paintings to your door by liveried chauffeur). Most of the galleries are divided among three general locations—Madison Avenue and its adjacent side streets, the 57th Street area, and Greenwich Village. It's a good idea to start at the galleries clustered around Madison Ave. and 79th Street, walking south along the avenue, and not forgetting the side streets to Fifth and Lexington. Then explore the concentration of galleries around 57th Street and Madison, and finally take the subway downtown for a short walk around the Village. The greatest variety, outstanding quality, and possibilities for bargains can be found in the art of the Madison Avenue complex. Fifty-seventh Street, the area where the first New York galleries located in the 1930s and '40s, now has the best quality, biggest names, and also the highest prices. The Village, with its East Village Tenth Street gallery complex, is no longer the good place to buy it once was, although it's still possible to find both quality and bargains if you look hard enough. Even in the very expensive galleries, your best buys will still be prints and drawings and smaller oils by major artists, especially during the Christmas sales when prices are much reduced.

Another area that may possibly develop into a new "Village," chiefly as a complex of "annexes" for small uptown galleries, is the downtown warehouse and loft district centered around Houston and Greene streets. It is here that many artists rent lofts in which to work and live. Dealers faced with the problem of squeezing outsized paintings and sculptures into shoebox-size brownstone galleries, removing stair rails and door frames, and hoisting whole shows through windows, no longer have the room to store art of this scale and make it constantly available to customers. As this book went to press, Richard Feigen, whose East 81st Street gallery often can't hold the environmental-scale art so popular today, had just rented a three-story former button factory in this downtown loft section. He feels the area may very well turn into a Sunday hangout for art buyers who can also get Chinese lunch while loft and warehouse hopping.

The New York art gallery situation has not always been this affluent and vibrant, however. New York's current art boom is a distinctly World War II and postwar phenomenon. In the 1930s and early '40s, you could count the number of galleries, especially those devoted to contemporary and modern art, on the fingers of one hand. But with the war, artists like Hans Hofmann, Marcel Duchamp, Léger, Mondrian, and the sculptors Jacques Lipchitz and Naum Gabo fled Europe for New York, and along with them came refugee collectors and some farsighted dealers. Perhaps the most influential gallery—really a combined museum and gallery— was heiress and art patron Peggy Guggenheim's ART OF THIS CENTURY, a Frederick Kiesler-designed, Cubist-Surrealistic show-place. Artists like Robert Motherwell, Jackson Pollock, Ad Reinhardt, Jimmy Ernst, Hans Hofmann, and Mark Rothko were introduced with great flair here, the architecture as much of a drawing card as the artists (the Cubist section of the gallery had a tent-like, dark blue canvas wall with unframed pictures suspended in mid-air on strings, while sculpture seemed to float, as it was also mounted on suspended pedestals).

Other art ventures, run by Charles Egan, Betty Parsons, and Curt Valentin, followed Miss Guggenheim's pioneering lead, but for many years it was a rough go for galleries in New York, even during the heyday of the Abstract-Expressionists in the 1950s. Now we see the other side of the coin when a prominent gallery owner like Samuel Kootz, for years the dealer for painter Hans Hofmann and an important representative for Picasso in the United States, closes his gallery because "it's all become too easy."

Not only have adventurous dealers and their galleries been the tastemakers of this city. The museums have also played an important role, especially that all-powerful arbiter of taste, the MUSEUM OF MODERN ART. An artist's reputation can be made or broken by a one-man show at the "MOMA," and a seemingly dizzying succession of art styles—Abstract Expressionism, Op, Pop—has been documented there in recent years.

It is true that the many styles, or "fashions," of art introduced here by both MOMA and the dealers may seem very transient; yet the one constant of the situation is the serious, continuous striving for valid new forms of expression. It is this exploration of new forms and of new aesthetics that is pushed by the dealers and which is copied throughout the rest of the country, in Europe, Japan, and the Middle East. More serious experimentation takes place here than in any other U.S. art center, and much of it reflects the vitality of the performing arts in New York—music, drama, dance. "Happenings," in which creative improvisation is the paramount aim; the various forms that collage and Constructivist art have taken; experiments with electronic music combined with the visual arts: all these are part of this exploration in which the traditional boundaries of the arts are crossed and in which the arts merge. It goes without saying that this leads to both the best and the worst in the arts, but it is these extremes of good and bad, with all their shadings toward the middle, that give New York City the uniquely avant-garde, experimental flavor which makes it distinct from the rest of the country.

It is obviously impossible to list all of the current art movements and galleries in this New York City section. The following listing is offered as a guide for your own explorations and selections. There is nothing static about the art world in New York—that is part of its excitement—and galleries come and go even quicker here than in other American cities, moving locations often. The artists, too, change galleries frequently. Because of this, and if you're interested in a particular gallery or artist, you can save yourself time by telephoning the gallery first and checking its hours, artists, and location. In the following guide, the three main geographical locations of art are chronicled in terms of the contemporary and modern galleries. Then, the names and addresses of galleries in the more specialized fields of buying, such as antiques, crafts, graphics, Middle and Far Eastern art, and primitives, are given. Other sources for buying—department stores, auction houses, places for renting art, and framing establishments—follow. Lastly, there is a selected listing of New York's major museums.

A few handy facts to remember about New York galleries: the art "season" runs approximately from September to June; shorter hours and less interesting "group" shows occur in the summer; the usual hours are 10 a.m. to 6 p.m., with the Village galleries opening and closing later in the day and evening; there is hardly ever an admission fee (except for benefit shows) to galleries; you may often have to ring a doorbell, especially for second-floor galleries (this is just so they'll know you're coming). Gallery openings, where it is possible to meet the artist, are available to anyone on the gallery's mailing list, and are usually held Tuesday evenings and on Saturdays. There are many of these openings during the season, as exhibitions run for about three or four weeks. However, even if the show of a particular artist has closed, it is always possible to see his work either at the gallery or at his studio. For this, it is better to make an appointment ahead of time.

Information about Art

It's also a good idea to do some reading on the galleries and artists you're going to see before starting off. There is a greater wealth of publications on art here than in any other city in the U.S. The national newsmagazines *Time* and *Newsweek* have regular sections devoted to the arts in New York. The weekly *New Yorker* reviews many New York exhibitions in its "Goings on About Town" section (artists are listed alphabetically by last names). *Cue* also has complete art exhibition listings.

Then there are the magazines devoted exclusively to art, such as *Arts, Art Voices, Antiques, Art International, Art in America, Art News, the Fifty-seventh Street Review* (a new bi-weekly mimeographed sheet available in the 57th Street galleries), and *Craft Horizons*. The *Art Gallery* is available in all New York City galleries and museums. You can look these magazines over in your local public library first and decide which ones you like best, then take out a subscription. Only a few of the art magazines are available on New York newsstands, such as some on 42nd Street.

The newspapers, in addition, have extensive art sections on Sundays, usually with topnotch critics writing on the shows. *The New York Times* is generally acknowledged as the best, with reviews on both Saturday and Sunday; these critiques, and the many advertisements by the galleries, will keep you well apprised of the current shows. For antique buffs, there is "The Antiques Directory" published every Saturday in the *Times*. *The Village Voice* publishes reviews of exhibitions all over town, as well as a listing of new exhibitions entitled "At the Galleries."

Guidebooks, such as Kate Simon's *New York Places and Pleasures* (New York, Meridian Books, Inc.) and Elizabeth Squire's *The New York Shopping Guide* (New York, M. Barrows & Co., 1961) can also be helpful. Two others are *The Greenwich Village Guide* and *The Village Guide,* available for fifty cents at Kaplan Stationery Store at the corner of 11th Street and Sixth Avenue.

Not exactly a guidebook, but even more useful, is A. L. Chanin's *Art Guide/New York* (New York, Horizon Press, 1965), an unusual picture-by-picture tour of key works in the leading New York museums. *The Art Collector's Almanac, #1, 1965,* by Marshall Matusow and available at Wittenborn's, is a good twenty-five-dollar investment if you want to make a very thorough study of the galleries.

Don't forget the NEW YORK CONVENTION & VISITORS

BUREAU, INC., at Pershing Square, 90 E. 42nd Street, which will arm visitors with maps and directions; the CULTURAL INFORMATION CENTER OF THE CITY OF NEW YORK, at 148 W. 57th Street, and the unique ART INFORMATION CENTER, 11 W. 56th Street, 247-2350, which can direct you to any artist or gallery in New York, and which will also give directions for buying in Europe.

Where to Buy

Galleries

Madison Avenue Area, Low Eighties to Low Sixties: Our tour will begin with the concentration of galleries around Madison Avenue and 81st Street; we'll then continue south. The nearest cross streets, floors, and the geographical location (east, west, north or south) of each gallery are listed.

Noah Goldowsky
1078 Madison Ave. (81st St., E., 4th fl.), LE 5-5571
Contemporary and modern painting, sculpture. M, F, A-R, Install. Open 11:30-6 Tues-Sat; noon-5 Mon-Fri summer.

Richard Feigen
24 E. 81st St. (Mad.-Fifth Aves., S., 2nd fl.), RE 7-6640
Modern Europeans and Americans, including Opsters such as Bridget Riley.

Barzansky Galleries
1071 Madison Ave. (S.E. corner 81st St.), LE 5-1137
Gatto, Messersmith, Fitzgerald, etc. M, F, A-R, Install. Open 10-5:30 daily.

Robert Elkon
1063 Madison Ave. (80th-81st Sts., E., 2nd fl.), LE 5-3940
A young, exciting dealer. Carries Friedel Dzubas and others.

Krasner
1061 Madison Ave. (80th-81st Sts., E.), RE 4-6110
This large, two-storyed gallery holds a great range of modern styles.

Kraushaar
1055 Madison Ave. (corner 80th St., E., 2nd fl.), LE 5-9888
An older, established gallery that carries Louis Bouché, John Heliker, William Kienbusch, Carl Morris, Karl Schrage, Marguerite Zorach, etc. Open 9:30-5:30 Mon-Sat.

Ligoa Duncan
43 E. 80th St. (off Mad. Ave., N.), YU 8-3110
Young Internationals. Open 11-5:30 Tues-Sat.

Crespi Gallery
1045 Madison Ave. (80th-79th Sts., E., 2nd fl.), 988-1950
Run by the colorful Costa Rican painter Pachita Crespi, this gallery offers twentieth-century contemporaries. Prices $100-$500. R, Install. Open daily 12-6.

La Boetie, Inc.
1042 Madison Ave. (80th-79th Sts., W.), 535-4865
An intimate, expensive little gallery featuring international names. 10:30-5:30 Tues-Sat.

Saidenberg
1035 Madison Ave. (N.E. corner 79th St.), BU 8-3387
An impressive gallery offering Picasso, Klee, Villon, and the American painter Balcomb Greene.

1018 Madison Ave. (79th-78th Sts., W.): Offers five galleries. Take the elevator to the top floor, and work down.

Twentieth-Century West
6th fl. Penthouse, 628-8647

Forum Gallery
5th fl., LE 5-6080

Borgenicht Gallery
4th fl., LE 5-8040
An excellent gallery that offers a variety of contemporaries: Avery, Bolotowsky, kinetic sculptor José de Rivera, Peterdi, etc.

Byron Gallery
3rd fl., YU 8-9570
When I visited this gallery they were showing critic Brian O'Doherty's Surrealistic "Boxes," which I liked. Also pre-Columbians.

Wittenborn One-Wall Gallery
2nd fl., BU 8-1558
In addition to its changing shows of graphics, this is one of the best outlets in the city for fine art books and European art publications. Open 9-12, 1-5 weekdays; 9-5 Sat; closed some Sats summer.

Graham Gallery
1014 Madison Ave. (79th-78th Sts., W., 2nd fl.), LE 5-5767
Twentieth-century paintings and sculpture. Also a large cache of
Americana, especially prints and drawings. Open 10-5:30 Tues-
Sat; 10-5 Mon-Fri summer.

Silberman
1014 Madison Ave. (79th-78th St., W., 3rd fl.), TR 9-6980
Mainly an Old Master dealer, but one who also offers moderns who
appeal to him.

Perls
1016 Madison Ave. (79th-78th Sts., W.), TR 9-7440
An elegant gallery that shows well-knowns like sculptor Alexander
Calder. A sunken pebbled sculpture garden presides behind the
gallery.

Bianchini
16 E. 78th St. (Fifth-Mad. Aves., S.), 582-0153
Contemporary European paintings, sculpture; figurative rather than
abstract.

Ira Spanierman
50 E. 78th St. (Mad.-Park Aves., S.), TR 9-7085
Traditional Americans.

The Contemporaries Gallery
992 Madison Ave. (N.W. corner 77th St.), TR 9-1980
Quality, contemporary art of a conservative, figurative nature.

World House Galleries
987 Madison Ave. (N.E. corner 77th St.), LE 5-4700
Its gleaming interior is unique in its visual embodiment of avant-
garde architect Frederick Kiesler's "flowing space" theories. Stark
white walls, a jet-fed black pool, tropical plants, and ceilings that
seem to undulate (they mask a complex lighting system) are the
setting for works by internationally famous artists—Brancusi,
Braque, Derain, Fantin-Latour, Kandinsky, Klee. Expensive, but
worth visiting even if on a budget. In the Hotel Carlyle.

Leo Castelli Gallery
4 E. 77th St. (off Fifth Ave., S.), BU 8-4820
One of the truly great galleries in New York, this art outlet reflects
the flair and taste of dealer and collector Leo Castelli. Emphasis is
on the "New," with a leaning toward "Neo-Dada" styles. Robert
Rauschenberg, Jasper Johns, Frank Stella, and Lee Bontecou are

Exhibition of sculpture by Lewis Iselin at the Larcada Gallery, New York, fall, 1965.

Exhibition of Aiko-Greenly sculpture at the Bertha Schaefer Gallery (Aiko and Greenly–two-man show), New York, September, 1964.

Exhibition of paintings by Alice Baber, A. M. Sachs Gallery, New York, fall, 1966.
(*Photograph by John D. Schiff*)

Exhibition of paintings by William Clote at the Bertha Schaefer Gallery, New York, summer, 1966.

Exhibition of textiles at the Scalamandré Museum of Textiles, New York.

The Parke-Bernet Galleries, New York.

An exhibition of 72 contemporary American printmakers at the Terrain Gallery, New York, spring, 1965. (*Photograph by André Kertesz*)

The Gallery of Modern Art, including the Huntington Hartford Collection, New York. (*Photograph by Arnold Eagle*)

Asia House, headquarters of the Asia Society
and the Japan Society, New York. (*Photograph
by Joseph Molitor*)

Interior of the Museum of Contemporary Crafts, New York.
(*Courtesy American Craftsmen's Council, New York*)

just a few of the well-known artists offered here. Open 10-6 Tues-Sat; 10-5 Mon-Fri summer.

Staempfli
47 E. 77th St. (off Mad. Ave., N., #209), LE 5-1919
One of New York's major galleries for contemporary sculpture. Not to be missed.

Lefebre Gallery
47 E. 77th St. (off Mad. Ave., N., #205), RH 4-3384 or RH 4-3340
A jewel of a tiny gallery offering art after 1945. 10-5:30 Tues-Sat.

Cordier & Ekstrom
978 Madison Ave. (77th-76th St., E., 6th fl.), YU 8-8857
You have to walk through the antique elegance of French & Co., back to the elevator to get up to these sixth-floor quarters. Once you're there, you'll find a beautiful, large space that shows the most avant of the avant-garde.

Burrell Galleries
955 Madison Ave. (76th-75th Sts., E.), YU 8-3112
Conservative Americans, French and Italians. Open 11-6 Tues-Sat.

Niveau Gallery
962 Madison Ave. (76th-75th Sts., W.), 737-1094
French Masters: Chagall, Rouault, Picasso, Vlaminck, Dufy, Léger, etc.

Stephen Hahn Gallery
960 Madison Ave. (76th-75th Sts., W.), LE 5-3520
Impressionists, Post-Impressionists, Modern French. Expensive.

Schweitzer Gallery
958 Madison Ave. (76th-75th Sts., W.), LE 5-5430
Ultra-conservative Realism. $125 up. M, F, A-R, Install. Open 9:30-5 Mon-Fri.

Phoenix
939 Madison Ave. (75th-74th Sts., E., 2nd fl.), RH 4-5166
An avant-garde cooperative gallery that used to be downtown.

Stable Gallery
33 E. 74th St. (Mad.-Park Aves., N.), RE 7-0100
The smells and space of the old Victorian stable over on Seventh Avenue are gone, but the same quality and adventurous taste that characterized the old place remain in these elegant new quarters.

Willard Gallery
31 E. 72nd St. (N.E. corner), RH 4-2925
Another of the pioneer women dealers who have made the New York gallery scene what it is, Marion Willard has long been Mark Tobey's representative. She also carries Lionel Feininger, sculptress Dorothy Dehner, Morris Graves, and the Hawaiian painter Tadashi Sato. Unusual items are Dorothy Dehner's bronze chess sets. Established in 1936, this handsome four-room gallery displays art in the setting of a private apartment. Open 10-5:30 Mon-Sat; closed Sun.

Royal Marks Gallery
19 E. 71st St. (Fifth-Mad. Aves., N., 2nd fl.), UN 1-3400
A small, avant-garde gallery that's worth watching. Open 10-5:30 Tues-Sat; 10-5 June 15-Sept; closed Aug.

Dorsky Gallery
888 Madison Ave. (S.E. corner 72nd St.), LE 5-4594
Nadler, Sainz, Schanker, Stout, $100-$9,000. Open 10-6 Tues-Sat; closed Aug.

Roko Gallery
867 Madison Ave. (72nd St., E., 3rd fl.), LE 5-7630
Contemporary American paintings, sculpture, graphics. Prices $50-$2,500. M, F, A-R, Install. Open 10:30-5:30 Tues-Sat; closed summer.

Nordness Gallery
831 Madison Ave. (68th-67th Sts., E.), TR 9-2250
Major contemporary artists.

A. M. Sachs Gallery
822 Madison Ave. (68th-67th Sts., W.), UN 1-4421
Mr. Sachs' kindly enthusiasm is infectious, and the young buyer is bound to find something here that suits both his taste and his pocketbook.

Martha Jackson Gallery
32 E. 69th St. (Mad.-Park Aves., S.), YU 8-1800
The adventurous taste of Miss Jackson has long selected the best of the international abstract avant-garde. Showrooms in this large town house occupy three storeys with high picture windows in front. Her roster includes painter Paul Jenkins and sculptor Phillip Pavia.

Galerie Foussats
30 E. 68th St. (Mad. Ave., S.), 535-9592
Contemporary Argentinians and Canadians, all media. Install. Open noon-6 Sat, and by appointment.

Rose Fried Gallery
40 E. 68th St. (Mad.-Park Aves., S.), RE 7-8622
Miss Fried feels "the most telling expression of our era is the School of Mondrian," and she has accordingly specialized in the Neo-Plasticists and the De Stael movements. Today she features the Uruguayan Torres-Garcia.

Terry Dintenfass
18 E. 67th St. (off Fifth Ave., S.), RH 4-1580
All media, $10 up. M, Appraisal, Install. Open 10:30-5:30 Tues-Sat; closed summer.

Hirschl & Adler
21 E. 67th St. (Fifth-Mad. Aves., N.), LE 5-8810
A well-established gallery specializing in eighteenth- to twentieth-century European and American art.

Larcada Gallery
23 E. 67th St. (Fifth-Mad. Aves., N., 3rd fl.), 249-4561
Contemporary and traditional works, mostly Americans. M, Appraisal, Install. Open 10-5:30 Tues-Sat.

Banfer Gallery
23 E. 67th St. (Fifth-Mad. Aves., N., 4th fl.), RH 4-2044
Contemporary Americans, all media. M, Install. Open 10-6 Tues-Sat.

Landau-Alan Gallery
766 Madison Ave. (66th-65th St., W., 2nd fl.), 535-3113
American and European contemporary paintings, sculpture, drawings. Install. Open 10-6 Tues-Sat; closed July-Aug.

Chase Gallery
31 E. 64th St. (Mad.-Park Aves., N.), LE 5-3991
European and American contemporary oil paintings. Prices $100-$100,000. Appraisal, Install; open 11-5 Tues-Sat.

FAR Gallery
746 Madison Ave. (65th-64th Sts., W.), RE 4-7287
In addition to the notable graphics FAR offers, it also displays fine watercolors and small, outstanding sculptures. F, A-R, limited Install; open 9:30-5:30 Mon-Sat; closed July-Aug.

Florence Lewison Gallery
35 E. 64th St. (Mad.-Park Aves., N.), 879-0810
This art outlet is devoted to a program of "Americans Remembered"—nineteenth- and early twentieth-century American artists

the gallery feels have been overlooked or underestimated. The roster includes Albert Bierstadt, Thomas Cole, Louis M. Eilshemius, George Inness.

Great Jones Gallery
645 Madison Ave., 421-9525
This gallery used to be downtown. Younger artists are shown.

Rehn Gallery
655 Madison Ave. (corner 60th St., 2nd fl.), PL 3-4694
Its roster of major American artists includes Burchfield, Hopper, Marsh.

The Tribune Gallery
26 E. 64th St. (off Mad. Ave., S.), 421-9533
Old and New Masters. Open 10-6 Tues-Sat.

Zabriskie Gallery
699 Madison Ave. (63rd-62nd Sts., E., 4th fl.), TE 2-9034
Miss Zabriskie has long specialized in showing younger, promising American painters.

The Fifty-Seventh Street Area: Sixth to Fifth Avenues: Many of New York's most avant-garde galleries are located on this block.

Bianchini Gallery
50 W. 57th St. (6th-5th Aves., S., 15th fl.), JU 2-0153
Contemporary American art and Master drawings from the nineteenth century to the present. M (for prints), F for clients, occasional Install. Open 10-6 Tues-Sat; by appointment summer.

Howard Wise Gallery
50 W. 57th St. (6th-5th Aves., S., 2nd fl.), CO 5-0465
This gallery offers one of the best facilities in the city for showing huge, modern canvases: the storage space in the back is as large as the viewing area in front. Architect Philip Johnson was an adviser, and the lighting was specially installed for modern paintings. At this writing, the emphasis is on minimal and neon-light sculptures.

Betty Parsons Gallery
24 W. 57th St. (6th-5th Aves., N., 3rd fl.), CI 7-7480
Mrs. Parson's philosophy of "how the show looks, its presence and style" has made her a successful art pioneer since she first opened her doors in 1946. A sculptress herself who studied with Bourdelle and Zadkine in Paris, she always displays great taste and flair for picking only the best. Jackson Pollock, Hans Hofmann, Adolf Gottlieb, Barnett Newman, and Ad Reinhardt have all been on her

roster at one time or another. She has a tremendous sense for what is alive at the moment, and she has given many younger, unknown artists their start.

Galerie St. Etienne
24 W. 57th St. (6th-5th Aves., N., 8th fl.), CI 5-6734
A friendly, intimate gallery full of sunlight and lush plants that seem to enhance the contemporary European paintings on the walls.

Tiber De Nagy Gallery
29 W. 57th St. (6th-5th Aves., N., 3rd fl.), RE 7-4130
A small, well-lighted gallery, its handsome parquet wood floor sets off the starkness of much of the avant-garde art exhibited here.

Dwan Gallery
29 W. 57th St. (6th-5th Aves., N., 8th fl.), 753-9280
Another of the very far-out galleries on this block. Open 10-5:30 Tues-Sat; closed July-Sept.

Fischbach Gallery
20 W. 57th St. (6th-5th Aves., N., 6th fl.), PL 9-2345
Very avant-garde styles are shown in the large gallery, while a smaller room is reserved for drawings and graphics. Install. Open 10-5:30 daily; closed July-Aug.

Pace Gallery
9 W. 57th St. (6th-5th Aves., N., 3rd fl.), HA 1-3292
Definitely avant-garde.

Crossing Fifth Avenue: You reach the extremely chic higher rent area on the East Side.

Findlay Galleries
11 E. 57th St. (5th-Mad. Aves., N., 2nd fl.), PL 8-1297
The walls of this attractive gallery are covered with what looks like raw silk. Mostly expensive School of Paris paintings.

Midtown Galleries
11 E. 57th St. (5th-Mad. Aves., N., 3rd fl.), PL 8-1900
Established in 1932, this tradition-oriented gallery offers works by Bishop, Cadmus, Thon, Vikrey. M, R, Install. Open 10-6 Mon-Sat; 10-6 Mon-Fri July-Aug.

Albert Loeb and Krugier Gallery
12 E. 57th St. (5th-Mad. Aves., S.), PL 3-7857
Contemporary Europeans include Ernst, Vieira da Silva, Arp.

M. Knoedler & Co.
14 E. 57th St. (5th-Mad. Aves., S.), PL 3-9742
Painter Willem de Kooning and sculptor Bernard Rosenthal are two avant-garde artists recently taken on by this staid old gallery.

Waddell Gallery
15 E. 57th St. (5th-Mad. Aves., N., 4th fl.), 421-4141
One of New York's most experimental galleries. Its roster includes Roy Kiyooka, Aleksandra Kasuba, Paul Van Hoeydonck, Will Barnet. Open 11-5 Tues-Sat; closed July-Aug.

Sidney Janis Gallery
15 E. 57th St. (5th-Mad. Aves., N., 5th fl.), PL 9-4241
If you had to pick New York's foremost gallery of modern and contemporary art, this would be it. Janis, who became an art dealer by way of personal collecting, has most of the great names of both the Abstract-Expressionist and Pop movements (Jim Dine, Claes Oldenburg, sculptor George Siegel) on his roster. Janis almost singlehandedly introduced the Pop movement and has also given theme shows that have chronicled the great modern art directions— Dadaism, Futurism, Cubism.

Wally F Galleries
17 E. 57th St. (5th-Mad. Aves., N.), HA 1-5390
A whole house devoted to modern French art. Expensive. Also Chicago and Palm Beach branches. Open 9:30-5:30 Mon-Sat.

Van Diemen-Lilienfeld Galleries
21 E. 57th St. (5th-Mad. Aves., N., 2nd fl.), PL 3-6634
An elegant velvet-walled gallery devoted to top Americans, Europeans and especially the German Expressionists and French Impressionists.

Crossing Madison Avenue to 41 E. 57th St. (N.E. corner): It would be possible, because of the excellence, number, and variety of galleries in this one towering office building, to do all your art buying here.

Berthe Schaefer
8th fl., 755-3330
Miss Schaefer, who used to be located directly across the street, has expanded her quarters in this location, still offering a wide range of styles and mediums, as well as her well-known interior designing service. Install. Open 10-6 Mon-Sat.

Marlborough-Gerson Gallery
6th fl., PL 2-5353
Associated with a major London art gallery, Marlborough-Gerson boasts the names of Robert Motherwell, Mark Rothko, Ben Nicholson, Kokoshka, Pasmore, Gabo, Armitage, et cetera on its roster. In addition, it offers the estates of the late sculptor David Smith and painter William Baziotes. In its Graphics Gallery (5th fl.), there is a wide selection, both as to style and price, of contemporary prints. M, Appraisal. Open 10-6 Tues-Sat.

André Emmerich Gallery
5th fl., PL 3-3180
This is one of the most stunning spaces in the city for showing large, environmental-scale contemporary art. There is also a small gallery for primitive art, an art area in which Emmerich is an acknowledged authority.

Pierre Matisse
4th fl., EL 5-6269
Son of the twentieth-century painter Henri Matisse, this dealer quite naturally leans to the great names of his father's era, such as Miró and Manessier. Open 10-6 daily; 10-5:30 June-Sept.

Allan Frumkin Gallery
3rd fl., PL 3-3180
A gallery that concentrates on quality, Frumkin features mainly contemporaries, as well as putting on beautifully installed shows of drawings and Pre-Columbian art.

Charles Egan
3rd fl., PL 5-1825
Long one of New York's pioneering dealers, Egan now largely devotes his shows to monumental sculpture by Reuben Nakian, George Sugarman, and Raoul Hague.

Frank Caro
2nd fl., PL 3-2166
New York's leading dealer in Oriental art (see Oriental section).

Harry Salpeter Gallery
42 E. 57th St. (Mad.-Park Aves., S.), MU 8-5650
Contemporary Americans. Prices $50-$1,500. Install. Open 11-5:30 daily; noon-5 summer.

Hammer Galleries, Inc.
51 E. 57th St. (Mad.-Park Aves., N.), PL 8-0409
French nineteenth- and twentieth-century art; Western Americana.

Prices $25-$400,000. M, F, A-R, Install. Open 9:30-5:30 Mon-Sat; closed Sat July-Aug.

Schoneman Galleries
63 E. 57th St. (Mad.-Park Aves., N.), PL 5-3020
French Impressionist and Post-Impressionist paintings. Prices $500 up.

ACA
63 E. 57th St. (near Park Ave., N., 2nd fl.), PL 5-9622
A well-known gallery of Realistic Americans such as Bellows, Burchfield, Chase, Eilshemius, Hassam, Henri, Kuniyoshi, Lucks. Open 10-5:30 Mon-Sat.

Downtown Gallery
465 Park Ave. (Ritz Tower Hotel, sub-street level), PL 3-3707
One of the first pioneering dealers in this city, director Edith Halpert has been thoroughly described in this book's introduction. She now offers her usual roster—Stuart Davis, Dove, Marin, O'Keefe, et cetera—and American folk art, by appointment only.

Acquavella
119 E. 5th St. (Park-Lex. Aves., N., 2nd fl.), PL 3-1296
This gallery sometimes puts on specialized, very handsome exhibits, such as the flower paintings of Fantin-Latour.

Burgos Galleries
127 E. 57th St. (Park-Lex. Aves., N.), TE 8-0017
Figurative oils, watercolors. F, A, R, Install. Open 9:30-5:30 daily.

Portraits, Inc.
136 E. 57th St. (near Lex. Ave., S.), PL 8-2852
The country's leading dealer for realistic portraiture, both for commission and exhibit. A roster of about one hundred artists from which to choose.

Swinging over to 56th and 55th Streets, you reach:

Grand Central Moderns
8 W. 56th St. (5th-6th Aves., S.), TB 7-3344
A non-profit organization that offers modern Americans. Prices $200-$5,000. Open 10-5:30 daily, except 1-5:30 Mon.

Westerly
8 W. 56th St. (5th-6th Aves., S.), 582-3395
A cooperative gallery for younger painters and sculptors. 11-5:30 Tues-Sat; closed Mon summer.

Capricorn
11 W. 56th St. (5th-6th Aves., N.), 581-5095
Contemporaries.

Poindexter Gallery
21 W. 56th St. (5th-6th Aves., N.), JU 6-6630
An excellent art outlet showing quality painters: Manoucher
Yektai, Nora Speyer, George Spaventa, Richard Diebenkorn, Nell
Blaine, et cetera. Prices $500 up. Open 11-5:30 Tues-Sat; closed
July-Aug.

East Hampton Gallery
22 W. 56th St. (5th-6th Aves., S.), CI 6-3118
An up-and-coming avant-garde gallery showing Sonia Gechtoff,
John Day, Ben Cunningham, Paul Reed, et cetera. Prices $30 up.
R, Install. Open 11-5:30 Tues-Sat; closed Sat summer.

Mexican Art Annex
47 W. 56th St. (near 6th Ave., N.), 246-0694
Tamayo, Cuevas, pre-Columbian art, et cetera. Open 10-5 daily.

Kennedy Galleries
20 E. 56th St. (5th-Mad. Aves., S.), EL 5-3740
High-quality American paintings and Western Americana. Also
fine prints.

Iolas
15 E. 55th St. (5th-Mad. Aves., N., 2nd fl.), PL 5-6778
An elegant floor-through gallery of gleaming white walls and jet-
black ceilings, this art outlet has long pushed European painters,
especially those with a Surrealistic bent. They include Max Ernst,
René Magritte, Matta, Jean Tinguely, Niki de St. Phalle.

The Village and East Village: The best way to start is to take
the IRT subway to Sheridan Square, taking along a map if you're
not familiar with the maze of streets down here.

Hinckley & Brohel
45 Christopher St. (off 7th Ave., N.), WA 9-7265
Good bargains in prints and drawings. The gallery has a Washington, D.C., branch as well. Open 1-11 p.m. daily; closed Mon; 2-10
summer.

Art d'Haiti
49 Grove St. (7th Ave.-Bleecker St., N.), CH 3-9040
Bright Haitian primitives make this tiny gallery a real pleasure to
visit. It also offers small primitive scpultures.

Terrain Gallery
39 Grove St. (Bleecker-Bedford Sts., N.), WA 4-4984
This gallery has excellent contemporary graphics, reasonably priced, in large, spare, white quarters. Open 1-6 Tues-Sun; 3-6 Tues-Sat summer. M, Install.

Park Place Gallery
542 W. Broadway (Bleecker-W. 3rd Sts., W.), 982-4580
Taking over the more exciting aspects and professionalism of the old Tenth Street cooperatives, this gallery is now the best place in the Village to buy avant-garde contemporaries. Prices $90-$10,000. Open 11-6 Tues-Sat, noon-5 Sun; closed summer.

Kaymar Gallery
548 W. Broadway (Bleecker-W. 3rd Sts., W.), GR 7-6510
Almost next door to Park Place, this outlet has a large sub-basement for contemporary art. A specialty is contemporary graphics, and printmaking is done continuously on the premises. F, A-R, Install. Open noon-6, and some evenings.

Zegri Gallery
10 E. 8th St. (off Fifth Ave., S.), GR 3-7510
Known for years as the Sudamericana Gallery, this outlet has a quality presentation of contemporary Latin American arts. There's also a case of pre-Columbian and folk art at the back. M, F, A-R, Install. Open 11-6:30 Tues-Sat; 1-6 July; closed Aug.

Gordon's Fifth Avenue
68 Fifth Ave. (12th-13th Sts., W.), WA 9-5171
New graphics, and contemporary foreign artists. Open 11-6 daily; closed summer.

East Village: Formerly the location of many avant-garde cooperative galleries, the area no longer has the excitement and professionalism it had in the 1950s. However, many new cooperative galleries have taken over the old quarters, all in the block between Fourth and Third Avenues, and it's still possible to find a good bargain now and then.

Aegis Gallery
80 E. 10th St., 477-9735

Aspects Gallery
100 E. 10th St., OR 4-9741

Brata
56 Third Ave. (10th-11th Sts., W.), GR 5-9361

Gallery 84
84 E. 10th St., OR 4-9772

Stryke Gallery
86 E. 10th St., 475-9329

Antiques and Old Masters

New York has quite recently become the world's major market-place for antiques. Most of the better quality, and higher priced, shops are clustered around Fifth and Madison Avenues in the East Fifties (especially 57th Street) and Sixties. The smaller shops where you can occasionally find a real bargain are concentrated on Third Avenue in the Forties, Fifties, and Sixties, with a scattering of shops mushrooming over onto Second and First Avenues. *Antiques* magazine has already been mentioned as the most valuable guide for antique lovers. Two directories, also cited, should prove helpful: those of the ART AND ANTIQUE DEALERS LEAGUE OF AMERICA, INC., and the NATIONAL ANTIQUE AND ART DEALERS ASSOCIATION OF AMERICA, INC. The following dealers and galleries have only quality wares, tending to be rather high priced, but many are also interested in starting off the modest buyer with less expensive items.

Arthur Ackerman & Son
50 E. 57th St., PL 3-5292
English antiques.

Antique Porcelain Co., Inc.
48 E. 57th St., PL 5-4190

Teina Baumstone
807 Madison Ave., RE 4-8360
American antiques.

Durlacher Brothers
538 Madison Ave., EL 5-3398
Old Masters.

Duveen
18 E. 79th St., TR 9-0476
Old Masters.

French & Company
978 Madison Ave., LE 5-3330
French and Italian antique furniture.

James Graham
1014 Madison Ave., LE 5-5566
American and Continental antiques, with an outstanding collection
of silver.

Josephine Howell, Inc.
41 E. 57th St., PL 3-5515
Eighteenth-century French furniture.

M. Knoedler & Co.
14 E. 57th St., PL 3-9742
Old and Modern Masters, with drawings and prints for the modest
buyer.

Edward R. Lubin, Inc.
17 E. 64th St., UN 1-3649
Old Master sculptures, paintings.

D. M. & P. Manheim
46 E. 57th St., PL 8-2986
English antiques, especially ceramics.

Needham's Antiques, Inc.
143 E. 57th St., EL 4-7493
Outstanding porcelain, furniture.

Newhouse Galleries, Inc.
15 E. 57th St., PL 5-4980
Old Master paintings and Americana of all periods.

Frank Partridge, Inc.
6 W. 56th St., CI 7-2050
Eighteenth-century English furniture.

James Robinson
12 E. 57th St., PL 3-7433
Antique English silver.

Israel Sack, Inc.
5 E. 57th St., 753-6562
Fine American antique furniture, paintings.

Jacques Seligmann & Co.
5 E. 57th St., PL 3-0250
Old Masters, especially Medieval and Renaissance sculpture, and
beautifully framed old drawings.

S. J. Shrubsole
104 E. 57th St., PL 3-8920
Old English silver.

A. Stair & Co., Inc.
59 E. 57th St., EL 5-7620
Eighteenth-century English furniture and porcelains.

John S. Walton, Inc.
16 E. 52nd St., PL 7-0484
Fine American furniture.

M. Wyatt
29 Cornelia St., No phone
A goldmine for the bargain browser and buyer: old prints, posters, playbills from 1600 to 1940. Prices $1 to $50. R. Install.

North American Indian Art

The American Indian Arts Center
1051 Third Ave., 861-2630

The Brooklyn Museum Gallery Shop
188 Eastern Pkwy., Brooklyn, 638-5000

The Museum Shop of the American Museum of Natural History
79th St. and Central Park West, 873-1300

The Museum Shop of the Museum of the American Indian
Broadway at 155th St., 283-2420

Tepee Town, Inc.
9 W. 42nd St., 563-4885

George Terasaki
200 E. 33rd St., 684-1352

Crafts

America House, Ltd.
44 W. 53rd St., PL 7-9494
Housed in a dramatic new building and affiliated with the Museum of Contemporary Crafts across the street, this outlet deals only in the best work by America's finest craftsmen. Many one-of-a-kind objects are for sale, with all types of crafts available.

Bonniers, Inc.
605 Madison Ave., PL 9-7985
Unusual glass, ceramic, and woven items from all over the world

are displayed on the second floor, and Bonniers is the only New York gallery to show Japan's top folk potter, Shoji Hamada. Expensive, but you'll find craft items here that are available nowhere else in the city.

Cepelia Corporation
5 E. 57th St., PL 1-0005
Unusual examples of Polish folk art. The handwoven woolen rugs are especially handsome. Don't miss the upstairs gallery. Open 10-6 daily.

Design Research, Inc.
53 E. 57th St., HA 1-2578
Bright textiles, toys, glass, et cetera, to complement any modern decor.

The Elder Craftsmen Shop
850 Lexington Ave., LE 5-8030
Custom-made items by talented Senior Citizen craftsmen.

Greenwich House Pottery
16 Jones St., CH 2-4106
Good quality, low prices. You can watch the pottery being made in the school in back.

Georg Jensen, Inc.
667 Fifth Ave., PL 1-2400
Handsome crafts from all over the world. On the third floor.

National Design Center, Inc.
415 E. 53rd St., MU 8-5200
Large-scale exhibitions of crafts are sometimes held here.

Phoenix Pan-American Imports, Inc.
793 Lexington Ave., TE 8-2522
Mexican handcrafts, mainly. Some Latin American antiques.

Scalamandré
977 Third Ave., EM 1-8500
Unusual fabrics, many handwoven. Their MUSEUM OF TEXTILES is at 201 E. 58th St.

SONA ("The Golden One")
11 E. 55th St., 752-4586
An export center for the Indian government, this shop displays lovely native crafts. The textiles are outstanding, as is the Indian antique sculpture. If you happen in on the right day, you may

be waited on by Mrs. B. K. Nehru, wife of the Indian Ambassador to the United States, who is chairman of the advisory committee for SONA.

Steuben Glass
Fifth Ave. at 56th St., PL 2-1441
Outstanding examples of glass by contemporary glassmakers. Mainly traditional designs.

United Nations Gift Center
Visitors' Entrance (First Ave. and 47th St.), PL 4-1234
Unusual quality crafts from all over the world. Reasonable prices.

Graphics (Prints, Drawings)

H. V. Allison
11 E. 57th St., PL 3-0305
Prints and drawings by nineteenth- and twentieth-century artists; George Bellows is a regular.

The Art Fair
123 Second Ave., OR 4-6545
International etchings, lithographs, drawings. Reasonable prices.

Associated American Artists
605 Fifth Ave., PL 5-4211
One of the largest and best print houses in the country, offering both Old Master and contemporary graphics (emphasis is on contemporaries, however). They publish the "Patron's Supplement," available on request. From this, they have an extensive mail-order business all over the country. Prices $10 up. M, F, Install. Open 10-6 Mon-Sat; closed Sat summer.

The Captain's Quarters
967 Madison Ave., 249-7770
A large cache of nautical prints and drawings, 65¢ and up.

Peter Deitsch Gallery
24 E. 81st St., RE 7-8279
The gallery has the atmosphere of an old English study with its fireplace, huge sofa, and paneled walls. The beautifully framed graphics are all stunningly lighted. Expensive.

The Drawing Shop
1078 Madison Ave., UN 1-4250
Selected European drawings, sixteenth to nineteenth centuries. Open 11-6 Tues-Sat, and by appointment.

FAR Gallery
746 Madison Ave., RE 4-7287
Modern European and American prints, drawings, and watercolors handsomely displayed. Be sure to look at their excellent publications on prints. F, A-R, limited Install. Open 9:30-5:30 Mon-Sat; closed Sat July-Aug.

Allan Frumkin Gallery
41 E. 57th St., PL 3-3180
Quality contemporary drawings.

London Arts-Macy's
Herald Sq. and 34th St., 9th fl., LA 4-6000
Inaugurated in 1966 with a Picasso graphics show, this gallery, part of a Detroit graphics concern that sends out packaged shows, offers first-rate prints and drawings to a wide public. Expensive. Open 9:45-9 Mon, Thurs, Fri; 9:45-6 Tues, Wed, Sat.

Lucien Goldschmidt
117 Madison Ave., TR 9-0070
Handsomely bound rare books, as well as outstanding prints and drawings, line the walls. Prints from 1500 to 1950. M, Install. Open 10-6 Mon-Fri, 10-5 Sat.

Kennedy Galleries
13 E. 68th St., EL 5-3740
Mostly conservative, mainly Currier & Ives. Catalog on request.

M. Knoedler & Co.
14 E. 57th St., PL 3-9742
Graphics are the only bargains that exist at this high-priced establishment.

Marlborough-Gerson Gallery
41 E. 57th St., 5th fl., PL 2-5353
Many contemporary graphics, often of an off-beat nature.

Multiples
929 Madison Ave. (74th St., W.), 249-3250
An important gallery for contemporary, quality graphics by such artists as Josef Albers, Barnett Newman, Larry Rivers, Claes Oldenburg. Also sculpture, objects, and banners in editions. Prints: $25-$350. Other art: $300-$1,500. Open 10-5 Tues-Sat.

Oestreicher's
43 E. 46th St., PL 7-1190
This gallery has carried fine lithographs since 1898.

The Old Print Shop, Inc.
150 Lexington Ave., MU 3-3950
There are rare and interesting finds at this famous shop. Maps
are a specialty, as are the Early American lithographs and engravings. Mail orders through their 25¢ monthly "Portfolio."

Poster Originals, Ltd.
16 E. 78th St. (Mad.-5th Aves.), 861-0422
An unusual gallery devoted exclusively to American and European
art posters.

Pratt Graphic Art Center
831 Broadway (12th St.), OR 4-0603
Prints by both students and professors of this graphics school. Good
quality and prices.

William H. Schab Gallery
48 E. 57th St., PL 8-0327
Dürer, Rembrandt, Goya, Manet, Degas are just a few of the
famous names you'll find here.

Walter Schatzki
153 E. 57th St., MU 8-6116
This is one of my personal favorites. Old Mr. Schatzki is always
there with his friendly, "Please, may I help you?" and actually
you may need some help with the wide selection here: the bins of
old maps, master drawings and watercolors ($1-$10); the large
cache of Daumier lithographs; the hand-painted fruit and flower
etchings that are $2 and up, etc. Charming old greeting cards are
also offered. No catalog, but written requests are happily filled.

Shickman
929 Park Ave., 249-3800
A major New York Old Master drawings dealer. Only the best
quality.

Charles E. Slatkin, Inc.
115 E. 92nd St., LE 4-4222
This gallery is located in the penthouse of an apartment building,
and you have to ask to see the stock of rare and beautiful drawings here. Open 10-5:30 daily.

E. Weyhe, Inc.
794 Lexington Ave., TE 8-5478
Another favorite of mine. You have to climb to the gallery from
the tile-fronted first-floor catacomb of art books. Weyhe first got

into art dealing when artists didn't have enough cash for books and paintings. Here you'll find Japanese, Goya, and Daumier prints, as well as the now very rare rubbings from Angkor Wat. Open 9:30-5:30 Tues-Sat; 9:30-5 Mon-Fri summer.

Wittenborn One-Wall Gallery
1018 Madison Ave., BU 8-1558
Contemporary and modern European graphics.

Oriental Arts

The following dealers are the leading ones for fine Orientalia (the arts of Japan, China, India, Southeast Asia, and the Middle East) in New York City. In addition, major Oriental art shows are listed monthly in the bulletin of the ASIA SOCIETY (Asia House, 112 E. 64th Street).

Asian Gallery
24 E. 80th St., 734-1379

Frank Caro
41 E. 57th St., 2nd fl., PL 3-2166
Successor to the famous Oriental arts dealer C. T. Loo, Caro has recently much enlarged his quarters and can now display magnificent large pieces of Indian and Cambodian sculpture. The pieces are all beautifully lighted, as in a museum. Caro is generally acknowledged as the foremost Chinese art dealer in the country.

Ralph M. Chait
12 E. 56th St., PL 8-0937
This gallery also has the feeling of a small museum. All kinds of ceramics, *objets d'art,* and jades abound here. Reference books on art line the back of the shop.

Therese M. Clayton
712 Madison Ave., 2nd fl., TE 2-8721
You'll find many good buys in this jumble of Orientalia, and Miss Clayton is always interested in helping you with your special field of buying.

Warren E. Cox Associates, Inc.
6 E. 39th St., MU 5-2580
This gallery specializes in Near and Far Eastern ceramics. Mr. Cox has written a two-volume book on ceramics of the world, so he knows what he's about.

J.H. Dildarian Rugs
762 Madison Ave., 2nd fl., BU 8-4948
Antique Oriental rugs of the first quality.

J.M. Eisenberg–Royal Athena Galleries
1000 Madison Ave., AG 9-7050
Long the leading New York dealer for Middle Eastern ceramics, many offered at bargain prices, Eisenberg recently moved into these dramatic, plush new quarters fronting on Madison Avenue. The stock now includes all kinds of Orientalia, beautifully displayed; and Eisenberg plans changing exhibitions as well.

N.V. Hammer
147 E. 72nd St., BU 8-0044

Nasli Heeramaneck
23 E. 83rd St., RE 4-8658
A top notch dealer. By appointment only.

Howard Hollis
923 Fifth Ave., 988-6377
You are sure to receive individual attention in this gallery that is also a private apartment. By appointment only.

S.H. Hoo
680 Madison Ave., 421-4179

Japan Folk Craft
167 W. 4th St., OR 5-2385
There are a few folk-craft (*mingei*) pottery items stored away on shelves behind the jumble of this tiny store.

Charles D. Kelekian
667 Madison Ave., PL 2-5263
Mr. Kelekian is a tremendously friendly, helpful dealer who says his father came here from Turkey in what was a real *America, America* story. Kelekian's Middle Eastern and antique Mediterranean objects are obviously of museum quality, but he's always happy to start off the new collector with less expensive pieces.

J.J. Klejman
982 Madison Ave., LE 5-5484
First-rate objects. Be sure to see the back room and second floor. By appointment only.

Mathias Komor
19 E. 71st St., TR 9-3840
A top-quality, friendly dealer who really knows his art. By appointment. Also fine Egyptian and primitive art.

Mahboukian Gallery
1078 Madison Ave., BU 8-7747
A small gallery with an obliging, friendly owner. He'll often give a break to new buyers in small Middle Eastern pottery, metal, and glass items.

Doris Meltzer
38 W. 57th St., CI 5-8936
Changing exhibitions on different Oriental themes.

Mi Chou
801 Madison Ave., YU 8-1840
The leading New York gallery for changing shows of modern Japanese and Chinese art. Also some older, traditional work on consignment.

The Oddity Shop
2455 Broadway, TR 4-4175
There are some real finds here, especially in South Indian wood sculpture, mixed with oddities from all over the world.

Safani Gallery
960 Madison Ave., UN 1-2160
A top-quality Middle Eastern dealer with a large mail-order business. Write for the handsomely illustrated catalogs.

Joseph Seo
756 Madison Ave., TR 9-9110
Seo has some good, low-priced objects, as well as museum-quality items.

J.T. Tai & Co., Inc.
810 Madison Ave., BU 8-5253
The Chinese furniture and ceramics are especially outstanding.

William H. Wolff
843a Madson Ave., YU 8-7411
Mr. Wolff's enthusiasm is infectious; and even though he usually deals with top collectors and museums he's also interested in finding less expensive pieces for the more modest buyer.

Primitive Arts

The following are only a selected few of the leading New York dealers. THE MUSEUM OF PRIMITIVE ART, 15 W. 54th Street, CI 6-9493, puts out a more extensive listing, which is available on request, free.

Julius Carlebach Gallery, Inc.
1040 Madison Ave., RE 7-0116
All kinds of primitive objects, from perfect little Mexican pots to shining African masks, are beautifully displayed in long cases against cheerful yellow walls. A pebbled bed of stone statuary occupies the middle of the gallery. There's also an unusual collection of both antique and modern jewelry, as well as antique ivory chess sets. Not to be missed.

Colombian Center Art Gallery
1091 Madison Ave., BU 8-5750
Occasional shows of Pre-Columbian objects are held here.

D'Arcy Galleries
1091 Madison Ave., BU 8-5750
This is a beautifully lighted jewel of a gallery with only first-rate objects. Open 10-6 Tues- Sat; closed Aug.

André Emmerich Gallery
41 E. 57th St., PL 3-3180
Emmerich has written and collaborated on books on primitive arts. The gallery specializes in quality pre-Columbian objects.

Aaron Furman Gallery
905 Madison Ave., UN 1-5513
First-rate objects in a dramatic, two-story setting. Smaller items are placed in the rosewood cases at the back of the store. Open 11-5:30 Tues-Sat.

Galerie Kamer
965 Madison Ave., YU 8-6920
Archaic and primitive arts. Open 10:30-5:30 Tues-Sat, 2-6 Mon.

Mayan Arts, Inc.
51 Grove St., 675-4866
A nice, small gallery devoted to pre-Columbian and American Indian art.

Everett Rassiga, Inc.
13 E. 75th St., UN 1-3720
This gallery concentrates on pre-Columbian art in its two floors of an imposing old town house. Oceanic, Asiatic, and African arts are also featured. Open 10:30-5:30 Tues-Sat.

Judith Small Galleries, Inc.
8 E. 75th St., YU 8-0260
A leading gallery for all kinds of primitive arts.

Auction Houses

New York abounds in auctioneering establishments. Four of the leading ones are here listed. For others, consult the Yellow Pages of the New York City Telephone Directory.

The Astor Galleries
754 Broadway at 8th St., GR 3-1658

Parke-Bernet Galleries, Inc.
980 Madison Ave., TR 9-8300
"My wish is that . . . these things of art which have been the joy of my life shall not be consigned to the cold tomb of a museum, and subjected to the stupid glances of the careless passer-by; I desire that they shall be dispersed under the Auctioneer's hammer, so that the pleasure which the acquisition of each one has given me shall be given again, in each case, to some inheritor of my own tastes . . ." from the will of Edmond de Goncourt. Goncourt's feelings best sum up the *raison d'être* and also the atmosphere of a Parke-Bernet sale (see the section on auctions). Even if you're not going to bid, it's always interesting to browse through the pre-auction exhibition rooms on the second floor.

The Plaza Art Galleries
406 E. 79th St., TR 9-1800

The Savoy Art & Auction Galleries
18 E. 50th St., PL 3-3941

Businesses that Sell Art

Many of the major New York department stores and business concerns now put on art shows. A few are listed here.

Abercrombie & Fitch
Madison Ave. at 45th St., MU 2-3600

Alexander's
Lexington Ave. at 58th St., 5th fl., CY 8-2000

Brentano's Galerie Moderne
586 Fifth Ave. (48th St., N. wing), PL 7-8600

Hallmark Gallery
Fifth Ave. at 56th St., JU 2-2810

E.J. Korvette
575 Fifth Ave., TN 7-7000
Douglaston, L.I. (Queens), 321-4500

Lever House
390 Park Ave., MU 8-6000

London Arts-Macy's
Herald Sq. and 34th St., 9th fl., LA 4-6000

Lord & Taylor
Fifth Ave. at 38th St., WI 7-3300

Pepsi-Cola Gallery
Park Ave. at 59th St., MU 8-4500

Stern Brothers
Sixth Ave. at 42nd St., 6th fl., LO 5-6000

Time & Life Exhibition Center
Sixth Ave. at 50th St., JU 6-1212

Renting Art

There are surprisingly few places to rent art in the city. Two are:

The Museum of Modern Art
11 W. 53rd St., 6th fl., CI 5-8900
Paintings, sculptures, and prints of almost any modern style can
be rented for a two-month period, prices $5 to $35, depending on
the price of the art. Rental is also possible through the illustrated
catalog, if you don't happen to live in New York City.

Circulating Library of Paintings
33 E. 74th St., UN 1-6260
Their plan is similar to that of the Museum of Modern Art.

Framing

There are many fine framing establishments in New York, and you
may well have a favorite, neighborhood framer already. Three of
the more prominent concerns are:

Dain-Schiff, Inc.
1018 Madison Ave., LE 5-1566
Boasts one of the largest framing stocks in the city.

House of H. Heydenryk, Jr.
141 W. 54th St., CI 5-2323
The King of U.S. framing establishments (see the section on framing). This knowledgeable firm provides only the best in framing,
and is expert in special lighting techniques as well. The House

also carries on a large mail-order business through its catalog, available on request.

Kulicke Frames, Inc.
43 E. 78th St. and 45 E. 10th St., AL 4-0140
Their gleaming brushed aluminum and brass frames are especially designed for modern paintings and graphics. Beautiful, but expensive.

Where to Look

New York City's museums and cultural institutions are so many in number that only the briefest descriptions can be given here. The reader is referred to the museum directories named at the beginning of this book, the museum section of Kate Simon's *New York Places & Pleasures,* and A. L. Chanin's *Art Guide/New York.*

Asia House Gallery
112 E. 64th St., PL 1-4210
Puts on notable exhibitions of art from all countries of Asia. Admission is free; bulletin and lectures for members. Open 10-5 daily, 11-5 Sat, 1-5 Sun.

The Brooklyn Museum
118 Eastern Pkwy., NE 8-5000
One of the world's great museums; unfortunately does not get the New York attendance it deserves because of its Brooklyn location. It is especially rich in primitive, Egyptian and Oriental arts, as well as in American painting. Its Museum Shop sells unusual folk items priced at 10¢ and up. Admission is free; authentication for members only; an extensive junior membership program; 50¢ parking lot. Open 10-5 Mon-Sat, 1-5 Sun and holidays; closed Christmas Day.

The Cooper Union Museum
Cooper Sq., AL 4-6300
An architectural National Landmark as well as the home of one of the country's great textile and decorative arts collections. Admission is free; authentication of decorative arts by appointment. Open 10-5 Mon-Sat Oct-May; 10-5 Mon-Fri June-Sept; closed holidays.

The Finch College Museum of Art
62 E. 78th St., BU 8-8450
Features fine changing exhibitions of all periods of art. Admission is free; open 1-5 daily; closed Mon.

The Frick Collection
1 E. 70th St., BU 9-0700
Housed in the old Frick Mansion facing Central Park, the museum has beautifully paneled rooms by Fragonard and Boucher, with notable period furniture and paintings by Rembrandt, Velasquez, Hals, Van Dyck, Titian, Bellini, El Greco, et cetera. Admission is free; open 10-5 daily, 1-5 Sun and holidays; closed Mon Aug. Children under 16 must be accompanied by an adult, children under ten not admitted.

The Gallery of Modern Art
2 Columbus Circle, LT 1-2311
Housed in a building inspired by Byzantine architecture and designed by architect Edward Durrell Stone (some wags call it "Stone's seraglio on 59th Street"). Opened in 1964, the Gallery, which includes the Huntington Hartford Collection, is dedicated to painters and sculptors representing "an alternative to the present dominance of abstract art." Admission $1 adults, 50¢ students, children under 12 25¢; open 11-7 Tues-Sat, noon-6 Sun and holidays; closed Mon, Christmas Day.

The Solomon R. Guggenheim Museum
Fifth Ave. at 89th St., EN 9-5110
Now so well known it hardly needs description. Designed by architect Frank Lloyd Wright on a dramatic spiral plan, the museum shows its art in bays on this spiral ramp (it is better to take the elevator to the top and walk down if you have any problems with vertigo). The permanent collection contains nearly three thousand works of art by such notables as Klee, Kandinsky, Brancusi, Miró, with major exhibitions organized from time to time throughout the year. Admission 50¢ adults, children under six free; open 10-6 daily, noon-6 Sun and holidays, until 9 Thurs; closed Mon, Christmas, July 4.

The Hispanic Society of America
Broadway near 155th St., 926-2234
Founded in 1904 as a museum and reference library devoted to the culture of Hispanic peoples, its collection of Spanish and Portuguese paintings, sculptures, textiles, metalwork, pottery, furniture, books and manuscripts, and prints is outstanding. Admission is free; 10-4:30 Tues-Sat, 2-5 Sun; closed Mon, July 4, Thanksgiving, Christmas, New Year's.

IBM Gallery of Arts & Sciences
16 E. 57th St., PL 3-1900, ext. 3150
Changing, high-caliber exhibitions. The permanent collection in-

cludes Western paintings and prints, chiefly American and Latin American; pre-Columbian sculpture; antique calculators and typewriters; models of the inventions of Leonardo da Vinci. The Gallery also sponsors traveling exhibitions to all parts of the country. Admission is free; open 9:30-5 Mon-Fri, 10-5 Sat; closed holidays.

The Jewish Museum
1109 Fifth Ave., RI 9-3770
Part of what was once the Felix Warburg Mansion, this museum now rivals the Museum of Modern Art in its program of very avant-garde contemporary exhibitions. There are also many Jewish ceremonial *objets d'art*. Original graphics, $15 and up, at the sales desk. Admission is free; authentication of Judaica decorative arts by appointment; credit courses with Hebrew University. Open noon-5 Mon-Thurs, 11-3 Fri, 11-6 Sun, closed Sat.

The Metropolitan Museum of Art
Fifth Ave. at 82nd St., TR 9-5500
The foremost museum in the United States; almost anything you're looking for is here. Its collections of more than three hundred sixty-five thousand works of art include European paintings from the thirteenth through the first half of the twentieth centuries; a cache of European drawings which is especially strong in works of the Italian eighteenth and French nineteenth centuries; an outstanding print collection dating from about 1450 to the present; a comprehensive survey of American art from Colonial times to the present; an unusual American Wing of decorative arts; the largest and most comprehensive Egyptian collection in the country; twenty thousand examples of Greek and Roman art; and the list could go on and on. It's best to get a free museum floor plan at the sales-information desk near the entrance, and to do one section at a time. Admission is free; limited authentication; credit courses with the Institute of Fine Arts of New York University and Columbia University; parking lot at south end of museum costs $1 for four hours. Open 10-5 Mon-Sat, 1-5 Sun, hols; the museum is experimenting with a 10 pm closing time Tues—call to confirm.

The Cloisters (Fort Tryon Park, WA 3-3700), a branch of the Metropolitan devoted to European Medieval art and architecture, incorporates sections from European Medieval buildings within a modern structure. These include a twelfth-century chapter house, parts of five cloisters from Medieval monasteries, a Romanesque chapel, and a twelfth-century Spanish apse. Included in the collection are the rare and impressive "Nine Heroes Tapestries" and the magnificent "Unicorn Tapestries," ranking among the world's great art treasures. This is a unique museum, with a commanding view of the Hudson River. Admission is free; public lectures every Wednesday afternoon; programs of Medieval music recordings Sunday and Tuesday afternoons. Open 10-5 Tues-Sat, 1-5 Sun and holidays; closed Mon.

Museum of the American Indian
Broadway at 155th St., AU 3-2420

Its collection of arts and crafts, both ancient and modern, of the American Indian cultures is the largest of its type in the world. Its museum shop offers a wide variety of high-quality, reasonably priced Indian art. Admission is free; authentication of Indian arts by appointment; occasional restoration, as time permits. Open 1-5 Tues-Sun; closed Mon, holidays, Aug.

Museum of the City of New York
Fifth Ave. at 103rd St., LE 4-1672

Devoted to chronicling the life and history of New York City. Admission is free; open 10-5 daily, 1-5 Sun and holidays; closed Mon, Christmas.

Museum of Contemporary Crafts
20 W. 53rd St., CI 6-6840

The only museum in the country devoted to displaying the best of United States and foreign contemporary crafts. The museum is beautifully designed, as are also the changing exhibitions. Admission 25¢; open noon-6 daily, 2-6 Sun.

Museum of Early American Folk Art
49 W. 53rd St., LT 1-2474

Puts on interesting, first-rate changing exhibitions of American folk paintings and sculpture. Admission 25¢, 15¢ for students; open 10:30-5:30 daily; closed Mon, Christmas, New Year's.

The Museum of Modern Art
11 W. 53rd St., CI 5-8900

The country's most notable museum devoted to modern art. It collects and shows not only sculptures, graphics, and paintings (Picasso's "Guernica" and "Demoiselles d'Avignon" are among its most famous masterpieces), but also industrial art, films, photography, architecture, and commercial design. Its bookstore at the entrance offers many fine books on this period of art, and the Art Lending Service on the sixth floor offers an extensive art rental selection. Admission $1 adults, 25¢ children; open 11-6 daily, except 11-9 Thurs, noon-6 Sun.

The Museum of Primitive Art
15 W. 54th St., CI 6-9493
Puts on first-rate, changing exhibitions devoted to the indigenous arts of Africa, the Americas, Australia, Oceania, and prehistoric Asia and Europe. Admission 50¢ adults, 25¢ students; open noon-5 Tues-Sat, 1-5 Sun; closed Christmas Day.

The New York Historical Society
170 Central Park West, TR 3-3400
Devoted chiefly to the history of New York State, the Society also boasts fine paintings by Benjamin West, Charles Willson Peale, Frederick Church, et cetera. Admission is free; open 1-5 daily, 10-5 Sat, 1-5 Sun; closed Mon, Aug.

The New York Public Library
Fifth Ave. at 42nd St., OX 5-4200
Has exhibitions mainly devoted to prints and rare books; you can get their events schedule to see exactly when and where. The Prints Division, Room 308, has a hundred twenty thousand prints and drawings from all periods. In addition, THE LIBRARY AND MUSEUM OF THE PERFORMING ARTS at Lincoln Center is quickly amassing an impressive collection on music, theater, and dance. Admission is free for all branches; as hours vary, phone the library branch first.

The New York University Art Collection
80 Washington Sq., SP 7-2000
Displays selections from its permanent collection at Loeb Student Center.

The Pierpont Morgan Library
29 E. 36th St., MI 5-0008
Rare books and manuscripts housed in the handsome Renaissance-style Morgan Mansion. Admission is free; open 9:30-5 daily; closed Sun; closed Sat June-July; closed Aug.

The Riverside Museum
310 Riverside Dr., UN 4-1700
Has an unusual collection of Tibetan and Japanese art, as well as an exhibition schedule of contemporary work. Art from the latter is always for sale. Admission is free; authentication of Tibetan and Pueblo art by appointment; open 1-5 Tues-Sun; closed Mon, holidays.

The Whitney Museum of American Art
945 Madison Ave., 249-4100
Recently reopened in a striking "inverted ziggurat"-designed build-

ing by architect Marcel Breuer; has an extensive collection of major American artists, as well as changing exhibitions devoted to an Annual Survey, young American artists, and individual artists. Works from the exhibitions can often be purchased directly from the museum. Admission 50¢; authentication of historical American art by written request; open 11-5 daily.

PHILADELPHIA, PA.

Where to Buy

Robert Carlen
323 S. 16th St., KI 5-1723
Eighteenth- to twentieth-century primitives and classical art. Prices $100 up. A-R, F, M, Install. Meter parking. By appointment.

Bernard Conwell Carlitz
121 S. 18th, LO 3-6608
Prints, drawings, watercolors, rare books. Prices $10-$2,500. A-R, F, M, Install. Open 11-6.

Dove Art Galleries
2036 Chestnut, LO 7-6142
Modern oil paintings and sculpture. New artists for collectors. Crafts. Prices $80-$600. Open 10:30-6 Tues-Fri, 2-6 Sat, 3-6 Sun; closed Mon; closed July-Sept.

Gallery 252
252 S. 16th, PE 5-0480
All mediums. Also ceramics, sculpture. Prices $25-$5,000. Coop, A-R, F, M, R, Install. Open 11-5 Mon-Sat, 11-9 Wed.

Makler Gallery
1716 Locust, PE 5-2540
American and European contemporaries. Paintings, sculpture, graphics. Coop; A,M,R, Install; Parking. Open 11-5 Mon-Sat.

Newman Galleries
1625 Walnut, LO 3-1779
850 W. Lancaster, Bryn Mawr, LA 5-0625
Nineteenth- and twentieth-century Americans and Europeans. All media, all schools, established in 1865. Prices $25-$15,000. Parking (Bryn Mawr); A-R, F, R, M, Install. Open 9-5:30 Mon-Fri, 9-9 Wed, 9-6 Sat; 9-5 Mon-Fri summer.

Pennsylvania Academy of Fine Arts
Broad and Cherry, LO 4-0219
Contemporary American artists and student art. Its Annual, from which work is sold, is famous. Prices $15-$27,000. Will refer buyers to artists. Open 10-5 Tues-Sat, 1-5 Sun; closed Mon, holidays.

Philadelphia Art Alliance
251 S. 18th, KI 5-4302
Changing exhibitions of contemporary art, crafts. One can buy work from the shows or from the second-floor sales desk. "Art Alliance Bulletin" is their calendar of events. Street parking; open 10:30-9 Mon-Sat, 1-6 Sun; 10:30-6 Mon-Fri July-Aug; closed mid-Aug to Labor Day.

Philadelphia Civic Center
34th and Convention
Contemporary arts and crafts, with emphasis on traveling shows. Have organized some excellent regional crafts shows, such as the 1967 Delaware Valley Craftsmen's Exhibition.

The Print Club
1614 Latimer, PE 5-6090
The Club was started in 1915 by a group of twelve art lovers to provide a focal center for the graphic arts; the membership now numbers over one thousand and the club is well known nationally. Over twenty graphics exhibits are held yearly; circulating exhibits are sent across the country; a workshop is maintained for professional printmakers, in which groups are given on-the-spot demonstrations of printing techniques; and a permanent collection fund purchases gift prints for the Philadelphia Museum. This is one of the best places in the United States to buy all kinds of prints at moderate prices. Open 10-5 Mon-Fri, noon-4 Sat; closed June 15-Sept 10.

Charles Sessler
1308 Walnut, PE 5-1086
Special shows and collectors' items. Graphics. A-R, F. Open 9-5; closed June-Sept.

Woodmere Art Gallery
9201 Germantown, CH 7-0476
Contemporaries. A community art center, non-profit. Parking; open 10-5 daily, 2-6 Sun; 10-4 summer.

YM/YWHA Arts Council
401 S. Broad, KI 5-4400
Their purpose is to bring new trends and expressions to the attention of the Philadelphia art world. They attempt to show exceptional area artists. Work is sold, but not on a profit basis. Their very attractive exhibit announcements are designed by Philadelphia artist Samuel Martin. Open 1-5 daily.

Environs

Gallery 1015
1015 Greenwood, Wyncote, TU 7-4547, TU 7-4645
Contemporary art: painting, sculpture, ceramics, prints. R, Install. By appointment (Gladys Myers, dir.).

Golden Door Gallery
Playhouse Inn, New Hope, 862-5529
Contemporary, international oils, watercolors, graphics, sculpture. Prices $10-$1,000. Parking; F, Install. Open 12:30-5 daily, 1-5 Sun; 11-5, 7:30-9:30 summer.

The Selective Eye
2 W. Bridge, New Hope, 862-2982
A furniture store that shows contemporary art. Low priced. M; open 10-5:30.

Upstairs Gallery
Lahaska
Traditional, modern crafts. To $1,500. Parking; Coop; Install; open 11-5.

Miscellanea

THE CLOTHES LINE EXHIBIT OF ART is an annual event in late May or early June. The two-week ARTS FESTIVAL takes place about the same time.

Where to Look

Atheneum of Philadelphia
219 S. 6th, WA 5-2688
Housed in a notable Italian Revival "Palazzo" (John Notman, 1847), in which handsome examples of American Empire furni-

ture and paintings are displayed. The independent PHILADEL-
PHIA MARITIME MUSEUM is part of the first floor. Free
admission to members and others, upon request; open 9-4 Mon-
Fri.

Atwater Kent Museum
15 S. 7th, WA 2-3031

A history museum that displays Philadelphia memorabilia. The
history of Philadelphia is traced from pre-William Penn Indian days
to the city of your grandfathers. Admission is free; parking lot
opposite building. Open 9-5 daily, 9:30-5 Sun.

The Barnes Foundation
Merion, Pa.

Houses the finest collection of French Post-Impresionist paintings
in the United States; its only rivals outside this country are
collections in Russia. Roomfuls of Renoirs, Matisses, Cézannes,
Picassos, et cetera, have dazzled the eyes of those lucky enough to
get in. Through the will of the late Dr. Albert C. Barnes, the bril-
liant, though eccentric, founder of the collection, only a few persons are admitted daily, usually by appointment. The State of
Pennsylvania is presently seeking to have this changed. Admission
at 9:30 a.m.

Buten Museum of Wedgwood
246 N. Bowman, Merion, MO 4-0342, MO 4-9069

Shows the comprehensive story of Wedgwood in seven thousand
items displayed in five galleries. All ten major varieties of the ware
are shown. Visitors are escorted individually or in groups throughout the museum by one of the nine associate curators. Gallery
talks at 2 p.m.; admission is free; open 2-5 Tues-Thurs Oct-May.

Commercial Museum
34th and Convention, MU 6-9700

Features permanent displays of primitive and folk art from the
Museum collections, as well as changing exhibitions of contemporary crafts, architecture, and industrial design. Admission is
free; open 10-5 Mon-Fri; 1-5 Sat, Sun.

Free Library of Philadelphia
Parkway at 19th and Vine, MU 6-3900

Contains one of the finest public library rare book collections in the
United States. Admission is free; 9-9 Mon-Fri, 9-5 Sat, 2-6 Sun;
hours change in summer.

Dove Art Galleries, Philadelphia, Pennsylvania.

The University Museum, Philadelphia, Pennsylvania.

Interior view, Newman Galleries, Philadelphia, Pennsylvania.

Interior view, Alverthorpe Gallery, Jenkintown,
Pennsylvania. (*Photograph by F. S. Lincoln*)

The Henry Francis du Pont Winterthur Museum
6 mi. N.W. of Wilmington, Del., on Rte. 52, bet. Greenville
and Centerville, OL 6-8591
Generally recognized as the best place in the country to view
outstanding seventeenth-through-nineteenth-century examples of
American decorative arts. Over one hundred period rooms are
furnished down to the smallest detail with objects—ceramics, woodwork, metalwork, textiles, paintings, prints, etc.—especially fitted
to the rooms' designs and periods. The building was once the
residence of Henry Francis du Pont. Open Tues-Sat by advance
appointment; full-day tour $2.50: half-day tours $1.25; ten rooms
in South Wing open without appointment 10-4 Tues-Sat. Admission to Gardens $1, open 1-4 Sun, except in the spring, when they
are open daily.

Institute of Contemporary Art
34th and Locust Walk, 594-7108
Features changing exhibitions. Tours, lectures. Admission is free;
open 10-5 except 1-5 Sun.

Pennsylvania Academy of the Fine Arts
Broad and Cherry, LO 4-0219
The oldest art institution in the United States. Dedicated primarily
to American art and artists, through its museum and its school,
the Academy was founded in 1805 and is uniquely American.
Some of the most distinguished names in American art—from
Colonial times to the present—have been associated with it:
Charles Willson Peale, Rembrandt Peale, Thomas Sully, Mary Cas-
satt, William Glackens, John Marin, Thomas Eakins. Admission
is free; open 10-5 Tues-Sat, Sun and some holidays; closed Mon.

The Philadelphia Art Alliance
251 S. 18th, KI 5-4302
Does not maintain a permanent collection, but presents a series of
high-quality exhibitions which change monthly. Programs in the
performing arts offered as well. Admission is free; open 10:30-9
Mon-Sat, 1-6 Sun; 10:30-6 Mon-Fri July-Aug; closed Sat-Sun
July-Aug and mid-Aug-Labor Day.

Philadelphia Museum of Art
26th and the Parkway, PO 5-0500
Ranks as one of the world's great museums. Thousands of visitors
annually enjoy its over ninety thousand works of art. Among its
treasures are many magnificent painting collections—Arensberg,
Stern, Johnson, Wilstach, Elkins, McFadden, Gallatin, and Tyson

—and period rooms and architectural units including a pillared temple hall from India, a twelfth-century Spanish cloister, a great French Renaissance stone court, the Chinese Palace Hall, the Japanese Ceremonial Tea House in a setting of bamboo and polished garden stones. Also maintained by the Museum are the RODIN MUSEUM, on the Parkway, filled with the largest collection of Rodin sculpture outside of France, and two COLONIAL HOUSES, also in the Park. Admission 50¢ adults, 25¢ children; open 9-5 daily and Sun.

University Museum
University of Pennsylvania, 33rd and Spruce, EV 6-1241
Built up mainly through the University's archeological expeditions, its stunning collections contain art from Egypt, China (Buddhist sculptures of the sixth to eighth centuries A.D. are housed in a huge domed room), Babylonia, India, the Americas, Oceania and Austronesia, and Africa. The Museum is one of the world's leading institutions in the study of ancient and primitive man. Educational services for groups and schools. Admission is free; open 10-5 Mon-Sat, 1-5 Sun.

Information about Art

Both the *Bulletin* and the *Inquirer* feature Sunday art columns; the *Bulletin* also includes a listing of the week's openings at the end of its column. *The Philadelphia Spot Lite*, available free at most hotels, has a listing of art galleries and museums, with names of exhibitions, addresses, phone numbers, and hours; it also lists interesting historical houses. THE CONVENTION AND TOURIST BUREAU of the Chamber of Commerce, Hospitality Center, 1525 John F. Kennedy Blvd., will guide visitors and residents alike to cultural events, and their reprint of "Our Philadelphia Museums" is a succinct and informative guide that's free for the asking. Another, more detailed article on the same subject appeared in *Museum News*, April, 1965.

Crafts in Philadelphia

By Olaf Skoogfors, Silversmith and Jeweler

The majority of the craftsmen listed here sell from their own workshops, located in most cases in their homes or on their own property. As a rule, the local craftsmen cannot depend on the shops in the area to supply adequate sales to support them. We are not a craft-conscious city, despite the fact that we have a great number of excellent craft programs in the major art schools. Just recently, a great deal of headway has been made on a civic and private level.

Some of the craftsmen sell large quantities of low-cost objects, while others market a few high-priced objects per year. The individual outlets vary greatly. The following craftsmen are located within a fifty-mile radius of Philadelphia.

Jewelry

Wesley Emmons
258 S. 16th

Naomi Davis
7509 Woodlawn

Stanley Lechtzin
6540 N. 11th

Olaf Skoogfors
433 E. Sedgwick
Also a silversmith.

John Ware
c/o Moore College of Art, 20th and Race
Also a silversmith.

Ceramics

Raymond Gallucci
837 N. 7th, Allentown

Rudy Staffell
1219 65th

Armand Mednick
RD #2, Doylestown

Julia Jackson
120 W. Tulpehocken

Robert Lease
c/o Tyler School of Fine Arts, Beech and Penrose
Also weaving.

William Daley
c/o Philadelphia College of Art, Broad and Pine

Warren Bakley
Hammonton, N.J.
Also metals.

Byron Temple
New Hope

John Costanza
44 Eastwood, Berwyn

Robert and Paula Winokur
c/o Tyler School of Fine Arts, Beech and Penrose

Wood

Wharton Eshercik
Box 595, Paoli

Richard Hoptner
c/o Kenmore Galleries, 122 S. 18th

Daniel Jackson
120 W. Tulpehocken

Richard Reinhardt
10 Fawn, Newton Sq.
Also metal.

Richard Koga
2310 Locust

George Nakashima
New Hope

Palmer Sharpless
c/o George School, Newtown

Paul Wahwlman
Royerstown

Phillip Powell
New Hope

Metals

Paul Evans
New Hope

Weaving

Ted Hallman Jr.
Souderton, or c/o Moore College, 20th and Race

Robert Stafford
1916-B Lombard

Gerald Marvin
640 Shawmont

Valli Korin
7604 Montgomery

Rubin Eshkanian
c/o Philadelphia College of Art, Broad and Pine

Craft Outlets

The Circle Craft Shop
2014 Sansom

The Little Nook
25 E. Highland
Open 10-5 daily, closed Mon; parking.

The Peasant Shop
17th and Spruce
Long established; quality crafts. Open 9-5, closed Sun.

The Philadelphia Art Alliance
251 S. 18th
Hours listed above.

PITTSBURGH, PA.

By Rebecca R. Berman,
Executive Director, Pittsburgh Plan for Art

The art climate of Pittsburgh is comparable to that of most cities its size, and to most areas where art interest per se is steadily rising. It is generated through such educational facilities as the CARNEGIE INSTITUTE OF TECHNOLOGY, whose art department is extremely progressive; through the various outlets created for art exposure; through the unique policies of the PITTSBURGH PLAN FOR ART, by which paintings, drawing, prints and sculptures are exhibited, circulated on a rental system, and eventually sold; through the cooperation of the MUSEUM OF ART OF THE CARNEGIE INSTITUTE, which, under the direction of Leon Arkus, has presented outstanding examples of Pittsburgh's artists to the public; and through the efforts of the ARTS AND CRAFTS CENTER, where most of the major art groups meet and exhibit their work in annual shows.

The recent upsurge of art interest has been notably apparent here. Audiences for galleries and museums have grown in considerable quantity, and tastes have been honed by looking. No specific type of art is pushed, but in the past few years more of the abstract, both non-objective and objective, has taken the lead. This can be attributed to the fact that many purchasers are in their twenties, have grown up with modern art, and are very much involved with the present time.

Pittsburgh has no local "school." The artists are recognized for their own idiom, and their work is highly professional. Most have studied—the word "self-taught" does not apply here.

Categories which are best for buying in the reasonable price ranges are varied. Prints and drawings can be purchased for as low as ten dollars. Small sculpture is available from fifty dollars, and oil paintings from one hundred to one thousand. The moderately priced oil is the most salable item. The acclaimed Pittsburgh printmakers are George Nama, Russell G. Twiggs, and Helen Ubinger. Drawings executed by Harry Schwalb and Marie Kelly have been favorably accepted. Henry Bursztynowicz ranks highest in the lower priced sculpture field. There are many serious and excellent artists whose oils are prime examples of this universal medium. Outstanding among them are Richard Beaman, Russell Twiggs, Samuel Rosenberg, Louise Pershing, Cecelia Lieberman, Eva Ada Weill, Gertrude Half, Aaronel Gruber, Gloria Karn, Thomas Quirk, Jr., Charlotte Rosenberg, Marjorie Eklind, Kamal Youssef, Anne Golomb, Rochelle Blumenfeld, and Rebecca Berman. Douglas Pickering, Virgil Cantini, and George Koren produce most sensitive sculptures, bearing comparison to the best in the country. Virgil Cantini is the most popular sculptor in the higher priced bracket.

Unique to Pittsburgh is the PITTSBURGH PLAN FOR ART, by which art can be rented or purchased in the low to moderate price range. This organization serves as a non-profit community agency for the display, rental, and sale of paintings, drawings, and sculpture, and as a focal point for the merging interests of those creatively and receptively concerned with visual-art appreciation and education. Founded in 1955 with a grant from the A. W. Mellon Educational and Charitable Trust, administered by the Carnegie College of Fine Arts under Dean Norman Rice's guidance and assisted by a Citizen's Committee, it is now an invaluable self-supporting service. A membership fee is required for participation in the Plan, and members are entitled to all benefits offered. One-man exhibitions are a monthly activity. Seminars are moderated by qualified leaders; and an Art Caravan program for school children on the elementary and secondary level is operated by the Women's Association of the Plan. The Plan, which occupies space in a city-owned building, serves both the community and the artist, and is chartered as an educational institution.

Information about Art

Information about art events is available in both the *Pittsburgh Press* and the *Post Gazette*. Critiques are published in the *Gazette* at least three times weekly for as long as there are new openings of shows. The Press' coverage is about as extensive, but theirs is presented as feature stories rather than as critical reviews. A weekly arts calendar is also carried by both papers, while *This Week In Pittsburgh* has a monthly calendar, listing all openings taking place during that month.

In addition, public service announcements about art are carried on various radio stations, and local television stations cover art openings which they consider newsworthy. The publications of the architectural groups, and the weekly calendars of the University of Pittsburgh and the Carnegie Institute of Fine Arts also list art events of merit, as well as those of their own galleries.

Where to Buy

There is no one particular area in Pittsburgh which includes the greatest concentration of art outlets. However, the downtown business area includes the following galleries which carry a cross-section of all art forms.

J.J. Gillespie Co.
306 7th, 281-0877
Open 9-5 Mon-Fri; 9-1 Sat; closed July-Aug; parking in Gimbel's lot.

Wunderly Galleries
901 Liberty, 281-2711
Established 1894. Original oils, graphics.

Western Side of Town

Art Unlimited
677 Washington, 563-6686
Open 10-5:30 Mon-Sat and Mon, Wed, Fri evenings. Available parking. Moderately priced art of all kinds.

Southern Side of Town

International Art Gallery
South Hills Village Shopping Center, 833-3788
Open 10-9:30 Mon-Sat. Available parking. Few locals, many European moderns.

The Civic Center

University of Pittsburgh Book Center
4000 5th, 621-3500
Open 8:30-8 Mon-Thurs; 9:30-5 Fri, Sat; 8:30-5 Mon-Fri during July-Aug. Prints and drawings by local and out-of-town artists, and some Europeans.

Visual Arts Gallery
5743 Ellsworth, 362-7095
Open noon-5 Tues-Sat; closed Mon; evenings by appointment; available parking. Local artists only.

Arts and Crafts Mart
6300 5th, 361-0873
Open 10-5 Mon-Sat, 2-5 Sun; closed first 2 wks. Aug; available parking. Arts and crafts executed by members of the Center's resident groups.

East End of Town

Pittsburgh Plan for Art
1251 N. Negley, 362-1234
Open 10-4 Tues-Sat, 2-5 Sun; closed Mon; closed July-Aug; available parking. Local, national, and international artists; accepts its stock under a jury system; no fee for entries; only contemporaries; sales and rentals. Located in the old King family house, "Baywood."

Haugh & Keenan Galleries, Pittsburgh, Pennsylvania.

Antiques and Objets d'Art

Haugh & Keenan Galleries
5879 Center, Cathedral Mansions, 682-6331
Open 9:30-5 Mon-Fri, 9:30-1 Sat; closed Sun. Antique paintings, English and American furniture, silver. C. J. Seibert, the proprietor, is an authorized appraiser.

Antique Art Shop
5112 Penn, 661-9903

Martha Brown
3610 Fifth, 681-6055

Bunkerhill Galleries
236 Shady, 441-1506

Delp's Pink Carousel
4933 Penn, 441-2110

Dillner Galleries
2747 W. Liberty, 341-3300

Encore Galleries
5125 Penn, 361-3800

Miscellanea

Embroideries Unlimited
121 S. Drive, 782-0719
By appointment only. Owned and operated by Mrs. Wilbur King, who has written several books on the subject of stitchery and who is internationally known. Individual sales and commissions.

Pittsburgh Playhouse Gallery
Craft and Hamlet, 621-4445
Open 2-5 for the public, 11 A.M.-midnight for members. A combined theater-club-school that sells paintings and drawings in the $75-$1,500 price range. New shows monthly. Inquire at the Headwaiter's stand.

Sears-Roebuck & Co.
328 N. Highland, 661-6500
Open 9:30-9 every day except Sun; available parking. Carries

original paintings and prints, mostly on a caravan basis when the Vincent Price Collection is sent to town.

Art Festivals and Art Groups

THE THREE RIVERS ARTS FESTIVAL, an annual cultural event, is held in Pittsburgh's Golden Triangle. It is sponsored by the Carnegie Institute under the directorship of Donald Steinfirst. It has been recognized internationally and is one of the few festivals recommended to visitors from abroad by the United States Travel Service. More than a hundred fifty thousand persons visit the festival annually and enjoy an impressive variety of visual and performing arts.

Thousands of dollars' worth of art is usually purchased. The work is submitted by artists and craftsmen from Pennsylvania, Ohio, and West Virginia. For ten days, starting the last week in May, the Gateway Center is a beehive of activity from 11 a.m. to 11 p.m. An outstanding jurist is invited to select the entries and also award the prizes offered by several large corporations and the Festival. Unless otherwise indicated, all work is for sale. The Festival is made possible by monies donated by foundations, corporations, the City of Pittsburgh, Allegheny County, and generous individuals.

The many active art organizations of Pittsburgh are housed in the ARTS AND CRAFTS CENTER, 6300 5th, 361-0873. A and C sponsors the monthly shows of these member groups and maintains a mart where art of all kinds is displayed and sold. It is open 10-5 Mon-Sat, 2-5 Sun; closed New Year's, Easter, Labor Day, Memorial and Independence days, Thanksgiving, Christmas.

These groups include the ABSTRACT GROUP, formed in 1944 as an informal group of professional artists who meet to discuss, produce, and exhibit paintings and sculpture; the AMATEUR ARTISTS ASSOCIATION OF PITTSBURGH, whose purpose is to assist members to obtain the maximum from a hobby; the ASSOCIATED ARTISTS OF PITTSBURGH, which is the largest of the groups and which puts on an annual juried exhibition in which the accepted works are put on view at the Carnegie Institute for five weeks; the PITTSBURGH WATER COLOR SOCIETY, comprised of professional artists dedicated to furthering interest in this medium; the PITTSBURGH SOCIETY OF SCULPTORS, which puts on an annual show juried by a prominent sculptor; and the CRAFTSMEN'S GUILD, EMBROIDERERS GUILD, and NATURAL COLOR CAMERA CLUB.

Where to Look

Museum of Art, Carnegie Institute
4400 Forbes, 621-7300
The Institute is famous for its Carnegie International Exhibitions of Contemporary Art and is a vital local, national, and international art force. The galleries contain a permanent collection of contemporary paintings and sculpture as well as the Old Masters. Admission is free; authentication by appointment; *Carnegie* magazine for members. Open 10-5 weekdays, 2-5 Sun, 10-9 Tues late Oct-late March; closed Christmas, New Year's, Easter, Thanksgiving.

For local historic points of interest, which often contain art, consult THE PITTSBURGH CONVENTION AND VISITORS BUREAU, INC., 3001 Jenkins Arcade, for maps, directions, and schedules.

BALTIMORE, MD.

By Barbara Gold, Art Critic, *The Baltimore Sun*

Baltimore is living in an aesthetic past. There are only two genuine galleries in town—FERDINAND ROTEN, which sells Old and Modern Master prints, and THE PHOENIX, which handles the more established local artists. The rest is antiques. Fortunately, these ancient objects are the redeeming feature of the artistic scene. There are excellent opportunities here to find refurbished furniture, old oddities, and attractive antiquities, many offered for sale by local families who have owned them since ante-bellum days. As in most antique purchases you have to know what you're buying, but prices are generally low, and most good pieces seem to exude gallant Southern emanations.

In the midst of such a city, it seems likely that artists with any modern inclinations would feel stifled. Strangely they thrive on it. There are hordes of painters in the city who practice a pleasant abstract style which they somehow make innocuous enough to blend into any traditional Southern interior decoration. Although most of them are friends and belong to the same painting clubs, these artists do not form any sort of local or regional school. Rather they are the contented victims of the bland Expressionist manner which has become an international provincialism.

Part of their conformity may be due to the influence of some of the more prominent artists who live in the area. Foremost among these is Grace Hartigan, whose work has been included in some of the Museum of Modern Art's most influential traveling exhibitions. She teaches at the Maryland Institute, the local art school, and continues to work in her powerful, slashing, abstract style. Others are Herman Maril, who uses a broad abstraction to create delicate landscape scenes, and Reuben Kramer, who sculptures finely finished women in tortured bronze.

A really avant-garde artist could not find a home in Baltimore, however. Someone like Lowell Nesbitt, an adherent of an inflated Pop Realism, must leave and go to New York.

Hopefully Baltimore will somehow slowly catch up and close the big gap between it and the contemporary art world.

There are no galleries in which any of these artists could make a living from sales. There are, however, many chances to buy area art productions from exhibitions in museums and schools. The prices are reasonable, although they can be what minor New York painters are charging, and the locals are well supported by their friends and co-residents in Baltimore. Many exhibitions are heavily sold out by the closing date.

Some efforts are constantly being made to offer wider opportunities for residents to buy non-Baltimore art. A number of entrepreneurs have tried and failed to get actual New York-type art galleries going in the city. There are many art displays in the lobbies and meeting rooms of the modern apartment buildings going up all over town. These usually show prints and small paintings. The Women's Committee of the BALTIMORE MUSEUM OF ART is also doing its part to fill the gap by pushing its Sales and Rental Gallery, which, in addition to the usual selection of familiar Baltimore artists, has many minor New York pieces cajoled from various New York galleries. The very proximity of New York may well be the reason for Baltimore's failure to support its own galleries; the serious buyers can and do go to the big city.

The art-interested group is, in any case, quite small. Every member knows what the other is doing and what is socially acceptable at the moment. This is the coterie which runs the museums and sets the tone of artistic life in Baltimore. It is a practical-minded group—most can announce in a minute the financial wisdom of their latest purchase, and this frequently comes before expressions of appreciation—which puts far more emphasis on the fluctuating values of the business ethic than on the more esoteric ones of aesthetics. It's almost impossible to run a good commercial gallery which will satisfy this in-group and the demands of aesthetic quality simultaneously.

Where to Buy

For the person who wants to shop in Baltimore's art outlets, the best place to start is at the top of North Howard Street on "Antique Row," where the most rewarding, active, and promising antique shops cluster together. The most important is the Harris Gallery; from here it's an easy walk down North Howard with stops for each shop that catches the eye to Mulberry Street, where the Roten Gallery of prints and jewelry may be found halfway up the hill. After seeing Roten's both upstairs and down, the buyer might then head either west to North Eutaw Street to the Phoenix Gallery or out to the scattered apartment house and suburban exhibitions. The most worthwhile establishments are listed below. Parking is generally easy, if sometimes expensive, everywhere in the city.

For up-to-date information on art events, consult the *Baltimore Sunday Sun's* "What's To Be Seen," and my column, "Art Notes." The *Baltimore Sunday News-American* also has a listing of arts events and an art-music-drama column by R. P. Harriss. In addition, most radio and TV stations make "community bulletin board"-type announcements, and these often include art events.

Antiques

The devotee will find other antique shops scattered throughout the city, but those listed here present a good beginning. Most shops are open 9-5.

AAA Antiques and Arts Shop
867 N. Howard, LE 9-4095

Antique Row
829 N. Howard, 752-2493

The Antique Shop
827 N. Howard, VE 7-5991

Golden's Antique and Silver Shop
863 N. Howard, SA 7-7868

Harris Galleries
875 N. Howard, VE 7-2045

Ferdinand Roten Galleries, Inc., Baltimore, Maryland.

The Peale Museum, Baltimore, Maryland.

Kashan ware. (Persia.) Twelfth century. Collection of the Walters Art Gallery, Baltimore, Maryland.

The Monument Antiques
859 N. Howard, 727-5552

Norton's Antiques
843 N. Howard, 685-8236

Read Antiques
899 N. Howard, LE 9-6298

Quality Galleries

Ferdinand Roten
123 Mulberry, VE 7-7723
G, Mods, Eu, F, Install, M. Open 9-5:30 Tues-Sat.

The Phoenix Gallery
604 N. Eutaw, 539-7290
A, Mods. Open 12-5 Tues-Sat.

Other Interesting Downtown Galleries

All Trends
Bolton at Dolphin
G, Baltimore Mods. Open 2-5 Tues-Sat.

Vertical Gallery
One Charles Center Bldg., 727-6800
One-man exhibitions on eleven floors of this building. Baltimore
Mods, G. Open 8-6 Mon-Fri.

Apartments

Highfield House, The Stephen Mazoh Gallery
4000 N. Charles, TU 9-4000
A, Eu, G, Mods. Open 10-10 daily.

Rumsey Towers
Rumsey Island, Joppatowne, 672-2000
A, Eu, G, Mods. Open 10-10 daily.
    Others will probably add art as the public-relations value
spreads.

Suburbs

Studio North
8 Allegheny Ave., Towson, 825-2022
Balt, A, Eu, Mods, G, F.

Miscellanea

The following institutions have regular exhibition space. Usually what they show is for sale and is by local artists.

Baltimore Junior College
2901 Liberty Heights, 523-2151
Open 2-4 Sun, 10-4 Mon-Fri, 10-2 Sat.

Goucher College
Towson, 825-3300
The exhibitions here are usually of high quality. Open 9-5 weekdays, 1-5 weekends, and evenings of public events.

Jewish Community Center
5700 Park Heights, 542-8130
Open 10-10 daily, 10-4 Fri.

Maryland Institute
Mt. Royal Station, 669-9200
Usually the work of undergraduate and graduate students of the Institute. Often colorful. Always of interest. In a particularly fascinating setting. Open 10-10 daily.

Morgan State College
Hillen Rd. and Cold Sp. Lane, CL 4-6870
Open 10-4 Mon-Fri, 10-12 Sat, 2-4 Sun, and evenings of public events. Changing exhibitions, plus a permanent collection.

Parish Hall Gallery
514 N. Charles
Open 12-4 Tues-Sun.

In addition, the DRUID PARK FESTIVAL is open to all artists and craftsmen resident in Baltimore. Held the first or second Sunday in June around the Druid Park lake. The work is primarily by Sunday-painter types, but good things can be found, particularly in the jewelry line.

Art Organizations

ARTISTS' EQUITY, Maryland division of the national organization, holds an annual exhibition at the Peale Museum. There are other, less active, local groups, such as the BALTIMORE PEN-WOMEN and the BALTIMORE WATERCOLOR CLUB.

Where to Look

The Baltimore Museum of Art
Wyman Park at N. Charles, 889-1735

Baltimore's major museum, specializing in American, contemporary, primitive, Asian, and French nineteenth-century art. Works in all media ($1-2,500) are available at the sales desk, right by the main entrance to the museum. There is also a Sales and Rental Gallery, ground level, that rents art from one dollar per month. It is open noon-4 Tues-Fri, 2-6 Sun, closed summers. Authenticating of American and European art by appointment; free admission. Museum open 11-5 Tues-Sat, 2-6 Sun, 8-10 p.m. Tues Oct-May; closed Mon and Independence Day, Labor Day, Memorial Day, Christmas, Good Friday, Thanksgiving, and New Year's.

The Walters Art Gallery
600 N. Charles, 727-2075

Houses an extraordinary collection gathered in a period of only ninety years by William Walters and his son, Henry. The range is enormous—from Egypt to 1925—and includes some twenty-five thousand objects. The building, constructed in 1905-8, is a copy of a Renaissance palace in Genoa. The Gallery is an aesthetic experience that shouldn't be missed, and is one of the outstanding museums in the United States. Admission is free; authentication by appointment. Open 11-5 Tues-Sat, 2-5 Sun, 1:30-5 Mon, 11-4 Mon-Sat during July-Aug; closed New Year's, July 4th, Thanksgiving, Dec. 24-25; open 2-5 other legal holidays.

The Peale Museum
225 N. Holliday, 752-2000, ex. 2361

The museum's little brochure reads, "When Rembrandt Peale opened his 'Baltimore Museum and Gallery of the Fine Arts' in this building in August, 1814, it was his ambition to 'establish a Scientific Institution such as the population and wealth of this City demand,' and which would be 'equally honorable to Maryland and satisfactory to himself.' " It was a bold scheme, for this building was the first in the United States to be erected expressly as a museum, and the third such institution in the world. Recently named a National Historic Site, the museum is partly' maintained by the City of Baltimore and is devoted to preserving historical objects that show the life of the city. A wide selection of paintings by the Peale family is also on view. Admission is free; authentication of Baltimore and Peale art by appointment; publications about

Baltimore. Open 10:30-4:30 Tues-Sat; closed Mon, Sun, New Year's, Easter, Decoration, Independence, Labor, Thanksgiving and Christmas days; shorter hours in summer.

Maryland Historical Society
201 W. Monument, 685-3750
Devoted to collecting materials relating to the history of Maryland, the Society also has a fine collection of American paintings, prints, furniture, silver, ceramics, and maritime and military items. The Society is also building a larger, modern brick building next door. Admission is free; extensive publications; authenticating of local art objects and documents. Open 9-5 Mon-Fri, Sept 15-June 15; 9-4 Mon-Fri, 9-1 Sat, summer; closed Sat, Aug.

Breezewood
Hess Rd., Monkton, Md., PR 1-4485
This little-known museum near Baltimore houses the finest private collection of Thai art in the United States. Collector Alexander B. Griswold kindly opens his doors the first Sundays in April through October. Not to be missed.

WASHINGTON, D.C.

By Joanna Eagle

Culture goes hand in hand with politics in the nation's capital. The fact that Washington has more museums per square miles than any other United States city excepting New York sometimes overshadows the many excellent art galleries located here. The diversity of art, both to look at and to buy, reflects the cosmopolitan flavor of this handsome city. Like Washington's spread-out districts and wide boulevards, art, too, is scattered, and there are no clearly demarcated areas for browsing and buying. Yet the galleries, auction houses, and antique shops fall into three general locations, usually too far apart for walking (blocks are long in Washington), but close enough for bus, taxi, or auto travel. They are the downtown section, centered around F and G Streets, from 7th to 14th; the Connecticut Avenue area, comparable to New York's Fifth Avenue in its smart shops of all kinds; and historic Georgetown, located in the western part of the city near the canal. that once brought it lively trade.

There is little really far-out contemporary art, and only a few cooperative galleries, here. Nevertheless, there is a lively coterie of local artists, mostly centered around American, George Washington, Howard, Catholic and Maryland universities, where they teach. All are competent and active. There was even what was known as a "Washington School" a few years back, and it's currently having a lively revival. The city has a few good antique shops, but is generally not the best place to buy in this category. Far Eastern and primitive arts are also hard to find, although a few galleries do handle them.

Perhaps the biggest art bargain in Washington is appraisal of art. With its many museums, many government owned, Washington offers a great range in appraising, whether it's for an Early American painting you may have inherited (for this go to the CORCORAN GALLERY OF ART) or for a T'ang pottery horse you may have bought in China long ago (consult the FREER GALLERY OF ART for Oriental objects). Most of the curators are only too willing to look at your treasures, with the usual reservations. (See the section on appraisal).

Another unusual art opportunity here is the buying of contemporary Latin American painters and printmakers. The PAN AMERICAN UNION is highly active in this field and has shows that change every three weeks.

As in many other American cities, Washington's restaurants, theaters, university art departments, art schools, and art festivals provide good buying opportunities. Several of the department stores have instituted art departments and, on occasion, display good visiting shows (watch the daily newspapers for announcements of these exhibitions). The CORCORAN and WASHINGTON GALLERY OF MODERN ART offer art-rental services.

For information on gallery shows and art auctions and reviews of exhibitions, consult the following publications: the *Washington Post*, the *Evening Star*, the *Washington Daily News; Shopping in Washington*, a small magazine available for fifty cents in most stores; *This Week*, a publication that lists art shows and art points of interest (it's free at most hotels); *Washingtonian* magazine, which features an art column; the out-of-town calendars of *Arts* and *Art News;* the art sections of *Time, Life, Newsweek*, and *The New York Times*, which often report on the bigger Washington exhibitions.

The DISTRICT OF COLUMBIA RECREATION BOARD annually publishes a *Survey of the Arts*, in which all D.C. libraries, museums, and art galleries, as well as other cultural organizations, are listed. The Survey is free for the asking. The Department also issues *A Summer's Cultural Profile,* a listing of cultural events. Similar to this is the monthly *Cultural Events* calendar published by HERMAN MILLER, INC., 1730 M St., NW, free to anyone on the firm's mailing list.

If you're visiting Washington and want to get around by bus, phone the D.C. Transit Company (FE 7-1300), and they'll give explicit directions for each point you want to visit. In addition, all transit routes are listed in the front of the Yellow Pages.

Where to Buy

Downtown Area

Mickelson's

709 G, NW (7th), NA 8-1737

Combines one of Washington's oldest framing establishments with one of the city's newest, most handsomely designed galleries. A family business, Mickelson's has been framing for the White House since Mrs. Calvin Coolidge once brought in a painting for framing. Mrs. Jacqueline Kennedy was a steady customer. You pay a little more here, but it's worth it. A hodge-podge of blue-and-white Danish plates, old prints, lamps, mirrors, and maps had long been Mickelson's stock-in-trade, until they opened their spanking white modern gallery in 1963. They concentrate on contemporaries with national reputations—Carl Zerbe, Adolph Dehn, Rico Lebrun, Milton Hebald, to name a few. Paintings start at $140, graphics at $25, sculpture at $300, and naturally, the price includes framing. There's also a print and watercolor bin. A, An, Eu, F, G, A-R, Install; free parking at Downtown Park and Shop, 9th & G. Open 10:30-6 weekdays, 10:30-5 Sat.

Hecht's

7th and F, NW, 628-5100

Right down the street from Mickelson's and the National Gallery of Art, Hecht's department store occasionally puts on a good showing, like the mammoth New Guinea art sale of January, 1964. Their general art stock needs building up, though. A, E, Eu, F.

S. Kriger, Inc.

712 12th, NW (G), DI 7-2607

You need an experienced Orientalia eye when browsing through these three floors of Far Eastern scrolls, *objets d'art,* furniture, jades, ivories, bronzes, et cetera. Kriger has both expensive and inexpensive things. In the lower price range are Japanese *netsukes* from $2.50 up, ivory carvings beginning at $15, and jades for $20. Certificates of authenticity provided. E; open 9:30-5:30 daily; closed Sun.

Woodward & Lothrop
10th-11th F, NW, 347-5300

Better known as "Woody's," this department store has special art shows from time to time in its seventh-floor Gallery of Original Art. A, G; open 9:30-9 Mon, Thurs; 9:30-6 other days; closed Sun.

G.G. Sloan & Co., Inc.
715 13th, NW (G-H), NA 8-1468

Sloan's is Washington's, and the surrounding area's, major appraisal and auction house. Its ad in the Yellow Pages reads "The trash of one generation becomes the treasure of another," and the house has been devoted to this motto since 1891. Consignments auctioned off include anything from ironing boards to valuable Georgian silver. If you know what you want, bargain opportunities abound here. Objects for the auction block go on display the day before the sale from noon on; catalogs of the sales are mailed upon request. Sales are scheduled every Wednesday and Saturday at 10 a.m. during Sept-May. During June-Aug, they take place Tuesday and Friday at 10 a.m. A, Eu, Au, A-R.

Corcoran Gallery of Art
17th and NY, NW, ME 8-3211

In addition to its permanent displays, the Corcoran carries on an active program of selling and renting contemporary art. For sale are art works from the Washington-area series of one-man shows, from loan exhibitions, and from bi-annual exhibitions. Prices are usually not marked on the paintings, so inquire for them at the sales desk. Also at the desk are works by Washington-area craftsmen, with ceramicists Richard LaFean and Teruo Hara usually featured. The Corcoran's art-rental gallery is one of the few in the country to display rentable items in actual room settings (see the section on rental). Rental fees, varying from $5-$47 monthly, are based on the price of the art object. A, An, C, R. Open 10-4:30 Tues-Fri, 9-4:30 Sat, 2-5 Sun and holidays; closed Mon. Rental gallery hours: 12-4 Tues-Fri, by appointment summer.

Pan American Union
Constitution and 17th, NW, EX 3-8450

The contemporary Latin American paintings and prints on sale are among the best art buys in town. One-man exhibitions rotate every three weeks on the main floor, where there is also a Latin American folk-craft shop. Downstairs are the print shows, near where the Union's permanent collection is also located. Visit the main floor bookshop for background reading. E, G; open 9:30-5:30 Mon-Fri, 8-4 Sat.

Department of the Interior
18-19th (C) NW, 343-1100

The recently re-opened Art Gallery, located on the C St. side, 7th floor, features excellent changing exhibits of American Indian art. Much is reasonably priced, especially those objects by Indian children. The Handicraft Shop on the first floor, also near C St., features Kachina dolls and handsome turquoise-and-silver jewelry. On the way out, you may want to browse in the department's well-stocked library. E, C.

Arts Club
2017 I, NW, FE 7-7282

Further up Pennsylvania Ave. is the staid Arts Club. Conservative in flavor, even down to the handsome old brick house in which it is quartered, this organization shows mainly realistic portraits, still-lifes, and landscapes. Price range is about $15-$500. During the winter there are rotating one-man shows, plus exhibitions by such local art groups as the Washington Arts, Landscape, and Watercolor Leagues. A; open 11-5 daily.

Franz Bader Art Bookshop and Gallery
2124 Penna., NW, DI 7-3623

In a city of monuments, Austrian-born Franz Bader is an art institution all by himself. For more than twenty-five years he has run a personalized art bookshop-gallery that has given many of Washington's artists, among them United States Fine Arts Commission head William Walton, their start. Famous for his book-autographing parties, Bader has a guest list that has included Harry Truman, Jacqueline Kennedy, Dylan Thomas, and Dame Edith Sitwell. Featuring mainly contemporary Washington artists, Bader's watercolors start at $25, while his prints and drawings average $25-$50. He also has a handsome ceramics gallery downstairs, in which contemporary and Far and Middle Eastern wares are featured at extremely reasonable prices. A, Eu, G; open 9-6 daily, closed Sun.

Connecticut Avenue and Environs: Ever since the famed New York art dealer Joseph Duveen rented a Dupont Circle apartment to sell most of the art treasures now in the National Gallery of Art to Andrew Mellon, Connecticut Ave. and its Dupont Circle hub have figured prominently in Washington's art trade. Beginning near the Mayflower Hotel are:

Mrs. Greer of Middleburg, Ltd.
1145 Conn., NW, 638-1031

As the name implies, this is a branch of the larger Virginia store. This tiny, but well-stocked, shop specializes in eighteenth-century English furniture, *objets d'art,* and Lowestoft china, but also carries lower priced items. I saw a set of six hand-painted 1860 French cups selling for $70; an old silver-plated English toast cooler for $16.50; a pair of yellowed antique world globes for $450. In summer, the shop sports a gay red awning. An; open 9:30-5:30 daily, closed Sun; closed July, Aug.

Herman Miller, Inc.
1730 M, NW, 296-6052

Amid costly Eero Saarinen womb chairs and Charles Eames' furniture designs, reasonably priced folk crafts from Mexico, Poland, England, South America, Belgium, and Italy are easily found. Selected by designer Alexander Girard, a hand-carved Polish figure sells for $28, a gaily painted Mexican wood ferris wheel is $125, and so on. Be sure to see the toy wool animals. E; open 10-5 daily, closed Sun; closed Sat, July-Aug.

Veerhoff Galleries
1512 Conn., NW, DU 7-2322

Located just above Dupont Circle, these staid, long-established galleries specialize in custom framing, restoring, and appraisals, as well as conservative European and American contemporaries. Good buys here are the old maps and prints starting at $5, and the soft paste porcelain horse statues by Kathleen Wheeler, which will appeal to horse lovers. The Veerhoff publication, *Miscellanea,* which is available for the asking, is an illustrated list of their stock. Au, A, G, F, A-R, M; open 9:30-6 daily, except Sun; closed Sat, June-Aug.

Duncan & Duncan Chinese Shop
1511 Conn., NW, 232-4884

Excellent quality objects in a beautifully decorated store; it's a pleasure just to browse. Though many items are expensive, the shop carries less expensive things as well: tiny jade screens on carved stands, $25-$125; Ch'ing dynasty amulets, $10 up; bronze ritual vessels, $135; a Sung oil pot, $275. Certificates of authenticity provided. Bi-annual sales. E; open 10-6 daily, closed Sun.

The Washington Gallery of Modern Art
1503 21st, NW, 293-1700
Located in a dignified four-story old Washington town house, one block over from the Circle, the museum and its Collector's Rental Gallery carry on an active program of contemporary exhibits. The Rental Gallery features both local and New York artists; all mediums, including graphics, are available for rental and purchase. A, G, R; open 10-5 Tues-Wed, 10-10 Thurs-Fri, 11-5 Sat-Sun.

Henri Gallery
1500 21st, NW, 234-5513
Run by the personable lady who calls herself "Henri," this gallery has quickly established itself as the leading avant-garde art outlet in the Washington, D.C., area. Henri offers exciting displays of both local and out-of-town contemporaries (mostly the latter) in a dramatic, spacious new gallery. One-man exhibitions are shown on the first floor, with group exhibits on the second. Sculpture, prints, constructions, paintings and light environments are all available. Prices $50-$3,000. Install; 10-8 Tues-Fri, 10-6 Sat, 2-6 Sun, closed Mon; openings of new shows the first Sat of each month, 10 a.m.-8 p.m.; summer, 10-10 Tues-Fri, 10-6 Sat, 2-6 Sun, closed Mon.

Jefferson Place Gallery of Contemporary Art
2144 P, NW, 483-3121
This is, perhaps, Washington's "farthest out" gallery, featuring such well-known Washingtonians as sculptor William Kalfee and painters Robert Gates and Joe Sommerford. Sam Gilliam is another standout. There's usually a special group show at Christmas, and the gallery encourages installment buying. A; open 11-5 Tues-Sat; closed summer.

Jewish Community Center of Greater Wash., Fine Arts Gallery
1529 16th, NW, DU 7-6162
Over on the southeast side of the Circle, this gallery rotates six changing shows yearly. Their exhibitions have included a Yugoslav folk-art exhibit and a "Prints for the New Collector" show. A, Eu, G; open 10-3 Mon-Fri, 1-5 Sun; closed Sat.

18th Street, near Columbia Road, NW: You can often find bargains in the clutter of second-hand and junk shops here.

Hoffmann's
2447 18th, CO 5-5116
The biggest, with three or four shops.

John Marin (1870–1953): *The Sea, Maine, 1921.* (American.) Watercolor and charcoal on paper. 1921. Collection of the National Collection of Fine Arts, Smithsonian Institution, Washington, D.C.

A gallery in the Corcoran Gallery of Art, Washington, D.C., during the exhibition "Past and Present: 250 Years of American Art," 1966.

One of the galleries showing the permanent collection of the Pan American Union, Washington, D.C.

Gonzalez
2408 18th, AD 4-3336
Unusual antiques.

Launay & Co., Inc.
2410 18th, NW, 234-5147
Launay specializes in rare French furniture and *objets d'art*. The very nice French couple who run it give certificates of authenticity, also restore and repair antiques.

IFA Galleries
2623 Conn., NW, DU 7-7537
The prints, drawings, and watercolors are among the best in Washington, and the framing is also good. Prints are usually in the bins or in portfolios. Harold Altmann, Jack Bookbinder, Gabor Peterdi, Leonard Baskin, Braque, Picasso, Miró, and Cuevas are just a few of the names they carry. A, Eu, F, G; open 9:30-6 daily; closed Sun.

Institute of Contemporary Arts
1630 Crescent Pl., NW, HU 3-3230
Among ICA's many cultural offerings is the art gallery that opened in the spring of 1964. Most of the shows are devoted to contemporary Americans, but they've also had exhibits from Spain and Latin America. Open 12-6 daily; closed Sun; closed Mon, summer.

Georgetown: A busy port in Colonial times, Georgetown has retained its early shopkeeping traditions and quaint brick architecture. Cargo ships from all over the world used to put in here, and among the goods they brought were art objects. The "town" has retained its tradition of good taste and has maintained a wide selection of all kinds of art. Many galleries and antique shops line Wisconsin Avenue—Georgetown's Rue de la Paix—and I can only list some of the many here. For an afternoon of browsing, it's a good idea to start "in the heights" and proceed down to M St., as I did.

Craft House
1669 Wisconsin, NW, 234-4945
The best place in town for contemporary American crafts. Unusual textiles, hand-wrought silver jewelry and flatware, heavy pottery are on display for extremely reasonable prices. The house is a cooperative venture, run by seventeen members on a non-profit basis. Made-to-order work is a specialty; and one-man and group exhibitions are featured all year long. Information about craftsmen

and their activities—shows, classes, et cetera—is also available here. C; Install; Coop; open 11-5:30 daily, closed Sun; closed Mon summer.

Hinckley & Brohel Galleries, Ltd.
1665 Wisconsin, NW, 387-2316
A branch of the New York gallery of the same name, Hinckley & Brohel specializes in younger artists, such as the children of Ben Shahn—Judith, Abbey, and Jonathan. Good bargains, especially in drawings and prints. A, G, Install; open 11-6 Tues, Wed, Fri, Sat, 11-10 Thurs, 3-6 Sun; closed Mon.

The Orientale
1520 Wisconsin, NW, FE 8-9203
Far Eastern scrolls, Buddhas, ceramics, sculpture, and furniture abound at this address. You have to have a trained eye to buy here, but James Wanveer, the Dutch proprietor, is only too willing to assist. E; open 10-5 daily; closed Sun.

The Phoenix
1514 Wisconsin, NW, FE 8-4404
The best selection of contemporary Mexican crafts in Washington. Every object is hand picked, from the brightly painted clay pigeons to the unusual flowers made of newspaper and magazine covers. Tiny pre-Columbian heads begin at $12.50. E, C, M; open 10-6 daily; closed Sun; closed Sun, Mon summer. Ask for the free catalog.

Le Bazar
1510 Wisconsin, NW, FE 8-9130
The sign on the door reads "From Cazbah to Ginza; Spoken French, Italian, Turkish, Spanish, Greek, Abrabian, Armenian," and this should give you an idea of the international flavor of the place. Yoù have to be selective here; the better items are upstairs. E.

Krupsaw's Antique Shop
1420 Wisconsin, NW, 338-2229
You can find two floors of excellent quality European and Oriental *objets d'art,* furniture, chandeliers, and porcelains in these elegant quarters; the collection of English silver is outstanding. An; open 9-5 daily, closed Sun; closed Sun, Mon, July-Aug.

Arpad & Henry, Inc.
1400 Wisconsin, NW (corner O), FE 7-3424
121 King, Alexandria, Va., KI 9-9225
Many treasures are available among the hodge-podge accumulated

here, many priced in the lower ranges. This charming corner shop, with its floor-to-ceiling bookcases in the back, provides many services for the art collector: advice on how to start a collection, appraising and authenticating, fine repairs such as china restoration, silver plating, silversmith and goldsmith work done on the premises. Mrs. Arpad tells me that fifty per cent of the business is in the low- and medium-priced brackets. You'll like this friendly shop. An, Authenticating, Restore; open 9:30-5:30 daily, closed Sun; closed weekends July-Aug.

Artist's Mart
1361 Wisconsin, NW, FE 3-5336
The stock is extremely varied, both in style and medium, in Washington's oldest cooperative gallery. There are two floors in which to browse, as well as the bamboo-lined sculpture courtyard. A, C, G, R, Install; open 10-5 daily, closed Sun; 10-4 daily, closed Sun summer.

Georgetown Graphics
3207 O, NW, 333-6308
This is the largest collection of good inexpensive graphics in town. A ten per cent discount is given to students and teachers. The gallery handles primarily contemporary printmakers like Leonard Baskin ($25 up), Sister Mary Corita ($25 up), and Zao Wou-Ki ($35), and has a stock of some four hundred Daumier lithographs for $10 apiece. G; open 12-5 Tues-Sat, 2-5 Sun; closed Mon.

The Early American Shop
1317-19-23-25 Wisconsin, NW, FE 3-5843
The city's largest selection of seventeenth- through early ninetenth-century American furniture is housed in this multi-roomed shop, with a choice ranging from the most formal to the most provincial styles. Everything is in excellent condition, and they will ship anywhere. An, A; open 11-5:30 Mon-Sat, 7-9 Mon-Fri; closed Sun.

Pagoda
3116 M, NW, 338-0671
Turning into M St., you find this handsome Oriental specialty shop. Everything is in the best of taste: screens, scrolls, lacquerware, toys, paper objects, et cetera. The store also carries Japanese lacquer, and Thai and Cambodian sculpture. E; open 10-6 daily; closed Sun.

Washington Gallery of Art
3005 M, NW, 337-9708
The gallery's name is somewhat deceptive, as it carries pre-Colum-

bian primitives as well as offering an extensive roster of European, Latin American, and U.S. contemporaries. A, Eu, E, F, A-R, Install; open 11-6 daily; closed Sun; 10-4 daily June-July; closed Aug.

Miscellanea

As in most United States cities, university art departments, art schools, churches, theaters, and restaurants in Washington feature art exhibitions. Or there are special art events, such as the annual WASHINGTON ANTIQUES SHOW, held every January at the Sheraton-Park Hotel (watch the newspapers for exact dates). Student art, some of which is good and can be purchased for lower prices, is available through the following:

Corcoran School of Art
17th and N.Y. Aves., ME 8-3211

American University
Massachusetts and Nebraska Aves., 244-6800

University of Maryland
College Park, Md., WA 7-3800

George Washington University
2029 G, NW, FE 8-0250

Mt. Vernon Junior Art Gallery
2100 Foxhall Rd., FE 3-1400

Howard University
2400 6th, NW, DU 7-6100

Catholic University
620 Michigan Ave., NE, LA 9-6000

All of these schools have student shows, and you can contact their art departments for the time and the place.

Where to Look

Before you buy, you should look, and the many public collections in Washington provide ample opportunity for educating your eye. There is also a *Brief Guide to Museums in the Washington, D.C.* Area available for 25 cents at all Smithsonian Museum branches.

American Art, Antiques

The White House
1600 Penna. Ave., NW
Since Mrs. Jacqueline Kennedy turned this home of Presidents into a national museum, it has become one of the best places to view our country's cultural and artistic heritage. Open 10-noon, Tues-Sat; guidebook: $1.25.

The Corcoran Gallery of Art
New York and 17th, 638-3211
One of the most notable American art collections in the country, ranging from the early eighteenth century to the present. The building, designed by Ernest Flagg in 1897, is an interesting architectural document of that period. Authentication of American art by appointment; will recommend appraisers, restorers, framers; metered parking on three sides of the Gallery; free admission. Open 10-4 Tues-Fri, 9-4:30 Sat, 2-5 Sun; closed Mon, Christmas Day, July 4th; open 2-5 other public holidays.

The Old Stone House
3051 M, NW
An authentic eighteenth-century American home, with furnishings of that period. Admission is free. Open 1-5 Wed-Sun.

Modern Art

The Phillips Collection
1600 and 1612 21st, NW, 387-2151
Displays modern art and its sources in a charming old home and its modern addition. It also features one-man exhibitions of contemporary artists. Concerts on Sundays. Admission is free; open 11-6 Tues-Sat, 11-10 Mon, 2-7 Sun; closed Christmas and Labor Day, July 4th.

The Washington Gallery of Modern Art
1503 21st, NW, 667-5221
W.G.M.A. has become a major force for contemporary art in Washington since its inception in the early 1960s. Admission is free to members, $1 for non-members; open 10-5 Tues-Wed, 10-10 Thurs-Fri, 11-5 Sat-Sun.

Graphics

The National Archives
Constitution at 7th, NW, 963-1110
Has changing exhibitions of prints and watercolors, as well as displays of important national documents. Admission is free; open 9-10 daily, 1-10 Sun and holidays.

The Library of Congress
Independence and First, SE, 783-0400
An excellent collection of all kinds of graphics can be found in its Print Department. Admission is free; open 9-5:30 Mon-Fri.

Smithsonian Institution, Graphic Arts Department
Museum of History and Technology, 12th and Constitution, 381-5235
A good, growing collection of prints with an interesting display of print processes on the floor below. Admission is free; open 8:45-5:15 Mon-Fri.

Primitive Art

The Museum of African Art
316 A, NE
The only museum in the United States devoted exclusively to African art. The collection is housed in a lovely old home once occupied by Abolitionist Frederick Douglass. Admission 35¢; open 11-6 Mon-Wed, 2-5 Sat, Sun; closed Thurs, Fri.

The Robert Woods Collection of Pre-Columbian Art,
Dumbarton Oaks Research Library and Collection
R and 32nd, NW
Part of the fun of going to this small, but excellent, primitive arts collection, is seeing Philip Johnson's jewel of an architectural design which houses it. An excellent handbook of the collection sells for $1. Admission is free; open 2-5 except Mon; closed summer.

Museum of American Indian Art
Department of the Interior, C (18-19th), NW.
Near the C St. entrance are some handsome examples of silver, basketry, and pottery work among the canoes and moose heads. Walking toward the building's center, you will find several cases of excellent Eskimo art. Admission is free; open 8-4 Mon-Fri.

Religious Art

B'nai B'rith
17th and Rhode Island
Houses a good collection of Hebraic art, as well as displaying changing exhibitions of contemporary Israel painters.

The Islamic Center Museum
2551 Mass., NW
Offers a good chance to see handsome Persian carpets and tile work from the Middle East.

Rare Books

The Library of Congress
Independence and First, SE
Has continuous displays of early printing examples on the first floor. It also owns the famed Lessing J. Rosenwald collection of rare books, which can be seen here and at Rosenwald's "Alverthorpe" Gallery in Jenkintown, Pa. Admission is free; open 9 a.m.-10 p.m. daily; closed Sun, holidays.

Oriental Art

The Freer Gallery of Art
Smithsonian Institution, 12th and Jefferson Dr.
One of the world's finest collections of Far and Middle Eastern art. Authentications, by appointment, Wed. afternoon; admission free; open 9-4:30 daily.

Textiles

The Textile Museum
2330 S, NW
One of Washington's least known museums, but one of its finest; the cache of several thousand Peruvian textiles is the best anywhere. There's also a complete library on the textile arts. Admission is free; open 1-5 Mon-Fri.

The Smithsonian Institution
The Mall, 628-1810
Endowed by James Smithson as an "institution for the increase and

diffusion of knowledge among men," almost a world unto itself, the Smithsonian is here listed separately because of its many different divisions, functions, and buildings. The best way of sorting them out is to buy the Institution's handy guide book. It is well to remember the Smithsonian is both a scientific and cultural conclave, and that only some of its many parts are devoted to art. Courses for adults and children, Associates of the Smithsonian. Admission is free; open every day except Christmas 9-4:30 Sept 1-March 31, 9 a.m.-10 p.m. Apr 1-Aug 31; authentications by appointment.

The National Gallery of Art
10th and Constitution, 737-4215
Perhaps the Smithsonian's most famous building; houses some of the world's great masterpieces of Western art. The collections are particularly strong in Italian Renaissance and seventeenth-century Dutch painting, while the recent addition of the Chester Dale collection of modern art has given strength in that field also. The Gallery features numerous free lectures, a radio program, concerts, publications, and films; be sure to get on their free mailing list for their monthly announcements. Authentication by appointment on Wed, call the curator's office first; credit courses offered with George Washington University; free admission; open 10-5 Mon-Sat, 2-10 Sun, except April 1-Labor Day 10-10 Mon-Sat, noon-10 Sun; closed Christmas and New Year's Day.

The Freer Gallery
12th and Jefferson Dr.
Has already been named for the excellence of its Orientalia collections. Free lectures are also featured.

The National Collection of Fine Arts
10th and Constitution, NA 8-1810
The Collection led a rather peripatetic life, but moved to the historic Patent Office Building recently. Parts of the Collection include a graphics division and the Smithsonian Traveling Exhibition Service. Not devoted solely to older American art, it is now providing stiff competition to the Corcoran and Washington Gallery of Modern Art with its lively, contemporary exhibitions.

The National Portrait Gallery
The Smithsonian's newest service is also located now in the Old Patent Building at 8th and E, NW. All the other buildings are located on the Mall, where there is free two-hour parking.

RICHMOND, VA.

By F. D. Cossitt, Art Critic, *The Richmond Times-Dispatch*

Richmond is dominated by the avant-garde art department of the RICHMOND PROFESSIONAL INSTITUTE on one hand and more conservative groups like the RICHMOND ARTISTS AS-SOCIATION on the other. Amazingly good work is being produced here, in spite of the provincial locale, by fifteen to twenty first-rate painters and sculptors. The hundreds of others range from good to ghastly.

The public is interested in art (although the avant-garde doesn't sell here and must go to Washington, D.C., or New York City) and is fairly good about buying. The VIRGINIA MUSEUM OF FINE ARTS is here, which helps, although its orientation is decidedly *not* contemporary.

The best low-cost art buying opportunities are provided by students (RPI), street sales, and auctions, although you need a good eye, most of the work being very bad.

The best source of information about Richmond art is the weekly art column in the Sunday paper.

Where to Buy

The Eric Schindler Gallery
2305 E. Broad, 644-5005
Schindler's is located in the historic Church Hill section of Richmond, site of the church where Patrick Henry made his "Give me liberty" speech, and now undergoing renewal like Georgetown in Washington. The Gallery has been in operation for nearly ten years and is the most stable in Virginia. It handles rather conservative work, some of which is run-of-the-mill, some of which is quite good. All is by living artists except for prints, of which they have a fair selection. Prices from $10 on prints, from $50 on oils. Parking next door. A-R, F, Install, R; open 9:30-4:30 Mon-Sat; by appointment Sun, evenings; 12-4 Mon-Sat summer.

Hand Work Shop
316 N. 24th St., 649-0674
Specializing in Virginia crafts of quality. Weaving, pottery, woodwork, jewelry—also some good reproductions (glass by Blenko, etc.). A non-profit organization that also teaches crafts and fills mail orders. Open 10-5 weekdays, 2-5 Sun.

The Hand Work-Shop, Richmond, Virginia.

Art Market
1037 W. Broad, 353-7893
Has a small gallery (it is basically an art supply and frame shop).
It handles a variety of work, occasionally avant-garde. R; open 9-5,
closed Sun.

Art Festivals and Competitions

The RPI SPRING ARTS FESTIVAL: an avant-garde affair with
Happenings, et cetera. In the past, they have had such artists as
John Cage, Barnett Newman, Larry Rivers, Roy Lichtenstein. The
Virginia Museum's BIENNIAL VIRGINIA ARTISTS show, is
juried and open to all residents of the state. THALHIMER'S DE-
PARTMENT STORE BIENNIAL INVITATIONAL is also
juried. There are many lesser affairs of this sort. The JEWISH
COMMUNITY CENTER, for example, sponsors a good exhibits
program featuring an annual invitational in painting and a separate
one in sculpture, plus an annual UNDISCOVERED ARTISTS
SHOW, at 5403 Monument, AT 8-6091, from 9-10 p.m.; parking
lot. Yearly group shows are also put on by the RICHMOND
ARTISTS ASSOCIATION, the WEST END ALLIED ARTISTS,
and the JAMES RIVER ART LEAGUE.

Where to Look

The Virginia Museum of Fine Arts
Blvd. and Grove, MI 4-4111
An energetic, hard-driving museum that has pioneered in many
areas of the arts, particularly in bringing arts to the people. It is,
in the best sense of the word, a culture center. Among its
many innovations are its Artmobile, a huge, air-conditioned
"gallery on wheels" that carries original art from the Museum
throughout the state; organization of a unique Statewide Con-
federation of Arts groups, whereby cultural centers are established
all over Virginia; a Collectors' Circle, a group of museum members who collect original art with a curator's advice; a resident
craftsmen program in weaving and ceramics; the Loan-Own art
rental service, which contains over one thousand works by qualified
Virginia artists; sales in the Council Shop of works by the resident
weaver and ceramicist; and strong, permanent collections in European and Oriental traditional arts. Admission 50¢ per visitor over
16, weekends free; authentication by appointment; credit courses
with RPI, for museum members only; parking. Open 1-5 and 8-10
Tues-Sat, 1-5 Sun; closed Mon.

The Valentine Museum
1015 E. Clay, 649-0711
The Valentine calls itself "The Museum of the Life and History of Richmond." It boasts the third largest costume collection in the country; material on North Carolina and Virginia Indians dating back to 1500 B.C.; a research library on the history of Richmond and Virginia; and the famous 1812 Georgian-style WICKHAM-VALENTINE HOUSE. Authentication of costumes, decorative arts, household furnishings. Admission 50¢ adults, 25¢ students except Sun when free. Open 10-5 Mon-Sat, 2:30-5 Sun.

The Richmond Public Library
101 E. Franklin, 649-4740
The Library has one gallery for professional art exhibits, another for amateurs. Also lectures and demonstrations by out-of-town artists. Open 9-9 Mon-Fri. 9-5 Sat.

WILLIAMSBURG, VA.

Colonial Williamsburg
229-1000
This is one of the most fascinating of the United States outdoor museums. For nearly a century the little city was the capital of the Virginia colony, and its eighteenth-century buildings, furnishings, and gardens have been restored to perfection. There are seven Exhibition Buildings and many other houses and shops where you can see craftsmen working with the early implements and materials. Reproductions of many Williamsburg antiques, carrying the Williamsburg label, are for sale at the Craft House, but here, I'm afraid, you pay for the name. The illustrated catalog, available by mail, is $2.50. Open 9-5 daily for most buildings.

Abby Aldrich Rockefeller Folk Art Collection
229-1000
The Collection is housed in a charming building adjacent to the Williamsburg Inn and Craft House. Designed as a museum but suggesting domestic interiors of the nineteenth century, the Collection provides a perfect setting for a topnotch cache of Early Americana. Over eight hundred examples—oil paintings, watercolors, pastels, pen drawings, wood and metal sculptures—are displayed in changing exhibitions. Scheduled gallery talks are provided. Free admission; open 12-9 Tues-Sat, closed Sun, Mon.

House of Eight Winds
Duke of Gloucester, 229-6699
One of the best outlets for authentic American Indian art in the country. The stock ranges from New Mexican pottery to Alaskan blockprints, from colorful basketry and beadwork to intricately woven rugs. The moderate prices are $10-$275. Parking; M, Install. Open 9-6 daily, 1-5 Sun; 9 a.m.-10 p.m. daily, 1-10 Sun summer.

The Twentieth-Century Gallery
Nicholson Street
A first-rate, non-profit operation, located in the restored area near the Gaol on Nicholson Street, the gallery carries much of the best painting and sculpture being done in Virginia, and also draws artists from up and down the Eastern seaboard. Open 12-5 Tues-Sat, 2-5 Sun; closed Mon.

The South

CRAFTS
IN THE MOUNTAIN AREAS OF
MARYLAND, THE VIRGINIAS, THE
CAROLINAS, GEORGIA, KENTUCKY,
TENNESSEE AND ALABAMA

By Robert W. Gray, Director
Southern Highland Handicraft Guild, Inc., Asheville, N.C.

In the Southern Appalachian region there is a demand for crafts which exceeds the supply, and many of the professional craftsmen of the region earn a very good living through the sale of their handmade items. A recent survey of the market in this area showed annual retail sales of handmade items to exceed five million dollars.

It is true you hear a few craftsmen here complain about not being able to sell their entire production. There are several reasons for these complaints: the craftsman is not making quality (salable) product and will not change; he is not skilled enough to produce efficiently so the price is right; or he does not know how to contact the market.

Our Guild sponsors four retail gift shops for members' work and two annual Craftsman's Fairs. The Guild also circulates exhibits of members' work, and some sales are made from exhibits.

The Guild has been actively promoting the sale of handicrafts for thirty-six years. We have on file a large number of gift shops which would like to buy from us at wholesale cost. If we could get the products from craftsmen in the quantity we need, we could more than quadruple the sales of handwork in this area.

Some of our members, of which a number are outstanding craftsmen, use only the Guild outlets for their wholesale market. Others use the Guild outlets and other shops; some use their studio for

A hound carved of native buckeye with a natural finish. Work similar to this is available through the Southern Highland Handicraft Guild, Asheville, North Carolina. (*Photograph by Edward L. DuPuy*)

wholesale and retail sales of their products; and a few do not use the Guild for any type of sales at all.

The crafts which are sold the most are jewelry, pottery, and woodcarvings. Others include dolls, doll furniture, blown glass, hooked items, marquetry, objects made of native materials (cones, burrs, nuts, and pods), whimmydiddles, et cetera. We also publish a booklet, *Crafts in the Southern Highlands*.

The major competition open to all craftsmen in the Southeast is the Piedmont Craft Exhibition at the Mint Museum in Charlotte, N.C.

The annual CRAFTSMAN'S FAIRS (for Guild members only) in Asheville, North Carolina, the third week in July, and Gatlinburg, Tennessee, the third week in October, are the major sales and craft demonstrations of the region. Various crafts are available from a dollar up.

The major crafts outlets in the region are the following Guild shops:

Parkway Craft Center
Blowing Rock, N. C., 295-3738
Open May 1-Oct 3, 9-6 daily.

Allanstand
16 College, Asheville, N. C., 253-2051
Open 9-5 daily; closed Sun. M.

Guild Gallery
The Mall, Shelbyville Rd., Louisville, Ky., 896-1834
Open 10-9 daily.

Guild Crafts
930 Tunnel, Asheville, N. C., 298-7928
Open 9-5; closed Sun. Mail orders.

Others in the area are:

Midland Crafters
Pinehurst, N. C.
Robert Stearns runs this shop.

Arrowcraft
Gatlinburg, Tenn., 436-4604
Open Mon-Sat, 8-8 June 1-Aug 31.

12 Designer Craftsmen
Gatlinburg, Tenn., 436-4198

Log Cabin Gift Shop
Berea, Ky.
Open 9-6 daily; closed Sun.

CHARLESTON, S. C.

The art flavor of Charleston is best expressed in an excerpt from *The Lively Arts of Charleston,* a booklet published by the Junior League of Charleston in 1963:

The same brisk spirit of individualism which characterizes the history of Charleston flourishes today in its lively arts. For the arts in Charleston are unique, personal and deeply rooted in the lives of the people. Scores of local artists, writers, actors, dancers, musicians, antiquarians strive, creatively, to enrich the present and work diligently to preserve the gifts of the past. The culture of any community begins with intangibles . . . ways of living and thinking, attitudes and manners, the character of the people. The grace and elegance of the eighteenth century has left Charleston not only a wealth of beautiful architecture but a strong respect for the value of continuity. The changing world of the twentieth century has brought new people, new ideas and the opportunity for fresh evaluation.

There are many artists in Charleston, but there is no one "school" of art. The local art museum and general museum are well attended, but have to share public support with four historical museums and three historic houses. The National Park Service also maintains two historic forts in the immediate vicinity.

Those paintings that portray the picturesque qualities of the city and area—chromatic façades, rooftop patterns, moss-hung live oaks, birds and other wildlife—are the best sellers with tourist buyers. However, the artists whose work most often reflects today's art trends, though not large in number, have no difficulty in selling their work. The only local professional sculptor receives commissions from many places in the Southeast.

Information about Art

For information about art events in Charleston, *The News and Courier* carries a "Lively Arts" calendar on Sundays (Oct-May). A monthly magazine, *Gateway,* lists an events calendar also. And

WCSC-TV carries a calendar of this type each Monday. Unfortunately, neither of the local papers carries art reviews or criticisms.

Where to Buy

Antiques

George C. Birlant & Co.
191 King
Also an auctioneer and appraiser.

Colonial Antique Shop
193 King

The Goat Cart
O St. Michael's Alley
Sells on consignment.

Jack Patla Co.
181 King

Garnier's
198 King

Schindler's Antique Shop
200 King
A very large collection of paintings by William Aiken Walker.

Contemporary Art

Carolina Prints & Frames
158 King
Run by Raymond Holsclaw, this gallery sells work of artists from the Eastern Seaboard states, as well as artists' supplies. Framing.

Emmett Johnson Decorative Arts
38 Queen
A frame and specialty shop.

The Art Store
183 King
Artists' supplies, framing.

Gordon's Art Shop
208 King
Local reproductions and framing.

View into the library, the Nathaniel Russell House, Charleston, South Carolina. (Photograph by Louis Schwartz—*courtesy Historic Charleston Foundation*)

Interior view, the Slave Mart, Charleston, South Carolina.

The Slave Mart
6 Chalmers, 722-0079
Local artists and arts and crafts from Africa; devoted specifically to showing Negro arts and crafts and showing how they relate to their cultural roots in Africa.

Local artists who sell from their studios include the following:

Contemporary Styles

William Halsey
38 State, 723-5966

Corrie McCallum
38 State, 723-5966

Cheves Clark
1447 Mataoka, Mt. Pleasant, 884-9478

John Muller
1767 Pittsford C1, 766-6010

Julia Homer Wilson
34 Chalmers, 722-8687

Ann Karesh
751 Woodward, 766-7716

Sallie Frost Knerr
Isle of Palms, 886-6882

Faith Murray
Edisto Island, S.C.

Willard Hirsch
17 Exchange, 723-1635
Sculptor

Landscapes (Pastels, Watercolors)

Elizabeth O'Neill Verner
38 Tradd, 722-4246
The studio is housed in Charleston's first "Sweet-Shop."

E. deMay Smith
3 Greenhill, 723-6354

Minnie Mikell
71 E. Bay, 723-3502

Primarily Portraits

Ray Goodbred
147 Beaufain, 722-0215

Alicia Rhett
59 Tradd, 723-4643

Birds and Nature

Anne Worsham Richardson
7 Arcadian Park, 766-2298

Edward Von S. Dingle
Middleburg Plantation, Huger, Moncks Corner, 825-1357

John Henry Dick
Dixie Plantation, Meggett, 766-9800

Sallie Ellington Middleton
17 Logan, 723-3815

Miscellanea

Kerrison's Department Store
260-62 King
Occasionally has exhibitions and sales of work by selected artists, usually Corrie McCallum and William Halsey.

Fort Sumter Hotel
On display in the lobby is work by E. deMay Smith and Elizabeth O'Neill Verner.

Charleston Artist Guild
This is an organization of about one hundred practicing artists, chiefly painters. It has two sales exhibitions annually: in February, in the Green Room of the Dock Street Theatre, and in late March or early April out of doors. It also has monthly meetings from October to April with lecturers, films, and workshops.

Where to Look

Gibbes Art Gallery–Carolina Art Association
135 Meeting, 722-0133
Gibbes holds monthly exhibits of local, regional, national, and international art, in addition to its permanent collections of American paintings and sculpture, European and Oriental graphics, and

Chinese decorative art. Original art sold only in connection with the annual state show and during certain exhibitions. The price range is usually $25 to $800, and the Gallery takes no commissions on sales. Admission is free. Authentication of American painting and miniatures may be had by appointment. The gallery is open 10-5 Tues-Sat, 1-6 Sun; closed Mon, New Year's, Independence Day, Labor Day, Thanksgiving, Christmas.

The Charleston Museum
125 Rutledge, 722-2996

This was founded by the Charleston, S.C., Library Society in 1773, the first museum in the U.S. Although essentially a natural and cultural history museum, its collections contain fine arts and decorative arts objects from the Near East, Mediterranean countries in the Classical periods, and the Orient. Its South Carolina collections are especially noteworthy, including period rooms, costumes, furniture, and silver, with emphasis on local cabinetmakers and silversmiths. The Museum also has two historic-house branches: the HEYWARD-WASHINGTON HOUSE, 87 Church St., dating from 1770, with Georgian architecture, Chippendale-style furniture; and the JOSEPH MANIGAULT HOUSE, 350 Meeting St., from 1810, an Adam-style house with early nineteenth-century furnishings. Admission is free; 10-5 daily, 2-5 Sun and holidays; closed Christmas.

Historic Charleston Foundation
51 Meeting, RA 3-1168

This is a non-profit foundation dedicated to the preservation of Charleston's historic and architectural heritage. The NATHANIEL RUSSELL HOUSE, an unusually beautiful example of Adam architecture, serves as its headquarters. The house, which was built shortly before 1809, has been called an "elegant exercise in ellipses." The Foundation also runs tours in the spring through other historic Charleston houses and publishes a map of its tours. The Russell House is open 10-1 and 2-5 daily, 2-5 Sun, Christmas Day; $1 admission.

ATLANTA, GA.

By Carlyn Fisher
Art Critic, *Atlanta Magazine*

If one had in mind the purchase of an original work of art, it would be possible to shop in some twenty-eight different establishments in the city of Atlanta. Swinging from the DZIRKALIS GAL-LERY, which for six years has successfully catered to lovers of antique European paintings, to the spanking new HEATH GAL-LERY, which recently has leaned toward those of modern per-suasion, there is quite a bountiful choice. However, of these twenty-eight, less than half should be classified as bona fide galleries whose main concern is the promotion and sale of original works of art.

None of the galleries is over six years old, and each reports a steady increase in sales and attendance. Each notes also that it is the students and young couples who are the most interested and who do the most buying. In an *Atlanta* survey of the leading deal-ers, all reported that they felt the taste in art of the Atlanta public is definitely on the upswing. Most think their future in the art busi-ness is bright and are generally optimistic.

However, the history of art dealings in Atlanta has not always been so rosy. It was in 1946 that the first real gallery opened its doors in a renovated house on Ellis Street and was resoundingly ignored by almost everyone. Called simply THE GALLERY, this pioneering effort was made by two well-qualified ladies, Eleanor Storza and Vienna-born Anna Felber. The gallery had an old-world elegance and was in every sense excellent.

Works by such famed masters as Peter Paul Rubens, Anthony Van Dyke, Jacob van Ruisdael, Amedeo Modigliani, and Jackson Pollock graced its walls. But at the time the High Museum was too poor, and the public too indifferent, to buy these treasures.

"Atlanta was absolutely not ready for the gallery," states Anna Felber. We had a magnificent Monet—"Waterlilies"—and people hardly looked at it. It seemed so bad to them. We also had a very good Picasso. We went to untold trouble, making four trips a year to New York to beg and plead for top quality work to exhibit. It was truly heartbreaking in many ways."

The two struggled doggedly on, hoping eventually the import-ance of what they were doing would be understood. In its seventh season, The Gallery offered shows of work by local artists. This proved to be their last valiant attempt. The Gallery died, with very few mourners.

A few months after the demise of The Gallery, Atlanta painter Ed Ross opened an exhibition of contemporary British paintings and drawings by such luminaries as Ben Nicholson, John Piper, and Graham Sutherland. The space was small, being a converted por-tion of his studio in the basement of an old wooden house on Thirteenth Street.

Here for the first time was established in the city a gallery devoted exclusively to the exhibition and sale of modern art. During the following months works by regional as well as local artists were shown. Selected and hung with care and discernment, the paintings in this little gallery offered a gourmet feast for anyone who bothered to make his way through the door.

Expenses were slight, and the gallery broke even its first year. But the effort and time involved in running it became a great burden to Ed Ross who was, first and foremost, a painter.

In 1953 the ARTS FESTIVAL OF ATLANTA burst into life with the avowed purpose of introducing the city to her artists, and her artists to the city. With its birth came an opportunity for people from all over town to see that there were some gifted and serious artists in their midst. Held in Piedmont Park in the spring, the Festival enabled crowds of Atlantans for the first time to see original drawings, paintings, sculpture, and handicrafts, and the seeds of interest in the visual arts were scattered throughout the community. But the Festival lasts only one week in May, and the other fifty-one were empty indeed.

Finally, in 1959, Judy Alexander, returning to Atlanta after a five-year study of art in Pennsylvania and New York, decided to open a gallery. Calling it first The New Arts, then changing the name to THE ALEXANDER, she founded it in a two-story white frame house on Peachtree Road.

Out of inner necessity on her part, Miss Alexander soon made the gallery the center of the most avant-garde activities in town. The then little-known James Dickey read his poetry to small but rapt audiences in the main room; painter Ad Reinhardt came from New York and talked to a packed house about his controversial purist philosophy of art, saying, "Art is art-as-art, and everything else is everything else. Art-as-art is nothing but art. Art is not what is not art . . ." and thereby stirred up a hot debate.

Talks on Zen Buddhism by a Japanese scholar, lectures on modern drama, politics, and music were equally welcomed. The gallery sponsored a concert of original compositions by two Atlantans, Dick Robinson and Margaret Fairlie; and Miss Alexander thus became the only one to have so honored these able composers in their own town, though both have received recognition in other parts of the world.

Not the least of her educational efforts was in the form of major exhibits from some of America's modern pioneering artists, including a show of important canvases by the late Franz Kline. Her primary energies were devoted to the promotion of those local painters and sculptors whom she felt deserved recognition. Being

A corner of the Signature Shop, Atlanta, Georgia.

(Left) Interior view, Heath's Gallery, Atlanta, Georgia. (Right) Interior view, Artists Associates, Inc., Atlanta, Georgia.

Interior view, Dzirkalis Art Gallery, Atlanta, Georgia.

possessed of a keenly sensitive and well-trained eye, she uncovered many unknowns, giving them one-man shows and generally promoting their work.

In December, 1965, the Alexander Gallery closed. The building in which it was housed had been sold and scheduled for demolition. Miss Alexander continues to act as agent for the artists she represents.

Wavering between optimism and pessimism over what she has or has not accomplished, she questions whether a gallery of the caliber of The Alexander can prosper in Atlanta. On the one hand, it has been greatly appreciated by those who knew what she was about, but, on the other, it had been a continual financial struggle. This was partly, she admits, because as a businesswoman she left something to be desired, but also because what she was sponsoring was understood by so few. The Franz Kline show, which was of prime cultural importance, had been unheralded and badly attended. And this was true of many of her most daring exhibits.

The past twenty years have been a tedious stretch for the art market in Atlanta, but times and tastes seem to be slowly changing for the better. New galleries, like the Heath, have opened, and somehow have managed to keep going. Perhaps at last it is no longer so much a decision of whether or not to shop the galleries, but more a question of which gallery to shop. That's a good sign.

Where to Buy

Academy Theatre
3213 Roswell, N.E., 233-9481
Art exhibits in lobby. Open 7-11 p.m. Wed-Sat.

Allison Art Acres
3940 N. Peachtree, Chamblee, 457-3080
A combined gallery and school run by the energetic Jean and Jack Allison, this art outlet features mainly American contemporaries. Also handmade and wheel-thrown pottery from Georgia clay. F, Install. Open 10-5 Tues-Sat, 7-9 p.m. Tues and Thurs, 2-6 Sun; parking available.

Catherine Hughes Waddell Art Gallery
Trevor Arnett Library, Atlanta University
Fine examples of contemporary art, including examples of contemporary works by William Thon, Robert Vickery, Edwin Dickinson, I. Rice Pereira, Lee, and Gaton. Also a very complete as-

semblage of works by contemporary Negro artists in America and an African art collection. Admission is free.

Artists Associates, Inc.
1105 Peachtree, N.E., 984-5228
An artists' cooperative that has fine shows by members and guests. You can always see the members' work in the back room. Paintings, prints, drawings, sculpture. Open 11-4 Mon, 10-5 Tues-Sat, 2-6 Sun.

Atlanta Jewish Community Center
1745 Peachtree, N.E., 875-7881
Tasteful, good exhibits. Open 9 a.m.-11 p.m. Mon-Thurs, 9-5 Fri, 9 a.m.-11 p.m. Sun.

Dzirkalis Art Gallery
33 Peachtree, N.E., 525-9994
Mr. Dzirkalis is a Middle-Eastern gentleman with some of the finest Old Master paintings in town at $500 up. Authentication. Open 10-5 Mon-Sat.

Fine Arts Gallery
935 W. Peachtree, N.W., 876-5610
A small, hole-in-the-wall gallery that features younger artists. Open 10-5 Tues-Sat, 2-6 Sun.

Georgia State College
33 Gilmer, S.E., 523-7681
The young, aggressive art department usually features good student and guest shows. Open 9 a.m.-10 p.m. Mon-Fri.

Hamilton House Gallery
3252 Peachtree, N.E., 237-3116
Exhibits local artists. Open 9:30-5 Mon-Fri.

Heart of Atlanta Art Gallery
255 Courtland, N.E., 688-1682
Representational European paintings in the motel lobby. Open 9 a.m.-10 p.m. every day; parking; American Express charge.

Heath's Gallery
62 Ponce de Leon, N.E., 876-1468
The gallery is housed in the Fox Theatre building, an eclectic "mosque" structure that is a landmark in downtown Atlanta. Specializes in quality prints and drawings by such artists as Matisse, Picasso, Miró, Arp, Baskin, and Pozzatti. One-man exhibitions

in other mediums also. Parking; A, F. Open 9:30-6 Tues-Sat, 3-6 Sun.

Gavant Gallery
3889 Peachtree, N.E., 233-3938
European contemporaries; contemporary Atlanta and regional works also, at $5-$500. Parking; F, R. Open 10-5:30 daily, 4-8 Sun.

Jens Risom Design, Inc.
351 Peachtree Hills Ave., N.E., 237-9223
A furniture-manufacturing firm that has continuing one-man, contemporary shows of paintings. Rental, installment arrangements with artists. Open 9-5 Mon-Fri.

Little Gallery, Franklin Simon
640 Peachtree, N.E., 872-8801
Contemporary paintings, prints. Open 9:30 a.m.-9 p.m. Mon and Fri, 9:30-6 Tues-Thurs, Sat.

Mandorla Gallery
40 14th, N.E., 875-8892
Colorful, high-quality art, displayed in a converted old house. Two owners, one a craftsman in leather, the other in handmade jewelry. Some of the best art being produced in the South. Parking; Install. Open 11 a.m.-9 p.m. Tues-Sat, 1-6 Sun, closed Mon.

O'Karma's Art Gallery
1050 Spring, N.W., 874-9461
All media, all styles except avant-garde. Specializes in eighteenth- and nineteenth-century oils and fine prints. Parking; F, A-R, Install, Credit Card Corp. of America charge. Open 8:30-5 Mon-Fri, 8:30-4 Sat.

Pocket Theatre
535 Courtland, N.E., 874-9751
Avant-garde art along with the theater offerings. Open 10-6 and at show time, Mon-Sat.

Signature Shop
3267 Roswell, N.W., 237-4232
Outstanding crafts and handwork, a first-class place to buy original and fine decorator items. Carries jewelry, weavings, ceramics from top Southern and national craftsmen. A good place to find unusual items of top quality. Parking; M, Install. Open 10-5 Mon-Sat.

Southwest Artists League Gallery
Fulton Federal Savings and Loan Assn.
2357 Sewell, 522-2300
Local artists shown here. Open 9-4 Mon-Fri.

Spelman College
Rockefeller F.A. Bldg., 350 Leonard, 523-1056
Student and guest exhibits in the Long Gallery. Open 9-5 Mon-Fri,
9-noon Sat, 2-5 Sun.

Willens Galleries
349 Peachtree Hills, N.E., 237-2991
Wall decor in all media, fine prints. By appointment.

Miscellanea

Atlanta's eight-day ARTS FESTIVAL, held in Piedmont Park
every May, is an outstanding event featuring really fine works of
arts and crafts (including weaving, pottery, jewelry, etc.) all by
local and regional artists. Evening performances by local perform-
ing-arts groups are also very rewarding.

Atlanta is now constructing a twelve-million-dollar CULTURAL
CENTER which will house our performing and visual arts as well
as the ATLANTA SCHOOL OF ART. It will provide a permanent
home for the Atlanta Symphony and also house our High Museum,
and is scheduled for completion in the fall of 1968.

Where to Look

The High Museum of Art
1280 Peachtree, N.E., 876-8332
The Museum, soon to be housed permanently in Atlanta's Cultural
Center, offers a collection of mainly Western art from the early
Renaissance to the present day. It includes the Kress Collection of
Italian paintings and sculpture from Northern Europe. Its Museum
Art Shop changes its sale-exhibit of juried original art every two
months. And the Museum's library recently received a Samuel H.
Kress Foundation grant for ten thousand dollars to enrich its
library. It is open 1-5 Sun-Mon, 10-5 Tues-Sat, 7-10 p.m. Tues.

Information about Art

Both newspapers and radio station WGKA have Sunday listings
art gallery shows. *Atlanta* magazine has a very detailed monthly

listing plus feature articles on art by its art critic. THE ATLANTA CONVENTION BUREAU, Suite 806, Peachtree Center Bldg., 230 Peachtree, is a good source of information on all the arts in Atlanta.

MIAMI AND MIAMI BEACH, FLA.

By Nellie Bower
Art Critic, *The Miami News*

Owing to the large number of retired residents—the so-called Senior Citizens—emphasis in the Miami area is chiefly on nonprofessional art. However, Miami can also boast of several painters who have achieved a more or less national reputation and a few who are even known abroad, having either lived or exhibited in Italy, Sweden, and Mexico.

Eugene Massin, instructor on the art faculty of the University of Miami, is pretty generally conceded to be number one here. Others among the top men are Tony Scornavacca, twice winner of the thousand-dollar award at the Atlanta High Museum competition; Jack Amoroso, the only Floridian represented at the New York World Fair's Pavilion of Art, 1965; and Robert von Zimmerman, whose larger than life portrait of President John F. Kennedy was purchased for the University of Berlin. In general, though, good women painters outnumber men three or four to one in this community.

I would also say that, in spite of the much vaunted boom in art, interest in galleries and museums is almost nil, except by artists, who pay regular visits when a change of exhibit is advertised or otherwise publicized. A hundred dollars still seems to be a price many buyers have set for a painting, going to three hundred if it's something special. Some painters claim to receive in the high hundreds and even over a thousand, but I take these figures with a grain of salt except in portraiture, where prices are higher.

Where to Buy

Roughly, Miami is divided into the following main areas of activity: Miami proper, Coral Gables (a city in its own right), Coconut Grove, North Miami, and the city of Miami Beach. South Miami, Perrine, and, further south, Homestead, all have their own art clubs and art stores where paintings are sold.

Coral Gables

Joe and Emily Lowe Art Gallery
University of Miami, 1301 Miller Drive, 661-2511

This is considered to be a museum, as it has had several gifts of major art collections. Besides showing sections of these from time to time, the Beaux Arts members, a group of dedicated young women working constantly for the welfare of the Lowe Gallery, have organized a "Lending Library" of paintings, to which local artists contribute. As with most rental galleries, the paintings may also be purchased, with the rental fee applied to the purchase price. Prices range from $50 for a watercolor to a top of $500 for paintings. Parking; authenticating by appointment. Admission is free; 10-5 Tues-Sat, 2-5 Sun, 8-10 p.m. Wed.

Granville Galleries
3929 Ponce de Leon Blvd., 448-8612

Directed by Granville Fisher, dean of psychology at the University of Miami, the Galleries began operations about seven years ago. At the time, the founder stated he wished to help local artists by giving them an opportunity to display their art advantageously. Now he has taken over the entire area of the gallery (a very large space) to use as a studio and showrooms for his own paintings. These range in style from Abstract Expressionism to Expressionistic Realism. Prices are $150-$300, occasionally $1,000. Open late afternoon and evening during school year, regular hours during summer.

Rogues Gallery Two
256 Giraldi, 445-5721

This is a nice-looking place in a new location, run by two women. Once in a while, they show extremely "way-out" work; but it's mostly that of local, moderately good painters. Charles Posner, Marian Smith, Eugenie Schein, Rosana McAllister, and Dionisio Perkins, as well as a rather good Cuban painter, Baruj Salinas, have shown there in the past. Prices run $50-$350.

Rudolph Galleries
338 Sevilla, 443-6005

Its proprietor (of the same name) spends half the year in Woodstock, N.Y., where she also has a gallery. The one here is a fine little place, very tastefully arranged, well equipped to handle sculpture and painting exhibits, of which she has about four a season. Every once in a while she adds a new name, but certain artists—

Milton Avery, Arnold Blanch and his wife, Doris Lee, Sadie Rosenblum, and Robert Phillips—have shown with the gallery since its beginning here twelve years ago.

Village Corner Gallery
1136 S. Dixie Hwy., 661-7411
Opposite the University of Miami, this is actually a shop run by a jeweler who has given space to a gallery. He features exhibits of local painters, plus pieces of sculpture.

Coconut Grove

Mirell Gallery
3421 Main Hwy., 443-9140
Mirell presents a wide range of stock, encompassing Old Masters, museum-quality Pre-Columbian and primitive art, some Oriental art, American art from about 1780 to today, and exhibits of both foreign and local artists. Kenneth Treister, Lisl Beer, McGibbon Brown, Carl Folke Sahlin, Florence Taylor Kushner, and Gertrude Barmat are on the gallery's roster. A-R, R; Old Masters.

Tony Scornavacca
In an alley around the corner from the Mirell is this little place: no exact address available. At one time, Scornavacca, who started out as a mailman and who has gathered quite a following, had a very posh gallery at Miami Beach, but for reasons best known to himself now conducts this one in the arty atmosphere of the Grove.

Robert von Zimmerman
19 Anthony Arcade
This artist shows his own watercolors and oils.

Down East Gallery
2983 McFarlane, 443-9609
Artie McKenzie, another painter who shows mainly his own work, runs this gallery. His big business is in seascapes, which he paints with great facility. It's closed May-Oct, when he is operating another gallery at Harwichport, on Cape Cod.

Others in the Grove, operated on a more informal basis, are:

Shore Leave
A young woman painter originally took the little shop to paint in, and made it open house when it became popular. She lives on a boat called the *Majority of One*.

Gallery 3007
3007 Grand

The place next door to Shore Leave is run by a young man called McKenzie, who has made a rather fancy place out of a former barber shop. Most of the wares are things he has brought up from Central America—native carvings, a type of batik, some Pre-Columbian art. Etchings from $7, paintings from $15, but the quality of work here is superior.

Grove House
3496 Main Hwy., 445-5633

This is a large, well-run, non-profit establishment, and its many facets have made it the center of art in the Grove at three different sites. A combination cooperative gallery and school, its stock ranges from paintings and ceramics to jewelry, serigraphs, tiles—in fact, anything that can be termed an art or craft.

The Old School House Gallery
2916 Grand, 445-7430

This gallery has been a success ever since its opening in 1964. Director Bill Clemmer did wonders with the oldest schoolhouse in these parts and, while retaining all the quaintness of the school, he has made the exhibits very attractive. He is the teacher of jewelry-making at Grove House, and his jewelry, which is always handsomely displayed in some portion of the gallery, is most unusual and popular.

Miami Proper

Robinson Art Gallery
627 S. Miami, 374-5713

This is the oldest gallery in the city, established in 1918 by F. A. Robinson and his wife. The firm does framing, restoring, and cleaning of paintings and it has some very fine painters on its roster, Gerald Leake for one.

Bacardi Art Gallery
2100 Biscayne Blvd., 377-8511

Features local contemporaries. Parking available.

Miami Shores Art Center
273 N.E. 79, Miami Shores, 949-0017

A husband-and-wife undertaking. Husband Peter Driben is a portrait painter and offers portraiture classes; wife Louise Kirby also shows her work. Irregular hours, plentiful parking.

A full-sized cast of Michelangelo's *David* dominates the west end of the central garden courtyard in the Ringling Museum of Art, Sarasota, Florida.

Artist unknown: *Madonna in Glory.* (Cusco School, Peru.) Collection of the Joe and Emily Lowe Art Gallery, the University of Miami, Miami, Florida. (*Photograph by David Greenfield*)

North Miami Art Center
688 N.E. 125, 751-2091

Frank Smik has been known up on 125th St. for many years, both as painter-teacher and as one-time president of the Miami Art League. He recently opened a fairly large place of business in a neighborhood where, to my knowledge, there was no other art emporium. He has given its use to several art associations for their annual exhibits. His regular stock consists of a mélange of painters in his neighborhood, with prices very moderate.

Vizcaya
3251 S. Miami, 371-3531

A majestic palazzo built on the shores of Biscayne Bay, Vizcaya's exquisite treasures and commanding site, along with its fantasy of formal ʒardens and grottoes, make it a Miami landmark not to be missed. Admission charge.

Miami Beach

Galerie Fontainebleau
Fontainebleau Hotel, 4441 Collins, 534-1000

This is a rather elegant place, operated by Mr. and Mrs. Ben Wendkos. The former maintains a studio in the Lower Level Promenade, where he does portraits. He is one of the area's top artists in this genre. Mrs. Wendkos directs the gallery, while her husband selects the artists who exhibit there—mainly New York and other out-of-state painters—though Edna Glabman, Fred Albert, and a few other good locals are invited to show there. Later hours, 7 p.m.-midnight; in summer, mostly by appointment.

Frederick Mueller Gallery
940 Lincoln, 538-1924

Only first-class merchandise of the nineteenth and twentieth centuries: Picasso drawings, and paintings by Chagall, Buffet, Dufy, etc. Open 9-5 winter, 9-4 summer; parking.

Eve Tucker Galleries
1240 Lincoln, 538-4941

Handles New York and locals—one or two very good ones, others fair. A small, long-established gallery. A-R, F; open 10-5.

Galerie 99
168 N.E. 40, 758-1990

Mostly rather far-out stuff. Also, a few very nice shows of graphics, and of one or two prominent artists.

Marble Arch Gallery
Americana Hotel, Collins and 96th

One of the more important Beach galleries. Mrs. Sascha Robbins, the director, has excellent taste and brings some fine exhibits here from New York and Boston, others from Paris. She also has a number of graphics and specializes in lithographs by Buffet. Contemporaries only. Expensive.

Miscellanea

Temple Beth-Sholom
4141 Chase, Miami Beach

Has had some very good shows.

Washington Federal Bank
17th and Meridian, Miami Beach

Features exhibits sent to it by an artist in Tallahassee.

Coconut Grove Playhouse Gallery
3500 Main Hwy., Coconut Grove

Invites the different galleries in Miami to furnish paintings and sculptures for sale. Different shows every month.

Gulf American Gallery
79th and Biscayne Blvd., Miami

The gallery of Gulf American, a large land-selling project. Changing exhibits with works of art for sale.

Environs

The Sand Dollar
Islamorada Key

Features work by Miami artists.

Artists Unlimited
Duval St., Key West

Martello Tower East
Key West

An old fortress which has been refurbished inside as an art gallery.

The Gallery
Las Olas Blvd., Fort Lauderdale

Contempora Gallery
E. 15th, Fort Lauderdale

Art Festivals

COCONUT GROVE ARTS FESTIVAL is a sidewalk art show held annually in April. Invitational and children's art exhibits are featured, along with garden tours, a historical exhibit, plays, concerts, et cetera. The FORT LAUDERDALE ART FESTIVAL is usually put on in the fall. Traffic is closed off on the main street and artists come from all over to exhibit. The Miami Art League is usually invited to sponsor an art exhibit which is part of the MIAMI INTERNATIONAL BOAT SHOW at Dinner Key. Many artists show at this annual event in late February, and the prices are usually reasonable. The POINCIANA FESTIVAL ART EXHIBIT is held annually at Burdines Department Store.

Elsewhere in Florida

St. Armands Gallery, Inc.
302 John Ringling Blvd., Sarasota, 388-1357
Carries contemporaries Rampolla, Rubadour, Pachner, Solomon, Zerbe, etc. A-R, F, M, Install. Open 10-5 daily; closed Sun; closed Sat summer.

The Ringling Museums
5401 Bay Shore Rd., Sarasota, 355-5101
Situated on forty-five tropical acres, these were the gift of John Ringling to the state of Florida. They consist of a MUSEUM OF ART, famous for its collection of Baroque art; a one-and-a half-million-dollar Venetian Gothic palazzo, the RINGLING RESIDENCE, including a marble swimming pool, great pine organ, and gold-fixtured bathroom and bar from Cicardi's Winter Gardens; and the MUSEUM OF THE CIRCUS, the first museum to survey the history of the circus. Admission fees; 9-5 daily expect 1-5 Sun; closed Thanksgiving, Christmas.

Cummer Gallery of Art
829 Riverside, Jacksonville, 356-6857
Presents a wide range from the history of art, as well as featuring loan exhibitions and a sales desk of original art chosen by the director. Objects available include pre-Columbian pieces, $15-$100; small statuary, such as Indonesian heads, $30-$70; drawings, prints, manuscript illuminations, $10-$150. The galleries are arranged around a central patio and loggia, and the glass windows afford a view from front to river. Authentication of American and

European art by appointment. Parking; admission is free; 10-5 Tues-Sat, 2-5 Sun; closed Mon, Christmas, New Year's, Independence Day, Thanksgiving.

Jacksonville Art Museum
4160 Blvd. Cntr. Dr., Jacksonville, 398-1558
Specializes in contemporary art and changing exhibitions. It also runs an art school and offers both credit and non-credit courses in conjunction with Jacksonville University. Authentication by appointment. Parking is available. Admission is free; open 10-5 Tues-Sun, 7-10 p.m. Tues-Fri; closed Mon, Thanksgiving, Christmas, Memorial Day, Labor Day, Independence Day.

BIRMINGHAM, ALA.

By Judy O'Beirne and Gene Smith
Littlehouse on Linden Gallery

Where to Buy

Alabama Artist Gallery
1 Cobb Lane, 324-9355
Gene Smith, director. A cooperative gallery dealing exclusively with Alabama residents on a membership basis. Monthly shows with groups of ten artists showing five works each. All media. $25-$750. Parking in back of gallery. Open 10-4 Mon-Sat.

Art Originals Gallery
1922 12th, S., 254-3726
Rebecca Jennings, director. Paintings and crafts of local artists. $1-$100. Parking across street Open 10-5 Mon-Sat.

Center Gallery
606 N. 20th, 323-2957
Bill Yeager, director. Avant-garde and non-representational shows. Changing monthly one-man exhibitions. All media, including graphics. $300 and under. Open weekdays.

Gallery 31, Inc.
1921 11th, S., 251-0403
Frances Loeb, director. This gallery is patterned after New York art establishments dealing primarily in already publicized names.

Graphics included. Associate shows with New York galleries. Keeps continuous shows in lobby of Parliament House and Relay House. Open 11-4:30 Mon-Sat.

Littlehouse on Linden
2911, 2915, 2914 Linden, 879-7022

Gene Smith, director. First permanent art gallery in Birmingham. Deals primarily in introducing new talent and well-known American artists for special festivals, openings, seasonal exhibits. A large selection of signed graphics by Picasso, Dali, Miró, Chagall, etc. At 2911 Linden there are fine-quality custom framing, restoration, old prints. The gallery at 2914 Linden has original big-name graphics and exchange shows with several New York galleries. Monthly receptions with general public invited. Monthly one-man exhibits of both name artists and new talents are featured at 2915 Linden. Monthly receptions. Open 8:30-5:30 Mon-Fri, 8:30-12:30 Sat, at all locations.

Cellar D'Or
2809 Carlisle, 323-2358

Cornelia Rivers, director. A cooperative regional group. Representational, modern in flavor. All mediums. School of art with weekly classes. Prices: $75-$250. Open 10-5 daily. Street parking.

Henderson's Fine Arts Gallery
2015 3rd, N., 251-5061
Henderson's Village Gallery
2847 Culver, Mountain Brook, 871-6221

Ernest and Don Henderson are the directors of these two galleries. Nineteenth-century paintings and graphics. Framers, restorers, dealers in printing.

Miscellanea

BIRMINGHAM-SOUTHERN COLLEGE and SAMFORD UNIVERSITY have excellent art departments and both sell quality art. THE LONDON BRIDGES SCHOOL OF ART, 3024 13th, S. (328-4184), and THE DRAWING BOARD, 606 N. 20th (323-2957), also sell quality art. A RELIGIOUS FESTIVAL OF ART was organized several years ago, and a number of local churches participate in this annual event. Religious paintings are submitted by local artists and are on exhibit for a one-month period. These paintings are for sale, and response is usually good.

Art Festivals and Art Associations

Birmingham's annual FESTIVAL OF THE ARTS, usually held for ten days in the spring, is one of the country's most successful because of the professionalism with which it is run. It features ballet, opera, concerts, plays, literary criticisms, radio and TV performances, and a costume ball, as well as its excellent juried art show. These art works are selected from submissions by artists throughout the state; the prizes and purchase awards encourage a high-caliber show. Huntsville and Gadsden, Alabama, also have festivals similar to the one in Birmingham, but on a smaller scale.

Several other competitions held throughout the year are the WATERCOLOR ASSOCIATION SHOW; the ART ASSOCIATION SHOW; the yearly ALABAMA STATE FAIR ART COMPETITION; the bi-annual show held at HORSE PENS FORTY, a site about forty miles from Birmingham, where Indians once used the natural rock formations as pens for their stock and which is now a natural for this art show, which usually draws large crowds; and occasional SIDEWALK ART SHOWS held during the year in Birmingham and sponsored by various organizations.

Where to Look

The Birmingham Museum of Art
2000 8th, N., 323-8714
Offers a permanent collection of Italian and Dutch painting, American Indian art, pre-Columbian and Oriental art, Palestine archeological objects, British silver, etc. It is possible to purchase works from local, regional and national exhibitions put on at the museum by inquiring at the sales information desk where they take purchase orders. Parking; authentication by appointment; will recommend A-R, F. Admission is free; 10-5 Mon-Fri except 10-9 p.m. Thurs and 2-6 Sun; closed Christmas, New Year's.

Arlington
331 Cotton, 788-6155
A fine example of antebellum architecture, this house was built in 1842 by slave labor. It features Southern antiques of the early 1800s and is also noted for its stately square white columns on the portico. Admission: 50¢ adults, 25¢ children; open 9-5 daily except 1-6 Sun.

The First White House of the Confederacy
Washington and Union, Montgomery, 265-2341, ext. 2116
As its name suggests, this was first headquarters of the Confederacy; it was built in 1840. Admission is free; 9-4:30 daily; closed Christmas all day and Easter Sunday until 12:30.

Information about Art

Art events are covered regularly in the Sunday *Birmingham News*. Radio and TV stations are usually glad to publicize art events, and the educational TV channel has many fine programs along this line.

NEW ORLEANS, LA.

By Alberta Collier
Fine Arts Editor, *The Times-Picayune*

Where to Buy

Most of the galleries listed here, with the exception of the auction house and the two places on Carrollton Ave., are in the French Quarter and within easy walking distance of each other.

331 Gallery
331 Chartres, JA 2-3966
The oldest of the galleries, 331 handles few local artists. Lucille Antony, the owner, specializes in bringing in competent contemporary work from other sections of the country and abroad. Also old and modern prints. Install; $50-$700.

Orleans Gallery
527 Royal, JA 5-2672
A non-profit organization with a supporting membership. Member artists are usually featured, but occasionally outside shows are brought in. Prices $10-$1,400; R. Open 10-5 Mon-Sat; closed Mon June-Aug.

Glade Gallery
621 Toulouse, 525-0623
Has an excellent stable of contemporary local people, among them Ida Kohlmeyer, Pat Trivigno, Leonard Flettrich, and Jesselyn Zurik. Also specializes in Old Master drawings. Install; open noon-5 Mon-Sat.

Lowe Gallery
1126 S. Carrollton, 861-0395

Handles local work, prints and printmakers from elsewhere. Its director, Janet Kohlmeyer, also has an exclusive on the paintings of the late Dr. Marion Souchon, an artist with a fine reputation here. A-R, F, Install; parking.

The Borenstein Gallery
519 Royal

Has work by Noel Rockmore, who also exhibits in New York, and by local artists. Larry Borenstein, the director, also has some very good pre-Columbian work brought in from Mexico and other Latin-American countries.

The Louisiana Crafts Council
1114 S. Carrollton

Contemporary craft work available here. Open 10-4 Mon-Sat.

Early American work, especially Louisiana pieces, is available at LIEUTAUD'S PRINT SHOP, 531 Royal, and at the LANSFORD ART GALLERY, 632 St. Peter. European paintings of the past are available at the OLD EUROPE GALLERY, 631 Bourbon. And almost any kind of art work can come up at auction houses such as FORSYTHE-SANCHEZ ANTIQUE GALLERIES, 1810 Magazine.

Where to Look

Isaac Delgado Museum
Lelong Ave., City Park, HU 2-2129

The museum is in a tree-shaded city park near a lagoon. High point of the collection is a romantic group of nineteenth-century paintings that include Bouguereau, Gérôme, and Alma-Tadema. A Samuel H. Kress Collection of thirty-one Italian Renaissance paintings should also not be missed. Group and one-man shows of Louisiana contemporary artists, with the works for sale. Admission is free; 10-5 Tues-Sat, 1-6 Sun; closed Mon.

Information about Art

Both daily newspapers feature articles on art. *The Times-Picayune* has an art-criticism column, which includes hours and addresses of current art exhibits.

The Midwest

CLEVELAND, OHIO

By Helen Borsick
Art Critic, *The Plain Dealer*

Cleveland has traditionally been a city of considerable art activity on the amateur and semi-professional level, owing in part to the encouragement of the CLEVELAND MUSEUM OF ART. For the past forty-eight years the museum has held an annual May Show of work by local artists in order to give them a place to exhibit and a chance to sell. Commercial galleries traditionally have been few. The art-for-sale offerings have mainly been shows of work by local artists sponsored by art clubs for their members. Taste over the years has largely been conservative, favoring Realism and giving very little quarter to the newer art styles coming along. Only within the last ten years has the climate noticeably changed to admit contemporary art. Works in the modern vein by nationally known as well as local artists are now routinely shown.

There are still only a few good commercial galleries that rate above the picture-store level. However, some thriving quasi-galleries have been established in places of other business—theater lobbies, restaurants, motels, the lobby of the Women's City Club, a flower shop, and even in car-wash shops and banks.

There are also frequent opportunities to buy good things from such shows as the annual festivals held in the JEWISH COMMUNITY CENTER and at PARK SYNAGOGUE; the annual three-day art show and sale of Cleveland artists' work held on the Mall at SHAKER SQUARE; import displays brought in by the department stores; shows put on by local art groups; and several exhibitions sponsored annually by AMERICAN GREETINGS CORPORATION for members of its creative staff.

THE CLEVELAND INSTITUTE OF ART maintains a small, permanent selling gallery of art by faculty members (the Cleveland Gallery) and also holds a monthly exhibition of works by faculty, students, or guest artists. The work is usually for sale. Over the

295

years, the Institute has been the principal training ground for the city's artists. Its faculty forms the professional elite of Cleveland art and the nucleus of the "Cleveland School." The faculty includes sculptors William M. McVey, John Clague, and C. E. Van Duzer; painters Louis Bosa, John Teyral, Edwin Mieczkowski, Peter Paul Dubaniewicz, Francis Meyers, Joseph McCullough, and Vikto Schreckengost, who is also an industrial designer of note; printmaker Carroll Cassill; enamelist Kenneth Bates; textile designer Brita Sjoman; and Frederick and John Paul Miller in silver, jewelry, and design.

Some other prominent artists in the area are painters Paul Travis, Paul Riba, Robert Laessig, Joseph O'Sickey, Michael Sarisky, William Grauer, Shirley Aley Campbell, Alberta Cifolelli Lamb, Thelma Winter, Richard Treaster, and Kinley Shogren; potters Lisa McVey, Claude Conover, and Clement Giorgi; and enamelists Edward Winter and John Puskas.

The newly reorganized COOPER SCHOOL OF ART is now also beginning a regular exhibitions program.

Public support of the museum and the rest of the art scene has improved in recent years. Cleveland art galleries have been prone to open and close in quick succession, but several have now proven that a well-run gallery can eventually hold its own. Low-cost art sells best to a growing new public of art buyers here. Gallery owners rate it as about "a $300 town." But there is also a new segment of highly sophisticated collectors who buy big—and sometimes in Cleveland as well as in New York. There are still remnants of the conservative-vs.-avant-garde argument. Between the supporters of both sides, the art diet increasingly balances out.

Where to Buy

University Circle is the geographic center of culture here. It is an area on the northeast side of town. This is the location of Western Reserve University, the Cleveland Museum of Art, the Cleveland Institute of Art, the Historical Society, the Natural Science Museum, and Severance Hall with its concerts. There is also an attractive and popular art gallery in the area:

Ross Widen
11320 Euclid, 421-1424
Primitive sculpture, contemporary paintings, and prints, also framing. Open 10-5 daily.

A few miles further east:

Gallery International
13218 Superior, 851-9708
The city's top commercial showplace of mostly other-than-Cleveland contemporary art. Open 11-5:30 daily.

Guenther-Mattox Galleries
2450 Fairmount Blvd., Cleveland Heights, 321-4386
A variety of paintings and sculpture at mixed prices. Stresses "art as an investment." Open 10-5:30 daily; closed Thurs, Sun.

The Cleveland Institute of Art
11141 E. Blvd., 421-4322
Has an active selling program in its Cleveland Gallery, where works in all media are offered. Work is also for sale from its faculty and student exhibitions. Main gallery: 9-4:30 Mon-Fri, 7-9 p.m. Tues-Wed, 9-noon Sat; Cleveland Gallery: 1-3:30 Mon, Wed, Fri and 7-9 p.m. Tues-Wed; closed national holidays.

Downtown Cleveland

Dezign House
2241 Prospect, 621-7777
Custom interior design, novelties, serendipities, and exhibits of work by Cleveland artists. Open 10-4 weekdays.

Vixseboxse Art Galleries
2258 Euclid, MA 1-0763
Fine eighteenth- and nineteenth-century British and American prints, seventeenth-century Dutch and other paintings and porcelains. Open 10-5 daily, 11-3:30 Sat; closed Sat summer.

The Bonfoey Co.
1710 Euclid, 621-0178
Paintings, prints, framing.

Strong's Art Gallery
207 Frankfort, off Public Square, 241-6940
Framing, reproductions, prints.

Gallery 1-2
1454 W. 3rd, near Public Square
A relatively new cooperative gallery run by a group of student and other young artists with works priced about $5 to $100. Open daily and some evenings.

Gallery 1-2, Cleveland, Ohio.

Ross Widen Gallery, Cleveland, Ohio.

West Side

Malvina Freedson Gallery
12700 Lake Ave., Lakewood, 228-1111
In the lobby-promenade of the plush Winton Place Apartments. Paintings and sculpture. Prices from about $100. Continuous hours.

Hixson's Flower Barn Gallery
14125 Detroit, LA 1-9277
A combination flower-gift-serendipity-curiosity shop and art show-place. Business hours Tues-Sat; closed Mon.

Environs: Practically every suburb in the Greater Cleveland area is flourishing with amateur and semi-professional art sales. These are usually held in an assortment of places: the sidewalks of shopping centers, bank parking lots, restaurants, suburban art clubs and fine arts associations.

There are also several picture stores and framers scattered in the eastern suburbs that sometimes have art for sale. None, however, have much in the way of a regular, quality exhibitions program.

Gallery 35
35 S. Main, Chagrin Falls, 247-7432
This gallery is an exception. It shows paintings—a show per month —by local artists and maintains a permanent crafts gallery of works mainly by the Chagrin artists group. Open 1-5 Thurs-Sun.

There are two other art outlets in the area reaching to Akron, but also fairly accessible to the Cleveland audience. Both hold monthly showings of current works by area artists.

Lattavo Gallery
Yankee Clipper Inn, Rte. 8 at the Ohio Tpke., 653-8111
Open 10-5 daily except Sun.

Ghent Art Gallery
3461 Granger Road, Akron, 666-9739

Miscellanea

Every college and university in the area holds art shows from time to time, and you can look for announcements of these exhibitions in the local newspapers. Not all that is shown is of the highest quality but, then again, some is.

The Play House Theater
E. 77th St.

The theater conducts a regular exhibition schedule in its lobby gallery. Usually it is the work of an outstanding Cleveland artist, sometimes a show of imported prints or of a guest artist.

Karamu Settlement House
E. 89th and Quincy, 795-3322

Also has a gallery in its theater lobby. At almost any time you can wander in and find a show of Cleveland artists' work, usually someone connected in some way with Karamu's art-school program. There is also a small permanent gallery of craft items by Karamu artists.

Sears, Roebuck & Co.
8501 Carnegie, 795-2233

Has had about two art exhibitions of the Vincent Price Collection in Cleveland in the last five years.

The May Company
158 Euclid, 241-3000

Usually brings in an annual sculpture show of special interest; one year it was New Guinea art, then African, then Greco-Roman, then Far Eastern. But that's once a year. In addition, this store sometimes shows local artists in their picture department and in lobbies of restaurants in its downtown and suburban stores.

The Higbee Company
100 Public Sq., 579-2580

Located downtown and with branches in the suburbs; brings an annual print show in from New York; opens its downtown tenth-floor auditorium to shows by suburban groups, and quite often, though not on a regular exhibition schedule, will sponsor exhibitions of guest artists from other cities.

The Halle Brothers Company
1228 Euclid, 621-2700

Opens its facilities to local and outside artists from time to time.

Art Festivals and Competitions

The biggest festival is the MAY SHOW at the Cleveland Museum of Art. Other competitive annuals include exhibitions sponsored by the JEWISH COMMUNITY CENTER, BAYCRAFTERS (an art organization based in the far west suburb of Bay Village), and the NEWMAN CLUB, a college religious alumni organization that puts on a religious art show.

There are also numerous festivals held by art organizations that either limit their shows to members' work or make their exhibits entirely invitational. The largest annual of this type is the early November PARK SYNAGOGUE ART FESTIVAL, which brings in about a thousand works from the New York City galleries. An additional section is devoted to Israeli art, and another to art by Cleveland artists on an invitational basis. The emphasis is on contemporary trends. Several other synagogues have annual art shows, usually emphasizing Jewish art or works by members of art classes sponsored by the congregations.

Art Groups

Most are suburban area groups, such as the Lakewood Art League, Parma Art League, Euclid Art League, Willoughby Fine Arts Association, Chagrin Valley Artists' Association, Bedford Art League, Cleveland Society of Artists, Women Artists of Cleveland, Baycrafters, Westlake Art League, Ashtabula Fine Arts Center, Mill Hollow Art Center in Strongsville, North Olmsted Arts and Crafts Association.

The shows are held annually—and sometimes irregularly in between—either in the meeting centers or in borrowed locations such as the department stores or galleries.

Where to Look

The Cleveland Museum of Art
11150 E. Blvd., GA 1-7340

This museum rates as one of the great United States museums, and is among the world's foremost art institutions. Blessed by benefactors who left it both fine collections and huge bequests, Cleveland has bought and can continue to buy the finest. Its special excellence in Oriental and Medieval arts reflects the interests of its present and past directors, Sherman E. Lee and William M. Milliken, but it is constantly adding to the already high quality of its other European collections. For purchase, there are small exhibitions of contemporary art in one gallery of the museum almost constantly; most works are for sale, and potential customers are referred to the commercial galleries that loaned the art. The museum also holds a highly successful annual regional exhibition— its May Show—in which close to ninety per cent of the work exhibited is usually sold. There is also an extensive educational program. Admission is free; open 10-6 Tues, Thurs, 10-10 Wed, Fri, 9-5 Sat, 1-6 Sun; closed Mon.

The Salvador Dali Museum
21709 Chagrin Blvd. (temporarily), WA 1-8816
Offers over three hundred works in many media by the artist, with a complete library of writings on him. By advance appointment only; authentication of Dali works by appointment.

Cleveland Public Library
325 Superior, 241-1020
The library contains an art gallery furnished by the Cleveland Museum of Art. Library open 9-9 Mon-Fri, 9-6 Sat; art gallery, noon-9 Mon, noon-5 Tues-Fri; closed Sat, holidays.

Western Reserve Historical Society
1085 E. Blvd., 721-5722
Founded in 1867, the Society has several interesting art collections, including the Napoleonic gallery, a room relating to early Cleveland, and an early log cabin showing the possessions of a frontier family. Its library is particularly rich in nineteenth-century Americana. The Society is housed in two Florentine Renaissance-style buildings containing seventy rooms, surrounded by beautiful, formal gardens. Admission is free; 25¢ parking lot at rear; open 10-5 Tues-Sat, 2-5 Sun; closed Mon.

Information about Art

The principal dissemination of art news is in the Sunday issue of *The Plain Dealer*, and on Saturdays it is in the *Cleveland Press*. There is also art news in the Cleveland weekly magazine entitled *Fine Arts*. Occasionally there are radio and TV program listings, and sometimes the appearance of an artist or gallery owner on discussion programs.

CINCINNATI, OHIO

By Arthur Darack
Former Book and Art Editor, *The Enquirer*

Local professional painting ranges in price from ten to six hundred dollars. Not much of the latter is sold.
The local atmosphere is conservative, and while some people

are experimenting, and taking full advantage of the new trends, nobody is starting any. The best of the experimenting group are Paul Wilhelm, Margaret Wenstrup, William Collins, William Leonard, Stan Brod, and Evelyn Marx (who now lives in Sarasota). Conservative artists include Paul Moscatt, Ed Douglas, Robert Fabe, Larry Zink, Janet Rappaport, Davira Fisher, Philip Olmes, and many others.

Galleries and museums are well attended indeed. Modern art is being sold more and more, but Impressionism still seems most salable.

Where to Buy

The outlets are not very numerous. The best galleries are Flair House and Closson's, both at Fourth and Race. This area is downtown in a "core renewal" section. It will be the most posh part of the city ten years hence, with high-fashion shops, restaurants, specialty shops, and the Contemporary Arts Center.

Flair House
113 W. 4th, 241-1366
A very modern gallery showing work by New York and European artists for the most part. Their only local artist is William Collins, who teaches at the Art Academy and is the only Cincinnati artist to be invited to the Whitney Museum's annual U.S. invitational show. Also a good selection of prints. Open 10-5 daily.

Closson's
421 Race, 621-1536
Somewhat more conservative, offering local painters but more imports, and also many prints. Open 9:30-5:30 weekdays, except 9:30-8:30 Mon.

Out in the suburbs there are a number of galleries specializing in local artists, and in Mt. Adams, Cincinnati's "Greenwich Village," galleries are always opening and closing. They usually feature new artists and sometimes, as in the case of the PAVILION GALLERY in "New Dilly's" Building, artists from New York and overseas.

Suburbs

Harriet Crane Gallery
7876 Montgomery, 891-1316
Located in the enormous Kenwood Shopping Center, Miss Crane's

gallery features a local roster with imports from Chicago and Canada. She is an amateur artist herself. Open 10-5 weekdays, 2-5 Sun; closed Mon.

Kkae Gallery
1547 N. Bend, 771-5898
Formerly in the Tri-County Shopping Center, this gallery was the first shopping-center art gallery in the United States. It features mainly local artists, with some imports from nearby Dayton, Louisville, Indianapolis, Lexington, and Columbus.

The Art House
11470 Springfield, Glendale, 771-0578
The gallery is run by an artist, Margaret Hallforth, who also features area artists. She has classes, too, for children and adults, and sells artists' supplies.

Universities and Schools

Edgecliffe Academy, Our Lady of Cincinnati
Edgecliffe and Victory, 281-2533
Offers periodic, but not regular, exhibitions of paintings by graduates, and by some local painters. The gallery is downstairs in an old renovated mansion and is called EMERY GALLERY. Prices in the $75 to $300 range. Open 9-5 daily, Sun afternoon.

College of Mt. St. Joseph Gallery
Delhi Pike, 941-4200
Its beautiful, large gallery is located in the Catholic Women's College, with exhibits of mostly out-of-town artists. Also features private area collections. Open 9-5 Mon-Fri, 2-5 Sun.

University of Cincinnati, College of Design, Architecture & Art
Burnet Woods Campus, 475-4933
The gallery exhibits almost exclusively work by faculty members and students. Shows are also held in the new Commons Building.

Department Stores

Sears, Roebuck & Co.
2900 Reading, 961-7820
Has had a showing of the traveling Vincent Price Collection.

Shillito's
7th and Race, 381-7000
Has regular exhibitions of unusual things—for example, a "Salon

des Refuses" from the 1966 Zoo Arts Festival. Also Picasso prints, etc.

Mabley & Carew Co.
Fountain Square, 241-7400
Occasionally has exhibitions of local work.

Art Festivals and Competitions

There are many community-sponsored events, too numerous to list here. Perhaps the two largest held are THE TRI-COUNTY ARTS FAIR and the ZOO ARTS FESTIVAL. The Tri-County show, held on the Shopping Center Mall in May, is the art event of the Cincinnati area. It offers more prize money than any other, and imports judges. It attracts persons from about a hundred fifty miles away, and has had over seven hundred entries. It has been called "a mile of art," with art in the store windows, on wires stretched between canopy poles, on easels, and on display tables. Artists bring their own folding chairs and spend the day near their displays. There are also numerous demonstrations in the various art media. The Zoo Festival isn't as big as the Tri-County affair, but is more important as it lasts a week and a half, brings in jurors from New York, and attracts more of the professional artists, fewer of the amateurs. It is usually held in September. A third festival, at the SWIFTON SHOPPING CENTER, is a smaller version of the Zoo Festival and is held in early summer.

Where to Look

The Cincinnati Art Museum
Eden Park, 721-5204
Permanent collections of original paintings, sculptures, prints, and decorative arts offer a review of the major civilizations of the world, with over one hundred galleries given over to the collections. Its building has been completed over an eighty-year period, with the latest wing added in 1965. Original art sold at the sales desk includes rotating exhibitions of works by Art Academy of Cincinnati faculty the year around, local artists usually from late November to January, and occasional traveling print exhibitions from which works are sold. Authenticating by appointment; staff restorer will do outside work, time permitting; M.F.A. program with Art Academy and University of Cincinnati. Parking; admission free; open 10-5 Mon-Sat, 10-10 Tues Oct-Apr, 2-5 Sun and holidays; closed Thanksgiving, Christmas.

Cincinnati Art Museum, Cincinnati, Ohio.

Leyman Gallery, Cincinnati Art Museum, Cincinnati, Ohio.

The Contemporary Arts Center
113 W. 4th, 721-0390
Devoted to bringing quality contemporary art to Cincinnati. From its humble beginnings—three dedicated women working with a letter file, a portable typewriter, and borrowed galleries—the Center now has its own galleries, its own professional director, and a membership of over seven hundred. Although works are not sold from the exhibitions, interested buyers will be referred to various places where the works are available. Organized tours; admission free to members, 50¢ non-members; open 10-5 weekdays, 10-3 Sat, closed Sun.

The Taft Museum
316 Pike, 241-0343
The Taft houses important collections of sixteenth- to twentieth-century masters, including paintings by Goya, Hals, Rembrandt, Turner. It also features intricate Chinese porcelains and elaborately painted French Renaissance enamels. These are arranged in a beautifully decorated historic house, an important example of early Federal Period architecture. Admission free; parking; limited authentication upon request; open 10-5 Mon-Sat, 2-5 Sun and holidays; closed Thanksgiving, Christmas.

Information about Art

The *Cincinnati Enquirer* and the *Post Times-Star* are the two basic outlets, with radio and TV offering only a trickle of news and coverage.

DETROIT, MICH.

Where to Buy

Art School of the Society of Arts & Crafts
245 E. Kirby, 872-3118
Student work for sale in entrance hall.

Arwin
222 Grand River W., 965-6516
Lester Arwin, the personable director, is dedicated to making Detroiters aware of Michigan art talent. The second oldest gallery in the city, Arwin displays the work of Michigan artists only. Open 10-5:30 Tues-Sat; 10-8:30 Mon.

Detroit Artists Market
1452 Randolph, WO 2-0337
Established in 1932 as a non-profit gallery, the Market exhibits and sells the work of artists living within a sixty-mile radius of Detroit. Monthly exhibits are selected by a jury from work submitted by approximately three hundred fifty area artists. Included are oils, watercolors, graphics, sculpture, ceramics, weaving, jewelry, etc. Look for the blue door. Prices $2-$2,000. Install; parking lots around building. Open 10-5 Mon-Sat; closed Aug.

Garelick's
20209 Livernois, UN 3-2944
Robert Garelick was trained by the late Herman Baron of New York's A.C.A. Gallery and his Detroit headquarters reflects the quality of his apprenticeship. He features changing shows of American and European contemporaries—Raphael Soyer, Philip Evergood, Richard Florsheim, etc.—in addition to a large graphic room that is a veritable paradise for the modest collector. M, Install, F, A-R; adjoining parking lot. Open 9-6 daily.

Hanamura's
1433 Randolph, WO 4-1650
Contemporary arts and crafts by such craftsmen as Murray Jones, Jens Plum, Harry Bouras. Install; adjacent parking lots. Open 11-5 daily.

The J.L. Hudson Gallery
1206 Woodward, 963-7228
Founded only a few years ago as the brainchild of Hudson's young, energetic president, Joseph L. Hudson, Jr., the Gallery has very quickly achieved a national reputation for excellence. Hudson had the good sense to appoint a first-rate art director, Albert Landry, who gave up a successful New York gallery to come to Detroit. Landry's 1964 inaugural exhibit of the German Expressionists was a memorial to the German art scholar and pioneer W. R. Valentiner. Since then, his exhibits have included Picasso engravings, the drawings and sculpture of Jacques Lipchitz, and selections from the Pittsburgh International Exhibition of Contemporary Painting and Sculpture. His "stable" includes Josef Albers, French artist Pierre Alechinsky, English sculptor Reg Butler, Robert Parker, Louise Nevelson. Parking; Install; A-R. Open 9:15-5:15 Tues, Thurs-Sat, 9:15-8:15 Mon, Wed.

International Art Center
132 Madison, 961-9129
Twentieth-century art, with emphasis on living artists. All media. Prices $100-$1,000. F, Install. Open noon-6 Mon-Sat.

Gertrude Kasle Gallery
310 Fisher Bldg., 875-2100
Contemporary paintings, sculpture, and graphics. Her excellent roster includes Robert Goodnough, Paul Jenkins, Grace Hartigan, Robert Natkin, Lowell Nesbitt, Jack Tworkov. F, A; parking around building; Install. Open 11-5 Mon-Sat; closed Aug.

London Grafica Arts, Inc.
903 Fisher Bldg., 872-7660
This is the headquarters for touring shows of quality prints. Package shows, ready-framed, of graphics and drawings by such artists as Picasso, Braque, and Odilon Redon are sent to galleries in cities across the U.S. Four gallery representatives also travel to different areas of the country presenting a large show of mixed graphics for one day at a time at different universities and colleges. Parking; open 10-6 Mon, Wed, 10-8:30 Tues, Thurs, Fri; closed Sun.

Donald Morris Gallery
20090 Livernois, UN 3-8212
Twentieth-century Americans and Europeans such as Avery, Dubuffet, Miró, Gorky. Features national and international artists in a sophisticated atmosphere. Install; open 10:30-5:30 Tues-Sat.

Franklin Siden Gallery
210 David Whitney Bldg., 962-7710
Excellent quality works set on the balcony of a large downtown office building. Twentieth-century art, both modern and contemporary. Siden also keeps an excellent stock of contemporary prints in a second-floor room. Metered parking; M, F, Install. Open 10-5:30 Mon-Sat.

Environs

America House
Englander's, 555 E. Maple, Bloomfield Hills, 647-1954
Superior handicrafts; all craft media. Price $3-$900. M, Install; parking.

The new South Wing of the Detroit Institute of Arts, Detroit, Michigan.

Sculpture Court, new South Wing, Detroit Institute of Arts, Detroit, Michigan.

Franklin Siden, director, the Franklin Siden Gallery,
Detroit, Michigan.

Gertrude Kasle, director, the Gertrude Kasle Gallery, Detroit, Michigan.

Cranbrook Academy Art Gallery
500 Lone Pine Rd., Bloomfield Hills, MI 4-1600
Changing exhibits of contemporary and applied arts, as well as changing selections from its permanent collection of Italian, Flemish, and contemporary painting, and Oriental and pre-Columbian art.

Where to Look

The Detroit Institute of Arts
5200 Woodward, 831-0360
The Institute dedicated a handsome new South Wing of dark pearl granite in 1966 and plans a similar North Wing addition in 1969. The collection in the original Italian Renaissance building of gleaming white Vermont marble is arranged chronologically, so that visitors may pass in logical sequence "from the beginning to the end." An unusual feature is the huge mural painting of industrial Detroit by Mexican muralist Diego Rivera. The rental gallery, open to Founders Society members only, presents more than two hundred and fifty originals by Michigan artists. Authentication by appointment; underground parking garage on south side; sales from contemporary art exhibitions. Admission is free; open noon-9 Tues-Wed, 9-6 Thurs-Sun; closed Mon, holidays; open in summer 9-6 Tues-Sat.

Archives of American Art
5200 Woodward, 833-2199
Located in the Institute, the Archives was founded in 1954 as a national research institution to document the arts of the United States as a whole. It preserves the papers of artists, craftsmen, collectors, dealers, critics, historians, museums, societies, and institutions. The manuscripts, letters, notebooks, sketchbooks, clippings, and catalogs preserved here are invaluable for scholars and for all those interested in Americana. Adjacent underground parking; open 9-6 weekdays.

Detroit Historical Museum
Woodward and Kirby, 321-1701
This museum presents an invitation to take a walk through Old Detroit. Re-created streets of pioneer Detroit feature cobblestone and woodblock streets, old shops, public buildings, and homes of the past. Changing exhibits of the city, presented in conjunction with community and special-interest groups, are presented from time to time. Admission is free; open 9-6 daily except Mon, holidays; parking lot, 10¢ per hour at W. Kirby.

The Detroit Public Library
5201 Woodward, 321-1000
Housed in a handsome Italian Renaissance-style marble building, the library is elaborately decorated with murals, carvings, and stained-glass windows. Its collections include rare books, manuscripts, old maps, and sound recordings. Admission is free; open 9:30-9 p.m. Mon-Thurs, 9:30-5:30 Fri, Sat, 1-6 Sun.

The Children's Museum
67 E. Kirby, TR 3-2670
Displays scenes from American history, toy shops, a craft room, and so on—all for children. It's part of the very important growing movement in the United States to have certain art displays directed at children. Admission is free; open 9-5 Mon-Fri, 9-4:30 Sat; 1-4 June-Sept; closed Sun, Aug, holidays.

Henry Ford Museum and Greenfield Village
Dearborn, LO 1-1620
Located on a picturesque 260-acre setting near Detroit, this is one of the great outdoor museums in the country. Outstanding examples of Early American art and a street of Early American shops are in the museum, as well as a huge Mechanical Arts Hall holding more than two hundred authentically restored automobiles, locomotives, and airplanes. The Village has a dazzling array of over one hundred craft shops, schools, homes and public buildings dating from the seventeenth to the nineteenth century. Among them are Thomas Edison's Menlo Park laboratory, the Wright Brothers' bicycle shop, and the courthouse where Abraham Lincoln practiced law. Admission is $1.25. Museum is open 9-5 weekdays, 9-6 weekends and holidays; Village, 9-5:30 weekdays, 9-6 weekends and holidays. Special rates for families, children, and educational groups.

Information about Art

Full listings available in the *Detroit Free Press, Detroit News* and some information given on radio as well as television. DETROIT ADVENTURE, INC. publishes a monthly (except during the summer) calendar of cultural events listing twenty-six cultural and educational institutions in the city; you can obtain it by writing to 100 W. Kirby or telephoning 833-1400, exts. 220, 278. The DETROIT CONVENTION BUREAU (626 Book Building) puts out its very useful publication, *The Museums, Parks, Libraries and Zoos of Detroit Invite You;* it includes a cultural map of the city with directions on how to get from place to place.

CHICAGO, ILL.

By Joshua Kind

Professor of Art History and Humanities, Illinois Institute of Technology, and Chicago Correspondent, *Art News*

For the last decade, a mood of optimism has prevailed in Chicago about the "potential" of the city's art life. Being the capital of the Middle West, and itself a huge metropolis, Chicago has logically enough seemed the place for a sizable artistic community to develop in both the commercial and the spiritual senses. And yet, for the most part, this has not occurred, at least not in the fashion envisioned by those who believe in the possibility of the vision.

The cliché for many years has been that all of the many sizable collections built up here in the years since World War II were acquired in New York or Europe, and that the collectors would not buy here because of the lack of prestige attached to any purchases made in the city itself. (And even more damning is the fact that Chicago artists have been bought outside the city— so it is said.)

Be all this as it may—and negativism is not at all a minor force here; *e.g.*, the strongest Chicago artistic direction of recent times for many has been the forceful work of the so-called Monsters— the city does boast a good number of fine collections of twentieth-century art. And through the guiding hand of Joseph Shapiro, himself the owner of one of the best of these collections, Chicago can now claim a MUSEUM OF CONTEMPORARY ART. The Museum, which recently opened in the midst of the gallery cluster at Michigan and Ontario, is both a sign of the new vitality here and perhaps also the signal for further growth.

This is not to say that both the ARTS CLUB and the ART INSTITUTE OF CHICAGO, the major exhibitors of traveling art shows in Chicago, have not established fine traditions here. For many the prevailing mood did need an infusion, however. New galleries, also, have come into existence to supplement the older, more prestigious, establishments. While KOVLER, HOLLAND and GRAY, for instance, do handle international figures, they will, in addition, show local artists; which are also the specialty of DELL.

Although several of the older galleries in town have reciprocal agreements with dealers on both the East and West coasts, it is rare that New York sensations are seen here in one-man shows;

and so, for the most part, the flavor of the city's gallery openings is mild. Furthermore, the phenomenon of the "sell-out" is very infrequent. Most sales in the private galleries still occur in a more sedate fashion.

Some of the serious failings of the art scene in years past have recently been alleviated. The city has long needed an Old Master dealer, even one offering relatively inexpensive objects such as prints and drawings, and the minor arts. It has now acquired one in THE DRAWING GALLERY. And it may well be that the presence of only one major Old Master collection in the city is but a reflection of the past situation. Perhaps now, also, the past tense should be used for the lack of more than one major journalistic voice commenting on the art scene. This has recently been altered with the establishment of a monthly art commentary magazine, *Chicago Midwest Art*.

So that, as ever, the presence of a "potential" for development is strong in Chicago. Galleries, managed by attractive and capable people, and offering a large spectrum of wares, are available; the city is large and energetic; the second museum has just opened; the Chicago Art Institute, under a new director, seems ready to begin a new era in its evolution—and the members of the art community of the city hope that these elements will all coincide to produce a fine future.

Where to Buy

The Arts Club of Chicago
109 E. Ontario, SU 7-3997
Traveling and self-originating exhibits of high quality, with annual professional members' show in the spring. Open 9:30-5:30 daily, except Sun; closed July 1-Oct 1.

Art Institute of Chicago Rental and Sales Gallery
Michigan at Adams (ground fl.), CE 6-7080
Juried works in many media by Chicago-area artists. Rental fees range from $5 to $40 for a two-month period. Parking; open 10:30-4:30 Mon-Wed, Fri, 10:30-8 Thurs, noon-4 Sat; closed July-Sept.

Benjamin Gallery
900 Michigan, DE 7-1343
Collectors' prints, contemporary sculpture and drawings, some local artists. Prices $35-$5,000. Art displayed as if in a home. Doorman of building will park car; M, F, A-R, Install, R occasionally. Open 11-6 Wed-Sat, or by appointment; closed Aug.

Conrad Gallery
46 E. Chicago, 943-1524
Paintings, graphics, and sculpture by contemporary and nineteenth-
and twentieth-century masters. Prices $50-$25,000. F, A-R, R, Install; sculpture bases and pedestals. Open 10-6 Mon-Fri, noon-5
Sat, closed Sun; by appointment only in Aug.

M. Dell Gallery Ltd.
620 N. Michigan, 642-0630
A, Mods; emphasis on a large group of younger Chicago artists.
Open 10-6 Mon-Sat.

I. Distelheim Gallery
113 E. Oak, 642-5570
European moderns, especially Italians; Midwest artists. Open 10-6
Mon-Sat.

The Drawing Gallery (Charles Frank & Co.-Antiques)
154 E. Superior, 787-0985
Old Master drawings, and antiques. Open noon-6 Mon-Sat.

Fine Arts Faculty Gallery
5211 S. Harper, 324-8090
A group-supported gallery selling only the works of teachers in
the professional art schools and art departments of the Chicago
area.

Fairweather-Hardin Gallery
141 E. Ontario, MI 2-0007
Modern art in many media; local artists featured. F,Appraisal, R,
Install; open 10-5:30 Mon-Sat.

Richard Feigen Gallery
226 E. Ontario, 787-0500
Nineteenth- and twentieth-century European and American artists.
Parking across street; Install. Open 9-6 Mon-Sat.

Findlay Galleries, Inc.
320 S. Michigan, WE 9-4481
Paintings by Impressionists, Post-Impressionists, and contemporary
French and Italian painters. Prices $150-$150,000. City of
Chicago underground parking across street; M, Install, Restoring.
Open 9-5:30 Mon-Sat.

Allan Frumkin
620 S. Michigan, 787-0563
A,Eu,Mods,G; a large nineteenth- and twentieth-century print
selection. Open 10-6 Mon-Sat.

M. Gilman Gallery
103 E. Oak, 337-6262
A, Mods; emphasis on younger Midwestern artists. Open 10-6
Mon-Sat.

R. Gray Gallery
620 N. Michigan, 642-8877
Mods, A, Eu.; sculpture, paintings, and drawings of well-known
national artists. Open 10-6 Mon-Sat.

Hanzel Auction Gallery
179 N. Michigan, FR 2-4878
Chicago's major dispersal agents for works of fine art and the
minor arts.

B.C. Holland Gallery
155 E. Ontario, DE 7-2700
A, Eu, Conts, Mods; G. Open 9:30-5:30 Mon-Fri, noon-5 Sat.

International Galleries
645 N. Michigan, 943-1661
Works by Calder, Dubuffet, Dufy, Ernst, Gris, Matisse, Magritte,
etc. Parking; Install. Open 9-5:30 Mon-Sat.

K. Kazimir Gallery
620 N. Michigan, 337-2236
Structurist reliefs and geometric abstractions by Eli Bornstein, Jean
Gorin, Henryk Stazewski, John Cannon, Hilton Brown, etc. R,
Install. Open 10:30-5:30 Tues-Sat; 12:30-5:30 summer.

M. Kovler Gallery
952 N. Michigan, 642-8420
The gallery is devoted primarily to showing younger quality artists,
as well as more established ones; has a large, permanent stock of
nineteenth- and twentieth-century graphics. Most works range between $200 to $2,500, with some lower, some higher. M, F, A-R,
Install. Open 10:30-6 Mon-Sat.

Main Street Galleries
642 N. Michigan, 787-3301
Modern Europeans and Americans; local artists; prints, drawings,
sculpture. Open 10-5:30 Mon-Fri, 10-5 Sat.

Merrill Chase Galleries
620 N. Michigan, DE 7-5190
Open 9:30-5:30 Mon-Fri.

S.H. Mori Gallery
83 E. Van Buren, HA 7-1274
Older and modern Oriental art in all media.

Oehlschlaeger Galleries
107 E. Oak, SU 7-6779
Contemporaries, mostly American. Prices $150-$3,500. M, Install.
Open 10-6 Mon-Sat.

Sergel Gallery
86 E. Randolph, RA 6-5814
Prints, all styles and periods. M, Appraisal, Install. Open 9:30-
5:30 Mon-Fri.

Galleria Roma
155 E. Ontario, 787-0005
Modern Italian paintings and sculpture. Open 11-6 Mon-Sat.

Welna Gallery
54 E. Oak, 337-2773
European and American art; some prints and drawings. Open
10:30-6 Mon-Sat.

Miscellanea

University of Chicago, Renaissance Society
Goodspeed Hall, 58th and Ellis, MI 3-0800, ext. 2886
Occasional shows of local and national artists, and yearly show of
"Contemporary Art for Young Collectors."

University of Illinois
Chicago Circle, Halstead and Polk, 663-2900
Shows of local artists, and various group shows.

The Blackhawk Restaurant
139 N. Wabash Ave., 726-0100
Monthly exhibits of local artists.

Bernard Horwich Center
3003 W. Touhy, RO 1-9100
Series of exhibitions of leading local artists.

Illinois Institute of Technology
Hermann Hall, 33rd and State, CA 5-9600, ext. 364
Scene of recent "Phalanx," a Chicago artists' group, recently merged
with Participating Artists of Chicago.

Kendall College
Lincoln and Sherman, Evanston, 869-5240
Series of exhibits, both individual and group, of well-known local artists.

Vincent Price Gallery of Art
Sears, Roebuck, Ontario and Michigan, 265-2500
American and European paintings and sculpture; prints and drawings.

Marshall Field & Co.
111 N. State, 2nd fl., ST 1-1000
Twentieth-century School of Paris art.

Korvette's
Morton Grove Store, Waukegan and Dempster, 965-4040

Art Festivals and Art Groups

A good number of the city's shopping centers, both urban and suburban, sponsor outdoor "Art Fairs" during the summer. Most are juried and invitational, and often attract the best of the city's lesser known artists. The heyday of these fairs, at least so legend has it, was in the early fifties when many fewer opportunities for exhibitions were present in Chicago, and so many more inventive artists were drawn to them.

The most notable open exhibition of the season is the VICINITY SHOW, held annually at the Art Institute of Chicago, usually in the early spring.

The most active art organizations holding exhibitions are the PARTICIPATING ARTISTS OF CHICAGO, with annual shows at various locations; the ARTS CLUB, listed above, with its annual professional member show; the NORTH SHORE ART LEAGUE, which sponsors both painting and sculpture exhibitions at various locations under the title of "New Horizons"; the HYDE PARK ART CENTER, 5236 S. Blackstone, and its series of exhibitions during the year; and the SOUTH SHORE ART LEAGUE, which sponsors various art events.

Where to Look

The Art Institute of Chicago
Michigan and Adams, CE 6-7080
One of this country's great museums, excelling in primitive, Early American, and French Impressionist art. Collected at the turn of

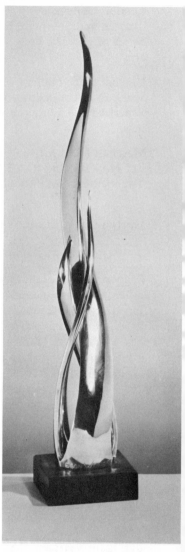

(Left) Artist unknown: Bull. (Assyrian, from the palace of Sargon II, 722–705 B.C., Khorsabad, Iraq.) Part of the collection of the Oriental Institute, University of Chicago, Chicago, Illinois. (Right) Egon Weiner: *Pillar of Fire*. Bronze. Height: 30 inches. Shown at the Conrad Gallery, Chicago, Illinois.

Exhibition of works by Milton Avery, November, 1966,
Richard Gray Gallery, Chicago, Illinois.

Exhibition of sculpture by Milton Hebald, 1966, the Kovler Gallery,
Chicago, Illinois.

the century by astute Chicago art lovers, the Impressionist and Post-Impressionist art cache includes whole roomfuls of Monets, Picassos, and Renoirs. (Chicagoans like to say, "We don't buy Monets here, we inherit them from our grandmothers.") Seurat's Institute masterpiece "La Grande Jatte" is world renowned and El Greco's "Assumption of the Virgin" is the largest major work of that artist in the United States. Another treasure of the Institute is its Print and Drawing collection. THE JUNIOR MUSEUM, which opened in March, 1964, and cost two hundred fifty thousand dollars, is the largest in the United States outside of New York City. The Institute's professional art school yearly holds its excellent student annuals, from which it is possible to buy work. Admission is free; open 9-5 daily, except 9 a.m.-9:30 p.m. Thurs, noon-5 Sun.

The Oriental Institute of the University of Chicago
1155 E. 55th, MI 3-0800, ext. 2471
This is a research institute and museum devoted to Near Eastern studies. The collection specializes in the prehistory and archaeology of the Ancient Near East, with objects and artifacts from Sumer, Akkad, Babylonia, Assyria, the Achaemenid civilization of ancient Persia, Palestine, Canaan, Choga Mish in Southern Iran, Anatolia, Egypt, and Nubia. Admission and guide service are free; credit courses with the University of Chicago; open 10-noon and 1-5 Tues, Wed, 10-5 Thurs-Sun; closed Mon, Memorial Day, July 4, Labor Day, Thanksgiving, New Year's Day, Christmas.

Field Museum of Natural History
Roosevelt and Lake Shore, 922-9410
Primarily a natural history museum, but also offers displays in Oriental archeological and ethnological material; Pacific and African artifacts, and Old World prehistory. Admission is 25¢ except free on Thurs, Sat, Sun; children, students, and teachers always free. Limited authentication of primitive objects by appointment. Credit courses with the University of Chicago. Free parking at north entrance. Open Nov-Feb: 9-4 daily, 9-5 Sat-Sun; March-April and Sept-Oct: 9-5 daily; May-Labor Day: 9-6 daily, except 9-8 p.m. Wed, Fri, Sat, Sun during mid-June to Labor Day.

Information about Art

Newspaper listings can be found in the "Panorama" section of the *Chicago Daily News,* in the *Chicago Tribune,* and in the *Chicago Sun-Times. The Chicago Arts Calendar* (The Adult Education

The Milwaukee Art Center galleries occupy the lower level of the Milwaukee County War Memorial Building (architect: Eero Saarinen; completed 1957). Milwaukee, Wisconsin. (*Courtesy Milwaukee Journal*)

Interior exhibit, the Milwaukee Art Center, Milwaukee, Wisconsin. (*Courtesy Milwaukee Journal*)

Council of Greater Chicago, 322 S. Michigan) is a bimonthly listing obtainable by subscription and in the galleries. The monthly magazines *Chicago Art Reviews* and *Mid-West Reviews* feature art columns. *WMFT Guide* is a radio-station guide with a complete calendar of local cultural events.

MILWAUKEE, WIS.

Milwaukee Art Center
750 Lincoln Mem. Dr., 271-9508
Located in the Eero Saarinen-designed Milwaukee War Memorial Building, the Center offers a fine permanent collection of Western art from the Renaissance to today; a major group of modern paintings and sculpture; and a strong selection of American art of all periods. Its third-floor rental and sales gallery offers the best of Wisconsin art to the public. Open 11-4 daily, 1-5 Sun. Rentals are as low as $5 to $25 for a two-month period. The Gallery Shop, located at the entrance to the galleries, makes available antique decorative arts, folk art, and pre-Columbian and Greco-Roman antiquities, ranging in price from $5 to $3,000. Occasional authentication by appointment; recommendation for A-R, F; parking lot 25¢; varied music, dance, drama, lecture, and film program. Admission is free; open 10-5 Mon-Wed, Fri, Sat, 10-10:30 Thurs, 1-5 Sun; closed Christmas, New Year's.

THE TWIN CITIES:
MINNEAPOLIS AND ST. PAUL, MINN.

By Dorothy Heckman Gregor

Where to Buy

Minneapolis

American Wildlife Art Galleries
822 Plymouth Bldg., 338-7247
The Gallery specializes in wildlife and Western Americana, subjects peculiarly suited to the Minneapolis area. Les Kouba is the director, and his very fine watercolors of Canadian duck-hunting scenes sell for $250 and $350. Besides watercolors and oils, Kouba also has sculpture, some etchings, and a few ceramics. The gallery, though

small, is attractively and efficiently arranged. Prices $25-$500, with a few paintings in the low thousands. Open 9-12 and 2-4 daily; closed Sat, Sun.

American Swedish Institute
2600 Park, 335-7621
A combined gallery and historic house, the Institute was erected as a thirty-three room mansion-castle at the turn of the century at a cost of a million and a half dollars. Inside, beautiful mahogany-paneled rooms provide the setting for eleven porcelainized fireplaces or *kakelugnar* and numerous glass, china, and textile artifacts. The permanent collection includes Swedish-American art, textiles, silver, wood carvings, and pioneer and immigrant items. The changing exhibits, in the sales and rental gallery, feature members of the Institute, usually Swedish-American artists. Art, priced from $25 to $500, can be purchased, or it can be rented for as little as three dollars a month. Most of the work is Realistic. Swedish crafts, mostly woodcarvings and glass, are also available in the gift shop. Parking; R; guided tours; folk-dancing recitals; library; Swedish classes. Admission: 50¢ adults, 25¢ children. Open 2-5 Thurs-Sun and open daily June-Aug except Mon.

Gallery 12, Dayton's Downtown
700 Nicollet, 332-6123
Located on the twelfth floor of this department store, the gallery has a good selection of American and European contemporaries. Examples include Arp, Calder, Chagall, Moore, Klee, Kirchner, and some Pop art by the American Jim Dine. Prices slightly higher here. Adjacent parking ramp; M, Install, F. Open 9:30-9 p.m. Mon, Thurs; 9:30-5:45 Tues-Wed, Fri-Sat.

Kilbride-Bradley Gallery
68 S 10, 336-0252
The unique feature of this gallery is a facetious monthly publication called *The Potboiler*. It, and the gallery, reflects the personalities of Byron Bradley and Robert Kilbride. As young graduates of the Minneapolis School of Art in 1950, they put in a year in Paris, then returned to found the gallery. You'll find mostly local artists here, and the opportunity to rent works of art. Prints are also included, as well as some nice pottery by Bradley. Parking lot across street; open 9:30-5:30 Mon-Sat; closed Sun.

Lucille Dahl
80 S 12, 336-3939
Just outside of downtown Minneapolis, this gallery offers American

and Oriental antiques, such as pewter, copper, a few Early American paintings. It's fun to browse. Parking; open 10:30-5 Mon-Fri, 10:30-3 Sat; other days 10:30-4; closed Saturdays in July.

Windsor Gallery
5019 France S., Edina, 927-6041
European artists, all media. Prices $10-$250. F, R, Install; parking behind building. Open 10-5 Mon-Sat; closed Sun.

M.A.S. "The Place" Gallery
1500 6th, 822-8027
Contemporary paintings, drawings, prints, mosaics; group and one-man exhibitions of young artists. Open 12-7:30 p.m. daily; closed Mon summer.

St. Paul

Hamline University Galleries, Dept. of Art
1536 Hewitt, 646-4843
Changing exhibitions of contemporary art, in addition to the permanent collections. Admission free; open 9-4:30 daily; closed Sat, Sun.

Keljik Oriental Rug & Antiques Galleries
600 Pleasant, CA 2-1197
Founded in 1898, this gallery is rather expensive, although you might find some buys among the Oriental vases and china, and the American etchings, paintings, and furniture. Parking; open 10-5:30; closed Sun; closed Sat July-Aug.

Suzanne Kohn Gallery
1690 Grand, 699-0477
A small gallery in the St. Paul suburbs that carries contemporary art by area artists. Oils, watercolors, ceramics, prints. Miss Kohn's pet miniature schnauzer, Fritzie, will greet you at the door. The gallery's commitment is to showing the best in regional art. M, F, Install; parking. Open 1-5 Mon-Sat; closed July-Aug.

Kramer Galleries
507 Wabasha, 225-5722
Devoted to featuring Minnesota and other U.S. painters, as well as local craftsmen. Mr. Kramer also has some more expensive work by Maurice Utrillo, Pierre Mignard, Samuel Waldo, etc. On the other hand, his 1847 German costume prints for six dollars each

are a real bargain. His Summer Craft Fair is an annual event. Open 9-5:30 Mon-Sat, 9-9 Thurs; closed Sun.

Where to Look·

The Minneapolis Institute of Arts
201 E 24, 339-7661

The permanent collection here runs the whole gamut of art history from Mesopotamia to the contemporaries. It also features sixteen thousand master prints and drawings. Housed in a Neo-Classic McKim, Mead & White building, the Institute has been one of the most active museums in the country in its art rental and educational programs. Its Little Gallery for Sales and Rentals has monthly exhibits of paintings, graphics, and sculpture, as well as a bin for browsing. All are twenty-five dollars and up, complete with frames or mats. Works are also sold from certain special exhibitions in the museum. Authenticating by appointment. Parking lot with charge. Credit/non-credit courses with University of Minnesota. Open 10-5 Wed-Sat, 10-10 Tues, 1-5 Sun, holidays; closed Mon, Christmas, New Year's.

Walker Art Center
1710 Lyndale S., 377-6234

Outstanding exhibitions of regional, national, and international art are initiated yearly by the Center and many are circulated to other major American and Canadian museums. Its permanent collection of twentieth-century painting, sculpture, drawing, and prints is one of the most important in the country, and its examples of Oriental jade, ceramics, and sculpture are also well known. Its catalogs and publication, *Design Quarterly,* are noted for their graphic design and reference value. The sales and rental gallery offers art by regional artists from $25 to $2,000, and visitors may often purchase art from the changing exhibitions in the Center. Parking; authentication of contemporary art. Admission is free; open 10-5 Fri, Sat, 10-10 Tues-Thurs, noon-6 Sun; closed Mon.

University Gallery, University of Minnesota
Northrop Memorial Auditorium, 3rd and 4th fls., 373-3424

A good permanent collection primarily of twentieth-century American paintings, sculptures, and prints, plus changing exhibits by the faculty and graduate students, and traveling exhibitions. There is a rental gallery, but it is available only to University staff and students. Admission is free; open 8:30-4 Mon-Fri, 2-5 Sun when announced; closed Sat, holidays.

Interior view, the American Wildlife Art Gallery, Minneapolis, Minnesota.

Director Suzanne Kohn and dog Fritzie, the Suzanne Kohn Gallery,
St. Paul, Minnesota.

Part of the Sculpture Court, Walker Art Center, Minneapolis, Minnesota, showing (left to right) *Winter Wall* by Peter Agostini, *Reclining Mother and Child* by Henry Moore, and *La Grande Chiave* by Giacomo Manzù.

The Minneapolis Institute of Art, Minneapolis, Minnesota.

Minneapolis Public Library
500 Nicollet, 338-0781
Although no exhibits of art are mounted, the library maintains a file of local artists' and galleries' addresses. Parking. Admission is free; open 9-9 Mon-Thurs, 9-5 Sat, 9-5:30 Fri; hours change in summer.

St. Paul Art Center
30 E 10, 227-7613
Special exhibits of outstanding contemporary painting, sculpture, drawings, and crafts are mounted in this handsomely designed modern building. Its permanent collection includes twentieth-century and primitive arts. Many of the works from the exhibits are for sale. Its "Fiber, Clay, Metal" biennials are rightly famous. Parking. Admission is free; open 10-5 Tues, Wed, 10-10 Thurs-Sat, 1-10 Sun; closed Mon, Christmas, New Year's, Memorial, Independence, Labor, and Thanksgiving days.

Information about Art

The *Minneapolis Tribune* regularly reviews art exhibits and publishes a complete art calendar each Sunday. Two magazines, *Minneapolis Guide to Dining, Entertainment and the Arts* (1000 Upper Midwest Bldg., 335-8821 or 332-2391) and the *Twin Citian* (400 National Bldg., 333-6331) have art listings and articles. The *St. Paul Pioneer Press* has Sunday listings of shows, while the newspaper of the University of Minnesota, the *Minneapolis Daily,* has excellent coverage of the U.M. Gallery as well as occasional art listings, announcements, and reviews.

ST. LOUIS, MO.

The roster of actively exhibiting artists could fill a large file drawer. About a hundred artists are consistently productive, with between twenty and thirty active on the national scene.

The leading St. Louis artists include: Kent Addison, young sculptor; Frederick Becker, printmaker; Edward E. Boccia, painter; Fred Conway, painter; Belle Cramer, painter; Patricia Degener, ceramicist; Fred Dreher, painter and sculptor; H. Richard Duhme, Jr., sculptor; William Fett, painter; Alexandra Korsakoff-Galston, enamels; Charles Galt, portraitist; Gustav F. Goetsch, painter; Sheldon Helfman, painter; Muriel Helfman, weaver; Fred Henze, ceramicist, mainly plaques and sculpture; Howard Jones, painter and constructor; Helen Jones, sculptor; Robert Jordan, painter; Myrtle Kornblum, painter and printmaker; Leslie Laskie, painter and designer; Arthur Osver, painter; Ernestine Betsberg (Osver), painter; Charles Quest, painter and printmaker; William Quinn, painter; Siegfried Reinhardt, painter; Joan Rosen, painter; Aimee Schweig, painter; Ann Scott, sculptor; Wallace H. Smith, painter; Stanley Tasker, painter; Marie Taylor, sculptor; Rudolph Torrini, sculptor; Ernest Trova, painter and constructor; Lee Wallas, painter; Rodney Winfield, painter and sculptor; and Simon Ybarra, sculptor.

Many of these, and other artists, are teachers. The principal school is the Fine Arts School of Washington University, with Arthur Osver and Siegfried Reinhardt, among others listed above, on its faculty.

All art categories can be purchased in the under-one-hundred-dollar price range with a lot in the more prevalent professional range of up to and around five hundred dollars. The top artists now display price tags of up to $1,500 or more.

Paintings are the most available, but prints, small sculpture, and crafts are becoming quite popular. Crafts include mainly weaving, ceramics, some metalwork, jewelry, and, occasionally, glass.

There is no St. Louis "school" stylistically. The style range is from barns to Op.

Nearby colleges and universities such as Southern Illionois University at Carbondale and the Alton campus of Missouri University, and several colleges in the immediate area have strong art departments. McCluer High School has nine art instructors.

The CITY ART MUSEUM, operated by city taxes with free admission, has around three hundred fifty thousand annual attendance and is picking up steam with a new administration of young staff members. The STEINBERG HALL GALLERIES of Washington University are especially active in contemporary exhibits. The ST. LOUIS ARTISTS' GUILD (812 N. Union Blvd., FO 1-6043), organized in 1886 and in its own building since 1908, is *the* prime art force here with a yearly schedule of exhibitions, competitions, and demonstrations. Parking lot; open noon-4 daily, 1-5 Sun, closed Tues.

Where to Buy

The main action is in the "West End," an area of turn-of-the-century houses and shops near the northeast corner of Forest Park.

It is an outlying section of St. Louis that was built up at the time of the 1904 World's Fair (Louisiana Purchase Exposition), and includes many blocks of nice old town houses of that vintage. Maryland, Euclid, and McPherson Avenues are in this neighborhood.

The "spine" concentration is roughly along Lindell Boulevard, between downtown and Clayton, which connects the West End galleries, Forest Park, Washington University, Clayton, and also St. Louis University.

The West End galleries usually have Sunday openings early in each month, with a "gallery walk" that encourages browsing in all, usually with refreshments at each gallery. These are very popular with the public.

This gallery concentration, in what is called the Maryland-Euclid-McPherson area, has:

The Martin Schweig Gallery
4647 Maryland, FO 1-4226
Director Martin Schweig, Jr., aims at showing work of outstanding quality, whether it is of St. Louis talent or from elsewhere. This is a long-established gallery of top rank. Parking in rear.

Norton's Gallery
325 N. Euclid, FO 7-9917
A frame shop that exhibits good paintings and prints. It carries signed, limited print editions by such well-knowns as Afro, Arp, Dali, Pissarro.

The following cooperative galleries were founded by groups of painters, sculptors, and craftsmen respectively. Like most "coops," all had rather shaky beginnings, but are now in the black and flourishing:

Craft Alliance Gallery
4738 McPherson, FO 1-2121
Craft coop.

Painters Gallery
386 N. Euclid, FO 1-7400
Painters' coop. Contemporary, local artists. All mediums. $50-$1,000. F, R to businesses only, Install. Parking; open 11-5 Mon-Sat.

Sculptors Gallery
388 N. Euclid, FO 7-1811
Sculptors' coop. Sculpture by the twenty-eight St. Louis sculptors who own the gallery. The only gallery in St. Louis solely devoted to

sculpture. Summer rental only; Install; Parking; open 10-4 Tues-Sat; 4-7 the first Sunday of every month.

Antiques

Margo Antiques
4428-30 Olive, JE 3-4865
Specializes in American furniture and glass, and English ceramics and porcelain.

Suburbs, Environs: Except for the Richelle Gallery, the outlying galleries are usually art-supply shops that offer classes and exhibit student work in a sort of a closed circle cycle. Some young talent does sometimes show up, however.

Richelle Gallery
8236 Forsyth, Clayton, VO 3-8150
This is a favorite of the new collectors, and is a full-time gallery. It carries mainly imports of paintings, prints, and occasionally sculpture. Prices are usually $200 to $300, with some also higher.

The Art Mart
31 N. Meramec, Clayton, PA 5-7858

Art Mart Gallery II
9983 Manchester, Clayton, TA 2-3900
Both have exhibits by students from their classes. Also art supplies sold.

Miscellanea

Most public libraries, even in the suburbs, have rentals of art reproductions. These are quite active. Galleries usually allow try-out periods of works they hope to sell.

Steinberg Hall, Washington University
6200 block, Forsyth Blvd., VO 3-0100
Has changing exhibitions of first-rate contemporary work, as well as showing the Washington University permanent collection of painting and sculpture. Open 9-5 Mon-Fri, 10-4 Sat, 1-5 Sun.

Pius XII Memorial Library, St. Louis University
3655 W. Pine, JE 5-3300
The library has exhibition space on three floors, and features changing shows of well-known artists tastefully displayed.

Loretto-Hilton Center for the Performing Arts, Webster College
135 Edgar, Webster Groves, WO 8-0500
This is a beautiful exhibition space set in the large foyer of the
theater auditorium. It was spanking new in 1966. Parking lot across
street; open 10-4 daily, 1-7 Sun.

South County Bank
110 S. County Centerway, IV 7-6000
Offers excellent exhibitions of contemporary art.

Famous-Barr Department Store
6th and Olive, GA 1-5900
Headed by Morton D. May, a foremost collector, the store has had
several major exhibition-sales of African, Polynesian, Greco-Roman, and pre-Columbian art, plus a topnotch show of Jacob Epstein sculpture. Prices (except for the Epstein pieces) range from
$50 to $4,000.

Sears, Roebuck & Co.
North Store, 1408 N. Kingshighway, FO 1-1000
Has had the Vincent Price Collection temporarily.

Scruggs-Vandervoort-Barney
10th and Olive, CH 1-7500

Stix, Baer & Fuller
601 Washington, CE 1-6500
Both the above department stores have had various art events,
usually by high school and elementary school students.

In addition, the suburban shopping centers often set up SPRING
ART FESTIVALS, sometimes for youngsters, sometimes for professionals, which are good for the general art scene.

Art Festivals and Art Organizations

THE MISSOURI SHOW, sponsored every odd-numbered year by
the City Art Museum, is an important competition judged by artists
or other authorities of national prominence.

THE SPRINGFIELD (MO.) ART MUSEUM NATIONAL
WATERCOLOR COMPETITION (1111 E. Brookside, Springfield, Mo., UN 6-2716) is an excellent place for the modest buyer
to purchase first-rate works of art, in this case the often neglected
medium of watercolor. An annual event usually held in May, the
competition attracts top artists through its stiff jurying and attractive
purchase prizes.

The KIRKWOOD OPEN AIR ART FAIR, in Kirkwood Park, initiated in 1951, is a two-day, mid-September event open to anyone who wants to enter work in any medium. Each entrant is assigned a panel of the cyclone fence around the Kirkwood Park tennis courts for hanging his or her work. The art is juried and cash prizes awarded. The fair is sponsored by the St. Louis County Art Association and the Kirkwood Chamber of Commerce.

The WEBSTER GROVES FESTIVAL OF THE ARTS, initiated in 1963, is an exhibition and competition open to St. Louis area artists of all ages. It is sponsored by the Gore-Lockwood Trade Association, a group of merchants of the area, and pulls in as many as five thousand persons during the one day in May that it is held. It is an out-of-doors, sidewalk show where it is fun to browse.

The ST. LOUIS ARTISTS' GUILD, mentioned earlier, has annual competitions in oil and sculpture; prints, drawings, and crafts; portraits; and watercolors and pastels; with prizes totaling around $300 to $500 for each. It also organizes the GREATER ST. LOUIS ART FAIR, another outdoor event.

The SOCIETY OF INDEPENDENT ARTISTS is a group that will appeal to more conservative tastes. They exhibit in the refectory of the Kiel Auditorium Opera House and have annual prizes.

Where to Look

City Art Museum of St. Louis
Forest Park, PA 1-0067
Designed by architect Cass Gilbert in 1904 as the central building of the Palace of Art for the Louisiana Purchase Exposition. Offers art from all major cultures in its permanent collections. Some original prints, decorative items, design objects, and quality jewelry and craft items are sold at the sales desk in the Sculpture Hall. The price range is $5 to $100. You may also purchase from certain exhibitions. Authenticating by appointment; parking; credit courses with Washington University. Admission is free; open 2:30-9:30 Tues, 10-5 Wed-Sun; closed Mon, Christmas, New Year's Day.

Missouri Historical Society
Jefferson Memorial Bldg., PA 6-2622
Established in 1866 to preserve objects and documents relating to the history of Missouri and the Louisiana Purchase Territory,

City Art Museum, St. Louis, Missouri. (*Courtesy City Art Museum, St. Louis*)

Webster Groves Art Festival, 1966, Webster Groves, Missouri.

Interior view, the Painters Gallery, St. Louis, Missouri.

"An Adventure in Thailand" exhibition, Gallery of Folk Art,
Halls, Kansas City, Missouri, May, 1966.

the Society has an interesting collection of early Midwestern arts and crafts.

St. Louis Public Library
1301 Olive, CH 1-2288
Like the Museum, the library is housed in a building designed by Cass Gilbert. Offers changing exhibitions of mostly St. Louis artists, with some showings of national art groups. Metered parking; admission free; open 9-9 Mon-Fri, 9-5 Sat; closed June-Sept, holidays.

Information about Art

The Sunday Music and Arts page of the *St. Louis Post-Dispatch* lists gallery events and has regular articles on art here and in other cities. Walter Barker is the New York City correspondent, and covers the shows there. The Arts Page was instituted in 1956, when eight gallery listings were a lot; now it may have thirty or more. The *Globe-Democrat* also has a Sunday page on art. The ST. LOUIS ARTS AND EDUCATION COUNCIL (532 De Baliviere) publishes a monthly bulletin of exhibitions, lectures, and related activities, sent free to anyone who asks for it. Radio and TV operate on a special-events basis, often doing good things when they do them at all; they are interested in the more spectacular events, however.

KANSAS CITY, MO.

By Donald K. Hoffmann
Art Editor, *The Kansas City Star*

The price range of ten to five hundred dollars covers a lot of ground in Kansas City. Because of the presence of the NELSON GALLERY OF ART here, the privately endowed KANSAS CITY ART INSTITUTE AND SCHOOL OF DESIGN, and numerous colleges and universities within driving distance, Kansas City is more than a Sunday-Painter art market.

Graphics generally run from about $20 to $150. Probably the strongest demand is for the lithographs of Thomas Hart Benton (mostly executed in the 1930s and 1940s), who lives here at 3616 Belleview Avenue. Their price range is generally $75 to $150, though the number of prints continues to dwindle. Other popular lithographers include Jack Lemon of the Art Institute staff and Thomas Coleman of the University of Nebraska.

Frederick James, a Kansas City artist, is extremely popular with his watercolor paintings, which sell from about $100 to $400. Cecil Carstenson, a local sculptor, sells very well at prices from about $60 to $400.

There is a marked lack of substantial oil paintings in the Kansas City area.

Perhaps the best place for buying art is the FRIENDS OF ART SALES & RENTAL GALLERY on the mezzanine floor of the NELSON GALLERY OF ART, 4525 Oak St. This is a volunteer organization that works closely with the professional curatorial staff of the Gallery, sometimes showing area artists, but often bringing in topnotch art on consignment from dealers in New York, Chicago, and San Francisco. A recent sculpture show included items priced at more than $20,000 and ranging down to $350, with pieces by Degas, Matisse, Daumier, Calder, Lipchitz, Moore, Braque, Léger, et cetera. Each fall the Friends of Art sponsors an "Art Market" in their galleries, with about five hundred pieces of art ranging from about $5 to $20,000. This organization provides the widest range of choice in buying art here, both in price and medium.

Where to Buy

The leading private galleries here are all in the southwest part of the city.

Palmer Gallery
6330 Brookside Plaza, DE 3-9334
The gallery offers one- or two-man shows nearly every month. It specializes in contemporary Mid-American artists such as Thomas Hart Benton (lithographs), Karl Mattern, Byron Burford. Prices $10-$3,000. Parking; F, A-R, Install.

Little Gallery Frame Shop, Inc.
5002 State Line, Shawnee Mission, Kansas, CO 2-2602
All mediums; local, national, and international artists; pottery and books. Parking; M, F, A-R, Install. Open 10-5.

Lawrence Gallery
901 Westport, JE 1-2423
American contemporary art, sculpture, prints, ceramics. Parking; Install. Open 10-5 Mon-Sat; 11-4 Mon-Fri summer.

Gallery of Folk Art, Halls
211 Nichols, CR 4-3486

The gallery offers a variety of authentic folk art from forty-five countries. Some of the objects offered in this modern, spacious gallery are soapstones carved by the Baffin Islands Eskimos; embroideries by the children of Peru; molas made by the Indians of the San Blas Islands of Panama. Part of the idea here is to get children interested in the idea of collecting original art. In addition, there are full-scale exhibits of six to eight weeks, including in the past a spectacular Art of Thailand show, a Japanese antiquities exhibit, and a collection of bronzes from India. Prices range from 10¢ to $20,000. M, Install. Open 9:30-5:30 except 9:30-8:30 Mon, Thurs.

Kansas City Art Institute and School of Design
4415 Warwick, LO 1-4852

The Charlotte Crosby Kemper Gallery, in which student, faculty, and guest work is exhibited and sold, is on the main floor of the Student Living Center. The Center is one of twelve buildings set in a beautifully landscaped twelve-and-a-half-acre campus. The Institute is the city's oldest cultural institution, organized in 1815, and is a highly active force on the Kansas City art scene. Drawings are $5 up, paintings and sculpture $25 up, prints $10 up, and ceramics $3 up. The pottery is of especially good quality. Parking; open 2-5 weekdays, 10-5 Sat, 2-5 Sun.

Antiques

Treasure House
7234 Wornall, HI 4-3033

Au Marche
320 Ward Pkwy., JE 1-6633

Miscellanea

All Souls Unitarian Church
4500 Warwick Blvd.
Features changing exhibitions of paintings and sculpture every six to eight weeks.

Plaza Art Fair
Sears' covered parking lot, Nichols Pkwy., Country Club Plaza
This art event, begun in 1931, is generally recognized as a model for community fairs.

Wichita Art Association
9112 E. Central, Wichita, Kansas, MU 6-6687
A wide range of work by living artists and craftsmen is shown. Install (by arrangement with artist); parking. Open 1-5 daily; closed Mon and during August.

Where to Look

Nelson Gallery of Art
4525 Oak, LO 1-4000
This is perhaps the most distinguished museum between the Mississippi River and the West Coast. It has outstanding examples of art of all periods, and is particularly strong in Oriental art with Asian art specialist Lawrence Sickman as the Gallery's director. THE FRIENDS OF ART SALES AND RENTAL GALLERY, already mentioned, is open 1-4 Tues-Sat, 2-6 Sun. It sells A, G, Mods, and Eu, and rents. Gallery hours: 10-5 Tues-Sat, 2-6 Sun.

Information about Art

The *Kansas City Star* carries a weekly art column and listing of exhibitions at galleries here and the museums of St. Louis, Wichita, the University of Kansas at Lawrence, Kansas, and the University of Missouri at Columbia, Mo.

The Southwest

COLORADO:
DENVER, COLORADO SPRINGS,
BOULDER AND ASPEN

Denver

Where to Buy

The Gallery
314 Detroit, 388-1498
Contemporaries in all media: twelve area artists; well-known printmakers. F, Install. Parking. Open 10-5 daily.

Hal Lipstein Interiors
3rd and Fillmore, 388-0831
Some original crafts.

Kohlberg's
429 17th, TA 5-4578
Mr. Kohlberg, the proprietor, is knowledgeable and honest about
the Indian arts material he sells.

Public Library
1357 Broadway, 266-0851
The library collaborates with the Denver Museum on its monthly
art exhibits, also carries many reference books on art.

Rubinstein-Serkez, Inc.
248 Fillmore, 355-5774
Contemporary art. F, R, Install. Open 12:30-4:30 daily; closed
Sun.

Two Squares Art Gallery
2737 E. Third, 355-8637
Contemporaries.

Where to Look

Colorado State Historical Museum
E. 14th and Sherman, 222-9911, ext. 2136
Offers Western and Indian exhibits. Admission is free; open 9-5
daily, 10-5 weekends and holidays.

COLORADO 343

The Denver Art Museum
W. 14th and Acoma, 297-2793

Founded in 1893 as the Denver Artists Club with no capital funds, no art collections, and no permanent building, the original organization has evolved into the largest historic art museum between Kansas City and San Francisco and serves an eight-state area. It is an important storehouse of art, noted for its Oriental, Indian, and Samuel H. Kress Renaissance arts collections, in addition to providing excellent buying opportunities with its annual "Own Your Own," Metropolitan, Western Annual, and Colorado Artist Craftsmen shows. A juried exhibition usually held in the spring, "OWN YOUR OWN" had its tenth anniversary in 1966 and usually offers over one thousand objects with prices ranging from $2 to $1,000. Crafts, as well as paintings, sculptures, and prints, are included. The METROPOLITAN is a juried show open to all artists in the Denver metropolitan area, while the COLORADO ARTIST CRAFTSMEN COLLECTIONS are juried from submissions of the organization and are regularly for sale in the Museum Shop. Currently in the works is a dramatic new six-story structure to house the Museum, designed by Gio Ponti of Milan. Admission is free; art history courses offered; credit courses with the University of Denver; authentication by appointment; will recommend A-R, F. Open 9-5 Tues-Sat, 2-5 Sun, holidays, 1-5 Mon; closed New Year's, Easter, July 4th, Thanksgiving, Christmas.

Colorado Springs

Colorado Springs Fine Arts Center
30 W. Dale, 634-5581

Puts on about thirty-five exhibitions of painting, drawing, watercolor, lithography, sculpture, crafts, architecture, and photography annually. The work of local students and children from the Center's Art School is also presented. The CONTEMPORARY ART SOCIETY has made possible the building up of a permanent collection of nineteenth- and twentieth-century American and European art, while the TAYLOR MUSEUM, the department of the Center concerned with arts from other cultures, evolved from Alice Bemis Taylor's lifelong interest in the arts of the American Southwest and Latin America. Especially notable are the *santos,* or Spanish-American religious art, the most extensive collection of its kind in the country. The Center also features a biennial exhibition of "Artists West of the Mississippi" and a Rental Gallery that is organized two or three times yearly in one of the exhibition galleries. Parking in

Interior view of the annual "Own Your Own" exhibition,
Denver Art Museum, Denver, Colorado.

Mr. and Mrs. Harry L. Baum, Jr., with the Harry Bertoia *Sound Sculpture* they
purchased for the Denver Art Museum, Denver, Colorado.

lot across street; admission free; authentication by appointment; will recommend A-R, F; credit and non-credit courses with Colorado College; art school on premises. Open Sept-May: 9-5 Tues-Sat, 1:30-5 Sun, closed Mon; June-Aug: 9-5 Mon-Sat, 1:30-5 Sun.

Boulder

The Boulder Historical Society and Boulder Pioneer Museum
1655 Broadway
Offers historical objects of all kinds, from collections of clothing, paintings, and glass plates to blacksmiths' and carpenters' tools. Parking lot. Admission 35¢ adults, 15¢ juniors, free to members, educational groups, and children under 12. Open 2-5; closed Sat, Sun mid-May to mid-Sept.

University of Colorado Museum
Broadway at 16th, 443-2211, ext. 6165
A combined natural history and art institution. It features changing monthly exhibitions of group shows, faculty work, and juried competitive exhibits in its Hall of Art; most of the work is available for purchase. Campus parking; admission free; will recommend A-R, F. Open 8-5 weekdays, 2-5 Sun, holidays.

Fine Arts Department Rental Gallery, University of Colorado
Fine Arts Building, Rm. 104, 443-2211
Offers contemporary art and graphics for rental. Open 8-noon, 1-5, Mon-Fri.

Aspen

Aspen Historical Society
328 E. Hyman, 925-3945
The Society's collections concentrate on antique furniture from old local homes, mining equipment, some Victorian clothing, maps and newspapers, and a large photographic exhibit pertaining to all aspects of Aspen history. Street parking; admission free; open 9-5 daily, 2-4 Sun.

The Aspen Institute for Humanistic Studies
P.O. Box 219, 925-7010
A non-profit educational institution which serves primarily as a conference and study center. It also mounts some first-rate art exhibits, such as the recent one of the 1964-65 work of Willem de Kooning, and the art of other well-known contemporaries. The Institute, in addition, has an Artists-in-Residence program under

which four leading contemporary artists are brought to Aspen each summer, working in the Brand Building, and holding panel discussions from time to time.

NEW MEXICO: ALBUQUERQUE, SANTA FÉ, AND TAOS

Albuquerque: There is a lot of American Indian art for sale here, but it takes a skilled eye to sort out the good from the bad. A few of the outlets are listed here; for others, contact the INDIAN ARTS AND CRAFTS BOARD, Room 4004, U.S. Department of the Interior, Washington, D.C. 20240, for their fact sheet titled *Potential Outlets for Indian and Eskimo Arts and Crafts* (see also the section on North American Indian art in this book).

American Indian Arts

El Toro Gifts
Patio, 2012 Plaza, N.W., 242-7204

Guild of American Indian Designer Craftsmen
308a San Felipe, N.W.

Livery Barn
14610 E. Central, 298-2290

Old Town Creative Art Shop
110 Romero, N.W., 242-5625

Wright's Indian Trading Post
518 Central, S.W., 247-8297

Other Arts

Jonson Gallery, The University of New Mexico
1909 Las Lomas, N.E., 243-4667
Director Raymond Jonson is a Professor Emeritus of Art from the University and also reputedly the driving force behind most Albuquerque artists. The gallery, devoted mainly to showing his own work while giving other artists one-man shows, takes no commission for works sold. Parking; open noon-6 daily.

New Mexico Arts & Crafts Fair
Old Town Plaza
This is an annual crafts display and sale held every June. It is open to all New Mexico artists.

New Mexico Art League Galleries
New Mexico State Fair Gallery of Fine Arts, 255-8427
Contemporary New Mexico artists and traveling exhibitions. Open 2-4 Tues-Fri, Sun; closed Mon, Sat.

University of New Mexico Art Gallery
Fine Arts Center, 243-8611
New Mexican art, both old and new. Open 12-5 Mon, Tues, Thurs, Fri, 12-5, 7-10 Wed, 1:30-5:30 Sun; closed Sat.

University of New Mexico, Museum of Anthropology
University 8 Roma, N.E., 243-8611, ext. 272
Navajo silver, rugs. Admission free; open 9-4 Tues-Sat; closed holidays.

Santa Fé: This community is an interesting art center for several reasons. Founded in 1610, Santa Fé was the second oldest settlement in the United States, and, while few early New Mexican art objects are left in the city, there are still many examples of early adobe architecture, *alacenas* or *trasterors* (heavily carved early cupboards or cabinets), and the little patron saint statues called *santos*. The presence of famed weaver Alice Parrott, who lives and works in Santa Fé with her husband, Allan, provides an excellent opportunity to see and buy from two topnotch craftsmen. In addition, designer Alexander Girard has founded the MUSEUM OF INTERNATIONAL FOLK ART at the Museum of New Mexico, an almost unique crafts museum. In Santa Fé, there are also many excellent opportunities to buy American Indian art, notably at the PLAZA in front of the Governor's Palace and at the INSTITUTE OF AMERICAN ARTS. Again, it is recommended that you consult the *Potential Outlets for Indian and Eskimo Arts and Crafts*, put out by the Indian Arts and Crafts Board, U.S. Department of the Interior.

Where to Buy

Indian Arts

Kachina House
610 Canyon, 982-8415

Institute of American Indian Arts, Student Sales Center
Cerrillos Rd., 983-8971
Although basically a school for the training of young Indian artists, the Institute also offers quality student art in its handsome adobe

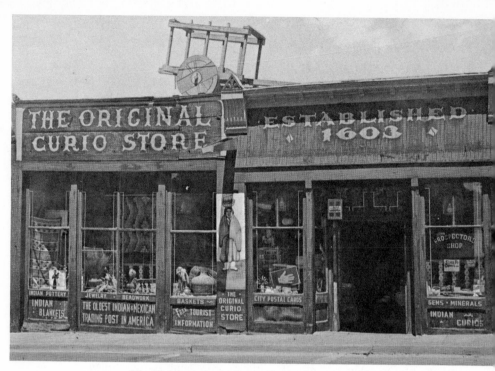

The Original Curio Store, Santa Fé, New Mexico.

Interior view, main gallery of the Blair Galleries, Ltd., Taos, New Mexico.

Institute of American Indian Arts, Santa Fé, New Mexico.

showroom building. It is run by the students, and all profits go for loans, scholarships, and special projects. Paintings, sculptures, graphics, and craft items are sold from $3 to $700. Open 8-5 daily.

The Morning Bird
720 Canyon, 983-7410

Arrowsmith Trading Post
402 College, 982-8141

Original Curio Store
201 W. San Francisco, 983-3451
Contemporary Indian art, mostly watercolors. Prices $15-$200. Parking; Open 8:30-5:30 daily winter; 8:30-9 p.m. daily summer.

Packard's Trading Post
61 Shelby, 983-9241

Other Arts

Doodlet's
111 E. San Francisco, 983-3771
Fine art and folk art, seventeenth through twentieth century. Prices $100 up. M, F, Install. Open 8:30-5 Mon-Sat.

Lippincott Studio
1270 Canyon, 982-0640
Work of Janet Lippincott only. Install; parking; open 9-5 daily.

The Market
111 E. Palace, 983-8920
Modern crafts; works by Alice and Allen Parrott. M, Install. Open 9-5 daily.

The Mud Palace
821 Canyon
An adobe mud hut that is a tourist attraction in itself, this gallery shows some of the best regional art of Santa Fé.

Where to Look

Museum of International Folk Art
Museum of New Mexico, Old Pecos Rd., 982-3628
A collection of folk arts from many countries all over the world, as well as *santos* and Spanish-Colonial art.

Dennis Beall: *Lone Star*. Three-color intaglio print. One of a limited edition of
twenty prints and two artist proofs commissioned by the C. Troup
Gallery-Codex Press, Inc., Dallas, Texas.

Museum of New Mexico
Fine Arts Bldg., 107 E. Palace, 982-3626
Southwestern U.S. art, traveling exhibitions. Admission is free; open 9-5 daily, 2-5 Sun, holidays.

Taos

Blair Galleries, Ltd.
Ledoux, Box 933, 758-4357, 758-4163 or 758-3094
Contemporary art, especially Western Americana and early American art. Styles are primarily representational to Expressionist. Prices $100 to several thousands. M, Install; parking. Open 9-5 daily.

Carl's Indian Trading Post
Kit Carson and Dragoon, 758-2378
Indian crafts, paintings.

Harwood Foundation
University of New Mexico, PL 8-3063
Taos artists, as well as Spanish Colonial art. Open 10-5 daily, closed Sun.

Manchester Gallery
Ledoux, El Prado, 758-3080
Just a short drive from Taos, this gallery offers contemporary southwesterners. Parking; Install. Open 9-5 daily summer; afternoon and by appointment winter.

DALLAS-FORT WORTH, TEXAS

Dallas

Atelier Chapman Kelley
2508 Maple, RI 7-9971
The gallery exhibits contemporary paintings, sculptures, and graphics by American and foreign artists. Prices $75-$4,000. Parking; Install. Open 10-5 Tues-Sat, 1-5 Sun; closed Mon.

Sanger-Harris
Akard and Pacific, RI 8-3611
All periods represented in oils, lithographs, etchings, et cetera. Moderate to expensive. Install; F. Parking in next-door garage. Open 9:30-5:45 daily and until 9 p.m. Mon, Thurs.

C. Troup Gallery, Inc.
2528 Fairmount, RI 7-2259

This gallery concentrates on well-known contemporary print-makers, but will "branch out of the print field when we find an artist that we enjoy." In the fall of 1964 the Codex Press Workshop was added to the gallery, enabling artists to print graphics at the Workshop. Trained printmakers can use the press for a small fee, while there are also several print courses offered for beginners. The gallery commissions print series from artists. M, F, A-R, Install. Parking; open 10-4 Tues-Sat, 2-5 Sun with 2-7 public openings; closed Mon.

Valley House Gallery
6616 Spring Valley, AD 9-2441

French and American contemporaries. Open 10-5 daily.

The Dallas Museum of Fine Arts
State Fair Park, HA 1-4189

Has a permanent collection of fine and decorative arts of the United States, Mexico, South America, and Europe. It is also noted for its Texas folk arts. About forty exhibitions are assembled each season, and its Museum School offers painting and art history classes for adults and Saturday classes for children. It is possible to buy art from its annual competitive exhibitions, and through the Art Rental Program, which has been going for some time. The Museum also features "Young Collections" shows. Admission is free; open 10-5 Tues, Thurs-Sat, 10-9 Wed, 2-6 Sun; closed Mon, Christmas.

Fort Worth

Carlin Galleries
710 Montgomery, PE 8-6921

Among the thirty local and United States contemporaries represented are Peter Hurd, Henriette Wyeth, Adolf Dehn, Luis Eades, and Joseph Domjan. Patio parking lot; Install. Open 10-5 Mon-Fri, 2-6 Sun; closed July.

Josephine Mahaffey
Jacksboro Hwy., CE 7-2181

European and American contemporaries, all mediums. Prices $5-$300. M, A-R, F, R, Install. Parking; open 10-5 daily, 2-6 Sun.

Amon Carter Museum of Western Art
3501 Camp Bowie, PE 2-2847

This handsome museum, designed by Philip Johnson, is devoted to the visual documentation of the culture of westering North America, with outstanding examples of the art of Frederick Remington and Charles Russell. The museum also maintains an excellent reference library specializing in Texana and Western Americana. Admission free; parking; authentication of Western Americana by appointment; will recommend A-R, F. Open 10-5 Tues-Sat, 1-5:30 Sun; closed Mon except June 1-Labor Day.

Heritage Hall
604 Main, ED 6-1223
Traces the history and heritage of the Old West through the first thirty-five years of the city of Fort Worth and also offers other relics of the Old West. An art gallery on the lower floor sells juried paintings, sculpture, pottery, and graphics by local artists. Admission $1 adults, 50¢ children; open 10-9 Sat, 11-6 Sun.

The Fort Worth Art Center
1309 Montgomery, PE 8-9216
A city-owned culture complex of museum, art school, and theater. It is possible to buy original graphics at the sales desk, to rent art of selected local artists, and to purchase a variety of types of art from visiting exhibitions. The permanent collection ranges from the sixteenth-century Salviati "Portrait of a Young Man" to the twentieth-century "Murder with a Sun Umbrella" by Paul Klee. About thirty exhibitions are scheduled yearly. Admission is free; parking; authentication by appointment; will recommend A-R, F. Open 10-5:30 Tues-Sat, 1-5:30 Sun; closed Mon.

Fort Worth Children's Museum
1501 Montgomery, PE 2-1631
Student work can be purchased from the Education Department. Admission free; parking; open 9-5 Mon-Sat, 2-5 Sun; closed holidays.

HOUSTON, TEXAS

Where to Buy

James Bute Gallery
1983 W. Gray, JA 8-0584
Contemporary painting, sculpture, crafts, graphics. Open 8-5 Mon-Fri, 8-noon Sat; closed Sun.

Long & Co., The Houston Galleries
2323 San Felipe, JA 3-9337
Nineteenth- and twentieth-century American, French art. M, A-R,
F, R for business firms. Parking; open 1-6 daily; closed Sun.

Louisiana Gallery
3312 Louisiana, JA 8-1281
Modern, pre-Columbian, Mexican Colonial arts. Open 8-5 daily;
closed June-Oct.

Galeria, Sakowitz
1111 Main, 4th fl., CA 5-6441
Contemporaries, graphics.

The Shamrock Hilton
Hilton Ctr., MO 8-9211
Paintings on display in the private International Club may be
purchased by members. An annual antiques show is also held at
the hotel.

University of St. Thomas Art Gallery
Sul Ross at Yoakum, JA 9-1919
Changing exhibitions. Open 1-6 Mon-Wed, Fri, Sat; 1-9 Thurs;
closed Sun.

Where to Look

Contemporary Arts Museum
6945 Fannin, RI 8-1680
Offers mainly traveling exhibitions and a rental gallery in the rear
of the main gallery. Admission is free; will recommend A-R, F.
Open 10-5 Mon-Fri; 1-5 Sat, Sun; closed New Year's, July 4th,
Labor Day, Thanksgiving, Christmas Eve and Day.

Museum of Fine Arts of Houston
1001 Bissonnet, JA 6-1361
Features changing exhibitions of contemporary art and special collections, such as the Kress Collection of Italian and Spanish Renaissance masters, works by Western artist Frederick Remington, primitive arts, et cetera. Its dramatic new wing, added in 1958, was designed by Mies van der Rohe. The Junior Gallery offers changing
exhibits of special interest to young people. Admission is free; open
9:30-5 daily, noon-6 Sun, 9:30-5, 7-10 Wed Oct-June; closed
Mon, holidays.

ARIZONA:
PHOENIX, FLAGSTAFF, PRESCOTT, SCOTTSDALE, TUCSON, AND YUMA

Phoenix

The Four Seasons
10012 Cave Creek
All mediums. Prices $5-$350.

Galaxy Gallery
4747 N. 7th
Contemporary European paintings and sculptures. Prices $25-$5,000.

Tewa
5305 N. 7th
All mediums. Prices $50-$500.

Heard Museum of Anthropology and Primitive Art
22 E. Monte Vista, 252-8848
Features paintings by American Indians, including works by early Indian easel painters and contemporary work by living artists. The art for sale from one-man and student exhibitions ranges from $35 to $1500. The permanent collection emphasizes crafts of the Southwestern Indian cultures. Admission is free; authentication of primitive arts by appointment. Open 10-5; closed Mon.

The Phoenix Art Museum
1625 N. Central, 258-5345
Offers a fine permanent collection of Oriental, primitive, American, and European arts, with a special selection of American and European contemporaries. Admission is free; will recommend A-R, F. Open 10-5 Tues-Sat, 1-5 Sun; closed Mon, New Year's, Memorial Day, July 4th, Labor Day, Thanksgiving, Christmas.

Flagstaff

Museum of Northern Arizona
Fort Valley, 774-2443
This museum is unusually housed in a volcanic-rock and tile-roofed building constructed around a patio. Original Indian art, from $10 to $500, is sold in the Museum Shop at the rear of the Ethnology

Oriental Gallery, Phoenix Art Museum, Phoenix, Arizona. (*Courtesy Phoenix Art Museum*)

Phoenix Art Museum. (*Courtesy Phoenix Art Museum*)

(Right) Maurice K. Grossman: *Sun Altar*. (Tucson, Arizona.) Stoneware construction. Height: 38 inches. (Left) Frank Patania, Jr.: *Necklace*. (Tucson, Arizona.) Sculptured silver with topaz.

Stable Art Gallery, Scottsdale, Arizona.

Rose Cabat: "Feelie" bottles. (Tucson, Arizona.) Narrow-necked pots with crystals in turquoises, greens, blues and browns.

Gallery, while the permanent collections feature Indian arts and crafts. Admission is free; parking; credit courses with several universities; authentication of Indian art by appointment; will recommend A-R, F. Open 9-5 daily, 1:30-5 Sun, March 1-Dec. 24.

Prescott

The Sharlot Hall Historical Society
W. Gurley, 445-3122

Shows Indian artifacts and the possessions of early pioneer families, including a campaign desk and chair belonging to General George Crook. The rustic house was built in 1864 as the first Territorial Capitol from hand-hewn pine logs. Admission is free; parking; historical books on the Territory sold at Information Desk. Open 9-12, 1-5 daily, 1-5 Sun; closed Christmas, New Year's, Memorial Day.

The SMOKI CEREMONIALS are held every August, on the first or second Saturday evening, and consist of a pageant of ceremonials, sand painting, and dancing. The Smoki peoples are a "tribe" of white persons living in Prescott, dedicated to the artistic reproduction of age-old Indian ceremonials, particularly those performed by the Southwest Indians. As only one performance is held, it is wise to make reservations ahead of time through The Smoki People, P.O. Box 123, or the Prescott Chamber of Commerce, P.O. Box 1147.

Scottsdale

J. H. Armer
60 W. Main, 947-2407

Eighteenth- and nineteenth-century decorative arts. M, R, Install, antiques appraisal. Parking; open 9:30-5:30 daily.

Camelback Galleries
4521 N. Scottsdale, 945-6104

Oils and watercolors, concentrating on Western subjects. Prices $50-$2,000.

Dick Seeger Design Gallery
75 W. 5th, 945-2935

Paintings, sculpture, graphics, plus selected folk art objects, archaeological pieces, and selected contemporary designer crafts. One-of-a-kind pieces emphasized. Open 9-5 daily.

Dos Cabezas
35 W. 5th, 945-0521
Contemporary crafts.

Gallery of Modern Art
40 W. Main, 947-7455
Paintings, sculptures, graphics. Prices $150-$5,000. Open 11-5
Mon-Wed, Fri, Sat; 7:30-9:30 Thurs; closed Sun.

Gatti Studio Gallery
1310 N. Hayden, 946-2925
Oils, watercolors, and authentic Pre-Columbian artifacts. Prices
$10 up.

Gold Key Fine Arts Gallery
88 W. 5th, 945-2118
Contemporary paintings. Prices $75-$10,000.

House of the Six Directions
101 W. 5th, 946-1361
Historic and prehistoric Southwest Indian and West Coast Mexican
material. Also Southwest Indian paintings. All prices.

O'Brien's Art Emporium
82 W. Stetson, 945-1082
Representational American paintings, watercolors, sculpture, with
the accent on Western subjects. Prices $150-$10,000. Parking;
Install; open 10-5:30 daily; closed part of summer.

Stable Galleries
7610 E. McDonald, WH 5-7020
Semi-modern European, local, and American art. Prices $50-
$8,000. Open 11-5 weekdays, 2-5 Sat, Sun.

Studio One
50 E. 1st (Pima Plaza), 946-0549
Mostly representational contemporary paintings and sculpture, $50-
$1,000.

Yares Gallery
125 W. Main, 947-3251
Contemporary art of the region. Prices $20-$2,000.

Tucson

Gallery in the Sun
6300 N. Swan, 299-9191
Primarily oils, sculpture, ceramics, jewelry. Prices $50-$5,000.
M, Appraisal, Install. Parking; open 10-4:30 daily, 12-4:30 Sun.

The University of Arizona Art Gallery
Olive and Speedway, MA 4-8181
Kress Collection of Renaissance Art; contemporary international art; American painting. Parking; open 10-5 daily, 2-5 Sun.

Tucson Art Center
325 W. Franklin, 622-0402
Works in oils, watercolors, and graphics, by local artists mostly. Prices $75-$450. R. Parking; open 10-5 Mon-Sat, 1-5 Sun; closed summer.

Arizona State Museum
University of Arizona, MA 4-8181, ext. 305 or 702
Southwestern archeology and ethnology. Admission is free; open 10-5 Mon-Sat, 2-5 Sun; closed holidays.

Crafts in Tucson

By Margot D. Panofsky
Tucson Craft Guild

Crafts in Tucson have been helped considerably by the TUCSON ART CENTER, 325 W. Franklin, and the TUCSON CRAFT GUILD, which is part of it. The Craft Guild has promoted programs for craftsmen and other Art Center members interested in crafts, such as workshops, lectures, and meetings in which common problems of craftsmen are discussed.

In addition, the Craft Guild has taken part in a FESTIVAL CRAFT FAIR for the past few years, which is sponsored by the Tucson Festival Society. This is done mainly to acquaint the general public with crafts and the craftsmen in our area. In a way, the Fair could be mentioned as a sales outlet for crafts; however, the emphasis here is not particularly on sales but rather on the educational value of demonstrations in various crafts techniques. It usually takes place one or two days during the week before Easter.

The crafts mediums most frequently sold in the area are ceramics, metalwork, and textiles.

The most prominent of the Tucson craftsmen are represented in the crafts and sales area of the Tucson Art Center. Only a few craftsmen sell directly from their studios; those that do have shop hours mentioned on the following list:

Edward Barker
2038 E. 7th, 622-2075
Jewelry, sculpture, metalwork.

Ella S. Bolster
6391 E. Printer Udell, 298-9741
Weaving and stitchery.

Thomas G. Bredlow
1827 E. Limberlost, 793-2031
Blacksmith designer of contemporary and traditional objects. Open
9-6 Mon-Sat.

Ruth Brown
3568 N. Campbell, 326-5018
All types of handwoven fabrics, wall hangings, needlework, and
accessories for the home. Open 9:30-3:30 Mon-Fri.

Rose and Erni Cabat
3204 E. Blacklidge, 326-8166
Pottery, concrete and ceramic sculpture, fountains, enamel on copper.

Lucille Clark
1415 W. Wetmore, 887-2494
Weaving for interior accessories: rugs, lampshades, pillows, draperies, etc.

Charles and Louise Clement
Rt. 9, Box 350, 622-7524
Architectural and interior murals in mosaics and concrete, wall
hangings, plastic panels, room dividers.

Eva Cossock
4511 E. 7th, 326-1837
Sculpture in welded metals, cement, stained glass.

Lou Davis
1041 E. Sixth
Custom-made leather articles and sandals. Open 9-5 Mon-Sat.

Donna J. Dudley
2038 E. 7th, 622-2075
Sculpture.

Maurice K. Grossman
2826 E. Calle Glorietta, 793-2293
Ceramics and sculpture.

Kathy Haun
2849 E. La Madera, 326-4881
Carved doors, architectural accents, sculpture, and utilitarian objects in wood.

Jack Hicks
325 W. Franklin, 622-0402
Stoneware and raku pottery, metal sculpture, jewelry.

Nik Krevitsky
1010 E. Tenth (school), 791-6201
Stitchery, appliqué and batik wall hangings, enamel on metal.

Olga G. Leser
Rt. 2, Box 824, 298-0008
Metal sculpture.

George and Joyce McCullough
1302 S. Beverly, 325-9790
Pottery, jewelry, metal sculpture.

Frank Patania
199 N. Stone, 623-1371
Sterling and gold jewelry, accessories for home and office. Open
9-5:30 Mon-Sat.

Ruth Phipps
5346 E. Ft. Lowell, 793-2758
Jewelry, metal lighting fixtures, accessories for home and garden.

Floy W. Sanders
1344 E. Greenlee, 325-5668
Pottery, Egyptian paste jewelry, batiks.

Al Schofield
2847a N. Campbell, 327-6712
Jewelry in gold, platinum with precious and semi-precious stones.
Hollow flatware in all metals. Metal appliqué wall plaques. Open
8:30-5 Mon-Sat.

Chester and Evangeline Scott
2045 E. Adams, 326-4939
Weaving: draperies, tweeds, stoles, rugs, table linens, and special-
ties.

Shirley Van Cleef
3568 N. Campbell, 326-5018
Decorative and gift candles. Open 10-5 Mon-Sat.

John and Elsie Waite
3442 E. Terra Alta, 793-2916
Ceramic jewelry, embroidery-appliqué pillows and wall hangings,
rya and hooked rugs.

Berta Wright
1736 E. Speedway, 325-2591
Handscreened designs for fabrics, fashions, and interior accessories.
Open 9:30-5:30 Mon-Sat.

Craft Sales Area of the Tucson Art Center
325 W. Franklin, 622-0402
Parking; open 10-5 daily, 2-5 Sun; closed June to mid-July, mid-Aug to mid-Sept.

Desert House Crafts, Inc.
2841 N. Campbell, 793-2123
Open 9:30-5:30 daily; closed Sunday; parking.

Thunderbird Shop
199 N. Stone, 623-1371
Open 9:30-5:30 daily; closed Sunday; parking nearby.

Wright Designs and Assoc.
1736 E. Speedway, 325-2591
Open 9:30-5:30 daily; closed Sunday; parking.

Craft Competitions

In the past fifteen years there have been regular, annual competitive craft shows in the TUCSON ART CENTER. They are generally on a high, professional level and judged by competent out-of-town specialists.

Other juried shows are regularly being held in Phoenix and are mainly for DESIGNER CRAFTSMEN of Arizona. They are either at the Heard Museum or at the Phoenix Museum of Fine Arts. The Tucson show is usually held in the spring, while the Phoenix one is generally scheduled for the fall. The specific dates change from year to year.

Yuma

Yuma Fine Arts Assn.
248 Madison, 783-5942
The Art Section arranges for exhibitions, tours of galleries, lectures, and occasional field trips. Exhibits of paintings, graphics, sculpture, and crafts, with some of the work for sale, are displayed in the gallery and the Rental-Sales Gallery. The Art Section also places small loan exhibits in the Yuma City-County Library, Somerton Library, Wellton, and other communities throughout the county. Parking; R; Install. Open noon-5 Tues-Fri, 2-5 Sat-Sun Oct-June; closed Mon, holidays.

The West

LOS ANGELES, CALIF.

By Henry J. Seldis
Art Editor, *The Los Angeles Times*

Los Angeles has recently become the second most important art market in the country, and its artists work in every possible manner, having furnished leadership for such vanguard directions as Minimal Sculpture while maintaining a healthy diversity of styles.

Because of the TAMARIND LITHOGRAPHY WORKSHOP here there has been a special reawakening of interest in the collecting of original prints. These graphic works and the paintings and sculptures by relatively unknown artists offer the best buys. Nearly all the reputable galleries among the more than one hundred operating in Greater Los Angeles show young and little-known artists along with established ones. All present excellent opportunities for both beginning and more experienced art buyers.

More than thirty galleries line North La Cienega Boulevard from the 500 to the 900 block, while other concentrations can be found in Beverly Hills and, increasingly, in the San Fernando Valley. Several galleries operate in the Wilshire District. Each Monday night La Cienega dealers have open house, and literally thousands of people, some customers, flock to the street for a weekly art browsing session.

In the first year of its existence—1966—the new LOS ANGELES COUNTY ART MUSEUM at Hancock Park counted 2.7 million visitors. It is well s. rted by public and private funds, having been built with private money on public lands. It is the most important museum to have opened in the United States since the National Gallery opened its doors in Washington twenty-five years earlier.

Important, especially in the area of modern and contemporary art, are the exhibitions of the PASADENA ART MUSEUM and the U.C.L.A. DICKSON ART CENTER, along with galleries of a score of smaller universities and colleges.

366

Where to Buy

Edgardo Acosta Gallery
441 N. Bedford, Beverly Hills, 276-1977, 276-2402
Mods, Eurs. Open 10-5:30 Mon-Sat.

Ankrum Gallery
910 N. La Cienega, 657-1549
A top-quality outlet showing Mods, A. Install; open 10-5:30 Tues-Sat, 10-5:30, 8-10 Mon.

Frederick Anthon Gallery
365 N. Camden, Beverly Hills, 271-2523
An, Eu, A-R. Open 11-6 Mon-Sat.

Adele Bednarz Galleries
902 N. La Cienega, 657-5680
A, Mod, G. Install; open 10-5:30 Tues-Fri, 1-5 8-10 Mon, 1-4 Sat.

The Canyon Gallery
137 S. Topanga Canyon, Topanga, 455-2108
A, Mod. Open 1-5 Wed-Mon.

The Carter Gallery
900 N. La Cienega, 652-9000
A, G, Mods. Install; open 10:30-5:30 Tues-Sat, 10:30-5:30, 8-10, Mon.

Ceeje Galleries
968 N. La Cienega, 652-7872, 657-0671
A, Mod, G. Install; open 10-5 Tues-Sat, 10-5, 8-10 Mon.

Comara Gallery
8475 Melrose, 651-2245
A, Mod, G. Install; Open 10:30-5 Tues-Sat, 8-10 p.m. Mon.

Cowie Galleries
634 S. Westmoreland, 382-7040
A, Eu, Conservative Mods. Open 9:30-5 Mon-Sat.

Terry De Lapp Gallery
521 N. La Cienega, 652-3015
An important gallery showing eighteenth- and nineteenth-century Americans. Open noon-6 Mon-Sat.

Interior view of the Atrium section, Ahmanson Building, Los Angeles County
Museum of Art, Los Angeles, California.

Ahmanson Building, Los Angeles County Museum of Art, Los Angeles,
California. (*Photograph by Julius Shulman*)

Potter Beatrice Wood in her studio. On the shelves are a portion of her four hundred formulas for special clays and glazes, and some of her pottery.
(*Photograph by Thelner Hoover*)

Gilles A. De Turenne Gallery
263 N. Rodeo, Beverly Hills, 276-7380
Eu, Mods, G. Open 10-5 Tues-Sat.

Julie Dohan Gallery of Contemporary Art
14314 Ventura, Sherman Oaks, 783-3867
A, Mod, G. Open 12:30-5 Tues-Thurs, Sat, 1-4 Sun, 12:30-5, 7:30-10 Fri.

Dwan Gallery
10846 Lindbrook, 474-0528
One of the city's top galleries that show the vanguard of the avant-garde. Also Mods, G. Open 10-5 Tues-Sat.

Emerson Gallery
17230 Ventura, Encino, 789-3383
A, Mod, G. The gallery sometimes imports artists from Hawaii. Install; open 10:30-5 Tues-Thurs, Sat, 10:30-5, 8-10 Fri.

Rex Evans Gallery
748½ N. La Cienega, 652-2256
Another top-draw gallery that shows A, Eu, Mods, G. Install; open 10:30-5 Tues-Sat, 10:30-5, 8-10 Mon.

Feingarten Galleries of Painting
816 N. La Cienega, 655-4840
A, Eu, Mod. Install; open 10-5:30 Tues-Fri, noon-5 Sat, noon-5, 8-10 Mon.

Feingarten Galleries of Sculpture
718 N. La Cienega, 655-5466
A, Eu, Mods. Install; open 10-5:30 Tues-Fri, noon-5 Sat, noon-5, 8-10 Mon.

Ferus Gallery
723 N. La Cienega, 654-0669
A, Eu, Mod, Vanguard, G. Open 10-5:30 Tues-Sat.

Harry A. Franklin
445 N. Rodeo, Beverly Hills, 271-9171
This gallery specializes in primitive art, with only the highest quality offered. Appraisal, Install; open 10-5 Mon-Sat.

Galerias Carlota, S.A.
Foreign Club Arcade, Avenida Revolucion 719-P, Tijuana, Baja California, Mexico, 385-4077
Contemporary Mexican painting and sculpture, and pre-Columbian artifacts. Open 11-5 Thurs-Tues; closed Wed.

Galerie Simon
94 W. Dayton, Pasadena, 795-3319
A, Eu, G. Open 10-5 Tues-Sat.

Dalzell Hatfield Galleries
Ambassador Hotel, 3400 Wilshire, 387-6702
An important gallery showing A, Eu, and Mod Masters. Also G,
C. Open 10-6 Mon-Fri.

Heritage Gallery
724 N. La Cienega, 652-7738
A, Mod, G. Install; open 10-5:30 Tues-Sat, 10-1, 8-10 Mon.

Martin Janis Gallery
710 N. La Cienega, 788-1836
G, Eu, A, Mod.

Jefferson Gallery
7917 Ivanhoe, La Jolla, 459-3020
A, Eu, Mods. Open 10-5 Tues-Sat.

Paul Kantor Gallery
348 N. Camden, Beverly Hills, 276-2673
A top notch gallery offering nineteenth- and twentieth-century master paintings. Open 11-5 Mon-Fri.

Kirck Gallery
17003 Ventura, Encino, 783-1220
A, Mods, G. Install; open 10-4:30 Tues, Wed, Fri, Sat, 1:30-10
Thurs.

Kramer Gallery
635 N. La Cienega, 652-0611
A, G, Mod. Install; open 10-5 Tues-Fri, 10-5, 8-10 Mon.

Laguna Beach Art Ass'n.
307 Cliff Dr., Laguna Beach, 494-6531, 494-6532
Contemporaries, especially California artists. Open noon-5 daily.

Felix Landau Gallery
702 N. La Cienega, 652-1444
Shows top Southern California and Los Angeles artists, as well as
A, Eu, Mods. Open 10-5 Mon-Sat.

Adolph Loewi, Inc.
904 N. La Cienega, 657-5995
Top quality An, Eu. Open 9:30-5:30 Mon-Fri, Sat by appointment.

Los Angeles Art Association
825 N. La Cienega, 652-8272
Local artists. Open noon-5 Tues-Fri, noon-4 Sat, 2-4 Sun, 7:30-10 Mon.

Los Angeles Public Library
630 W. 5th, 626-7555
Varied exhibits. Open 10-9 Mon-Sat.

P. N. Matisse
356 N. Camden, Beverly Hills, 271-1189
Top-grade Eu, Mod, G. Open 10-5:30 Mon-Fri, Sat by appointment.

Oscar Meyer, Antique Works of Art, Inc.
847 N. La Cienega, 652-0064
Classical antiquities, Asian art, primitive and pre-Columbian arts. Open 9-5:30 Mon-Fri.

Municipal Art Galleries, City of Los Angeles
Barnsdall Park, 4800 Hollywood Blvd., 665-6966, 666-9462
Local exhibitions. Open 1-9 Tues-Fri, 1-6 Sat, Sun.

Municipal Art Galleries, City of Los Angeles
Tower Gallery-City Hall, 27th fl., 624-5211, ext. 2433
Local exhibitions. Open 10-4 Mon-Fri, 11-5 Sat, Sun.

Rolf Nelson Gallery
736 N. La Cienega, 657-3482
Top-quality vanguard artists. Also A, Eu, Mods. Install; open 10-5 Tues-Sat.

Occidental College
Thorne Hall, 1600 Campus Rd., 255-5151, ext. 254
Student art. Open 9-3 Mon-Fri.

Orlando Galleria
17037 Ventura, Encino, 789-6012
A, Mods, G. Install; open 10-4:30 Mon-Wed, Sat, 10-4:30, 7:30-10 Thurs, Fri.

Paideia Gallery
765 N. La Cienega, 652-8224
A, Mods, G, C. Install; open 11-5 Tues-Sat, 11-5, 7-10 Mon.

Herdert Palmer Gallery
515 N. La Cienega, 652-1961
A quality outlet showing vanguard art. Also A, Eu, Mod. Install; open 10-6 Tues-Fri, 10-5 Sat.

Palos Verdes Community Arts Ass'n.
2400 Via Campesina, Palos Verdes Estates, 378-4646
Varied exhibitions. Open 1-4 Mon-Sat, 3-5 Sun.

Pavilion Gallery—Fine Arts Patrons of Newport Harbor
400 Main, Balboa, 675-3866
Contemporaries. Open 1-5 Wed-Sun.

Frank Perls Gallery
9777 Wilshire, Suite 815, Beverly Hills, 275-5217
International top-quality masters, one of the city's leading galleries.
Open 10-5 Mon-Sat.

Gerhard Pinkus
Beverly Hills, 271-3918
G, Mods, Eu, A. By appointment only.

Pomona College Gallery
Bonita and College, Claremont, 626-8511, ext. 2241
Changing shows. Open 1-5 daily.

Poulson Galleries
910 San Pasqual, Pasadena, 792-7410
G, Mods, Eu, A. Install; open 10-5:30 Tues-Sat.

O. P. Reed, Jr.
521 N. La Cienega, 652-5500
A top-quality graphics outlet, including drawings. All periods.
Open noon-5 Mon-Sat.

Esther Robles Gallery
665 N. La Cienega, 652-1265
An important area gallery. A, Eu, Mods, G. Install; open 2-5,
8-10 Mon, noon-5 Tues-Fri, 2-5 Sat.

Scripps College, Rand-Lang Galleries
9th and Columbia, Claremont, 624-2616
Changing exhibitions of both old and new arts. Open 1:30-5 daily.

Stephan Silagy
305 N. Rodeo, Beverly Hills, 274-7229
Eu, Mods. Open 10-5:30 Mon-Fri.

Silvan Simone Gallery
11579 Olympic, 477-2416
A, Eu, Mods, G, C. Install; open noon-5:30 Tues, Thurs, Sat,
noon-10 Mon, noon-6 Sun.

Stendahl Art Gallery
7055-65 Hillside, Hollywood, 876-7740
One of the top dealers in the country for primitive arts. Phone for gallery hours.

David Stuart Galleries
807 N. La Cienega, 652-7422
A, Eu, Ex, G, C. Install; open 10-5 Tues-Fri, 11-4 Sat, 8-10 p.m. Mon.

University of California, Los Angeles, Dickson Art Center
405 Hilgard, 478-9711, ext. 3137
Changing exhibitions and student art. Open noon-5 Mon-Fri, 1:30-5 Sun; closed Sat.

University of Southern California
Harris Hall, University Park, 746-2799
Changing exhibitions. Open noon-5 Mon-Fri, 2-5 Sun.

Westside Jewish Community Ctr.
5870 W. Olympic, 938-2531
Changing shows. Open 3-6:30 Mon-Thurs, 2-5 Sun.

Nicholas Wilder Gallery
814 N. La Cienega, 657-6877
A, Eu, Mods, Vanguard. Open 11-5 Tues-Sat, 8-10 p.m. Mon.

Miscellanea

Two department stores in Los Angeles show art regularly. They are:

Sears, Roebuck & Co.
8487 Melrose, 653-0323
Open 10-10 Mon, 10-6 Tues-Sat.

W. & J. Sloan
9560 Wilshire, Beverly Hills, 275-5441
Open 10-5 daily; closed Sun.

BULLOCK'S, THE MAY CO., and MAGNIN have occasional exhibitions. Every July the Municipal Art Department sponsors the ALL CITY OUTDOOR ART FESTIVAL for one week, 9-9 daily, at Barnsdall Park. About 2,800 works are displayed; and $7,800 in prize money is awarded. Open to both professionals and amateurs.

Among active art organizations sponsoring art shows in Los Angeles are:

Fine Arts Patrons of Newport Harbor
Pavillion Gallery, 400 Main, Balboa

Los Angeles Art Ass'n.
825 N. La Cienega

Palos Verdes Community Art Ass'n.
2400 Via Campesina, Palos Verdes Estates

Santa Monica Art Ass'n.
1343 Sixth, Santa Monica

South Gate Art Ass'n.
9829 Walnut, South Gate

Westwood Art Ass'n.
1386 Westwood

Where to Look

Among the many museums within the city or driving distance of
Los Angeles are the following art institutions:

California Museum of Science and Industry
700 State Dr., Exposition Pk., 749-0101
Offers some art exhibits among its many scientific ones. Open 10-5
Mon-Fri, 10-6 Sat, Sun.

Casa De Adobe of Southwest Museum
4605 N. Figueroa, 225-8653
An authentic replica of Spanish Colonial architecture with antiques
of that period. Open 2-5 Wed, Sat, Sun.

The J. Paul Getty Museum
17985 Pacific Coast Hwy., Malibu
Another gem of a small collection. Housed in a wing of Getty's
residence on a sixty-five-acre estate, the gallery contains one of the
finest collections of French eighteenth-century decorative arts in
the world. Advance appointments required for 2-4 Wed and Sat.

Henry E. Huntington Library and Art Gallery
1151 Oxford, San Marino, 792-6141, 681-6601
Founded on a lovely estate by this famous collector and his wife,
the Gallery is noted for its English portraits and late eighteenth-
century French art. "The Blue Boy" and "Pinkie" are the chief
drawing cards of this small, but dazzling, collection. The botanical
gardens and research library are equally famous. Open 1-4:30
Tues-Sun.

The Los Angeles County Museum of Art
5905 Wilshire, Hancock Park, 937-4250

Constructed in 1966 in a series of linked buildings of striking design, this is truly a "culture center of tomorrow" and may well set the pace for new museums all over the United States. Present plans include the building up of its permanent collections, the bringing of more major international exhibitions to the museum, the originating of important traveling exhibitions at the museum itself, and the increased encouragement of contemporary art in the area. The Rental Gallery (1st level, Leo. S. Bing Bldg. open 10-4 Tues-Sat) offers a wide selection of contemporary art priced from $6 to $28 for a two-month period, while the Junior Art Workshop for children of museum members seeks to instill a love of art in the very young. Changing Exhibitions Gallery, adults 50¢, children 25¢; authentication by appointment (Fri); will recommend F, A-R; scheduled gallery talks 1 and 2 p.m. Tues-Fri; admission fee for traveling exhibitions; Acoustiguide tours, 50¢ for one, 75¢ for two. Open 10-5 daily except Mon, Lytton Gallery till 10 Tues, Fri; closed Mon, Christmas, Thanksgiving.

Pasadena Art Museum
946 N. Los Robles, 793-7114

The very large Galka E. Scheyer bequest of over six hundred works of modern art, with emphasis on the Blue Four (Feininger, Klee, Jawlensky, Kandinsky) set the course for the focus on twentieth-century art at this very fine small museum. Despite its limitations, the museum tries to organize its own exhibitions instead of depending on traveling ones, and has initiated several of international importance. Some works from its exhibits are for sale. Plans are currently being made for an enlarged museum to open in 1968. Admission free; open 10-5 Wed-Sat, 10-9 Tues, 2-5 Sun; closed Mon.

Southwest Museum
234 Museum Dr., 221-2163

Features contemporary Northwest Coast Indian and Eskimo art. Open 1-5 Tues-Sun.

Information about Art

The *Los Angeles Times* has a calendar listing and several art pages on Sunday. There are gallery reviews on Monday and Friday in the Family Section. *The Art Calendar*, published quarterly by the Art

Museum Council of the Los Angeles County Museum of Art and free to all museum members, is a very extensive and thorough listing of public art exhibits and events held in museums, professional galleries, and major institutions of Southern California. There are Sunday reviews and brief listings in the *Los Angeles Herald Examiner*. The magazines *FM and Fine Arts Guide* and *Los Angeles Magazine* also have listings and reviews. KFAC radio has spot announcements.

SANTA BARBARA, CALIF.

By Harriette von Breton
Art Critic, *The Santa Barbara News-Press*

Long before Los Angeles blossomed on the Southern California scene as its major cultural greenhouse, Santa Barbara was a well-known center for art and artists. The concentration of great wealth, sophisticated residents, and well traveled, internationally minded art collectors endowed the community with a high level of taste and brought collections of major works of art to the area.

Today, Santa Barbara is one of the most productive areas in California, with its large grouping of artists, collectors, and art traditions and with its museum, the only major museum between Los Angeles and San Francisco.

The Santa Barbara area is basically divided into three centers: Montecito, Santa Barbara, and the University of California at Santa Barbara in Goleta. Each of these makes a unique contribution to the community at large.

Where to Look and Buy

Santa Barbara

The Santa Barbara Museum of Art
1130 State, 965-8569
Founded in 1941 with Donald Bear as its first director, this beautiful Museum has benefited from its remarkable patrons and is one of the best small museums in the United States. Besides focusing the artistic wealth of the community, it has instituted an art education program and helped develop some of California's major artists, such as the late Rico Lebrun. The Museum produces over thirty exhibitions annually, and much of this work is for sale. It

also organizes exhibitions of outstanding local artists. At Christmas, a sale of rare prints selected by the Museum's director is mounted. The permanent collections are strongest in Greek and Roman sculpture and in American painting, but the rooms of Oriental art and Old Master drawings are also outstanding. Admission is free; admission for some special exhibits 50¢ general, 25¢ students, members free; will recommend F, A-R; art classes for children. Open 11-5 Tues-Sat, noon-5 Sun; closed Mon, holidays.

The First Press
19 W. Carillo, 963-5000
Owned and operated by Gary Chafe, this Gallery concentrates on younger area artists. All of them have unusual ability, while some are outstanding. Chafe holds down prices for young art buyers—$25 up. Street and lot parking; open 9-6 Mon-Sat.

Faulkner Gallery
Anapamu and Anacapa, 962-7653
The gallery is housed in the Santa Barbara Public Library and exhibits primarily the work of the SANTA BARBARA ART ASSOCIATION. All works by these hundred or so artists of both contemporary and traditional persuasions are sold at surprisingly low prices, making this a beginning art buyer's paradise. Street and lot parking; open 9-9 Mon-Fri, 9-6 Sat; closed Sun.

The El Paseo Complex of Studios
Anacapa and State Sts.
This is a unique shopping area in the heart of the city. Housed in colorful early Spanish Colonial-style buildings across from the City Plaza, these shops market mainly folk art. It is an interesting area to browse around for unusual moderately priced items. Open 9-5 daily.

The Three Sisters
19 W. Anapamu, 963-5400
Primarily a folk art store, the gallery also carries Santa Barbara locals. Street and lot parking; open 9-5 daily; closed Sun.

Montecito Area: This is a fast-growing art center with the following galleries:

The Esther Bear Gallery
1125 High, 969-0685
This is one of the major galleries in Santa Barbara; it is highly

professional and deals only in top-quality art. Mrs. Bear is the widow of the first director of the Santa Barbara Museum of Art. She has a large stable of local artists and imports works by others. Her exhibits have included William Dole, Howard Warshaw, Donald Lent, Jack Baker, William and Teresa Ptszinsky, Selden Spaulding, Tom Cornell, Julius Schmidt, Jack Zajac, William Theo Brown, Sam Francis. Numerous Los Angeles collectors travel here to buy. Open 2-5 Wed, Fri, Sun, and by appointment.

Gallery de Silva
1479 E. Valley, Montecito Village, 969-3533
Operator-owner Wally Silva represents several major Santa Barbara artists such as DeWitt and Douglass Parshall and presently exhibits the work of Donald Borthwick, probably one of the most exciting artists working on the West Coast today. He also carries a number of northern California artists and some Orientals like Matabee Goto. You'll find rare Japanese prints here, too. Parking; open 10-5 daily; closed Sun.

Galeria Del Sol
516 San Ysidro
This is a small, beautifully situated gallery that is presently expanding its exhibits from prints and etchings to include paintings and sculpture. Prices moderate to high. Open 11-5 Mon-Sat.

El Establo Gallery
1475 E. Valley, 969-2082
Director Rosemary Ball exhibits the artists of Southern California, Morro Bay, and other outlying Santa Barbara areas in addition to her own work. Reasonable prices. Parking; open winter 1-5 Mon-Fri, 10-5 Sat; closed Sun; summer 10-5 Mon-Sat, 2-5 Sun.

Galeria Del Monte
549 San Ysidro, 969-2512
Exhibitions of contemporary art from the United States, Europe, and South America. Moderate prices. Parking; open 10-5 Mon-Sat.

Mas O Menos
1482 E. Valley, 969-2433
This is a Mexican import shop that specializes in Mexican folk arts and handicrafts. Many tasteful, colorful things can be found here and are moderately priced considering the import duty. Parking in Village Sq., open 10-5 Mon, Thurs, Sat.

Interior view, Santa Barbara Museum of Art, Santa Barbara, California.

Sculpture Court, Esther Bear Gallery, Santa Barbara, California.

Elizabeth Clemens
1482 E. Valley, 969-5245
Located right next to Mas O Menos, this is a fine import shop for Scandinavian, German, Swiss, and other European items. Moderate to expensive prices. Parking in Village Sq.; open 10-5 Mon, Thurs, Sat.

Village Frame
1483 E. Valley, Montecito Village, 969-0542
Proprietor Merle Shore, himself an artist, specializes in custom framing, rare antique prints, original graphics, and the crating and shipping of fine art. Parking in Village Sq.; open 10-5:30 Mon-Sat.

Goleta

The University of California at Santa Barbara Art Gallery
Art Department, U.C.S.B., 968-1511, ext. 2288
At the annual Student Exhibition much excellent graduate-level work is for sale in the mediums of graphics, paintings, drawings, ceramics, and sculpture. Prices are extremely low. There are also outstanding changing exhibitions of major local, West Coast, and other American artists, and unique private collections; some work is for sale at prices in line with regular gallery rates. The permanent display includes the SEDGWICK COLLECTION of Renaissance paintings, pre-Columbian sculpture, Indian baskets, and the unusual MORGENROTH COLLECTION of Renaissance medals and plaquettes. Campus parking; open 10-4 Mon-Sat, 1-5 Sun; closed Christmas, New Year's, Easter, Thanksgiving.

Antiques

London Towne
25 E. De La Guerra, 962-2858
Offers a fine collection of eighteenth-century furniture and some unusual and rare old paintings. Street and lot parking; open 10-5 daily.

Lewis' Antiques
37 E. De La Guerra, 965-4058
539 San Ysidro, Montecito, 969-0213
Fine antique furniture, art objects, and some paintings. Parking; open 10-5 daily.

Environs: Thitry miles to the east of Santa Barbara is OJAI, a very art-conscious community that has a number of good artists living and working in it. Famed ceramicist BEATRICE WOOD lives in the upper part of the Ojai Valley at 971 McAndrew Road (646-3381) and sells her magnificent work from her large studio. Other well-known Ojai artists are Irene Koch, Francis Johnson, and Wes Johnson. There is an art gallery in the Community Center. Most of the outlying communities such as Ventura, Oxnard, Santa Maria, Paso Robles, Pismo Beach all have their art-association exhibits. There are many producing local artists, but the quality varies. SOLVANG, a Danish community about thirty miles to the northeast of Santa Barbara, has a number of shops with a vast array of Danish imports. This includes some very nice crafts.

Miscellanea

The SABADO (Saturday) and DOMINGO (Sunday) ART EXHIBITS are sponsored by the City Recreation Department and are held every week in the year unless rained out. The exhibits are open to all area artists with no entrance fee and are well attended by Sunday painters, tourists, and residents. The *Sabado* show now reaches almost a mile down Cabrillo Blvd.; it is popular and the prices are low. The quality varies. Open 10-5 each day.

The Artists Workshop
2779 Foothill, 962-5607
A hard-working group of artists with a pleasant studio, regularly scheduled classes, and two exhibits a year. Many of them are members of the Santa Barbara Art Association and also exhibit regularly at the Faulkner Gallery. Their work is reasonably priced.

The Adult Education Program
914 Santa Barbara, 962-8144
Includes a large, active art program: classes in all media and annual exhibitions.

Information about Art

The *Santa Barbara News-Press* carries full coverage of all major art events and is supportive and helpful in stimulating events and artists. *The Goleta Gazette* carries listings of exhibits. There are occasional radio and TV programs for special art events. *Art Forum* magazine covers many Santa Barbara exhibits and sometimes has feature articles on its artists.

SAN FRANCISCO, CALIF.

By Anita Ventura
San Francisco Art Writer

Art activity in San Francisco and the communities around the Bay has three focal points: the art schools, the museums, and the commercial galleries. Most stimulating, at present, are the several schools where art is taught, both the professional schools and the universities. In San Francisco itself is the SAN FRANCISCO ART INSTITUTE (800 Chestnut, OR 3-2640), formerly the California School of Fine Arts, near the North Beach area. The Institute, the oldest professional art school west of the Mississippi (founded in 1872), is directed by Fred Martin, himself a well-known local painter and printmaker, and has a teaching staff comprised of some of the area's outstanding painters and sculptors. The painters James Weeks, Julius Hatofsky, Richard Graf, Joe Otto, and Don Weygandt teach here, as do the sculptors Alvin Light, Jeremy Anderson, William Geis, Rodjer Jacobsen, and Bruce Nauman.

In the Institute's galleries, the exhibitions directed by the San Francisco painter and resident critic of *Artforum* magazine, James Monte, offer high-level selections of lesser known local artists, and a program of bringing exhibitions of work from other art centers that would not otherwise be seen in the city. The work of students who are exceptionally mature, even for a professional school, in technique and imagery, may be seen in the Institute's informal courtyard galleries at various times throughout the year. Open 10-4 Mon-Sat, noon-4 Sun; closed all national holidays.

Across the Bay, in Berkeley, the UNIVERSITY OF CALIFORNIA faculty is equally noteworthy. The sculptors Peter Voulkos, Harold Paris, James Melchert, Sidney Gordin, and painters Elmer Bischoff, Erle Loran, Karl Kasten, David Simpson, and Felix Ruvolo are among the regular staff members. The work of these artists, as well as that of visiting instructors from New York, may often be seen in the WORTH RYDER GALLERY of the University's Kroeber Hall (2620 Bancroft, 845-6000, ext. 2582; open 10-5 Mon-Sun) where studio courses are taught. It was in Berkeley that the first artist-operated metal foundry in the area was started by U.C. faculty members Don Haskin and Peter Voulkos. Shortly thereafter a foundry for student use was put in operation in the University's sculpture department and by now most of the sculptors working in cast materials in this area operate their own foundries in their studios.

The UNIVERSITY ART MUSEUM (after 1968: Bancroft Way, 845-6000), under the directorship of Peter Selz, will open in 1968. Until then, Museum exhibitions are held at the UNIVERSITY ART GALLERY (Barrow Lane, 845-6000, ext. 1207), located on the campus. Exhibitions of international interest may be seen there. In recent years, these have included "The Viennese Expressionists" (Schiele, Klimt), Jungendstil art posters, René Magritte, kinetic sculpture, and the paintings of Jules Pascin, among others. Admission is free; open noon-6 daily with extended hours when new building opens; closed Christmas Day.

At Mills College, in Oakland, are the painters Ralph Du Casse and the sculptor Robert Rhaemers. THE MILLS COLLEGE ART GALLERY (632-2700), directed by Carl Belz, often plans exhibitions of a type unique in the area, such as a large room ensemble of cast-rubber sculpture by Harold Paris, the first public showing of this work. Limited parking; authentication by appointment of modern and Oriental art; will recommend A-R, F; open 1-4 Sun, Wed, Fri.

The CALIFORNIA COLLEGE OF ARTS AND CRAFTS (5212 Broadway, 653-8118) also attracts outstanding local artists to its staff: F. Vredaparis, Mary Snowden, Mel Moss, Robert Bechtle, Jacques Fabert, and William Wiley, among others. It is increasingly apparent, too, that student work from Arts and Crafts merits the attention of those who are looking for developing artists of unusual talent who are likely to sustain production.

At STANFORD UNIVERSITY (Museum and Art Gallery, 321-2300, ext. 4177), about an hour's ride on the freeway from San Francisco, an artist-in-residence program has in recent years brought the French sculptor François Stahley to the area, and has also included the Italian sculptor Arnaldo Pomodoro, and the painters Frank Lobdell (now permanently on the staff) and Richard Diebenkorn. An exhibition program at Stanford under the direction of Ninfa Valvo, who was for some years director of contemporary exhibitions at the De Young Museum, promises to provide contemporary local artists an important and serious showplace. Limited parking; 10-5 Mon-Fri, 1-5 Sat, Sun.

As for museums, San Francisco proper has three of them: the CALIFORNIA PALACE OF THE LEGION OF HONOR (Lincoln Park, 221-5610; admission free; parking; open 10-5 daily; 1-5 holidays); the M.H. DE YOUNG MEMORIAL MUSEUM (Golden Gate Park, 558-6161; admission free; parking; open 10-5 daily); and the SAN FRANCISCO MUSEUM OF ART (Mc-Allister at Van Ness, 431-2040; admission free; open 10-10 Tues-Fri, 10-5 Sat, 1-5 Sun; closed Mon). The work of local contemporaries may be seen intermittently at all of these, although it is the MUSEUM OF ART, with its affiliated SOCIETY FOR THE ENCOURAGEMENT OF CONTEMPORARY ART AND RENTAL SERVICE, that offers the widest range of selections. An exception to this is in the area of printmaking, at the ACHENBACH FOUNDATION FOR GRAPHIC ARTS. Its galleries at the Palace of the Legion of Honor offer occasional exhibitions of California printmakers among its exhibits drawn from extensive holdings in Old Master prints and drawings.

A museum of crafts was recently inaugurated, MUSEUM WEST of the American Craftsmen's Council in the Clock Tower of Ghirandelli Square on the city's waterfront (900 N. Point, 474-0077). While the Museum has no permanent collection, its exhibitions are of the highest level. Its shows of the work of local and national craftsmen are contributing to the increasing difficulty of differentiating "fine" and "craft" work. The reason for the local difference lies in the Expressionist uses to which ceramics have been put by Peter Voulkos, Ann Stockton, James Melchert and others, and the extension of the possibilities of woven forms by Dominic di Mare and Ed Rossbach (parking; 10:30-5 Tues-Sat).

Outside the city, apart from the museum activity of the schools and universities previously mentioned, the ART GALLERIES OF THE OAKLAND MUSEUM (1000 Oak, 832-2738) concentrate on California painting and sculpture, showing the work of contempories in one-man exhibitions and being host to many art association shows (parking garage; admission free; 10-5 daily with some evening hours). The RICHMOND ART CENTER (Civic Ctr., 234-2397) held its fifteenth Painting Annual in 1966, and has also shown the work of artists not of the area but important to contemporary development, such as Jasper Johns. One-man and group exhibitions of important local contemporaries are also held here. (Open 9-4:30, 7-9:30 Mon- Thurs, 9-4:30 Fri; 2-5 Sun).

The San Francisco art galleries that handle contemporaries draw upon these teaching artists for exhibitions, for the most part, although the work of a number of people who have been influential in the area cannot be seen in them. Some of these are Frank Lobdell, James Weeks, and Elmer Bischoff, all of whom show their work either in Los Angeles or New York. And, of course, a number of professional artists do not teach, but confine their public activity to art exhibitions. A familiarity with both the art schools and the galleries is more necessary in San Francisco than it is, say, in New York for a comprehension of contemporary art activity.

San Francisco artists are scattered over a large geographical area, and the galleries and museums themselves are so widely dispersed that there is not the sense of a common front that is available in other cities, chiefly New York and Los Angeles. The logistics of geography and the sense of isolation of individual artists may account to some extent for the rather eccentric direction of the imagery apparent here. Schools of art that originate elsewhere are here transformed into something more personal and less uniform in approach. To this extent they soften in impact upon their appearance in this area, yet they gain, often, in personal expression. This is the chief benefit of a provincial situation, well known to the artists who choose to work here.

There is no San Francisco school of painting at this time. Art in this area is as diverse as it is everywhere else. Two directions, however, have been powerful in the past, and echoes of them live on in the newest work, while their chief practitioners have continued to develop within the mode they themselves may have originated. The first to appear was of an Abstract-Expressionist inclination, and was motivated by the presence in San Francisco in the 1940s of Mark Rothko and Clyfford Still, who with Clay Sphoon and Hassel Smith were teaching at the California School of Fine Arts, now the San Francisco Art Institute. It was there that Frank Lobdell and Richard Diebenkorn, among others, started to produce a rigorous abstraction, which in Lobdell's case was accompanied by a certain stiff and heavy use of paint that came to be identified with the Bay area and chiefly with the Institute itself. This was influenced generally by New York painting of the time, but more particularly by Clyfford Still and his heroic demands on himself as a painter. This sort of concern for painting—a high moral seriousness—has been passed on to younger painters through Lodbell's years of teaching at the Art Institute. And while its anthropomorphic imagery has been to some extent dissipated by the inroads of Pop Art and Object Sculpture, it may still be said to have influenced a number of artists in imagery as well as attitude whose work today may bear no resemblance to that of their teachers. Among these artists are William Geis, Robert Hudson, and William Wiley.

In the 1950s Paul Mills, curator of painting at the Oakland Art Museum, noticed and named a local trend when he exhibited a group of paintings under the title "Bay Area Figurative." This school was characterized by broadly brushed figures, executed with an Expressionist concern for gesture and color, but influenced by developments in abstraction as evidenced in the demands the totality of the painting made upon the generalized figures. Among the painters whose work continues to display these characteristics, although the brushwork is somewhat tamed by now, are James Weeks and Richard Diebenkorn (the latter, however, now teaching at U.C.L.A.).

These schools have dissipated, and there exists today a welter of styles and tendencies. As elsewhere, art for the collector of contemporary work who wants to buy something in a price range under $500 is available chiefly in prints, drawings, and small sculptures and paintings, even of fairly well-known artists. The number of artists here who are relatively unknown on the national scene makes it a field day for those who want to venture their judgment on the future, for there is in San Francisco no noticeable boom in the buying of art. The buyer may well find this uncompetitive market a boon to the purchase of even sizable paintings and sculptures in a price range that would elsewhere be considerably higher.

Where to Buy

Jackson Square: An area of San Francisco which has in recent years attracted a number of art galleries as well as decorators is the Jackson Square vicinity. This is one of the earliest settled parts of the city, and with its nineteenth-century brick buildings and the restoration of Jackson Square, now chiefly occupied by decorators and antique shops, the area offers the feeling of a homogeneous neighborhood most pleasant to stroll in. A greater number of selective contemporary galleries are located here than elsewhere in the city, and they are all in easy walking distance of each other. Parking on the street is difficult and usually limited to specific hours, with tow-away laws strongly enforced.

Berkeley Gallery
855 Sansome, 3rd fl., 397-0308
The gallery opened as a cooperative in Berkeley in the 1950s, with its members drawn from students and recent students of the University of California Art Department. In 1966 it moved to its present location in San Francisco. Its membership is limited to twenty, with occasional invitations to non members to exhibit. A sense of freshness and adventure pervades the gallery exhibitions, and this is furthered by the feeling of the gallery space itself, which was formerly a manufacturing loft but is now a handsome showplace

Edouard Manet (1832–1883): *The Milliner*. (French.) Oil on
canvas. Height: 33½ inches. Width: 29 inches. Collection of the
California Palace of the Legion of Honor,
San Francisco, California.

California Palace of the Legion of Honor, San Francisco, California.

The San Francisco Museum of Art occupies the fourth floor of the
Veterans Building, Civic Center, San Francisco, California.

Interior view, San Francisco Museum of Art, San Francisco, California.

Interior view of the Berkeley Gallery, San Francisco, California, showing work by Howard Margolis, Mol Moss, Karla Moss, Robert Hartman, Richard McLean and Nancy McCauley. (*Photograph by Gardiner McCauley*)

for art. One of the area's outstanding sculptors exhibits here: Tio Giambruni, who teaches in the sculpture department at the University of California at Davis. The media is often mixed at this gallery, making the distinction between painters and sculptors difficult. The other members include Lee Adair, Boy Allen, Tom Akawie, Robert Bechtle, Margot Campbell, Richard Graf (an excellent printmaker), Robert Hartman, Mel Henderson, Robert Loberg, Harry Lum, Howard Margolis, Gardiner McCauley, Nancy McCauley, Bud McKee, Richard McLean, Robert McLean, Mel Moss, and Pat Tidd. Good for purchases under $500. Open 11-4 Tues-Sat; closed July-mid Sept.

John Bolles
729 Sansome, 2nd fl., 392-4919
John Bolles opened this gallery in 1958 as an adjunct to his architectural practice. His interest is in presenting "contemporary art for the adventurous collector," and, because of his profession, he furthers the commissioning of painting and sculpture for architecture. The artists he exhibits here are chiefly Californians; some among them may also be seen in New York. Open 11-4:30 Mon-Fri.

Dilexi
631 Clay, 433-4260
Gallery director Jim Newman has brought professional standards to the handling of contemporary art in this city since 1958. In this most recent location, he has created the enlarged space and luxurious environment in which the art he handles can be seen to its best advantage. Monthly one-man shows and occasional group exhibitions of some of the most outstanding artists in the area are seen here. For those seeking the best in contemporary local art, as well as exhibitions of interest of foreign artists, a visit to Dilexi is a necessity. The prominent local sculptors Jeremy Anderson, Sidney Gordin, Rodjer Jacobsen, Alvin Light, and Charles Ross show here, and the gallery represents the work of Wilfred Zogbaum and H.C. Westermann in San Francisco. Among painters at Dilexi are Joel Barletta, Roy De Forest, Alan Lynch, Deborah Remington, Hassell Smith. Small works in all categories may be bought here for under $500. Open 11-6 Tues-Sat; closed mid-Aug to Sept.

Hollis
510 Clay, 2nd fl., 986-1263
Marvin Hollis shows mostly Western artists, some of whom have

moved to New York and the Midwest but maintain their connection with the gallery. The exhibitions are customarily of the work of one or two artists, and the diverse styles include Hard-Edge (Frederick Hammersley), shaped and painted canvas (Darrell Crisp), and abstract (Karl Benjamin). The work of the well-known painter and printmaker Karl Kasten, a member of the art staff of the University of California at Berkeley is exhibited here. Prices usually under $500. Open 11-5 Mon-Sat; by appointment July-Aug.

Pomeroy
449 Pacific, 981-1290
The paintings shown here have a somewhat decorative quality and are usually smaller in scale than the work at the above-mentioned galleries. Among the exhibitors are George Kars and Elizabeth Charleston. One-man as well as group shows are arranged. Open 9-5:30 Mon-Sat.

Quay
521 Pacific, entrance 2 Jerome Alley, 392-5532
The director of the gallery, Ruth Braunstein, infuses her premises with a swinging, enthusiastic attitude toward innovation and an appreciation of the work she exhibits. This is most attracitve in itself and the more so when the viewer, as often happens, agrees with her enthusiasm. An offshoot of the gallery is located in Santa Rosa, at 636 4th, for visitors who approach the city from the north. The Quay handles the important work of sculptors Peter Voulkos and Manuel Neri, and the painters John Altoon, Frank Hamilton, James Suzuki, and Nell Sinton. The work shown is characterized by a sort of edgy assurance: Erotic Art is at home here, as are all the various styles of contemporary art as they are practiced by artists whose individual mode is quite confirmed. Prints, drawings, paintings of some size by young but accomplished artists, and some sculpture may be purchased here for under $500. Open 11-6 Tues-Sat; closed 3 weeks July 1, 1 week at Christmas.

Union Square-Sutter Street: This area is the heart of San Francisco's shopping area, comparable to New York's Fifth Avenue in the Fifties blocks. The visitor staying at the St. Francis Hotel need walk only a short distance to the row of galleries, and those who come in town to view can take the cable car to avoid driving in downtown traffic. A number of parking garages are available, however.

Gump's Gallery
250 Post, 982-1616

The gallery is located in the outstanding shop in the West for the purchase of fine china and *objets d'art*. At Gump's, too, are galleries of Orientalia for the most discriminating collector (see the earlier section on Far Eastern art). The Gallery, on the fourth floor, handles the graphic work of internationally known artists, as well as that by West Coast printmakers. New York and West Coast painters and sculptors are shown here as well: Bryan Wilson, Walter Snelgrove, Howard Hack, Robert Harvey, Gregory Kondos, Art Holman, and Yektai, among others. The selection of American and European twentieth-century Master drawings, watercolors, and graphics may include some in the $500 vicinity, and there are some small paintings by well-known regional artists and some Europeans also around that price. Open 9:30-5:30 Mon-Sat.

Hansen
14 Tillman Pl., entrance also at 315 Sutter, 982-4212

This gallery is strong on prints and sculpture, with its top floor usually given over to the display of one of these media while the first floor may be occupied by a painting exhibition. The artists are almost all from the West Coast. Dennis Beall, one of the most notable local printmakers, exhibits here, as do John Ihle, Gordon Cook, Kathan Brown, Beith von Hosen, and Gerald Parker. The representation of local sculptors is especially fine, among them Harold Paris, F. Vriedaparais, Don Potts, and James Melchert. Wanda Hansen Ashe, director of the gallery, has been active here for a number of years and is hospitable to the new directions the gallery artists' work take. Art buyers interested in sculpture should certainly visit Hansen, where work in all categories and small sculptures will be under $500. Open 10-5:30 Mon-Fri, noon-5 Sat; closed Aug.

Ed Lesser
685 Sutter, 885-5903

Prints and paintings of an international Cubist-Expressionist bias are shown here. The gallery handles also, for instance, the work of Karl Schwoon, a student of Kandinsky who works in Hamburg. The paintings are elegantly framed, this work being done on the premises. The gallery has a sort of European warmth to it, and the director has strong personal tastes which, though they may not be in the mainstream of contemporary art, can be interesting examples of non-academic Cubist and Surrealist tendencies. Prices under $500. Open 10-6 Tues-Sat.

R. E. Lewis
555 Sutter, 2nd fl., 392-3175

One of the foremost print outlets in the West for over fourteen years, this gallery offers everything from rare Incunabula woodblocks to prints of the present time. It is rewarding to browse through the drawers in which prints and drawings and Eastern miniature paintings are stored. An Indian miniature of good quality may be purchased for $25 and a larger Indian transfer drawing, of exceptional appeal to the contemporary taste, was recently on sale for $150. For the moneyed buyer, a complete fifteenth-century manuscript is available for $5,000; although this sounds expensive, these mss. are sure to increase in value as they become more rare. A few American contemporaries are handled here, but the gallery does not represent any artists. The gallery issues monthly lists of graphics available. Open 10-5:30 Mon-Sat.

Maxwell Galleries
551 Sutter, 421-5193

Fred Maxwell established this gallery in 1940 and its present position may be expressed by saying that it is the only place in San Francisco where one can find work by Othon Frieze and Ernest Lawson, for example. No prints are handled; and the prices for paintings range from $500 to $75,000. There are three floors of galleries, each divided to provide space for the various exhibitions that concurrently occupy them. A sign at the entranceway advises, "The paintings displayed represent only a small portion of our collection—other paintings include . . . Bernard, Boggs, Bohrod, Bonnard, Boudin, Breughel, Charlot, Chase, Couleter, Courbet, Daubigny, Daumier, De Chirico, Delacroix, Derain, Dufy, Durpre, Frieseke, Friesz, Harpignes, Hassam, Hill, Hudson, Jawlensky, Keith, Kislin, Laurencin, Lautrec, Lawson, Lebourg, Lurçat, Manet, Marquet, Matisse . . ." and the list goes on and on. Quite a stellar array, though it's all below stairs. Open 9:30-5-15 Mon-Sat.

Paris
505 Post, 474-9079

The School of Paris, with its contemporary manifestation of decorative Cubism-Surrealism, is shown here. An example is Abram Krol who as a printmaker puts this style at the service of interpretations of Hebrew legend, illustrations of poetry, and the like. Prints and drawings of international artists may be seen, and fine framing is also done here. Prices under $500. Open 10-6 Mon-Sat.

Triangle
579 Sutter, 982-3498
Formerly on Polk St. for six years, the gallery is now gathering a stable of contemporary artists of various stylistic tendencies in a new location. Several Japanese painters are included as well as local, New York, and Northwest Coast artists. The director plans one-man shows throughout the winter and group shows in the summer. The work of Ronald Chase, poetically precise collections of emphemerae applied to large constructions, and of Jack Carrigg, large color-field paintings, may be taken as examples of the gallery's offerings. Small paintings, constructions, and collages will be available here for under $500. Open 9:30-5:15 Mon-Sat.

Union Street, west of Van Ness Avenue: This area has recently developed as an antique and import center, and it is in the antiques field that one will often find paintings of high quality. Outstanding in this regard is, for instance:

Clipper Ship Antiques
1775 Union, 776-9200
Specializes in maritime artifacts and paintings. Open 11-5:30 Mon-Sat.

The walker may cover as many as six blocks and find on both sides of the street interesting and entertaining sources of *objets d'art,* antiques, clothing, luncheon, and modern imported wares. Several galleries are hidden away in this shoppers' delight, and the most interesting of them are discussed below.

Artist Cooperative
2224 Union, 567-0464
These large, barnlike premises have every inch of wall space covered by paintings of decidedly various qualities. The sharp-eyed and sure buyer may well, however, find something worthwhile at a low price. There are 125 members of this cooperative, all of whom may be seen at the December showing. Open noon-6 Mon-Thurs, Sun; noon-9 Fri, Sat.

Original Prints
1747 Union, 885-5185
The name of the gallery defines its offerings; and the prints included, all of internationally known quality artists, may be purchased at low prices. The gallery has been in existence for fifteen years, and plans very shortly to expand its quarters for a larger

display area. Such exhibitions as the color engravings of S.W. Hayter titled "Contemporaries of Atelier 17" and selections from Paris galleries may be seen here, while portfolios of the work of both local and international graphics of fine quality are also available for inspection. Open 11-5:30 Mon-Sat.

Union Court
2124 Union, 921-1600
European contemporaries, for the most part, with decorative interpretations of current and not-so-current high styles, are offered by this gallery. The premises are small in scale, and so are the paintings. The encaustic Italianate fantasies of Losi Cinello, for instance, may be purchased here for around $500. Open 11-5 Mon-Sat.

Also on Union Street

Cloutier Et Cie
1878 Union, 567-7252
Open 10-5 Tues-Sat.

H. P. Corwith
1833 Union, 567-7252
Open 10-5 Tues-Sat.

Hunter
1814 Union, WA 2-4646
Nineteenth-century Americana. Open 10:30-5:30 Mon-Sun.

Pantechnicon
1849 Union, 922-1104
Open 10-5 Mon-Sat.

Watrous Fine Arts
2036 Union, 931-6434
Nineteenth- and twentieth-century Europeans, emphasizing Dutch-type landscape. Open 10:30-5:30 Mon-Sat.

Winblad
1814 Union, WA 2-4646
One-man shows of contemporaries of an academic nature. Open 10:30-5:30 Mon-Sun.

Other sections of the city: Somewhat off the beaten track. An automobile is the best way to get here but public transportation is also possible.

Lucien Labaudt
1407 Gough (near Civic Ctr.), 567-1850

This gallery is run by the widow of the gallery's founder, the painter Lucien Labaudt. The roster of artists included in annual exhibitions held since 1946 cover a large plaque on one wall, and in the spacious rooms of the old house occupied by the galleries the works of local contemporaries such as Ann Richner, Ella McLeroy, Sergei Scherbakoff, Benison Linde, and Rosinda Holmes may be seen. One of the chief attractions here is Labaudt's paintings. Prices under $500; and it would be wise to call before going. Open 1-6 Tues-Sat.

San Francisco Art Center
425 14th (Mission St. area), 431-9034

Strange constructions, many with an attitude of social protest, have been seen here, for the gallery is chiefly a showcase for the work of its owner, Frederic Hobbs. Truly for the adventurous, who need not invest more than $500. Open 12:30-5:30 Mon-Sat.

Arleigh
1812 Pacific, 2nd and 3rd fls., 474-4300, 771-0277

Under the directorship of R. Lee Carlson, this Gallery, now two years old, is gaining in prominence among the contemporary exhibition places in the city. A number of different approaches to exhibitions are evident here. Each year the gallery has a "Brotherhood" show, in which the paintings, to greater or lesser extent depending on the style of the artist, carry out this theme. In addition, the director is interested in showing the work of older artists which may not have been seen in the current emphasis upon the new, but, at the same time, he has the temerity to exhibit young artists not previously seen. Prints and drawings, and a few oils, are priced under $500. Open 1-5:30 Mon-Wed, Sat, Sun, 1-9 Thurs; closed Dec 24, Jan 17.

Gordon Woodside
3381 Sacramento (Presidio Hts. area), WA 1-6740

Gordon Woodside has been the leading dealer in contemporary art in Portland, Oregon, for the past five years, and the gallery in San Francisco, which has been open for one year, regularly shows work from Portland while adding to its list of exhibitors Bay Area artists. It has offered, for instance, the work of local painter Patrick Humble, which had not before been seen in the city. According to director Hugh Trutton, the gallery tries to keep the price of exhibit paintings in the three-figure range, and welcomes collectors whose budgets are confined to that. Open 11-7 Tues-Sat, 1-4 Sun.

Rose Rabow
2130 Leavenworth (Russian Hill area), 776-1720

Contemporary paintings and pre-Columbian artifacts are shown in the gracious setting of Mrs. Rabow's home. The artists shown vary in style: Gordon Onslow-Ford, Fred Reichman, Lee Mullican, and Richard Bowman. Open noon-5 Tues-Sat, and by appointment.

Vorpal
1168 Battery, EX 7-0413

The gallery was the scene of police investigation and the occasion for discussion on censorship of the arts for its 1965 exhibition of sculptures of couples in various love-making attitudes. This is not typical, however, of the work of the group shown here, which includes sixty-five artists of various inclinations and caliber. Prices under $500. Open 11-6 Mon-Sat, and by appointment.

Bill Pearson—Primitive Arts
3499 Sacramento, WE 1-2712

Pearson deals in African, American Indian, Mexican Colonial, Oceanic, and pre-Columbian art. The price range is typical of these fields. Open 11-5 Mon-Sat, or by appointment.

Miscellanea

For opportunities for buying in the very spread-out suburbs and environs of San Francisco, many of which contain excellent galleries, consult the *Bay Area Art Calendar,* a tri-monthly guide put out by the Arts Council of the University of California Art Museum, Berkeley. Phone the Museum, 845-600, ext. 1207, for copies.

The major yearly art festival of the Bay area is the San Francisco Art Commission's MUNICIPAL ART FESTIVAL, the biggest and oldest in the West. Usually held in the city's Civic Center Plaza in the late fall, from 10 to 10 daily, the exhibit is a five-day affair in which literally acres of paintings, sculpture, ceramics, graphic arts, weaving, jewelry, and structures are shown.

Some of the art groups that exhibit regularly in the city are THE SOCIETY OF WESTERN ARTISTS (annual exhibition at the De Young Museum); the SAN FRANCISCO WOMEN ARTISTS (annual show at the San Francisco Museum of Art), and the ASSOCIATION OF SAN FRANCISCO POTTERS (annual exhibit at the De Young).

Sears, Roebuck & Co.
Geary and Masonic, 567-7360
Holds special sales from the collection gathered by Vincent Price, the movie actor and collector. The sales go on for a month, generally, and present a miscellany that may include, for example, a drawing by Bonnard that sells for its normal market value, as well as the work of lesser known painters, which can be bought on a lower budget.

Information about Art

The two daily newspapers, the *San Francisco Chronicle* (morning) and the *San Francisco Examiner* (evening), regularly review art exhibitions and their combined Sunday edition devotes space to both local and international exhibitions of interest. In Oakland, the *Tribune* has offered serious art commentary for some years.

National and international publications fairly regularly cover the art scene: *Artforum* (New York), *Arts* (New York), *Art News* (New York), *Art International* (Switzerland), and *Studio International* (London). The art scene is also covered by such local publications as *San Francisco* and *West Art*.

As noted above, the Arts Council of the University of California, Berkeley, publishes, a tri-monthly guide to art events in the Bay area, while the San Francisco Convention and Visitors Bureau, 1375 Market, 863-2615, publishes a cultural listing titled *Coming Events in San Francisco* that includes selected art exhibitions.

Local television stations frequently preview important exhibitions in a format that may include a discussion with the exhibition's director of the work to be shown. Occasionally the new work and views of local artists are discussed on Channel 9, the local educational TV station. Pacifica Radio, KPFA, has regular art commentary both in the form of news and in extended discussion by various critics and artists.

PORTLAND, ORE.

Where to Buy

Arts & Crafts Society
616 N.W. 18, 228-4741
Invitational sales of Northwest artists. All periods and mediums.

Interior view, Contemporary Crafts Association, Portland, Oregon.

Front entrance, Portland Art Museum,
Portland, Oregon.

Juried work of instructors and students. Coop; Install; M. Parking; open 9-4 Mon-Fri.

Contemporary Crafts Association
3934 S.W. Corbett, 223-2654
A combined art association and gallery originally known as the Oregon Ceramic Studio, the Association is devoted to presenting vigorous and promising young talents. Such name artists as Franz and Margaret Wildenhain, Dorothy Liebes, Bernard Leach, and Robert Sperry were shown before they became well known. The EXHIBITION OF NORTHWEST CERAMICS, a biennial, is another attraction. Lectures and demonstrations are also regular events. Prices $5 to $50. Catalog 10¢. Parking. Open 11-5 Mon-Sat; closed Sun, holidays.

Fountain Gallery of Art
115 S.W. 4th, 228-8476
Contemporary painting, sculpture and prints. Full price range. Install; F, A-R. Open 11-5 Tues-Sat.

Image Gallery
2483 N.W. Overton, 222-5277
Contemporary paintings, drawings, prints, and sculpture, primarily by Oregon artists. This gallery shares artists with the Gordon Woodside Gallery in San Francisco and Seattle. Install; M; F; A-R; R. Parking; open 1-6 daily except Mon; closed Aug.

Oregon Society of Arts
2185 S.W. Park Pl., 228-8976
Traditional or representative art only. All mediums. This is a nonprofit organization that offers paintings by its artist members and takes no commission. Member artists number Ed Quigley and Arthur Selander. The Society's monthly bulletin is *Brushmarks*. Parking.

Window Gallery
1225 Commercial S, Salem, 362-1478
Contemporary Northwest artists. Oil, watercolor, sculpture. All prices. Coop; parking; R; Install. Open 11-5 daily.

Museum of Art, University of Oregon
Eugene, 342-1411, ext. 1101
Contemporary Pacific Northwest art available in the Rental-Sales Gallery. F, A-R. Open 11-5 Tues, Thurs; 1-5 Wed, Fri-Sun.

Where to Look

The Portland Art Association
1219 S.W. Park, 227-5626
The Art Association is notable for its extensive holdings of first-rate Northwest Indian Art, as well as its collections of Japanese prints, Renaissance art, classical antiquities, and English silver. Its Rental and Sales Gallery provides a good opportunity to rent or buy paintings and sculptures by Northwest artists. Sales prices range from $25 to $500, while rental fees are $7 to $15 for a three-month period. Work is often for sale from special exhibits such as the Artists of Oregon Painting and Sculpture Annual, regional group exhibits, and one-man and group shows by Northwest artists. Admission is free; parking; authentication by appointment; will recommend A-R and F; credit and non-credit courses with Reed College; art school on premises. Rental Gallery open 2-5 Tues, Thurs, Sun; Museum open 12-5 Tues-Thurs, Sat, Sun, noon-10 Fri; closed Mon, Christmas Eve, Christmas Day, New Year's Eve, New Year's, July 4th, Labor Day, Memorial Day.

The Junior Museum
3037 S.W. 2nd, CA 7-1505
Boasts a collection of shells, guns, sea life, Doll Room, and House of Minerals. It also offers guided tours and art classes. Admission is free; parking. Open 10-6 Mon, Wed; 2-10 Tues, Thurs; 9-5 Fri; closed Sat, Sun; 9-5 Mon-Fri summer.

The Oregon Historical Society
1230 S.W. Park, 226-4521
Comprises a history museum, a historical association, and a library. The collections concentrate on Pacific Northwest and Western Americana. The Society will soon move into the new Oregon Historical Center. Limited parking; admission free; authentication by appointment of manuscripts, books, museum objects, etc.; credit courses with Portland State College. Open 9-5 Mon-Sat; closed New Year's, Memorial Day, July 4th, Labor Day, Veterans Day, Thanksgiving, Christmas.

Information about Art

The *Sunday Oregonian* prints weekly art reviews by a staff art critic.

SEATTLE, WASH.

By Anne Todd
Art Reviewer, *The Seattle Times*

It was said some time ago that homes in Seattle have more "live art" on the walls than do those of any city of comparable size in the world. Seattle is keenly interested in its artists, and many persons of every economic bracket make a point of buying the works of Seattle painters, sculptors, printmakers, and potters. The dealers' galleries hold artists under contract and work actively to promote them, while the city's museums and institutions draw heavy attendance for their shows.

There are too many producing artists to name them and do justice to the accomplishments of each, but exhibition catalogs and brochures would provide some index of those of whom to be aware.

THE UNIVERSITY OF WASHINGTON'S SCHOOL OF ART, with a present faculty of forty-five professors, instructors, and lecturers and with its undergraduate and graduate students, is a strong factor in Seattle's art life. In addition to the University, Seattle has the CORNISH SCHOOL OF ALLIED ARTS and the BURNLEY SCHOOL OF PROFESSIONAL ART. WASHINGTON STATE UNIVERSITY in eastern Washington, plus EVERETT JUNIOR COLLEGE nearby, is also a source of training, as are WESTERN WASHINGTON STATE COLLEGE in Bellingham and CENTRAL WASHINGTON STATE COLLEGE in Ellensburg. They all have strong art departments.

For much of the Northwest, Seattle is the cultural capital, sharing that position to some extent with Portland, Oregon, and Vancouver, B.C. Artists from Montana, Idaho, eastern Oregon, and eastern Washington have gallery connections with the large coast cities, and add art works of admirable quality to Northwest exhibitions held here.

Visitors who come to Seattle from other parts of the country usually remark on how much less expensive painting, sculpture, and crafts are in this area than they would be if sold elsewhere. And, for this reason, many buy from our galleries while they are here. For the most part, dealers attempt to keep prices low on new performers to let them build an audience before their prices can climb. It is surprising, though, that some of the area's more secure artists charge as little for their works as the younger ones, and seem content with a steady sale at unspectacular rates.

Visitors also remark on the independence and diversity of Northwest artists, their seeming indifference to national fads, and the integrity with which they develop as individuals with individual styles.

To discerning visitors, the emphasis on handsome, buyable craft objects in the area is a pleasant surprise. Our potters, weavers, stitchers, and metalworkers are very accomplished, and their work is valued by those who live here. Fine craft shops feature them; and, as creative personalities, the craftsmen of the region are as much admired as the painters and sculptors.

As for a local "school," we are said to be influenced by the Orient, using an earth-toned pallette to imply a mystical involvement with nature as exemplified by the works of Mark Tobey, Morris Graves, and Kenneth Callahan. Artists living here stoutly deny the existence of such a school, claiming that the days of regionalism are past and that our artists work in the mainstream as much as artists anywhere in the world. It is my impression, however, that our artists *are* influenced by the soft quality of light here and *do* reflect an interest in nature. "Realistic" painting is not much admired, but most artists retain a sense of subject (often landscape) and include an emotional attitude toward it in their work.

Where to Buy

Dealers' galleries come and go but, at the moment, the chief ones are:

Otto Seligman Art Gallery
4727 University Way, N.E., LA 4-4512, LA 4-4556
Otto Seligman died in 1966, and his gallery was purchased by Francine Seders, the Parisian lawyer-librarian who acted as his assistant for the six months before his death. She hopes to bring more European art to Seattle, feeling that the city sees too little abstract art of the "School of Paris" variety. Seligman himself went to Europe each year to find painters to show in Seattle, but said he found Seattle almost impossibly chauvinistic about work produced outside the area. People came to his shows of European are but did not buy. This gallery is the western U.S. dealer for Mark Tobey.

Gordon Woodside Gallery
803 E. Union, EA 2-6689
Gordon Woodside directs this gallery, in its fifth year of operation.

Seattle Art Museum Pavilion, Seattle,
Washington.

Interior view, Seattle Art Museum Pavilion, Seattle, Washington.

Seattle Art Museum, Seattle, Washington.

Pacific Northwest Arts and Crafts Fair, 1966, Bellevue, Washington: a young visitor watches an artist in action.

One-man exhibition of pottery by Robert Sperry, Henry Gallery, University of Washington, Seattle, 1965. (*Photograph by James O. Sneddon*)

Recently it established a branch in San Francisco which is an apparent success. The gallery carries a relatively small stable, over which it exercises rigid control. With the branch in San Francisco, it has begun bringing California artists to Seattle and sending Northwest artists into the Bay area. It also has a strong connection with Portland, Oregon, sharing artists with the Image Gallery there. Since the space it occupies was once a dwelling, work shown in it suggests how it will look in a home.

The Collectors Gallery
Crossroads Ctr., Bellevue, SH 7-2155
This is a suburban gallery but is often visited by Seattleites since it shows many fine Seattle artists in a remarkably good space. It also represents artists from eastern Washington, Oregon, Montana, and Idaho. The gallery has a reciprocal arrangement with the Bau-Xi Gallery in Vancouver, B.C., to show Canadian artists here and Northwest artists in Canada. It also conducts an annual COLLEGE ART SHOW (CASCA) for art students enrolled in eighty-five Northwest art schools. In September, 1966, it held an American Indian art show with work by artists from many parts of the country. Robert Carpenter is the director.

The Northwest Craft Center and Gallery
Seattle Civic Center, JU 3-2889
Ruth Nomura directs this handsome selling facility, an outgrowth of the Seattle World's Fair, which included among its tenant exhibitions one mounted by the Northwest Designer Craftsmen. The exhibition was so popular during the Fair that permanent space was provided in the resulting Center for a fine retail craft outlet. In addition to pottery, selected weaving, jewelry, and craft items of all sorts, the Craft Center carries the works of individual print-makers, painters, and sculptors. The level of quality is high, and special artists are occasionally featured in monthly shows.

PANACA
240 Bellevue Sq., Bellevue, GL 4-0234
PANACA's easy proximity to the city makes it more of a Seattle gallery than a suburban one. Its name is an acronym from the Pacific Northwest Arts and Crafts Fair, which is held in Bellevue the last weekend of each July. The Fair is an enormous and very distinguished event that has become, in the last twenty years, one of the country's biggest art-selling occasions. PANACA was established to make the work of those who are in greatest demand during the Fair available throughout the year. In addition to its well-

chosen, well-displayed craft items, this facility conducts an art rental service, permitting members to rent paintings for a minimum of six months, and to apply rental on purchase. Margaret Reeves is director.

Artists Sales Gallery
University Village, 4700 25, N.E., LA 3-7264

Margaret Mattocks directs this artists' cooperative to which seventy-five member artists contribute time and money. The gallery offers low-priced paintings constantly on exhibition in quantity. Occasionally featured are "guest artists" who also designate "juror's choice" works. As a bootstrap operation that has been successful, the Artists Sales Gallery is a solace to its members and a source of inexpensive paintings for those who know what they like.

Attica
426 Broadway E., EA 2-5482

Attica opened in September, 1966, to show contemporary painting and sculpture and imported *objets d'art*. The director, Vernon Gray, is a professional actor and an amateur sculptor, with a wide acquaintance in America and Europe among artists. He will import contemporary art for exhibition as well as art objects. The gallery is new and very attractive.

The Gallery
311 Occidental, MU 2-7015

One of the most successful of the Pioneer Plaza restorations, The Gallery does much to insure that Seattle's version of San Francisco's Jackson Square will actually come to pass. It deals mostly in furnishings and art objects, but has begun to schedule monthly shows of paintings. These will be chosen for the way in which they complement the other items on display, but since the director is obviously a man of great taste and imagination, it may be assumed that his choices will be good. His first painting show was by a Yakima artist who had completed a series of "Old Master" paintings on themes by Velazquez. Witty studies of infantas and duchesses smirking serenely from deep Spanish glooms looked most appropriate with the ornate lighting fixtures and carved mirrors nearby.

Environs

Cellar Gallery
96 Kirkland Ave., Kirkland, VA 2-8451

An artists' cooperative, the Cellar Gallery mainly aims to serve the communities on the east side of Lake Washington in most of its shows and competitions. However it also imports guest artists from Seattle for invitational shows from time to time. It carries craft items as well as paintings, prints, and sculptures; and, like the PANACA Gallery, has a rental gallery for the convenience of its members.

Miscellanea

The Henry Gallery
University of Washington campus, 15th N.E. at Campus Pkwy., 543-2280
The Henry Gallery is operated as part of the Art Department of the University of Washington. Its shows pertain to the department's programs and needs, but it also includes in its schedule an annual exhibition by the Northwest Printmakers, in which works are for sale, and the biennial exhibition of Northwest Craftsmen, in which most of the work is for sale. Occasional one-man shows by members of the faculty also include work which is for sale. Prices $20-$1,000. Charge campus parking. Open 10-5 Mon-Wed, Fri, Sat, 5-10 Thurs, 1-5 Sun.

Seattle University
Broadway at Madison
Each year, shortly before Christmas, the Seattle University Art League holds a religious art show open to all artists who work with themes from the Old or New Testament. The show is juried and money prizes are given. Most of the works selected for the show are for sale.

The Jewish Community Center
1017 4th, MA 4-8431
For several years the Center has held an arts festival that included an invitational show of paintings, most of which were for sale. The building in which this event was held each year has been demolished to make room for a new office building, and the new center will not be built for some time yet. When it is built it will be on Mercer Island, and the festival will undoubtedly resume in an expanded form.

University of Washington
N.E. 42nd St.
Each Spring, the school of art holds a STUDENT ART AUCTION for one night in the Health Sciences auditorium. Students donate a part of what they get for their works to an art-school scholarship

fund, and keep the rest. The event in this way is a benefit for a great many people. Often the faculty members contribute work to this occasion, and fine paintings can be purchased for very reasonable figures when the crowd thins out toward the small hours of the morning. The promise is that all paintings will be sold by the time the event is over, so the reward for those who had naps in the afternoon can be substantial.

Sears, Roebuck & Co.
9105 Sunset, Renton, BA 6-2323
Although Sears has several stores in the Seattle area, this one makes the most of its Vincent Price art department.

Frederick and Nelson
5th and Pine, MU 2-5500
"The Little Gallery" is on its eighth floor. This is the oldest gallery in Seattle, having opened in the late 1930s. Its usual program is to ask eight artists each month to hang two or three paintings. The list usually includes four established artists and four younger ones. The Little Gallery also holds occasional shows of paintings by members of a painting group, imports shows from out of the state, and keeps a supply of paintings on hand in its files, which are easy to riffle through. A case contains changing shows of work by local potters and jewelers. On the fifth floor, near the picture-framing department, is a gallery of commercially supplied "original" paintings by professional painters who specialize in European landscapes, seascapes, and florals.

The Bon Marché
4th and Pine, MA 4-1234
Has "The National Gallery" on its seventh floor. Monthly shows by one or two artists are chosen by William Hixson, Professor of Art at the University of Washington.

Festivals and Art Groups

As soon as school is out in the spring, the surrounding suburban areas begin a series of art festivals, which are usually held outdoors in the shopping malls of the communities that sponsor them. The 1966 season began with a festival in Renton. Then came Edmonds, Bellevue, Kirkland, and Burien. The shows are divided into professional and amateur categories. They are juried, and prize money is given. Most works are for sale.

The major art competitions of the year are the NORTHWEST ANNUAL, held by the Seattle Art Museum in the Seattle Art

Museum Pavilion, Seattle Center, for artists of the five Northwest states. This show is juried, and prize money is given. Most work is for sale.

Another important competition is the ANNUAL WATER COLOR SHOW in the Seattle Art Museum Pavilion. Although paintings are restricted to works in water-soluble media, the conditions are similar to those of the Northwest Annual.

The FRYE ART MUSEUM holds an Annual Oil Painting Show for artists of the three coastal states, and a Puget Sound Area Exhibition for artists of the fourteen Puget Sound Counties.

The MUSEUM OF HISTORY AND INDUSTRY holds a show called "The Changing Scene in Washington" each fall, for artists who have painted subjects with some historical content to them. The works must have a recognizable subject, although they need not be realistic. The show is juried, and prize money is given. Much work is for sale.

The alumnae of CHI OMEGA, a sorority, hold an annual ART COLLECTORS TEA in its chapter house (4549 18, N.E.). Tickets to the tea permit would-be purchasers to come in and look at paintings brought to the chapter house by artists who have been invited to participate. Any works that are sold enrich the artists. Chi Omega does not take a commission.

The LAMBDA RHO ALUMNAE (University of Washington honorary group) holds a sale each year in November to which its members may contribute work. No work may be over $25. The show is held at the Henry Gallery.

Many orthopedic groups hold art shows to raise money for the CHILDREN'S ORTHOPEDIC HOSPITAL.

There are many other groups that put on art shows, but often they are of a try-it-once character, and are not annual events.

Where to Look

The Seattle Art Museum
Volunteer Park, EA 5-2000

Seattle Art Museum Pavilion
Seattle Center, 2nd N. and Thomas, MA 4-6550
The Museum opened its Pavilion in June, 1965, primarily as a showcase of contemporary art. The Museum and Pavilion are the outstanding cultural institutions of Seattle. The Museum is mainly

devoted to showing items from its superb collections, which are globally strong in Asiatic art. The Eugene Fuller and Thomas D. Stimson Memorial Collections are especially noteworthy for the latter. Original art from annual competitive exhibitions, Northwest regional shows, invitational group and one-man shows, and traveling exhibitions is often for sale. These are also shown at the Museum Pavilion, originally built as the British Pavilion at the 1962 Seattle World's Fair, and a dazzling exhibition facility. (For the Museum, admission is free; free floor plan; authentication by appointment; will recommend F, A-R; open 10-5 daily with an additional 7-10 p.m. Thurs, noon-5 Sun and holidays. For the Pavilion: admission is free; open 10-5 and 7-10 daily in summer; 10-5 Mon-Sat, closed Sun and holidays in winter.

Charles & Emma Frye Art Museum
704 Terry, MA 2-9250
Noted for its conservative taste, the Frye Art Museum emphasizes academic painting of the late nineteenth century, but it also brings in many shows circulated by the American Federation of Arts and the Smithsonian Institution Traveling Exhibition Service. It holds two main competitive shows during year, and invitational exhibits from local artists at its own discretion. Some of this work is for sale. Admission is free; open 10-5 daily, noon-6 Sun, holidays; closed Christmas Day.

The Costume and Textile Study Collection
School of Home Economics, University of Washington,
543-1739
Many cultures and techniques from the world over are represented. There are fragments of Italian velvets, brocades and damasks from the fourteenth to the seventeenth centuries; a large group of complete costumes and embroideries from Central Europe and the Balkan area; a 1958 gift of more than a thousand textiles from India; a group of Guatemalan fabrics; and many textiles that round out the world-wide collection. Special storage facilities both protect the fabrics and make possible their easy display. Open by appointment only; charge for University parking.

Seattle Public Library
4th and Madison, MA 4-3800
In addition to its comprehensive art reference collection, the library collects original prints and displays original work by local artists. Admission is free; open 9-9 Mon-Fri, 9-6 Sat; closed Sun.

Information about Art

Seattle's two daily newspapers, the *Seattle Times* and the *Seattle Post Intelligencer,* carry Gallery Guide listings, and reviews of shows in the main galleries and museums.

Seattle Magazine occasionally carries an article on art, as does also *Puget Soundings*, published by the Junior League of Seattle.

The SEATTLE CONVENTION AND TOURIST BUREAU (215 Columbia) publishes a very comprehensive *Calendar of Events* which lists theatrical, musical, and artistic offerings.

Occasionally the gallery dealers will buy advertising in the newspapers and on the radio.

CRAFTS IN THE PACIFIC NORTHWEST

By LaMar Harrington
Administrative Assistant, Henry Gallery, Seattle

Interest in both arts and crafts is lively in the Northwest, and most established craftsmen, of which there are many, can sell much of what they produce. This, of course, takes constant thought and planning on the part of interested individuals in this part of the country, but has resulted in a fine climate for the handcrafts. There is no craft-marketing problem here as there is in many parts of the United States.

Interest in the crafts began about twenty years ago and has continued to grow, with many activities and exhibitions for both interested public and craftsmen. The most recent undertaking was the formation of the FRIENDS OF THE CRAFTS, INC. (c/o Ruth Penington, President, Decorative Crafts Council, Fidalgo Allied Arts, P.O. Box 476, La Conner, Wash.), an organization devoted to promoting interest in the crafts.

Pottery is the most popular craft by far, with weaving and architectural accessories as close seconds.

As there are so many fine producing craftsmen here, it would be impossible to name them all. However, in going over the catalogs of the past four annual NORTHWEST CRAFTSMEN'S EXHIBITIONS, I find there are fifty to one hundred craftsmen in the area who produce and are accepted in competitive exhibitions consistently. For visitors trying to locate craftsmen in this area, these catalogs are very useful. Visitors can also contact Kenneth

Shores (Director, Contemporary Crafts Association, 3934 S.W. Corbett, Portland, Ore.), who is the Craftsman-Trustee for the Northwest Region of the American Craftsmen's Council.

Major Area Crafts Outlets

PANACA
240 Bellevue Sq., Bellevue Shopping Ctr., Bellevue, Washington, GL 4-0234
All types of crafts, all prices. Open 10-5:30 Mon-Thurs, Sat, Fri. 9-10 winter. Same summer, except Fri 10-7.

Northwest Craft Center
Seattle Center, Seattle, JU 3-2889
All types, all prices. Open 11-6 daily; closed Mon.

Collector's Gallery
Crossroads Shopping Ctr., Bellevue, Wash., SH 7-2155
Handicrafts, as well as paintings, sculpture. Open noon-5 daily, plus 7:30-9:30 Thurs, Fri.

Bainbridge Arts and Crafts Ass'n.
Box 161, Bainbridge Isle, Winslow, Wash., VI 2-3132
All types, all prices. Open 10-5 Mon-Sat, 1-5 Sun.

Craft Center
9623 Firdale Art Ctr., Edmonds, Wash., PR 6-5191
Located in an art center for teaching, this outlet is a working and teaching studio for enameling. Some forty painters, potters, jewelry makers, woodcarvers, serigraphers, and so on, are also represented. R; First Bank Card charge. Parking. Open 1-5 Tues-Sat.

Windigo Shop
408 Commercial, Anacortes, Wash.
Fine Indian artifacts, arts and crafts. Prices $2.50-$750. Parking. Open 9:30-5:30 daily.

Major Craft Competitions

The NORTHWEST CRAFTSMEN'S EXHIBITION, Henry Gallery, University of Washington, Seattle, is the region's only regular competitive exhibition. It is of as high a quality as possible within the limitations of a survey-type exhibition. Held biennially in the spring, it alternates with a biennial craft invitational.

The largest and most important market for crafts is held in conjunction with the PACIFIC NORTHWEST ARTS AND CRAFTS

FAIR in Bellevue, Washington, the weekend nearest July 26 (the day it is least likely to rain in the Puget Sound area). An outdoor show lasting three days only, it had its twentieth anniversary year in 1966.

Other smaller and younger exhibitions held somewhat irregularly throughout the area are the BAINBRIDGE ARTS AND CRAFTS ASSOCIATION show, Winslow, Washington; the ARTS AND CRAFTS ASSOCIATION exhibition, Tacoma, Washington; and such suburban summer fairs as the CREATIVE ARTS FESTI-VAL, Renton (early June); the EDMONDS ARTS FESTIVAL (mid-June); the ANACORTES ARTS AND CRAFTS FAIR (early August); the KIRKLAND SUMMER ARTS FESTIVAL (late July); and the BURIEN ARTS AND CRAFTS FAIR (late August). Although the dates of these exhibitions shift from year to year, all are usually three-day events held every summer.

HONOLULU, HAWAII

By Joanna Eagle
Former Art Critic, *The Honolulu Advertiser*

The particular vitality of both the art and the life here owes much to the melting-pot culture of Hawaii. Chinese, Japanese, Koreans, Filipinos, Hawaiians, Caucasians, and Portuguese have all con-tributed their unique aesthetic sensibilities to the rich variety of art produced in the islands. Rather than suffering from its isolation in being more than two thousand miles from the nearest art center, Hawaii now provides an important link between East and West. Its international flavor is further underlined by the presence of the EAST-WEST CENTER here, a graduate institute for the study of Asian, Pacific, and American cultures.

The Island artist could easily be overwhelmed by the lush sensuousness of his environment. But while there is the usual amount of "tourist art"—sunsets, beaches, nudes, paintings on black velvet—that any large resort area seems to produce, the quality art remains largely individualistic.

There is much good art and art activity in Honolulu, but it does not center around the commercial galleries. These usually have a rough go here, and only one, GIMA'S ART GALLERY, has managed to survive for any period of time. However, you can't very well avoid art in Honolulu. Go into the banks, to the HAWAII

Pauahi Hall, the Bernice P. Bishop Museum, Honolulu, Hawaii.
(*Courtesy Bernice P. Bishop Museum*)

Art exhibits surround the patio of the Hawaii State Library, Honolulu.

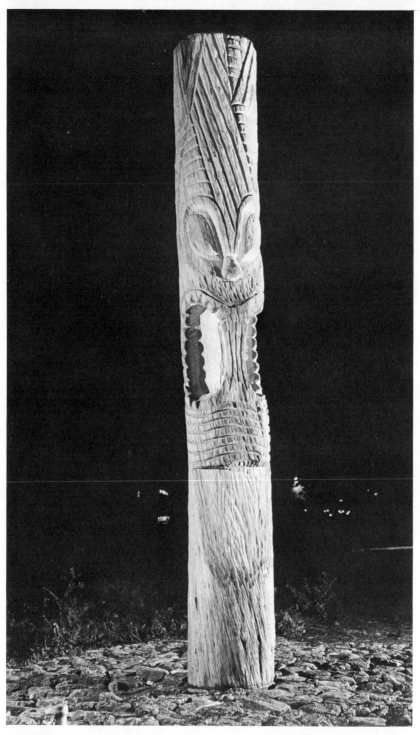

A Hawaiian temple image of carved wood stands at the main entrance to the
Bernice P. Bishop Museum grounds, Honolulu, Hawaii. (*Courtesy
Bernice P. Bishop Museum*)

STATE LIBRARY, to the dramatic new HONOLULU INTER-NATIONAL CENTER, even to the NEWS BUILDING with its art gallery, and you will usually find excellent art displays. Art is all around you, thanks to the encouragement of local merchants at the ALA MOANA and WAIALAE SHOPPING CENTERS; the art displays in the schools and universities; the churches that have given over space to exhibits; the commissioning of art by architects in the city's dramatic new buildings; and in the homes of many Honoluluans who are avid collectors.

The integration of art with architecture is typical of a tropical environment. However, the cooperation of artist and architect is even more emphasized here because of the presence of Mexican Mural Renaissance painter Jean Charlot, who brought many of the ideas of that art movement from Mexico to Hawaii. Now retired from the University, Charlot continues as an active muralist, painter and writer, and the influence of his, and his students', work is still felt throughout the community.

For a relatively small city, Honolulu boasts a high percentage of quality artists, many of whom teach at either the Honolulu Academy of Arts or at the University of Hawaii. Among them are painters Webster Anderson, J. Halley Cox, Juliette May Fraser, Helen Gilbert, Hon Chew-Hee, Tom Litaker, Ben Norris, Louis Pohl, James Rosen, Tadashi Sato, Edward Stasack, Wilson Stamper, Tseng Yu-ho, and the "dean" of Honolulu artists, Madge Tennent; sculptors B'umpei Akaji, Edward Brownlee, and Mamoru Sato; potters Isami Enomoto, Claude Horan, Roger Lintault, Harue McVey, and Toshiko Takaezu; stained-glass artist Erica Karawina; and weaver Jean Williams, to name just a few.

The museums and the University have played important roles in building up the arts in Hawaii. The HONOLULU ACADEMY OF ARTS is an exquisite repository for both Western and Eastern art objects, and is well known for the excellence of its Oriental collections. It also has group and one-man shows of Hawaii artists from time to time. Its art school, along with the dynamic art department of the UNIVERSITY OF HAWAII, employs many of Hawaii's foremost artists. The University and the Academy, in addition, both import recognized mainland artists as guest professors. The BISHOP MUSEUM is an important research and display center of Pacific ethnology and archeology, and Hawaiian artifacts.

In addition, there is a newly formed STATE CULTURAL COMMISSION, under the directorship of Alfred Preis, that coordinates local activity in all the arts, including the visual ones.

Where to Buy

Ansteth Ltd. Interiors
2126 Kalakaua, 932-361
Chinese furniture, Oriental paintings and screens, silks, and art objects.

Asia Room, East-West Center
University of Hawaii Campus, 918-111
Changing exhibitions of international art.

Gima's Art Gallery
Ala Moana Center, Lower Level, 997-526
In a town that sees art galleries come and go all too frequently, Gima's has managed to hold on through the years due to the generally high quality of its exhibitions and its Ala Moana shopping-center location. Gima's features both established and beginning Island artists in its small but choice space. All media are included, as well as Oriental antiques, paintings, and objects. Parking; F; A-R; Install; china repairs. Open 9:30-5:30 Tues-Thurs, Sat, 9:30-9 Mon, Fri.

Grossman Moody
2200 Kalakaua, 935-788
In addition to its "Jewels from the Seven Seas," this elegant shop features a dazzling array of Oriental antiques, porcelains, bronzes, and paintings.

The Honolulu Advertiser's Contemporary Arts Center of Hawaii
News Bldg., 605 Kapiolani, 52-977
One-man and group shows of top Island artists displayed in a handsome, well-lighted gallery. At one time or another, the Center has given space to all of Hawaii's foremost artists. Prices $50-$3,000. A; M; Install. Open 8-6 Mon-Fri, 8-3 Sat.

Hawaii Arts Council Gallery
Church of the Crossroads, 1212 University, 992-220
Right down the street from the University and the East-West Center, this Gallery offers all media as well as crafts. The Gallery is run by the Hawaii Arts Council, an organization of the Islands' best artists, which also offers art classes at the church. Parking; open 9:30-4 Mon-Sat, 9:30 a.m.-12:30 p.m. Sun.

Honolulu Community Theatre
Makapuu and Alohea, 740-274
Features art displays by local artists in its lobby.

Iida's
Ala Moana Center, Lower Level, 960-888
8 S. Beretania, 502-049
Japanese decorative objects, chiefly of the tourist variety.

John F. Kennedy Theater, East-West Center
University of Hawaii Campus, 918-746, 918-747
Changing art displays by local artists in the lobby.

John Young Gallery
2119 Kalakaua, 939-933
Contemporary prints, paintings, oils, watercolors. Parking; Install;
open 10-5 daily.

Joji's
1259 S. Beretania, 506-869
Be sure to stop at Joji's when visiting the Honolulu Academy of
Arts, just down the street. This is perhaps the most tasteful shop in
Honolulu, and features hard-to-get Japanese folk arts selected by
Joji Wago himself in Japan. Joji occasionally puts on one-man
shows of the foremost Japanese folk potters.

Lamoi
942 Maunakea, 581-523
Located in the old Chinese section of the city, this Gallery presents
shows by Chinese artists from Hawaii, Hong Kong, and Taiwan.
Parking; M; open 9-3 daily.

Hawaii State Library Art Circuit
478 S. King, and Oahu Public Library branches, 506-081
Shows at the main library, which are then circulated to branches
on the island of Oahu, are selected by the Hawaii Arts Council.
This is the most extensive program for sending quality art exhibits around the Island. All media by local artists are offered. The
art gallery at the main library surrounds a cool patio in the center
of the building. Parking; open 9-9 Mon-Fri, 9-5 Sat, 1-5 Sun.

The Little Gallery
1943 S. King, 966-838
One-man shows of important Island artists with New York representation. Open 10-4 daily.

Royal Hawaiian Art Gallery
Royal Hawaiian Hotel, Main Hotel Bldg., Front Lawn Level,
938-003
The gallery features top Hawaii artists, such as Ed Stasack, Bumpei Akaji, Ed Brownlee, Jean Charlot, Louis Pohl, and Wilson Stamper.

Shirokiya
Ala Moana Center, 941-9111
Japanese decorative arts, with special shows of Japanese artists and art on its top floor.

Unitarian Art Gallery
2500 Pali Hwy., 554-047
Changing exhibitions of local artists. Install; parking; open 9-3 daily; mornings only during summer.

University of Hawaii, George Hall
University of Hawaii campus, 918-111
Quality exhibitions of student art are featured, and usually changed monthly. A more extensive exhibition program is planned when the new art building is completed in 1969.

Environs

Windward City Gallery
Mall, Windward Shopping Center, Kaneohe, 241-862
Offers local artists, especially members of the Windward Artists Guild.

Hunnicutt Art Gallery
53-346 Kamehameha Hwy., Punaluu, 247-485
Local paintings, crafts. A good stop as you drive around the island.

Diamond Head Gallery
Kahala Hilton Hotel, Main Lobby, 5000 Kahala Ave.,
744-2211
One-man and group shows of Island artists; paintings and sculpture.

Polynesian Cultural Center
Laie, 299-291
It is well worth the thirty-eight-mile drive from Honolulu to see this fifteen-acre complex of Polynesian villages and art, representing Samoa, Fiji, the Maoris, Tahiti, Hawaii, and the Tongans. The

Sales Shop offers hand-made objects and art from these Polynesian cultures. Admission: $2 adults, $1 children under 12.

Art Organizations

Some of the main art groups putting on exhibits are the HAWAII HAND WEAVERS HUI, the HONOLULU PRINTMAKERS, the HONOLULU PAINTERS & SCULPTORS LEAGUE, THE WINDWARD ARTISTS GUILD, THE HAWAII WATER-COLOR AND SERIGRAPH SOCIETY, and the HAWAII ARTS COUNCIL. Their shows are usually put on at the Honolulu Academy of Arts, Ala Moana Shopping Center, or through the Hawaii State Library Art Circuit.

Art Festivals and Competitions

There is usually some kind of art festival being held at ALA MOANA CENTER, Lower Level, at almost any time of the year. Regularly scheduled competitions, some put on by Honolulu's varied ethnic groups, include the art display at the NARCISSUS FESTIVAL in January (Chinese); the art exhibit of the CHERRY BLOSSOM FESTIVAL, usually held in February-March-April (Japanese); the EASTER ART FESTIVAL, Honolulu's biggest, most professional show organized by The Windward Artists Guild at Ala Moana Center, in which a prominent mainland art expert is usually brought in as juror (past judges have included Alfred Frankenstein, art critic, the *San Francisco Chronicle* and Henry Seldis, art critic, the *Los Angeles Times*); the art display at the FIFTIETH STATE FAIR in July; the combined ANNUAL OF The HONOLULU PAINTERS & SCULPTORS LEAGUE And The HONOLULU PRINTMAKERS, and the various branches of the Armed Forces with their shows. You can check the local newspapers for announcements of these events.

Where to Look

The Bernice P. Bishop Museum
1355 Kalihi, 855-951
Founded in 1889 by Charles Reed Bishop as a memorial to his wife, Princess Bernice Pauahi, the last direct descendant of Kamehameha the Great. It is a major scientific and art research center devoted to answering questions about the Pacific. Its visual displays are devoted mainly to Hawaiiana and to artifacts of Pacific peoples. Its expeditions and research activities are chronicled by the Bishop

Museum Press; their books are available in the Main Floor Hawaiian Hall Book and Gift Shop. Parking; authentication of primitive Pacific arts by appointment; exhibit halls: admission $1.50 adults, 50¢ juniors, includes the Planetarium Show; open 9-4:30 Mon-Sat, 1-5 Sun and holidays.

The Honolulu Academy of Arts
900 Beretania, 583-693

With its galleries surrounded by landscaped courtyards, the Academy can surely be called one of the world's most beautiful museums. It is a sheer delight to wander through the cool galleries, passing through the bright court sunshine at intervals, listening to the birds and the splash of water. Though small, the Academy is world famous for the excellence of its Oriental collections, built up by Chinese art scholar Dr. Gustav Ecke and former director Robert P. Griffing, Jr.; the James Michener collection of Japanese prints; and a select, but fine, collection of Western art including a gallery of Kress Collection paintings. There are also many changing exhibitions; for example, the Academy was the second United States museum to show *Art: U.S.A.: Now,* the collection of the Johnson Wax Company, on its way back from Japan. Admission is free; art school; lending collection; parking; open 10-4:30 Tues, Wed, Fri, Sat, 10-9:30 Thurs, 3-6 Sun; closed Mon.

201 Prospect, 506-952

Tennent Gallery

Presents the work of Hawaiian artists, with a large group of Hawaiiana paintings and drawings by Madge Tennent. Admission is free; open 10-noon Tues, 7-9 p.m. Thurs, 3-5 Sun.

Information about Art

Chief sources of art news in the Islands are the Music & Arts page of the combined *Sunday Advertiser-Star Bulletin* and the art column written by Jean Charlot in the Wednesday *Star Bulletin.* During the week, there are occasional art stories and reviews in both papers. The local magazine *Honolulu Today,* which recently took over the venerable and famed *Paradise of the Pacific,* has some art coverage. Radio and TV coverage is extremely spotty, if practically non-existent, but the new ETV station has regular programs on the creative arts on Channel 11.

Sources and Obligations

I wish to thank the many persons and organizations who made this book possible. It is they, rather than I, who are the authors of *Buying Art on a Budget*. So many friends and individuals gave selflessly of their time, knowledge, and hospitality that they are almost too numerous to list.

This book could never have been put together without the many contributors in some thirty cities and locales across the United States who became interested in the project, and who gave generously of their time and specialized knowledge of art in their cities. To all of them go my heartfelt thanks.

To the many museums and art organizations who contributed photographs and answered questionnaires also goes my deepest appreciation.

Several publishers generously contributed reference books: Farrar, Straus & Giroux, Inc. (Pierre Cabanne's *The Great Collectors*), the Museum of Modern Art (Caroline Keck's *How to Take Care of Your Pictures*), The Macmillan Company (*Great Private Collections*, edited by Douglas Cooper), and Charles E. Tuttle Co., Inc. (*The Ceramic Art of Japan*, by Hugo Munsterberg).

I wish to thank especially JoAnne and Charles Murphy, without whom this book would probably never have been written; Lisa Suter and Meda Mladek of Washington, D.C., who provided valuable introductions to collectors in that city; Seymour Slive of Harvard University and Gustav Ecke of the University of Hawaii, who taught me much about "looking" and taste; my agent, Anita Diamant; and my husband, George, who did the preliminary editing of this manuscript.

I have indicated my primary sources, and noted the books to which I am particularly indebted, in the text. No bibliography is included, therefore, aside from certain recommended readings which are also cited in the text. In addition, the reader is directed to the bibliographies of these books for further reading in specialized areas of art.

425

Further acknowledgments are listed under the appropriate chapter headings:

THE JOY OF LOOKING: For their help with information on United States museums, I wish to thank the American Association of Museums, Smithsonian Institution, Washington 25, D.C. I also wish to thank *Art News* and Mrs. Frederick Kiesler for the use of Frederick Kiesler's statement on galleries; the many private collectors in Washington, D.C. who so generously threw open their collections to me; Arnold Gingrich, publisher of *Esquire,* and The New York Board of Trade for their information on U.S. businesses and art; the cartoon so kindly loaned by *Punch* in the section on art reproductions; and the information provided by The Art Dealers Association of America and the Appraisers Association of America, Inc.

HOW AND WHERE TO BUY: For the information on renting art, I am indebted to the Washington Gallery of Modern Art, Washington, D.C.; Inga Heck of the Corcoran Gallery of Art, Washington, D.C.; and the Art Lending Service of the Museum of Modern Art, New York City. Collector Henry Hecht, also of Washington, gave a great deal of valuable information on buying art, especially on purchasing in galleries, on exchanging art, and on prices. It was through the kind permission of Farrar, Straus & Giroux, Inc., that I was able to quote the art dealer Paul Durand-Ruel's statement about gallery dealers (excerpted from Pierre Cabanne's *The Great Collectors*). My deepest appreciation for their valuable contributions to the auction section go to Mary Vandegrift of the Parke-Bernet Galleries, Inc., and Edward N. Beck of Clark, Nelson of London, Ltd. Mrs. Howard de Vis-Norton of the Honolulu Academy of Arts, the Smithsonian Institution, and the Museum of Modern Art provided necessary information on traveling exhibitions. And for the advice on Buying What You Like, I had the kind permission of *The Washington Post* to reprint collector Paul Mellon's thoughts on this subject.

YOUR ART IN YOUR HOME: Valuable information for this section was quoted from two books by Henry Heydenryk, Jr., *The Right Frame* and *The Art and History of Frames,* both published by James H. Heineman, Inc., New York City, and used with the publisher's kind permission. Advice on the care of art was gleaned from Carolyn Keck's *How to Take Care of Your Pictures* and from art restorer John Steele of Washington, D.C.

ORIGINAL ART PRICED UNDER $1,000: The following individuals gave generously of their advice, time, and knowledge, and some of the information given by these art specialists was used also in the Sources of Low-Cost, Original Art in the United States section of this book. Yet, none of these persons are to be held responsible for what I have here written. The interpretations and evaluations are my own.

Americana: Edith Halpert, director, The Downtown Gallery, New York City; George Hamilton Montgomery and Mary Black, former and present directors respectively of the Museum of Early American Folk Arts, New York City.

North American Indian Art: Frederick J. Dockstader, director, and Mary W. Williams, manager of the Museum Shop, the Museum of the American Indian, New York City; James McGrath of the Institute of American Indian Arts, Santa Fé, New Mexico; Robert Hart, General Manager of the Indian Arts & Crafts Board, U. S. Department of the Interior, Washington, D.C.

Antiques: Babette Craven, former antiques editor of *Art News;* James Ketchum, Curator of the White House, Washington, D.C.; and Lawrence Ross of *Connoisseur.*

Crafts: Craft Horizons and the American Craftsmen's Council, New York City; potter Teruo Hara, Warrenton, Va.; and collector Martin Amt, Washington, D.C.

Exotics: Far Eastern Art: James Cahill, Professor of Oriental Art, the University of California, Berkeley; Asia House, New York City; Walter Spink, Associate Professor of Art, the University of Michigan, Ann Arbor; John Pope, director of the Freer Gallery of Art, Washington, D.C.; Simon Kriger of S. Kriger, Inc., Washington, D.C.

Middle Eastern Art: Richard Ettinghausen, Professor, the Institute of Fine Arts, New York University, New York City. *Primitive Art:* Allen Wardwell, Curator, Primitive Art department, The Art Institute of Chicago; Julie Jones of The Museum of Primitive Art, New York City; the sculptor and collector Jacques Lipchitz; Elizabeth Benson, curator of the Pre-Columbian Collection at Dumbarton Oaks, Washington, D.C.

Graphics: Jacob Kainen, consultant on prints to the Collection of Fine Arts, Smithsonian Institution, Washington, D.C.; collector Lessing J. Rosenwald, Jenkintown, Pa.; Katherine Shepard and William Morrison of the National Gallery of Art, Washington, D.C.; the Pratt Graphic Art Center, New York City; the Print Council of America, New York City; Frank Getlein, art critic of *The Evening Star* (Washington, D.C.) and author of *The Bite of the Print;* A. D. Lublin, art dealer, New York City; the International Graphic Arts Society, Inc., New York City; the Master

Drawings Association, New York City; Riva Casteleman, the Print Room of the Museum of Modern Art, New York City.

Modern and Contemporary Art: The Washington Gallery of Art, Washington, D.C.; A. L. Chanin of the Museum of Modern Art, New York City; and Ramon Osuna, the Pan American Union, Washington, D.C.

SOURCES OF LOW-COST ORIGINAL ART IN THE UNITED STATES: In addition to the contributors who wrote the chapters on buying art in individual United States cities, I wish to thank the many tourist and visitors' bureaus across the country who sent information. I would also like to thank the many art organizations, individuals, museums and galleries who contributed information and photographs.

Special thanks go to the following in the East: the Institute of Contemporary Arts in Boston for their booklet, *The Cultural Resources of Boston;* painter Alice Baber for her help on art in New York City; Leon Arkus of the Museum of Art, the Carnegie Institute, for information on Pittsburgh, Pa.; the Philadelphia Civic Center for its listing of craftsmen in the Philadelphia, Pa. area; Frank Getlein, art critic for *The Evening Star* (Washington, D.C.), for his help on Washington.

In the South, my thanks are due Helen G. McCormack, former director of the Carolina Art Association, and Marian Rivers; in Birmingham, Alabama, to Gene Smith, Littlehouse on Linden; and in Atlanta, Ga., to Carlyn Fisher, art critic for *Atlanta* magazine, to the magazine for allowing certain reprints, and to Paul Valentine, former art critic of the *Atlanta Constitution.*

I am grateful for the help received from the following in the Midwest: Detroit Adventure, Inc.; Betty L. Zimmerman and Mary Louise Baskett of the Cincinnati Museum of Art; George McCue of the *St. Louis Post-Dispatch,* the Artists' Guild and the City Art Museum, all of St. Louis, Mo.; James Harithas, presently Assistant Director of the Corcoran Gallery of Art, Washington, D.C., for his help on Phoenix, Arizona, where he was formerly associated with the Phoenix Museum.

In the West, much appreciation goes to Gerald Nordland, director of the San Francisco Museum of Art; Thomas W. Leavitt, director of the Santa Barbara Museum of Art; Alfred Frankenstein, art and music critic, the *San Francisco Chronicle;* and painter Edward Stasack of Honolulu, Hawaii.

Index

NOTE: *Galleries, museums, and other institutions that appear in the second part of this book may be found in this index by consulting the name of city in which they are situated.*